BANDITS, GANGSTERS AND THE MAFIA

Bandits, Gangsters and The Mafia:

Russia, The Baltic States and the CIS since 1992

MARTIN McCAULEY

An imprint of **Pearson Education**

Harlow, England · London · New York · Reading, Massachusetts · San Francisco
Toronto · Don Mills, Ontario · Sydney · Tokyo · Singapore · Hong Kong · Seoul
Taipei · Cape Town · Madrid · Mexico City · Amsterdam · Munich · Paris · Milan

PEARSON EDUCATION LIMITED

Head Office:
Edinburgh Gate
Harlow CM20 2JE
Tel: +44 (0)1279 623623
Fax: +44 (0)1279 431059

London Office:
128 Long Acre
London WC2E 9AN
Tel: +44 (0)20 7447 2000
Fax: +44 (0)20 7240 5771
Website: www.history-minds.com

First published in Great Britain in 2001

© Pearson Education, 2001

The right of Martin McCauley to be identified as Author
of this Work has been asserted by him in accordance
with the Copyright, Designs and Patents Act 1988.

ISBN 0 582 35764 0

British Library Cataloguing in Publication Data
A CIP catalogue record for this book can be obtained from the British Library

10 9 8 7 6 5 4 3 2 1

Set in 9/13pt Stone Serif
Typeset by Graphicraft Limited, Hong Kong
Printed and bound in Great Britain by Biddles Ltd., Guildford and King's Lynn

The Publishers' policy is to use paper manufactured from sustainable forests.

CONTENTS

LIST OF MAPS, FIGURE AND TABLES

PREFACE

RUSSIA IS ALWAYS REGARDED AS THE coming country but never seems to arrive. And so it turned out during the 1990s. Euphoria, inside the country and outside, greeted the demise of communism in December 1991. It was presumed that the application of western economic theory to Russia would transform the failed planned or command economy into a flourishing market economy in almost the twinkling of an eye. There would be some pain, like the pain of childbirth, but it would be short-lived. Russia would join the ranks of the 'civilised' countries. This expressive Russian term implies that Russia was previously viewed as barbaric, outside the gates of paradise. Paradise was a capitalist paradise. Russia was inebriated with the wine of hope. Sobering up was a traumatic experience. In 2000, Russian Gross Domestic Product (defined as the total flow of goods and services produced by the economy over a specific time period) had fallen to 55 per cent of that of 1990 (the Soviet GDP only declined by 24 per cent between 1941 and 1945). About 30 million persons (about 20 per cent of the population) had maintained or improved their living standards, of whom about 10 million had attained western living standards. Those living in poverty totalled about 60 million (about 40 per cent) of whom about 30 million had incomes below the minimum subsistence level of $35 a month. Only 10 per cent of newborns were without health problems, 50–80 per cent of school-age children were classified as having a physical or mental defect, contagious diseases were increasing by leaps and bounds – the list is endless. Why had it all gone so horribly wrong? Given the human (a highly educated population) and material capital at Russia's disposal, who was to blame for the debacle?

Instead of civilised capitalism Russia got gangster or bandit capitalism. Homo economicus and femina economica took over. They were only concerned with naked self-interest; they grabbed everything within reach and in so doing corrupted the government and weakened the state.

The sign reads: I demand the repayment of Tsarist debts.
A wry comment on state loans. The government never honours its debts to the
population. Created by Igor Revyakin.

The gangsters took over the state and ran it in their own interests. In fact, given the opportunity, gangsters will take over any state, even an advanced one. The reason why they do not in the latter is that core institutions, such as parliament and the legal system, are strong enough to stop them. Once the state weakens the gangsters strike. This simple verity was overlooked by Russian and western economists in 1992.

Marx analysed English and French nascent capitalism and did not like what he saw. He regarded capitalists as short-sighted exploiters who were digging their own graves. The level of exploitation of labour was too high to be sustainable. His analysis was economic and ignored other factors such as culture and religion. In this he was following in

Russia is so poor that a beggar makes off with the traditional offering of bread and salt intended for the guest. Created by Igor Revyakin.

a long tradition. Adam Smith's *Wealth of Nations* is about economic self-interest. The materialistic nineteenth century appeared to confirm the dictum that man was concerned about money and getting more of it. It was the heyday of liberalism which in reality is about economic self-interest. Marxism regarded liberalism as its great enemy but they were two sides of the same coin; they only took different routes to riches. Liberals understood that capitalists could become monsters if not restrained by the state. The state would always be needed since capitalists would never change. Marx thought that the state could fade away because men and women would behave rationally if there were no private property. Money would also disappear.

Marxism worldwide has a dismal record. It has failed economically everywhere to compete successfully with capitalism. However, many would argue that it achieved higher levels of social justice than under capitalism. Nevertheless citizens in communist states were more concerned with their falling standards of living. Many were willing to sacrifice their social benefits to return to capitalism. They were reluctant to believe that a communist system could be reformed successfully, meaning a standard of living which was comparable to that enjoyed in rich capitalist states.

The communist economies were planned economies in which the state owned and ran the factories and other sources of wealth. The Soviet model began to break down in the 1980s. Planners then cast their eyes at capitalist models. They were unlucky with their timing. Capitalism almost collapsed in the United States after 1929. The New Deal saved it. The war in Europe almost killed capitalism. The Marshall Plan saved it in western Europe. The thinking behind the Marshall Plan came from the classic work of John Maynard Keynes, *The General Theory of Employment, Interest and Money*, published in 1936. Keynes was concerned with national security (military-industrial complex, food production, high technology, basic science, information systems and the basic industries which provide employment and raw materials). In order to ensure it the state needed control over the above sectors of the economy. Small and medium-scale production and services could develop in a free market. Private initiative should be promoted and entry to production made easy. Hence government should play a role both in macro-economic demand management and the micro-economics of allocating scarce resources. Keynes was applied with great success in West Germany and Japan after 1947. He contributed much to the unprecedented prosperity and economic growth of the west until the 1970s. Had the planned economies collapsed in 1970, the capitalist model to have been recommended would have been the Keynesian one. A strong state and much state intervention would have been proposed. The state could take up to 50 per cent of the GDP in taxes. However, the Keynesian recipe did not have much effect in the 1970s because of powerful interest groups, especially labour unions. They were more concerned with increasing wages than productivity. A backlash set in and it became political wisdom on the right in politics to attack the state and see it as the source of all economic ills. One of the consequences of this was the rise of Milton Friedman and monetarism. The market (with the Central Bank of key importance – setting interest rates and determining the money supply) should regulate the economy and the smaller the government the better.

The neglect of Keynes in 1992 was not due to ignorance about his work. Keynes's books were translated into Russian in 1921, 1922 (two editions) and in 1924. At the second Comintern Congress no less a luminary than

Vladimir Lenin praised him and recommended his insights be studied. Keynes lectured at Moscow university in 1925, that is, during the heyday of the New Economic Policy (NEP). His classic work on employment was published in Moscow in 1936, and in 1948, and was praised by Stalin (because Keynes criticised Trotsky), and in 1978 when it was warmly recommended by Aleksei Kosygin, the Soviet Prime Minister. Keynes's correspondence with Lenin was published in 1994. Gorbachev was effusive in his praise. The young reformers may have believed that an economist praised by Lenin and Stalin was beyond redemption. They would have learned more from Keynes than Friedman.

When communism collapsed in 1989–91, monetarism was all the rage. It was wholly inappropriate for Russia. What was needed was Keynesian economics, not the economics of shock therapy. President Putin may dip into *The General Theory* and find policies which will promote economic growth and a more stable society. One of the attractions is that Lenin's NEP is reminiscent of Keynes: the commanding heights of the economy in state hands and light and consumer goods industries in private hands. The state determines the priorities of the economy.

The astounding story of this remarkable decade is the material of this book. Who are the heroes and who are the villains? Russia was full of bandits and gangsters. In fact one can say that in the realm of human history never has so much been stolen from so many by so few. It is a story of failure which cost many their lives, many their livelihood and cast many into the pit of despair. In 2000, the haves constituted about 10 per cent of the population. The amazing thing is that such a social revolution has not led to civil war in Russia. Western Europe would have descended into anarchy if something similar had happened there. Russia is different, as western theorists have learned to their cost.

In mid-2000, a popular 1980s poem by Dmitry Prigov was all the rage in Moscow.

The Plumber Will Come

The plumber will come and smash the toilet,
The gas man will come and break the gas stove,
The electrician will do all the rewiring,
However, the policeman arrives to say, enough, enough of your carrying on.

Gorby is the plumber, Yeltsin is the gas man, Berezovsky, the electrician, or perhaps it is the other way round. However there is no doubt who the policeman is: Vladimir Putin.

The author had some personal experience of the events related in this book. In the years 1989–95, he had various Russian business partners. The most successful relationship was with Mikhail Pasternak, who died prematurely in 1995. Together, they amassed a large archive on Russian banking and banks which has remained unpublished. This book is dedicated to his memory. All the Russians were pessimists about the future, especially Mikhail. None had any faith in politics or politicians. The author had a grandstand view of Russian corporate culture. Banking was an eye opener. Needless to say, he lost money in Russia. Westerners who turned in a profit in Russia had to be very smart indeed. Those who did, played Russian business by Russian rules, not those of the west. What is called corruption in the west is part and parcel of Russian business culture.

The author spent many years studying communism in Russia. One of the questions which always intrigued him was why such a naturally entrepreneurial people as the Russians should adopt such a profoundly anti-business ideology as Marxism. It only dawned on him, in the late 1980s, that Marxism was observed only in theory and not in practice. It was the ideology of the ruling class, the nomenklatura. It provided them with the moral high ground while living off the labour of the masses. The working class knew that the claim that they ruled Russia was a myth. However they did not attempt to make it a reality and thereby cemented a system which developed two faces. The public face glorified the Marxist myth but the private face lived in the real world. This is why the nomenklatura became so practised in hypocrisy. The author's first experience of these two faces was at the World Youth Festival, in Moscow, in 1957. He was approached by two young men who spoke superb English. They wanted to buy English pounds and dollars, indeed any hard currency. These young men would become members of the nomenklatura but they were not interested in building up a law abiding state. They were not inspired by the goals of communism, only the prospect of making money on the side. In 1991, communism passed away but the nomenklatura carried on. Its most skilful members became effortlessly the new capitalist nomenklatura. The only difference was that there was no longer any need to engage in hypocrisy. A spade could be called a spade. The mask could be thrown away. The communist nomenklatura learned through time how to exploit the state in their own interests and thereby to enrich themselves. They put everything they had learnt to good use after 1991. Unimaginable riches flowed into their pockets.

The Russian intelligentsia was and is the conscience of the nation. However, it has never exercised power and, indeed, is quite incapable of becoming a ruling class. It was very influential during the late Gorbachev and early Yeltsin eras. Russian *intelligenty* are charming, highly cultured and extremely good company. They make wonderful friends. The author has often thought that a Russia ruled by these men and women would be a wonderful place. But that is daydreaming. The other Russians, hard headed, materialistic, ruthless in defence of their privileges and totally unconcerned about the welfare of others, rule. Whereas the Russian *intelligenty* are honest, the other Russians are instinctive liars. Cheating and robbing are as natural as breathing. In business, the author learnt that a contract is only valid until the ink is dry. Russians then start trying to undermine it in their own commercial interests. Short-term gain is put before everything else.

The author has retired from the Russian business scene. His experience has made him sceptical of those who believe that Russian political and business culture will change and become more like the west. Corruption is systemic; in other words, it is in the genes of the system. Russia is Russian and should be accepted as such.

No attempt has been made to write a comprehensive account of the period. Important areas such as culture are rarely mentioned. The goal has been to highlight the most important actors and occurrences and attempt to explain the extraordinary course of events.

I wish to thank Judy Twigg and Dr Tim Allen for their valuable help and many other scholars and friends.

The major sources of this book are Aron (2000), Freeland (2000), Gustafson (1999), Hough (2001), Huskey (1999), Klebnikov (2000), Nagy (2000), Reddaway and Glinski (2001) and Shevtsova (1999).

Throughout this book a billion is a thousand million. All dollars are US dollars.

ACKNOWLEDGEMENTS

We are grateful to the following for permission to reproduce copyright material:

Plate 2 – Russian President Vladimir Putin. With permission from Associated Press [Trans Ref. No.: MOSB131].

Plate 3 – Anatoly Chubais, Chief of Staff of Boris Yeltsin. Photo by Steffen Schmidt, Reuters – with permission from Popperfoto [DAV10: Swis-Forum: Davos, Switzerland, 3 February 1997].

Plate 4 – Russian President Boris Yeltsin, right, during a meeting with leading Russian bankers. With permission from Associated Press Photo/ITAR-TASS/President's Press Service [MOSB102].

Plate 5 – Boris Berezovsky, left, and Roman Abramovich. With permission from Associated Press Photo/Ivan Sekretarev, Staff [Trans. Ref. No.: MOSB109].

Plate 6 – Balkan's special envoy Viktor Chernomyrdin. With permission from mf/Photo by Alexander Natruskin Reuters [MOS01: Yugoslavia-Russia Teltsin: Moscow 17 June 1999].

Plate 7 – Acting Prime Minister Sergei Kiriyenko. With permission from Pool Associated Press/ - /VG/nie/ao [Russia-Kirienko Smiles – 19980424 - Moscow - Russian Federation].

Plate 8 – Primakov. With permission from Novosti [PRAVIT-1].

Cartoons – Created by Igor Revyakin.

MAP 1: The Russian Federation.

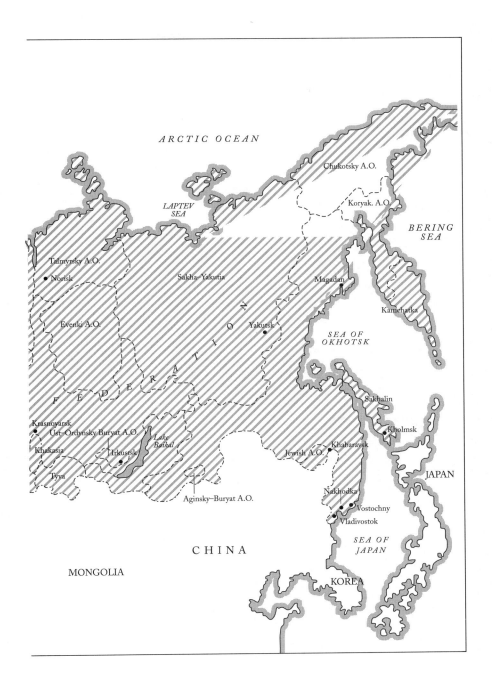

ARCTIC OCEAN

Chukotsky A.O.

LAPTEV
SEA

Koryak. A.O.

BERING
SEA

Talmyrsky A.O.

● Norisk

Sakha-Yakutia

Magadan

Kamchatka

Evenki A.O.

Yakutsk

SEA OF
OKHOTSK

F E D E R A T I O N

Sakhalin

Krasnoyarsk

Ust–Ordynsky Buryat A.O.

Lake
Baikal

Kholmsk

Khakasia

Irkustsk

Jewish A.O.

Khabaravsk

Tyva

JAPAN

Aginsky–Buryat A.O.

Nakhodka

Vostochny

Vladivostok

CHINA

SEA OF
JAPAN

MONGOLIA

KOREA

1

HOW AND WHY DID IT HAPPEN?

THERE ARE SIX MAIN EXPLANATIONS WHY Russia took the course it did after 1991:

1. The roving bandit and the stationary bandit
2. The hedgehog and the fox
3. *Khalyava*
4. Power and property
5. Property rights
6. The Marxist-Leninist legacy

THE ROVING BANDIT AND THE STATIONARY BANDIT

Every businessman is a roving bandit. He is always on the look-out for something to steal. Seize everything which is not nailed down and why not try to take it as well? With apologies to Karl Heinrich Marx, he engages in primitive theft accumulation. He only thinks about himself and has no concern about the impact of his activities on the rest of the population. The roving bandit needs to keep the state weak in order to flourish. The simplest way to achieve this is to steal the great offices of state, the office of Prime Minister, the ministry of finance, the ministry of foreign trade and so on. When roving bandits take over the government or state they have to amass wealth very quickly because this will create social tension. If there is unrest it could lead to the roving bandits losing much of their wealth. This is the moment they think of becoming stationary bandits. They acquire an interest in law and order because it can guarantee them security of tenure. They need a stronger state, one which can deliver public goods to the population, health, education, law and order and defence. This means they have to begin paying more and more tax. However it is highly unlikely that all roving bandits will simultaneously decide that it is opportune to become stationary bandits. The result is the roving bandits go to war. Gradually the stationary bandits take over, and with time one becomes dominant. They become the state.

There are four main reasons why Russia fell prey to roving bandits (Nagy 2000: 4).

- The manner in which the Soviet state dissolved in 1991
- The type of economic reform which was chosen
- The accumulation of power by the President and the manner in which he wielded it
- The chaotic and state-threatening process of decentralisation within Russia

Boris Yeltsin set out to destroy Gorbachev's Soviet Union from within by challenging all Soviet institutions. They exploited Russia and the sooner they were destroyed the better. Only then could Russia rise from the ashes and become a great state again. In 1991, he declared war on the Union on two fronts. He ordered Russian banks to withhold tax payments made by enterprises to the Union budget. He also encouraged regional administrations to ignore revenue-sharing arrangements by not transferring their share of taxes to the Union budget. In order to wean Russian regions away from the Union he exempted them from paying taxes to the centre. Regions were being given the opportunity to reduce their dependency on the centre and to learn how to haggle with Yeltsin in order to benefit themselves. Yeltsin was in the business of granting tax concessions for political favours. The other tactic was to challenge the centre for the ownership of enterprises and farms on the territory of the Russian Federation. Until 1991, most important enterprises belonged to the Union while lesser enterprises were under the jurisdiction of the Russian Federation. In the chaotic days of 1991 they could choose under whose aegis they wished to be. Ownership of Russian enterprises (Russia produced about 75 per cent of the Soviet GDP) was absolutely crucial in the political struggle between Gorbachev and Yeltsin. The level of taxation and the amount of state social benefits which were distributed through the enterprises depended on whether the enterprise was Soviet or Russian. Yeltsin began to outbid the Union authorities, promising lower taxation and higher social benefits. For instance, Union enterprises paid 35 per cent profit tax whereas Russian ones only paid 32 per cent. Social benefits in Russia were 20–40 per cent higher. This was unashamed bribery but it was highly successful. Yeltsin revealed his talent for populism. The short-term goal was to ensure that the Union government received less and less revenue until it collapsed.

However, dishing Gorbachev was a two-edged sword. It taught enterprise managers that fiscal favours could be the reward for political support. Yeltsin, without meaning to do so, was laying down the fiscal rules of the new Russia. Managers were stronger as a consequence of perestroika and were learning quickly that they could also become political actors. Enterprise directors were to prove the most powerful political interest group in the new Russia. Regional authorities also soon learned to take advantage of the situation in Moscow. Fiscal advantages could be gained by astute bargaining. Yeltsin was creating a rod for his own back when it came to dealing with authorities in the new Russia. Revenue collection by the Soviet Union dropped from about 40 per cent of GDP in 1990 to about 28 per cent in 1991. The government compensated by printing more money which resulted in higher and higher inflation. Since price controls were still in place a huge monetary overhang built up (Nagy 2000: 66). It may have reached 500 billion rubles or half the Soviet GDP. There were two ways of liquidating it, pro-market Soviet and western economists agreed. One was to offer ruble-denominated state bonds to the population with the principal and part of the interest paid in US dollars or other convertible currencies. The other way was privatisation. The state would start with small-scale privatisation, apartments, plots of land, shops, small workshops and move gradually to large-scale privatisation, enterprises, mines and oil and gas fields. Citizens would end up owning much of the country's fixed assets. The core of the 500-day programme was privatisation. However Gorbachev could never bring himself to adopt it (Klebnikov 2000: 51). Gorbachev's solution to the monetary overhang was to borrow $30 billion from western banks, purchase consumer goods and then sell them at ten times the price in the Soviet Union. However, the West would not lend him the money.

When Yeltsin took over in Russia in December 1991 a strong state was out of the question. Indeed there was a fear that Russia could disintegrate as well. The threat of shortages of food leading to a situation reminiscent of February 1917 was real. Yeltsin had banned the communist party which had been the glue which kept the Soviet Union together.

However he had no similar institution to take its place but did not think a presidential party was necessary in the new Russia. No attention was paid to state institutions when shock therapy or wham-bang-thank-you-ma'am economics was introduced in January 1992. Prices were liberalised or freed while only the prices of a few necessities were still controlled by the state. No thought was given to a safety net for the most vulnerable. The young reformers, headed by Egor Gaidar, believed fervently that the market would liberate Russia and make it rich quickly. The state's role was to stand back and allow the raw energy of Russia's entrepreneurs free room.

When it all began to go wrong in the spring of 1992 an attempt was made to strengthen the state but Moscow found that its words were not heeded. The weakening of the state had gone too far for the President and government to wave a magic wand and expect to be obeyed (Nagy 2000: 87–8). The enterprises and regions had begun to learn how to negotiate politically with the centre. Whereas under Gorbachev the goals had been economic they were now political and economic. The enterprise directors, the red directors, were well represented in parliament, the Supreme Soviet, and, after April 1992, began to act as a coherent interest group which was opposed to the new economic order of shock therapy. The President was gradually forced to make concession after concession to them. This involved placing their members in government and, in December, one of them, Viktor Chernomyrdin, became Prime Minister. Yeltsin attempted to strengthen the state, mainly through presidential decrees because parliament was not amenable, until he gave up in frustration in the summer of 1993. The conflict between the President and parliament was resolved by force. No consensus was sought when introducing shock therapy and no consensus could be achieved in resolving the conflict this policy produced.

The bloodletting of October 1993 revealed how weak the President really was and in the December 1993 Duma elections this was clear to all and sundry. The pro-government parties were in the minority. The majority of voters had voted against economic reform mainly because there was no gain only pain. A major belief of the young reformers was that the privatisation of state enterprises was absolutely essential if a market economy were to get off the ground in Russia. Rapid privatisation was embarked upon and the motto was bad privatisation is better than no privatisation. Bad privatisation meant dirty privatisation when crooks acquired state assets. The IMF began lending money to Russia and imposed its own conditions. Two of these were that the state had to collect more tax and reduce the budget deficit. Given the weakness of the Russian state these objectives were beyond it. It also got itself embroiled in a war with Chechnya, from 1994–96, and thereby wasted some of its limited resources. The situation became desperate in early 1996 when opinion polls revealed that President Yeltsin's chances of re-election in June 1996 were slim. The President did a deal with some businessmen which resulted in his re-election but the price he paid was huge. The businessmen became politically very influential and had a major say in the way the government was run.

The bankers and businessmen entered the government and influenced the management of the state in their own interests. They did this in various ways (Nagy 2000: 91):

- The privatisation process had all the hallmarks of being designed to benefit insiders most.
- Many tax concessions were granted after the re-election reflecting rewards for political favours.
- Since the government did not have the budgetary means to meet all its obligations it had to decide who took priority when payment was due. The businessmen ensured that they were top of the list.
- State revenues were channelled through private banks and the banks paid no interest on this money. The banks were lax in paying it back to the government. In the meantime, among other things, they bought GKOs and other government bonds. In reality, they were lending the government its own money and being paid handsomely for the privilege. In return, they facilitated the government system of off-budget subsidies.
- Necessary economic reforms were delayed so that insiders could continue to benefit from their transactions. Large companies sometimes had their energy bills cancelled. Duty free imports could be arranged.
- An increasing amount of tax could be paid in non-cash form, either by goods (at inflated prices) or by a reduction in budgetary transfers.
- Companies which had contributed to the President's re-election fund received tax breaks, exemption from VAT payments and other financial rewards.

It is interesting that the roving bandits who entered government made no attempt to set up political parties to provide them with an electoral support base. They did not regard public support as important. It also reveals that political parties in Russia were not considered vehicles for increasing one's influence in the state. The quickest route was to steal state assets. Another factor was that the roving bandits did not collude collectively against the state, they fought one another for supremacy in the state. This is not surprising since it is elementary economics.

When the state is weak one can make up the rules of the game when the market economy is launched. Moscow's reach in the regions was limited and its energies were consumed by the conflict between the executive, the President, and the legislature, the Supreme Soviet. In Germany, in May 1945, the first from under the rubble were the wheelers and dealers, pimps and conmen. The same happened in Russia. The most successful became roving bandits. However the roving bandits were already in place in Russia in January 1992. Gorbachev's reforms had unleashed a lot of economic energy but not in the direction he had hoped. Almost all the leading roving bandits of the 1990s were ready for the off in 1991. They became household names very quickly: Boris Berezovsky, Mikhail Fridman, Mikhail Khodorkovsky, Vladimir Potanin, Vladimir Gusinsky, Aleksandr Smolensky and Vladimir Vinogradov. They possessed special talents. They linked up with members of the government and the presidential administration and this resulted in their mutual enrichment. Some members of the government and presidential administration thus became roving bandits. Of course, government ministers had an interest in ensuring that the state remained weak. Another person who became a roving bandit was Aleksandr Korzhakov, head of the presidential guard. Theft became a way of life in the government and the presidential administration. The President contributed to this development by setting up his own slush funds in 1992.

In order to ensure their own security the roving bandits set up their own private armies. They normally recruited a senior officer from the former KGB to run it. They also had their own economic and political analytical centres which provided them with vital intelligence and security information. Since they placed their own men inside the government, the presidential administration and the Central Bank, they had top-level contacts. They also had the funds to buy any information they needed and bribe any official or judge they had to. It was not unknown for a roving bandit to hire the police to deliver a hit against another roving bandit.

The above make up a proportion of the roving bandits but the largest group of roving bandits are enterprise directors. How and when did they emerge? They emerged over the years 1992–94 because of the weakness of the state and the means chosen to privatise state assets. Until privatisation the industrialists were a managerial pressure group, albeit a powerful one. They became roving bandits step by step. In 1992, they realised that the absence of state authority permitted them much lee-way for theft. Then privatisation handed them their enterprises. By 1994 they owned about 60 per cent of Russia's industrial assets. Not every enterprise director is a roving bandit but the vast majority are. It was not inevitable that the roving bandits would emerge in Russia. After all they did not surface in the Baltic states, which chose the path of democracy, or in the Caucasus and Central Asia. Authoritarian rulers in these regions have prevented their emergence.

After President Yeltsin was re-elected in July 1996 some of the roving bandits realised that the state was too weak and was not delivering the public goods the population expected (Nagy 2000: 97–100). First and foremost was Anatoly Chubais. He and others entered the government. He held an auction for Svyazinvest, the telecommunications holding com-pany. The result was that Vladimir Potanin won and Boris Berezovsky and Vladimir Gusinsky lost. Such was their anger that they unleashed the banking war which tore Russia apart. Chubais's bid to turn the rov-ing bandits into stationary bandits (his most implacable roving bandit opponent was always Boris Berezovsky) had spectacularly failed and threat-ened the integrity of the Russian state. In 1997–98 another attempt was made to force the roving bandits to pay substantially more tax and fund the necessary public services. However Viktor Chernomyrdin, the Prime Minister, opted out at the last moment in March 1998 and was sacked. This undermined Russia's standing abroad and the East Asia crisis in the summer of 1998 engulfed a weak Russia. The crisis revealed that Russian government decision making was negatively influenced by rov-ing bandits who were pursuing their own personal gain and ignoring the long-term interests of the Russian state. The President was too weak to influence events decisively.

The concept of the roving and stationary bandit is derived from the work of Mancur Olson (1993 and 2000) on interest groups. The roving bandits during the period 1992–96 pursued short-term interests which consisted of maximising their theft and robbery of state assets. They were managers and bankers in the main. They became immensely rich very quickly because of the once-in-a-lifetime opportunity of privatis-ing state assets at a fraction of their real value and sometimes free of charge. Due to the uncertainty about how long the window of oppor-tunity would stay open, the roving bandits hoovered up voraciously every asset they could. They immediately engaged in asset stripping and transferred the money to offshore accounts. They had no interest in invest-ing in Russia as their assets could be confiscated by the state. In order to ensure that the state did not confiscate their wealth they needed a weak and corrupt state. Indeed their ideal state was one which belonged to them. If the roving bandit wants to stay he has to become a stationary bandit. The reasons why some roving bandits in Russia in 1996–97 had concluded that it was time for a stronger state were that all the major privatisations were over and the time had come to safeguard their existing holdings. The millions of voters who chose the communist candidate in the presidential elections of 1996 sent shivers down the spines of some roving bandits. The public had concluded that it had paid too high a price for economic experimentation since 1992. Perhaps 40 per cent of the population were below the poverty line. There was a real possibility of a social and economic crisis which, if it occurred, could spell the end of the roving bandits. A more equitable distribution of wealth in Russia was needed to stabilise the state (Nagy 2000: chapter 6).

In this book those who end up as roving bandits start off as small-time entrepreneurs, gravitate into clan chiefs, then roving bandits and oligarchs. All oligarchs are roving bandits but not all roving bandits are oligarchs. To qualify as a clan chief one needs to be a dollar millionaire. To become an oligarch a billion dollars is the signing-on fee. The term oligarch was first used by Berezovsky in 1996. He understands the impact of exaggeration so he claimed they ran the Russian state, including the government. It also reveals that he was not afraid of a public backlash.

A remarkable fact about the most successful roving bandits, the oligarchs, is that they are almost all Russian Jews. Indeed if one lists the top seven oligarchs six are Jews,* the odd man out being Vladimir Potanin. But he is of Old Believer stock. Before 1917 many of the most successful merchants were Old Believers. An honorary oligarch, Anatoly Chubais, is of Baltic German-Jewish-Latvian stock. The dominance of Jews is astonishing in a country such as Russia with its anti-Semitic tradition. These Jews seldom acted in unison. Indeed the norm was for them to fight one another. A case in point is the rivalry between Boris Berezovsky and Vladimir Gusinsky who represent the two traditions in Moscow Jewry. Hence there is no Jewish conspiracy to take over Russia.

---

* Boris Berezovsky was baptised into the Russian Orthodox Church in the mid-1990s. This gave rise to some wry jokes. A Chief Rabbi is visiting Jerusalem and goes to the Wailing Wall. 'I am the most miserable of men, my son has disgraced me and converted to Christianity. What have I done to deserve this? Is there no justice in this world?' He goes on in like vein for a while until he is interrupted by a voice from Heaven: 'Isaac, I have the same problem myself!' Boris's conversion was not well received. The problem is that no one believes he has any other god but money and completely lacks a spiritual dimension.

What special talents have produced their success? Jews were outsiders in the Soviet Union and were excluded from top positions in the communist party, industry and the security services. Instead they had to hone their skills at progressing in an often hostile environment. Jews were used by enterprise managers to acquire scace goods in order to fulfil the plan. They were known as *tolkachi* or go-getters. If they were arrested they were disowned by the enterprise. In national scandals those executed were the minnows and a Jew was often among them. It was high-risk work which required considerable entrepreneurial skill. In order to achieve their objective they had to know whom to bribe and how much. They became masters of working the communist system. They went into business on their own after 1991. This wealth of experience was a pool into which others who were astute could dip. Some such as Khodorkovsky developed their skills in the Komsomol, the young communist league. He rose as high as he could go. It also helped that he had a degree in chemistry. Others such as Berezovsky are talented mathematicians. Potanin, of Old Believer stock, has also inherited the drive, acumen and talent to accumulate great wealth. The Old Believer attitude to wealth was almost Calvinist; the eleventh commandment was to become rich but not to engage in conspicuous consumption.

Does it follow that the roving bandits are all criminals? Are they all master thieves who should be locked up for the good of society? No, they are all acting rationally from an economic point of view. Given that the state is weak and that there are assets to be acquired at knock-down prices and also free of charge a rational economic actor accumulates as much as he can. The political uncertainty means that he has to work very fast and possibly get out very fast. This means he engages in asset stripping and then moves the money offshore. He does not invest. In order to acquire more cheap assets he needs favours from government. Indeed top contacts can make him an instant millionaire. He must ensure that the state is weak and the best way of doing this is to place his nominees in government. The best officials are those that can be bribed. Public opinion is important and in order to mould it he needs to buy up newspapers, TV and radio stations. In order to gain immunity from prosecution he needs to get elected to a representative body such as parliament or a local council (in 2000, there were an estimated four million citizens who enjoyed immunity from prosecution). All this is rational economic and political behaviour given the incentives created by economic reform. Only when a roving bandit concludes that the time of the quick theft is over will he start thinking about the long term. Then he will be willing to pay more tax in order to secure his wealth. He will start investing in Russia. No sentiment is involved about helping Mother Russia, again it is a rational economic decision. The roving bandit is homo economicus and homo politicus personified. Thomas Hobbes and Niccolò Machiavelli would have no difficulty in understanding contemporary Russia.

All those involved in organised crime are roving bandits. A striking fact is that the mafia is dominated by Jews. The tactics employed in building up a business empire are employed to build up a criminal empire. Again the secret is asset stripping and then the transfer of wealth offshore. The only difference is that the businessmen asset strip the state whereas the mafiosi asset strip the businessmen. The mafiosi are a necessary part of the economic system. The state is weak and ready for plucking. However officials are still in charge of state assets and need an organisation to help them collect bribes, enforce deals and so on. The mafia performs this role. The mafiosi function in a competitive market environment. The rule 'expand or die' applies to them. They must always be trying to expand their reach and to take over smaller organisations. Some of the money they collect is invested at home but most of it flows abroad. Hence it was impossible for a businessman to become rich in Russia in the 1990s and ignore the mafia. He had to collaborate with it to survive. If he did not, his life span would be cut short. Oligarchs used the mafia to take out their competitors. The mafiosi penetrated the police and judicial system and hence could act almost with impunity.

Konstantin Borovoi, chair of the Russian commodities and raw materials exchange, sees the mafia as a shadow government. 'It has its own tax system, its own security service and its own administrative system. An entrepreneur, in addition to paying taxes to the government, has to pay taxes to this shadow government: bribes to the health inspectors, local police, tax inspectors, government landlords, and, of course, protection money to the gangsters guaranteeing him security.' Another businessman commented: 'the power of the government has collapsed but individual bureaucrats retain control over the nation's resources. They want to profit from their position'. In order to become really rich they need an organisation which will handle negotiations with other bureaucrats and hit men to enforce the rents they have levied. So they link up with organised criminal groups for mutual enrichment (Klebnikov 2000: 36).

What then were the prospects for democracy in Russia? Democracy can only develop when roving bandits become stationary bandits.

Eventually one becomes dominant and he takes over the state. He acquires the right to impose taxes (which, after all, is legalised theft) in return for providing security and law and order. In order to facilitate and legitimise the collection of taxes, the state needs to promote representative institutions, first and foremost parliament. In this way democracy develops. However there is always tension between capitalism – the market economy – and democracy. The battle between those who wish to enrich themselves and those who wish to force them to share their wealth is constant.

Democracy needs a pluralistic dispersion of power. The state should be strong enough to prevent mini-autocrats re-emerging. The number of political parties should be small enough to allow them to act in concert against the emergence of a mini-autocrat. In order for this to happen there have to be a minimal level of harmony within society and also an acceptable standard of living. A society in economic crisis may choose an autocrat as an escape from its misery. For a democracy to function in the long term there have to be independent institutions which can mediate conflicts among the power-sharing elites. The powers of each elite have to be clearly and transparently articulated and regulated. Fundamental to successful democracies is a legal system which regulates property and enforces contracts. Representative institutions, first and foremost parliament, have to establish bodies which develop and protect the human rights of all and those of market participants in particular. A democratic state which provides the above also delivers basic public goods, such as law and order, health and education and defence and thereby is viewed as legitimate by its subjects. Judged by the above criteria, Russia is only beginning its journey to democracy.

Where does all this leave Boris Nikolaevich Yeltsin? Is he the roving bandit of all roving bandits? Boris made his career in the communist party and knew a lot about the construction business. He also knew a lot about how to climb the political ladder and cut deals. In so doing he developed a talent for being ruthless and deadly. He was also a risk taker. He threw away his party career in 1989 and went to war with almost everyone's favourite uncle, Uncle Misha Gorbachev. Luck was on his side and he made it into parliament which provided him with a platform to lambaste Uncle Misha and everything he stood for. In June 1991, he was elected President of Russia and his glory days reached a peak in August 1991 when he mounted a tank in front of the White House and called on everyone to defend freedom and Uncle Misha. He had become Boris the Bold. He cared nothing about economics but believed he had picked a winner in Egor Gaidar – after all he came from an illustrious lineage – and so shock therapy was launched on an unsuspecting population. Boris did not heed advice that he should adopt a new constitution, strengthen the state, call parliamentary elections, streamline the legal system and set up a presidential political party. He knew better. He had demolished Uncle Misha's state so why should he resurrect it? He did not want to be restricted by law and party politics. He was the father of the Russian people. In a short while he would start thinking of himself as a latter-day Tsar. When things began to go awry, Egor Gaidar kept on telling him that things would soon work out. The problem with Egor was that he got his knowledge of markets from US economic textbooks, first and foremost the classic text by Samuelson. With this knowledge he could bemuse Boris. If economic certainty had been an Olympic sport, Egor would have been groaning under the weight of his gold medals. But Boris had not got to the top by being bemused by clever young things like Egor Gaidar. He was a hardheaded realist. He went behind Egor's back and cut deals with his arch-enemies, the communists. When Egor wanted him to sign some outlandish decree, he could not say no to his face, he just signed it, then put it in a drawer and pretended it had been lost. Boris had to rule by decree because parliament would not pass his legislation.

As the economic situation worsened Boris was guided by only one principle, how to maintain his power. If enterprise directors became too clamorous, he made concessions to them. If the communists in parliament, many of the red directors were deputies, he made concessions to them. The young reformers were livid but Boris lived in the real world. He set up a slush fund to dip into when he had extra-budgetary expenses. He was under such pressure that he turned a blind eye to theft by his associates. His rule was that if an official was loyal to him he could steal. There was a lot to steal. Since the government was only partially loyal to him – many ministers were forced on him by parliament – he set up his own shadow government, the presidential administration. He needed his own personal guard which could be trusted. Aleksandr Korzhakov, who became known as Sasha the Knife, became its head and quickly established his own empire.

The 1993 constitution made the President a Super-President. He was allowed to issue decrees with the force of law but there were certain areas where this could not be done. These were taxation, pensions and social benefits, conditions governing the use of land, principles for the structure of state power in the subjects of the Federation, rules on elections to the Duma and the formation of the Council of the Federation, the appointment of judges, and the organisation of the procuracy

(Remington 2000: 506). All these had to be regulated by Duma laws and Boris could not issue decrees which contradicted them. When a law exists it may only be amended by another law, not by decree. When a subsequent law is passed it supersedes a decree. The new constitution ended the President's ability to call a referendum when it pleased him. Parliament also lost this ability. A referendum can only be held if two million citizens sign a petition to this effect. Over time presidential decrees have taken second place to Duma legislation in the eyes of Russian bureaucrats.

Privatisation offered riches to insiders. There was a quota system for the export of oil, timber and other commodities. A licence was a passport to riches. All that was needed was Boris's signature on a decree. His tennis coach hit on the idea that if he could import goods duty free he could become rich. Boris liked him so he agreed. The Orthodox Church was short of cash as most of its parishioners were poor. Why not give it a concession to import cigarettes and alcohol duty free? Done. Very quickly everyone realised that the nearer one got to Boris the nearer one got to riches. Boris needed favourites and to be known as being generous. He was quite rational in his relations with people. He had two faces. In public affairs he could be hard, uncompromising, a ruthless exploiter of human beings. In private he was considerate, polite and a good friend. However, power was his mistress and he loved wheeling and dealing.

The roving bandits surrounded him like a pack of wolves. Many of the young reformers had become roving bandits as the lure of lucre became too strong. One of the best places to be was in the Central Bank which extended loans to other banks and also helped to finance the budget. One wheeze was for some officials to leave the Central Bank, set up their own bank, arrange a large ruble loan, exchange it for dollars, transfer it to an offshore account, liquidate the bank and skedaddle. Boris did not bat an eyelid. Another lucrative perch was the ministry of finance. The roving bandits fought one another and Boris played one off against the other. The situation became serious in 1996 when it looked as if Boris would not be re-elected President. This threw the roving bandits into a panic. For the first and last time they all came together to ensure his re-election. Afterwards they set about tearing one another apart. Boris was in command of the situation until late 1996 and then his health went. Constantly in pain, he took drugs and chased them down with vodka. Tsar Boris the Bruiser died in late 1996. He was succeeded by Tsar Boris the Boozer. When coherent he would roar at subordinates: 'obey the Tsar's command'. He cut a rather pathetic figure on the domestic and world stage. He was an embarrassment to himself, his family and colleagues. No one was sure what Boris would say next, least of all himself. His foreign minister became skilled at damage limitation as he contradicted Boris's outlandish statements. All the while Boris's family had been increasing in influence, especially his daughter Tatyana. The family's main financial adviser was Boris Berezovsky. Family members were promoted, money moved offshore and villas bought abroad, including one in Bavaria. Those in his personal apparatus followed suit. Sergei Yastrzhembsky once expressed the opinion that officials should not fill one pocket but both pockets: 'Nado brat v obe zhmeni'. The last word is Polish Yiddish for hands. In other words, help yourself while you can. The financial crisis in August 1998 sent the family into a panic and they came up with a desperate solution. Another war in Chechnya was needed and the man to head the government was Vladimir Putin. On 31 December 1999 Tsar Boris handed over the reins of power to Vladimir Putin. The roving bandits could manipulate the media so as to ensure his election as President in March 2000.

Tsar Boris started off very promisingly but came to a sad end. In 1999, he was presiding over a chaotic, anarchic state in which the roving bandits had free rein. The regions were in disarray and the territorial integrity of Russia could no longer be taken for granted. His personal tragedy was Russia's tragedy. Counsel for the defence would argue that this picture is too bleak. In 1999, the cumulative drop of GDP was smaller in Russia than in seven of the former 14 successor states to the Soviet Union. However it was also greater than in another seven. Some had tried shock therapy and had taken western advice and IMF and World Bank money. There is no direct correlation between western advisers, IMF and World Bank money and economic performance. In 1990, about one Russian family in six had a car; in 1998 one in three had. Access to home telephones increased 40 per cent and the number of international calls multiplied by twelve.

A neat way of summing up Yeltsin as President of Russia would be to regard him as a master Bolshevik. His main concern was to amass and retain power. In order to do this successfully he needed to wheel and deal endlessly. Sometimes he was as sweet as honey, on other occasions as deadly as a viper. He was in his element in dealing with other Bolsheviks. He understood them and preferred their company. Young reformers and democrats made him uneasy. There is always only one concern: what does one do to come out on top? This is Lenin's question: who does whom (kto-kogo)? One does not have political friends, only colleagues. When they have served their purpose, dump them. Yeltsin had a great talent for populism. He was a natural when it came to pressing flesh and giving the impression that the person he was addressing was the only intelligent being, next to the President, on the planet. He is reminiscent of David Lloyd George, the Welsh wizard, in this respect. He had no ideology apart from the ideology of power. He understood that the exercise of power involves the use of force. He was willing to spill blood when necessary. As a master Bolshevik, he was the wrong man to guide Russia towards a liberal market economy and democracy. Chubais, his most influential economic aide, was a market Bolshevik. Impose fundamental economic change from above, untrammelled by law or morality. Yeltsin lacked the moral dimension which made Gorbachev so attractive to westerners. The latter could not bring himself to spill blood to stay in power. Yeltsin chose Putin as his successor, someone who was schooled in the Bolshevik tradition. Putin looks back with nostalgia at the Soviet era. Yeltsin does not. He hates the communists who ended his party career. He likes those who came over to his side. He ruled Russia with them, deploying the political skills honed in the communist party. A major objective for Boris was to prevent a democratic revolution in Russia. There was a real possibility at the end of the Gorbachev era and the beginning of the Yeltsin era that democrats could come to power and redistribute state assets among the population. Yeltsin categorically opposed this and wished to redistribute state wealth among his supporters. An important factor in nipping any democratic revolution in the bud was the dissolution of local soviets. They were full of newly elected deputies who wanted to kick out the communist nomenklatura and redistribute state wealth. A key centre was Moscow. Yeltsin seized the opportunity offered him by the attempted coup of October 1993 to disband the Moscow city and Moscow oblast soviets. He worked closely with Gavriil Popov, the mayor, to take control in the interests, not of the local population, but of the new nomenklatura.

Given that Boris was almost always in control, one can view Russia as a strong state (Hough 2001). The President was powerful enough to redistribute wealth among the ruling class. He could also force the Central Bank and ministry of finance to provide credits to enterprises, farms and regions. Off-budget funds were always available and used to keep the President in power. The oligarchs had also to take over weak companies and provide credits to others in need.

THE HEDGEHOG AND THE FOX

This metaphor comes from Sir Isaiah Berlin's masterful analysis of Tolstoy's view of history. Those who rule Russia can be divided into two groups: the hedgehogs and the foxes. They vie for supremacy and so far the hedgehogs are in the ascendancy. They are fascinated by everything they see around them and are not concerned about the national interest, only their own. They work on the principle that if there is anything to steal, steal it and steal it quickly. The nature of the state, the political system, political philosophy and other intellectual pursuits do not interest them. They are driven men (there are no successful female hedgehogs), driven by money. It buys political privilege and economic concessions. They engage in conspicuous consumption although they do not enjoy a high reputation among madams. Their energies are not channelled into sex but into business.

Foxes, on the other hand, are more concerned with the future of Russia than the future of their offshore accounts. Indeed they may not even have any. They prefer a centralised system since it permits more control. They believe that their prescriptions will restore Russia to its great power status. They are patient and are willing to make short-term concessions so as to achieve long-term goals. The hedgehogs think short-term, the foxes long-term. Everything comes to him who only stands and waits, is their motto. The foxes need an all embracing programme, a vision for the future. Their view of human beings is misanthropic. Without firm guidance a person's potential cannot be realised. The best way to achieve the objective of making Russia great again is to concentrate the nation's energies on certain tasks. A consensus is needed to achieve this and once arrived at should be enforced. Dissent weakens the national resolve.

Hedgehogs easily dominated the 1990s. The foxes were overwhelmed. Some were in the democratic movement and sought to create in Russia a liberal democratic political order and market economy, all regulated by the rule of law. The more visionary they were the easier it was for the hedgehogs to defeat them. Then there were the communist foxes masquerading under the guise of nationalists. Many of them found that being hedgehogs was more profitable. Cutting deals with the hedgehog President turned out to be a lucrative business. There were communist foxes who remained foxes, the unreconstructed Marxist-Leninists, but they were so small in number that the hedgehogs lost no sleep over them. Zhirinovsky's nationalists, in a crisis, would always turn into hedgehogs. Under no circumstances did they want a fox in the Kremlin. General Aleksandr Lebed, for a time, threatened to become a fox but the hedgehogs soon got together and framed him.

An unkind critic has likened Vladimir Putin to a frog. He is not a frog but a fox. He gives the impression of being afraid of some of the hedgehogs but his media adviser, Gleb Pavlovsky, is quoted as saying that the surest way to improve the President's approval ratings is for him to engage in hedgehog-bashing. The public is suspicious of both hedgehogs and foxes as it has grown weary of promises for a better tomorrow. Many in the police, security and military are looking to fox Putin to become their champion. If the foxes win the hedgehogs will have to roll themselves up into tight balls and wait for better times. However they have accumulated great wealth at home and abroad and the foxes may invite them to enjoy their ill-gotten gains abroad.

KHALYAVA

This slang term has five meanings: a cheap railway station prostitute; to satisfy one's wants at someone's else expense; a female thief; a floozy, whore; something which is easily done. Mikhail Bulgakov, in *Master and Margarita*, uses the word to describe a visit to the theatre without paying. This is the meaning which is adopted here. Some regard it as a modern instinct which is depriving Russia of a bright future. It may be driven by the Russian desire for egalitarianism. Only when Russia has overcome its communist past will *khalyava* be overcome. There is a common view today that it appeared first under communism. It arose out of envy because others had more than oneself. Some would claim that the popularity of Gennady Zyuganov's communists in today's Russia is based on this instinct. However it is a universal trait, according to other Russians. They would point to the experience of western advisers in Russia who under the guise of advice were lining their own pockets. *Khalyava* is something for nothing and this makes it sweeter. The less one pays for something the greater the profit. There are those who delight in seeking out opportunities to eat and drink well at someone else's expense. Some have special suits, the jackets of which have many deep pockets in which they can slip litres of vodka and kilograms of delicacies. This is free-loading with a vengeance but some Muscovites have turned it into an art form. They can usually be recognised by their chubby cheeks and extended waistlines.

In communist times, the family of the leaders lived well at the public's expense. Brezhnev ate strawberries in January and his family enjoyed trips abroad, without paying a kopek, of course. In the Brezhnev era officials expected bribes. An official visiting a farm came away with a chicken or some other meat. The ruling class, the nomenklatura, had special shops where they obtained everything they needed at nominal prices. On official occasions, vodka flowed and food was abundant.

All free for the chosen few, it goes without saying. Long vacations were the right of the ruling class. Payment was never mentioned. There were special rest homes where there were always many beautiful young ladies who appeared to have nothing else to do but to be accommodating to the wishes of the guests. The local big boss rewarded his subordinates with a weekend of pleasure.

When the Soviet state collapsed it was a natural that the nomenklatura would help themselves to the assets which they had been enjoying. Now the chance to own them was irresistible. Best off were those involved in the military-industrial complex. The Soviet state stockpiled large quantities of strategic goods in case of war. The country was divided up into zones with each zone capable of carrying on if others were wiped out. The young reformers in Moscow did not know how much was piled away and where it all was. The local bosses had no intention of telling them. Gradually they discovered that they could steal these reserves, sell them and put the money in offshore accounts. Everyone involved in *khalyava* learnt a new term, *offshorny schet*, offshore account. The first thing they asked when they arrived in the west was how to set up their own *offshorny schet*. If the nomenklatura could do this others were not far behind. Some, like Boris Berezovsky, were astute enough to promise to make members of the ruling class fabulously rich. Their ingenuity knew no bounds. One scam was to produce 35,000 cars with the same number plate and declare that only one had been manufactured. The rest could be sold off at 100 per cent profit. If the state inspector became suspicious he could be cut in on the deal.

Khalyava was much more democratic than communism. Previously there was a strictly observed hierarchy with the big boss getting the most, the middle boss getting less and the little boss getting the least. In public, conspicuous consumption was banned; it could only be enjoyed in private. In reality, the nomenklatura were building a communist system for themselves where they could have everything they desired. The more they consumed the less the people consumed. An astute move by Khrushchev and Brezhnev was to wage a campaign against the theft of public property from time to time. This permitted them to confiscate whatever they liked from whomever they liked. The nomenklatura thus appropriated, or rather, misappropriated, this property as their own.

The hierarchical system disappeared under Gorbachev when he introduced perestroika. This permitted the emergence of private bankers, businessmen, enterprise owners and capitalists. Those who had been restricted previously to the black market could now go legitimate. The skills they had learned in the black economy could now be deployed in full in the legal economy. Since there had been no wholesale market, inputs had had to be stolen from factories. Workers made goods in the factory on the side by stealing inputs and time. Almost everything had a price. No one thought that stealing from the state was wrong, only stealing from one's friend was wrong.

Khalyava led to managers privatising their factories overnight and then engaging in asset stripping. The same applied to the armed forces where soldiers could sell their equipment and uniforms. Officers sold guns, aircraft, indeed anything anyone would buy. The Chechens bought much of the matériel which they used against the Russian army from the Russian army. Whereas the communist party had its property confiscated in Moscow, the Komsomol, the young communist league, retained its property. All its buildings, theatres, sports facilities, gymnasia, hotels, medical facilities and the like throughout Russia were privatised by Komsomol leaders. This was *khalyava* on a grand scale.

Pyramid schemes became enormously popular in the early and mid-1990s because Russians believed that one could get something for nothing. Companies were founded and offered huge dividends in return for vouchers. A few received huge rewards but most lost their investment as the companies were quickly dissolved. The owners could then use the vouchers to acquire state property. The most notorious pyramid scheme was the MMM, run by Sergei Mavrodi. He became a Duma deputy to escape criminal prosecution but he was stripped of his immunity by his fellow deputies. However the belief that one can become rich overnight without any effort is not restricted to Russia. Lotteries are very popular in rich countries. *Khalyava* can lead to accidents. Russians have been known to steal railway lines to sell as scrap metal. They are not concerned about the inevitable derailment of a train. A powerful factor behind *khalyava* is the impoverishment of the people. If it is a choice between stealing and starving, stealing wins every time.

POWER AND PROPERTY

The struggle between power and property began in 1991 and is still going on. The struggle has gone through four phases so far:

- 1991–93: The young reformers concentrated on parcelling out political power among themselves while others concentrated on acquiring property. These included the red directors, the clan chiefs and aspiring oligarchs.

- 1994–96: Those who had acquired power gradually realised that they had given away much of the state's property. They began to think about acquiring property for themselves but found that the most valuable pieces had already been snapped up. These included state cash flows through private banks. There was also the perennial need to borrow money from private banks to augment the state budget. Those with property sought to influence those in power in order to protect and augment their holdings. Those in power gradually realised that they had carried out the reforms in such a way as to leave themselves without property and money. Even worse, it was easy to steal money from them, by not paying tax, or simply by theft of state property, for instance.

- 1996: Power holders began to panic in the light of the December 1995 Duma election results and the upcoming presidential elections. The authorities put together a plan to declare a state of emergency and to cancel the presidential elections. In stepped the property holders who were more self-confident but also had more to lose and proposed a plan which could keep the authorities in power (the Davos pact). The proposal was that the elections would go ahead and appear democratic but the property holders' control of the media would ensure that public opinion could be endlessly manipulated. There was also the point that the authorities would count the votes. As Stalin once remarked, it does not matter how people vote, it matters who counts the votes. Needless to say the property owners drove a hard bargain, a huge swathe of Russia's most valuable state assets in return for winning the presidential election for Yeltsin (loans for shares scheme).

- 1996–2000: The men of property developed an appetite for power. Through their use of the mass media they had resurrected the careers of those in power. The owners of the mass media realised how powerful a weapon the media could be in acquiring and retaining power. Had the mass media barons not intervened the people would have got what they wanted: the communists back in power. Yeltsin's physical frailty led to Chubais coming back as head of the presidential administration and Potanin as deputy Prime Minister, responsible for the economy. However the men of property found that government is more complex than they had envisioned. They were used to taking quick decisions and implementing them even faster. This was the route to riches. Government is much slower, requires patience, consensus building, implementation and a fine understanding of the policy process. Then there was parliament, the procurator general's office and officials and the audit chamber. The men of property had neither the desire nor the patience to master the art of government. They left the government but retained their influence over the President and his family. However the authorities were still large property owners so power was still attractive. The property owners understood how to manage enterprises and those who work in them but not the Russian state. The route to managing the nation was through the media and the media barons set about this task with gusto. Those property owners who had no media outlets were at a grave disadvantage.

Again elections were on the horizon – the Duma elections of December 1999 and the presidential elections of June 2000. The men of property busied themselves with founding political parties and movements, seeking election to the Duma and hunting for a presidential candidate who would win and leave them with their property. Chubais, realising that the state was the largest property owner of all, moved to the United Energy Systems of Russia, the power monopoly. It afforded him property and power. The authorities, the bureaucracy, were not agitated by the prospect of elections because they would remain in power, irrespective of whoever moved into the Kremlin. Those who were agitated were power holders who would be blown away if the communists or someone inimical to their interests succeeded Yeltsin. The President was scouting around for someone who would succeed him and remain loyal to him. This would guarantee him immunity from prosecution and block the sequestration of his and his family's assets.

Founding political parties and movements is not the route to manipulating public opinion and becoming influential. The only route for a new party or movement is through the mass media. There were two main groups, NTV, controlled by Vladimir Gusinsky, and ORT, by Boris Berezovsky. They gave air time to their chosen politicians, governors and opinion makers. In so doing these luminaries became more popular with the public. The Gusinsky clan or party was more conservative and chose Evgeny Primakov. This may have appeared a strange choice: a man of property, as Primakov was, on the political left. His foreign policy was distinctly NATO-unfriendly and he was no admirer of America, the west and the Russian-American pseudo market economy. However it was a case of *faute de mieux*. The alternative was Yury Luzhkov but the Moscow mayor was seen as too ambitious and not to be trusted. He also prevailed over a formidable property empire as the manager of the capital's assets. Berezovsky had always competed with Gusinsky (the exceptions were the Davos pact and the Svyazinvest fracas) and could not choose Luzhkov as Primakov and Luzhkov were joint leaders of the OVR coalition. Berezovsky and his party looked hard and long and eventually found their man, Vladimir Putin. The latter was a brilliant choice. He met one of the most important criteria, loyalty to Yeltsin, even more, personal loyalty to the President.

The Berezovsky media had to transform Putin into a real, Russian hero. There were two routes: cleaning up corruption and cleaning up Chechnya. However Putin was in a hurry and needed instant appeal. Cleaning up corruption cannot be done in a few months. An even more important consideration was that this would have involved cleaning up Berezovsky. Boris had certainly not chosen Vladimir to do that. It had to be Chechnya and it had to be a successful, short war. The Chechens were enticed into Dagestan, Moscow and other cities suffered terrorist attacks and the way was open for violent reprisals. The second Chechen war was reported in two fundamentally different ways, the ORT and the NTV versions. Berezovsky's ORT was less concerned about human rights violations in Chechnya than in making Putin look a great leader. NTV did not want Putin in the Kremlin and therefore reported human rights violations, the suffering of Russian soldiers and how terrible and unnecessary the war was. It also aired doubts that the bombs in Moscow and other cities had been planted by Chechens or Dagestanis. Gusinsky's print media speculated about conspiracy theories. Was Putin behind the bombings? Who had fooled Basaev into invading Dagestan? Unfortunately for Gusinsky and the NTV party, the average Russian wanted the Chechen problem dealt with once and for all. The Moscow bombs had changed the public mood. If this involved wiping out every Chechen, so be it. Putin caught the public mood when he warned, with a string of obscenities, that every Chechen fighter (every Chechen between the ages of 16 and 60 was considered a fighter) would be followed into the shit house (*v sortire*) and wiped out.

And so Putin was elected President. The Berezovsky camp thought that he would complete building the edifice that Yeltsin had begun. This would have made Boris an even greater man of property. They were in for a big surprise. But that is another story.

The key to the story is that Berezovsky and his clan believed they had selected Vladimir Putin as the incoming President. In reality it was Evgeny Primakov and others in the military and intelligence communities who had selected Putin. The beginning of the saga was the sacking of Primakov as Prime Minister and the failure of the Yeltsin camp to force through the nomination of Viktor Chernomyrdin as his successor. That was the moment the Yeltsin camp lost control of events. Sergei Stepashin became Prime Minister and the police did not hide their delight at his elevation. They thought that they were on the road to dominating Russia. Yeltsin claims that he thought of Putin as Prime Minister but put in Stepashin as a stopgap (Yeltsin 2000). One interpretation of this revelation would be that he is putting a gloss on his defeat. Berezovsky believed that by using his media to boost Putin he was benefiting himself in the long term. He was deluding himself. Gusinsky supported Primakov and Luzhkov and may have actually believed that they were serious about going for the presidency. Primakov went through the motions but his interests were elsewhere. Luzhkov was master of Moscow and Moscow oblast and worked out a division of power with Putin. To underline his control of the capital Luzhkov once put 1.5 million demonstrators on the streets of the capital. Moscow is more than the capital of Russia, it is a budding international centre. Of the 10 million inhabitants of greater Moscow there are about 1.5 million Tatars, 500,000 Chechens and Ingushi, 300,000 Azeris, 200,000 Koreans and Chinese, 200,000 Vietnamese, Jews, and many other nationalities. Within a decade or less the majority of Muscovites will be non-Russian. Moscow's economy is divided among these groups, who live in well-defined parts of the city. The Tatars used to sweep the streets of Moscow but have moved economically upwards; the Azeris control the wholesale and retail markets, the Koreans the semi-finished food market and so on. The mayor manages this increasingly dynamic economy. President Putin is at the centre of a new interest group, the military-intelligence community or clan, which is now attempting to dominate Russia. Berezovsky and Gusinsky have lost, for the present but possibly for ever. Neither has been in intelligence and this is a serious drawback when attempting to second guess and outmanoeuvre the Putin clan.

PROPERTY RIGHTS

Karl Marx was fascinated by capital. How was it created? The problem was that it was invisible. He thought one had to go beyond physics to find the 'hen that laid the golden eggs'. Adam Smith wrote that one had to 'create a wagon-way through the air' to get to the hen. But where does the hen live? What then is capital, how does one produce it and how is it related to money? Why is only a small proportion of the population able to create it while the vast majority fails to do so? Capital is not the same as money which is an expression of the value of capital. Capital is the ability to create money out of thin air (de Soto 2000: 10).

There are twenty-five rich capitalist countries in the world and over two hundred poor capitalist countries. What distinguishes the rich from the poor? A functioning legal system which confirms who owns property. Property can be a building, a factory, tangible assets, even intellectual, as in the case of copyright. In all rich countries it is easy to discover who owns what, and to buy and sell that property. There is a central land register and when property changes hands it is recorded in the register. The major advantage of this is that those who own property can go to a bank and obtain credit using their property as collateral. It is quite simple to demonstrate that one has legal title. In this way capital is created. The more property one has the more credit one can obtain. The credit may be used to buy other property and in this way greater wealth is created. Hence the state's recognition of legal title to property is the route to wealth creation.

In poor capitalist countries this is not so. There may be hundreds of central and local government offices which register the legal title to property. Getting registered may take from two to twenty years as there are many steps to go through. Each step requires payment to some official and also payment for the registration. In almost all poor countries the process of the registration of title may cost more than the property is actually worth. Not surprisingly, the owner gives up. The disadvantages of non-registration are severe. The owner cannot use the property as collateral to obtain a loan from a bank and has to save money if he wishes to expand his activities. Since he is already poor this takes a long time. If he does not have legal title – it is estimated that 80 per cent of property in poor countries is not registered – he is outside the law or extralegal. As such he is at the mercy of the tax collector, policeman, bureaucrat and every other servant of the state who grasps the opportunity to extract a bribe to leave him alone. Then there is organised crime. The mafiosi offer to give him protection from the law if he pays up to 20 per cent of his turnover to them. Hence the extralegal economy spawns corruption and organised crime. The state's servants and the mafia benefit most when the extralegal sector expands as this provides them with additional revenue. The imposition of the rule of law is against their interests.

Russia is a poor capitalist country. The Washington whiz kids who advised Gaidar in the early years did not understand that the most important economic reform is legal reform. Land is the most valuable form of property. In 2000, Russia had still not enacted legislation permitting the private ownership of land. All land is still leasehold, meaning that the final owner is the state. As such the state can terminate an individual's lease without due compensation. In the capital, rent has to be paid to the city government of Moscow on all property. The Duma has consistently failed to act on the advice of western lawyers who point out that a functioning market economy is based on legal title to private property. Why not? Because leaving legal ownership murky benefits too many people. Setting up a legal business in Russia is immensely complicated and involves dozens of steps. At each stage a bureaucrat has to be bribed in order to move on to the next stage.

The complexities of becoming legal mean that the vast majority of new businesses remain extralegal. About half the economy may now be extralegal. Some businesses are located behind doors on which there is no indication that a business is operating there. Business cards routinely have no address, only a name. They avoid paying taxes but have to pay bribes.

The greatest drawback of the extralegal economy is lack of credit; those operating there cannot use their property as collateral for a bank loan. It is not surprising that the Russian banking system is mainly concerned with buying and selling government securities, obtaining government accounts and distributing state subsidies. Extending loans to private businesses is a very small part of their activities. Banks normally only deal with big business. There are no private bank accounts, in the western sense, in Russia. Although individuals and private companies have bank accounts, according to Russian law certain entities, such as the tax authorities and some public utilities, are entitled to remove money from these accounts without the prior permission of the account holder. This naturally promotes capital flight, and cash, barter and offshore transactions. In some regions there is private ownership of land. However, legal title is revoked if there is a change of use of the land – for example, if the farmer sells the land to a developer to build houses on it.

According to this analysis, Russia needs to effect a legal revolution before it will take off economically. There is no point leaving the revolution to the lawyers, they are mainly concerned with the status quo. There has to be political will from the centre because the goal is to ensure that a uniform legal system comes into being. A central land register has to be set up. Has the centre the power at present to do this, even if it so desired? The advantage for the centre is that if hundreds of thousands of businesses were brought into the legal sector, tax revenue would increase dramatically. Taxes could also be collected on legally owned property.

THE MARXIST-LENINIST LEGACY

Adherents of this view take ideology seriously. They believe it can subconsciously shape mind patterns even after it has officially been repudiated. Hence it is possible to be an ardent capitalist and democrat but also continue to be influenced by the world view imbibed in one's youth. Take the young reformers, for instance. They believed they could effect an economic revolution from above by introducing the market economy by fiat. All major Russian economic reforms since 1861 have been introduced from above. The state decided it had to catch up with the west and in order to do that it had to imitate the west. Economic reform from above is very Marxist. Change the economic base by fiat and the superstructure (politics, etc.) follows suit. It could also be called Bolshevik capitalism or capitalist Bolshevism. The new capitalists, the oligarchs, were taught, in their Marxist-Leninist classes, that capitalists become rich by theft, coercion, murder and corruption of the state. An honest capitalist is an oxymoron. Every one was a scoundrel. How do capitalists accumulate capital? By exploiting workers, paying them starvation wages. In order to get away with this, they need to have at their command the instruments of coercion of the state, the police and the military. In other words, they have to take over the state and run it in their own interests. The goal of every capitalist is to become a monopolist because if he corners the market he holds everyone else to ransom. Violence between and among big bosses is natural. How else is one to become a monopolist?

The above scenario is natural when capitalism is being established. It is the way it developed in the United States. This is primitive capitalism. When big business has taken over and agreed on a mutually beneficial distribution of the spoils, the country can then move towards civilised or advanced capitalism. In the United States it took almost a century. Russia is still at the stage of primitive capitalism. The language of the oligarchs is instructive. Berezovsky is fond of the expression 'primitive capital accumulation'. This is Marx's term. His view of US capitalism, in its formative years, is from Marx's interpretation of history. The same is true of Chubais. From a Marxist perspective, the new bourgeoisie runs the state in its own interests. State officials are there to facilitate the rule of the bourgeoisie and help it to distribute the spoils. The young reformers shared Marx's view that the state plays no useful role in a capitalist economy. It does not facilitate economic growth, capitalists do that. However the young reformers did not take on board Marx's insight that in a capitalist system illegal and corrupt activities are rational if they are profitable. In many successful capitalist countries high levels of corruption fuelled rapid economic growth during the early and middle stages of capitalist expansion (England in the eighteenth century, the United States during the 1850s). The reason why Russia is different is that the government permitted the flow of corruptly acquired wealth abroad. Had the money been invested in Russia, the situation now would be quite different. From this perspective they did not learn enough from Marx. Another aspect, which may go back to Marx, was the young reformers' neglect of small business. They concentrated on medium and large scale enterprises and did not create the incentives for small entrants to the market. New commercial banks to provide capital for small businesses were not encouraged to emerge. As a result, many small businesses operate in the informal economy. The lack of understanding of the importance of secure property rights appears to flow from the young reformers' formative Marxist years. Marx's economic theory is derived from studying companies in the mid-nineteenth century. They are light years away from modern corporations. Hence the young reformers had little understanding of modern capitalist companies. The corollary is that American advisers were well versed in the behaviour of modern corporations but did not grasp that Russia's companies were still at the pre-corporate stage of development.

This view sees Russia's move to capitalism as a replay of Marx's analysis. Even though Berezovsky, the oligarchs, Chubais and the young reformers thought they had repudiated Marx and Marxism, in reality, Marx was exacting his revenge on them. The subliminal influence of Marx has been very pervasive. The new ruling class in Russia has a Marxist view of capitalism. Accepting a western view of capitalism will be a slow process. Tony Blair's capitalism and the capitalism flayed by Charles Dickens are about a century and a half apart. A civilised capitalist Rome cannot be built in a day.

WHO IS TO BLAME?

Russian analysts tend to fall into two groups: the optimists and the pessimists, with the latter in a large majority. Both groups present Russia as a morality play, a battle between good and evil. The optimists search for heroes and the pessimists for villains (Treisman 2000). Leon Aron (2000) casts Yeltsin as the hero, battling indomitably against the forces of backwardness, fraud and deceit to lead Russia triumphantly into a brighter future. Lilia Shevtsova (1999) is in like vein. Stephen Cohen (2000), on the other hand, is a convinced pessimist and has been one since 1991. Like Archie Brown, he mourns the passing of Mikhail

Gorbachev. Cohen thinks that the Soviet Union in 1991 was a successfully reforming state. Most of the essential social and economic institutions were still intact. This evolving system was destroyed by an American political crusade to transform Russia into a 'replica of America'. The 'missionaries and evangelists' who preached the gospel of 'tight-fisted monetarism' were the advisers from the IMF and Harvard. The result was the 'demodernisation' of Russia. By allowing Jeffrey Sachs and his cohorts to 'swarm' over the Russian plain, President Clinton did more damage to US interests than did the war in Vietnam. Cohen made his reputation with an acclaimed biography of Nikolai Bukharin, the Bolshevik who favoured a more gentle road to socialism than the one chosen by Iosif Stalin. Stalin was not impressed and devoured him. In turn, Gorbachev's Soviet Union, according to Cohen, was devoured by wild American monetarists. This is far from the case. The Soviet Union's economy was in a state of collapse in 1991. Inflation, for instance, was over 160 per cent. The budget deficit was out of control. Asset stripping by enterprise directors was in full flow and the extralegal economy was approaching half of the whole economy. In stepped Gaidar with his liberalisation of prices and free market economics. With the wisdom of hindsight, he might have held off freeing prices for a year or two. However Ukraine did so and suffered even more severe inflation and asset stripping than Russia.

Just how influential were the American monetarist gurus? Cohen and others, for instance Janine Wedel, assume that they were dominant. They waltzed through the Kremlin as modern-day Pied Pipers of Hamelin. Gaidar and the young reformers were entranced by them and followed them to their doom. The Russian people also joined the queue of admirers. This gives the impression that central government was strong and radically changed Russia. Reality was different. Central government was weak and could not raise enough revenue to balance the budget. Russia's economic policies were unsuccessful but would different polices have been much more successful?

Chrystia Freeland (2000) does not believe that the Harvard conmen caused the downfall of the Russian economy. She hunts for villains and eventually identifies them: Russia's own oligarchs. To her the oligarchs laid the foundations which distorted Russia's development. The main fault lay with the Russian government who struck an infamous deal – the loans for shares deal – and thereby ruined the country. One cannot build a sound economy on such treacherous foundations. The main objection to this argument is that Russia's economic foundations were unsound before the loans for shares scheme. It was a product of the way the country was being managed or rather mismanaged. Gorbachev created the conditions for the emergence of the oligarchs and they initiated the infamous deal. They did not bring original sin into the country, they merely took advantage of a fallen society. Given the huge natural monopolies that existed, it was almost inevitable that a small number of oligarchs would emerge. The key question was whether they would emerge from the red nomenklatura or would be young economic upstarts. They turned out to be mainly Jewish mathematicians and theatre people. Again they did not create the economic environment, they were just smart enough to take advantage of it. The oligarchs took risks but one does not become super rich without taking big risks. They gambled that Yeltsin would win the 1996 presidential election and ensured that he did. Looking after their investment took top priority. The affair damaged the government and it failed to attract any bidders for Rosneft, the oil company. The problem with identifying the oligarchs as the arch-villains is that the Russian economy improved during the period when their influence was greatest. Foreign direct investment, in 1996–98, was three times that of the three preceding years. Real GDP dropped on average by 8.5 per cent during the years 1993–95 but by only 2.4 per cent annually during 1996–98; the percentage of those in poverty also fell in 1996–98. Yeltsin was almost persuaded to cancel the presidential elections of 1996 because he thought he could not win. Had he done so the result could have been civil war. Those who dissuaded him were Chubais and General Anatoly Kulikov, the minister of the interior. The former is an honorary oligarch and no one has ever accused Kulikov of being a democrat. Yet they saved Russian democracy.

Paul Klebnikov (2000) sees original sin entering Russia through one man, Boris Berezovsky. He is the arch-villain whose machinations and nefarious influence distorted Russia's development. He is the Don Corleoni of Russia and deserves the sobriquet, Don Boris. He transformed corruption into an art form. Again one can rejoin that Boris was just bright enough to take advantage of the world in which he found himself.

Peter Reddaway and Dmitri Glinski (2001) have no doubts about the origin of the disease which has crippled Russia. Master Bolsheviks Boris Yeltsin, Anatoly Chubais and probably also Egor Gaidar set out in 1991 to nip the democratic revolution in the bud and prevent the middle class from taking over Russia. They sought to restrict power and wealth to elites. In other words, the communist hierarchical system was retained. Those on top ruled and those underneath accepted their decisions. Shock therapy and privatisation added up to market Bolshevism. The market was imposed from above and geared towards bringing into being a new nomenklatura. It succeeded beyond their wildest dreams. Gaidar, Chubais and the other members of their team saw themselves as gods, not accountable to the rest of the population. The most successful businessmen, the oligarchs, also acquired political influence. This is one reason why political parties, or interest groups embracing the whole population, have not developed in Russia. Politics under Yeltsin can be seen as a conflict among clans, elites and groups for wealth and influence with the rest of the population as bystanders.

All six explanations given above, from roving bandits to the Marxist-Leninist legacy, assume that Russia was the master of its own destiny. To argue that the United States 'lost' Russia is to accord to Washington an influence which it never enjoyed. Russians are brilliant at saying one thing and doing another. The most one can claim is that Americans gave advice but Russians decided themselves what to do. Chubais was a master at giving Washington the impression that he was their man while pursuing his own policies. With hindsight it was fortunate for Russia that most foreign advice fell on deaf ears. Many claimed to know the best route for Russia to take from communism to something better; however, no one actually knew or knows what should be done to transform Russia. How is one to overcome corruption in public and private life? How should one enact legislation promoting the private ownership of land and securing legal title to it? How should one promote economic growth so as to make Russia competitive on the world stage? To repeat, no one knows. There are no simple recipes which, if applied, will succeed. Russians themselves will have to find the way out of the maze they are in. The US economy is not a universal model. It is the result of a combination of circumstances which has proved uniquely successful. Its policy preferences cannot be transferred to Russia. Mother Russia must give birth to her own economic model. It may never be as successful as the American or it may become in time more successful. At present, no one knows which of these two possibilities is more probable.

2

BRILLIANT TACTICAL BUT DISASTROUS STRATEGIC POLICIES: THE GORBACHEV ERA

JESUS CHRIST JOINS AN AEROFLOT FLIGHT from Irkutsk to Vladivostok in Siberia. He approaches a passenger. 'I can grant you any wish you like.' 'Oh, I should like all communists to disappear from the face of the earth.' 'Yes, that can be arranged.' He moves on to another passenger. 'And do you have a special wish?' 'Yes, I want all fascists to be done away with.' 'All right, I can arrange that.' He then comes to another passenger, a Jew. 'Is it really true that you are going to do what those two gentlemen asked?', he asks doubtfully. 'Of course. After all, I am the son of God.' 'Well, in that case, I should just like a cup of coffee.'

The moral of this story is that it would take divine intervention to get a cup of coffee on an Aeroflot flight. The planned economy is so inefficient it cannot deliver such a simple request. This is the economy that Mikhail Gorbachev set out to restructure or reform in 1985. He was unaware at the time that he needed divine intervention to succeed but by 1991 he would ruefully have to admit that this was so. The fundamental reason why Gorbachev failed was because he did not fully understand the forces which shaped the Soviet political and economic system. What he was trying to do was to reform the economy by issuing orders from the centre at a time when enterprises had developed considerable skill in protecting their own interests. They pursued techniques which served self-interest but which did not serve the national interest. Gorbachev eventually introduced elements of the market to the

Soviet economy but they led to its disintegration instead of transforming it into a more efficient economy. How did the Soviet command or planned economy come into existence and why did it prove impossible to reform it successfully? Reform here is understood as providing enough quality goods to satisfy the demand of the Soviet population.

THE PLANNED ECONOMY

Karl Marx did not like the market economy. It should be replaced by an economy which produced for need, not for profit. Lenin and the Bolsheviks were enamoured of this way of thinking and set about implementing it as quickly as possible after taking power in 1917. An extreme version came into being during the Russian civil war of 1918–20 when one of the prerequisites, the abolition of money, was almost achieved. The failure of this first attempt forced a rethink in 1921 and the New Economic Policy was introduced to keep the Bolsheviks in power. It was a mixed economy, public and private ownership, and money again played an important role. The fierce succession struggle which broke out after Lenin died in 1924 was resolved by the end of the decade, with Stalin the clear victor. Now he could turn his mind to introducing the centrally planned economy. This economy was based on the logical assumption that if the resources of society were assembled and deployed optimally, the result would be superior to anything achieved in a market economy. Implicit in Stalin's economic model was the belief that no economic actor (managers, workers) harboured interests which ran counter to the interests of society as a whole. Hence self-interest and the national interest coincided. The reason for this was the belief that conflict only arose if private property still existed. If all property were nationalised, or belonged to society as a whole, then conflicts of interests which could harm the economy (called antagonistic contradictions by Marx) could not arise. However this logical analysis turned out to be fatally flawed.

The Bolsheviks sought to manage the Soviet economy as a single economic space. The Five Year Plans became law and each enterprise had to follow the orders of the planners in Moscow. The state was eliminating the risk faced by every producer. Factories and farms did not need to work out the optimal mix of output. Their inputs were provided and their output was disposed of by the state. Enterprises were paid in money by the state but the money went immediately into state banks. The money to pay wages was forwarded by Moscow and the money in circulation was equal to the amount necessary to purchase all the consumer goods, pay for services such as transport, etc. Since enterprises could incur harsh penalties for not fulfilling the plan they learnt to stockpile resources to provide a cushion if inputs failed to arrive on time. They also became clever at reporting what the planners wanted to hear. A major problem for Stalin was to discover the true potential of each factory and farm since he was aware that they cheated by underreporting. He wanted to squeeze more work out of the workers and thereby increase labour productivity. Many campaigns were launched to achieve greater output from available resources. In the 1930s they were reported as great successes but under Gorbachev it was revealed that they had achieved very little. Workers realised that they were treated as a cheap resource as they had been before 1917. Quality suffered in the race to increase output. This reduced interest in innovation. Another reason was that if an innovation did not achieve its potential and the factory underfulfilled the plan it was penalised. Economic problems were looming in the late 1930s but the onset of war in 1941 transformed the situation. Rigid central planning collapsed and enterprises maximised output from available resources by using their own initiative. As a consequence when the central planners attempted to reassert their control after 1945 they were never really successful.

The Soviet economy was a wholly militarised economy. Such was the fear of invasion that the production of war matériel took precedence. Consumer goods were produced to keep labour at the workplace and to ensure that capacity was fully utilised. Machinery was dual purpose. Macaroni and cigarettes were produced at the same calibre as rifles. Stalin accepted that workers expected rising living standards but to him the amount available for consumption was equal to the surplus of the war economy. After 1945 prices were reduced annually making it possible to abolish money in the future.

REFORMS FROM KHRUSHCHEV TO GORBACHEV

After Stalin's death in 1953 Nikita Khrushchev promised to raise living standards (average living standards were still below those of 1913) as part of his bid to win the succession struggle. The major problem was raising labour productivity. In order to do this there had to be incentives. However since Khrushchev had abandoned coercion as a motivating force he had to fall back on persuasion. He held out the glittering prospect of the beginnings of communism (to each according to need, from each according to ability) in 1981. Almost all his reforms were concerned about getting more production out of the workers. Some aspects of the economy were highly successful under Khrushchev – the first Sputnik, the first man in space, the first woman in space and the first dog in space. However they ate up resources at an alarming rate. He did attempt to trim the military budget but his bellicose foreign policy ensured that defence expenditure had to be increased. Khrushchev believed that the economy was ready for take off but, in reality, it had almost reached its zenith. The slow decline then began.

The first attempt to introduce elements of the market into the planned economy occurred in 1965, the Kosygin reforms, named after the Prime Minister. Enterprises were permitted greater decision-making powers and were encouraged to link up with end-users. They could also sack workers. It all came to grief in 1968 when the Soviet Union and its allies invaded Czechoslovakia to put an end to 'socialism with a human face'. The need to produce more consumer goods led to the emergence of the consumer sector of the Soviet economy in the late 1960s. This complicated the task of the central planners because there were always political pressures to invest more in the consumer sector thereby draining resources from the primary, military economy.

There was much debate during the 1970s about improving the economic mechanism (an expression much employed in the early Gorbachev era). It was code for increasing labour productivity. A key question, that of ownership, was evaded. Proposals that cooperatives could be more efficient than state-owned enterprises and private farming more productive that collective and state farming were ruled inadmissible by the communist party. There could be no private ownership under socialism. However the economy, in the 1970s, did start producing a surplus not needed by the military or the civilian population. The Soviet Union began to export increasing quantities of oil, natural gas and raw materials. As the output of these resources increased, however, the rest of the economy began to slow down. Agriculture was, as before, the Achilles heel and export revenues helped to pay for mounting food and grain imports from the west, primarily the United States. As Brezhnev became addicted to drugs from the mid-1970s so the Soviet ruling class (nomenklatura) became addicted to the good life. This bred corruption which previously had lubricated the wheels of the economy but was now becoming a brake on development. The workers took the nomenklatura as their role model. Lazy bosses meant lazy workers. Boozing became a national disease (except in the Muslim republics). The invasion of Afghanistan, in December 1979, suggested the leadership was drunk when they took the decision but they were stone-cold sober. America and the west, the Muslim world and, it appeared, everyone else turned on the

Soviet Union. The Americans began to increase their defence budget thereby forcing Moscow to devote more resources to defence in an economy which had almost ceased to grow.

From the mid-1970s the planners proved unable to manage a mixed military and consumer economy. A major reason for this was that resources were running out. Previously achieving growth had been simple: invest more resources. Now quantitative growth had to give way to qualitative growth and, not surprisingly, the planners were not up to the task. Brezhnev gave way to Andropov who was dying when he took over – an apt metaphor for the Soviet Union. He was on a dialysis machine and this gave rise to some terrible jokes. 'Comrade Andropov will illuminate any discussion.' He is the 'most switched-on man in Moscow'. At least he did try. He knew what was wrong but that was not a great achievement. It was obvious to every beggar in Moscow. People were not working and when they were not working they were drinking. Get them all back to work and this would solve two problems: how to increase output and how to cut down on alcoholism. However no one was afraid of comrade Andropov, even though he had been head of the KGB for years. Some enterprising gentlemen borrowed militia uniforms and fined workers found in shops on the spot. Andropov discovered that a Russian and his drink cannot be parted. As vodka disappeared it was replaced by samogon (hooch), toothpaste, shoe polish and other illicit beverages. All this gave an enormous boost to the black economy and swelled the ranks of the crooks and criminals (called the *mafiya* or mafia under Gorbachev). Private property was not protected by the communist state so the new entrepreneurs had to turn to the criminals for protection. The road to hell is paved with the best intentions. Andropov was duly followed by the dying Chernenko whose emphysema was so bad that he could not speak coherently most of the time. He soon died. This produced the joke about two foreign heads of state meeting at Chernenko's funeral. 'Do you attend many funerals in Moscow?' 'Yes, I have a season ticket.'

ENTER GORBACHEV

Mikhail Gorbachev was a breath of fresh air in the Kremlin: 'What support does Gorbachev have?', 'None, he can walk unaided.' The old men in the Politburo thought they were putting a younger, more dynamic version of themselves in power. Andrei Gromyko, the veteran foreign minister – dubbed Grim Grom and Mr Nyet after his habit of saying no to anything the west proposed – waxed eloquent on the talents of the new comrade general secretary. He repented at leisure as Gorbachev set about dismantling the Soviet communist edifice. All Grim Grom could do was to grind his teeth and look even more morose. Gromyko had graduated from the Stalinist school of politics – the boss was always right. Hence he did not join any conspiracy against Gorbachev – he was dead before the attempted August 1991 coup.

Gorbachev's record before he became general secretary in March 1985 was unremarkable and this was one of the factors which led to his election as communist leader, the second most powerful man in the world after the American President. He had grown up in the north Caucasus and missed some schooling during the German occupation of his village. This was always evident in his command of Russian. It was replete with wrong endings and stresses and he never overcame his habit of not completing some sentences. Given his rural, farm background it was even more remarkable that he gained entry to the prestigious Moscow University. He spent five years studying law, a subject which was not taken very seriously in the Soviet Union. However it opened his eyes to foreign legal systems and philosophies and this was to prove valuable later. At university he met and married his great love, Raisa Maksimovna Titorenko. She was brighter and was to develop a greater insight into human cunning than her husband. They were a remarkable couple and he was always ready to express his great debt to her – he delighted in pointing out that she had better academic qualifications than he had. How many husbands would do that?

Gorbachev moved back to Stavropol krai after graduation and, after a stint in the local procurator's office – long enough to convince him that a legal career would bore him to death – he moved into Komsomol or young communist work. The ambitious Gorbachev was often appalled by the poverty, both material and intellectual, that he encountered. Nevertheless he mastered the rules of the game and eventually became communist party leader in his home territory. An ambitious politician had to get to Moscow, and Gorbachev was convinced he was a cut above the others in Stavropol. His big break came in 1978 when he was appointed (in Politburo speak, elected) secretary for agriculture. As such he was the party's top man for the rural sector and above the minister of agriculture. The rural economy did not flourish under his management, indeed it continued its decline, proving incapable of feeding the Soviet population. So why did Gorbachev progress up the ladder? Leonid Brezhnev, the general secretary, regarded agriculture as his pet project, and could only concentrate for short periods of time. Agriculture was just one of the sectors which was in terminal decline from the later 1970s onwards. After Brezhnev came Yury Andropov, who had a soft spot for Gorbachev and had promoted his career, then Konstantin Chernenko who did his breathless best to spoil Gorbachev's chances of succeeding him.

THE NEW TEAM

A new leader always chooses a new team. Gorbachev did not have the freedom of action of a US president or a British prime minister. He was mindful that he had been elected leader but that many saw him as first among equals. His task was to clear out the deadwood of the Brezhnev era and to appoint over time those who would provide dynamic management after the drift of the previous ten years. He made Nikolai Ryzhkov, an industrialist from the Urals, his Prime Minister and Eduard Shevardnadze, first party secretary in Georgia, his foreign minister. Ryzhkov was not a controversial appointment but Shevardnadze's elevation surprised even him and outraged the foreign ministry. Andrei Gromyko had not even been consulted and expected one of his clones to take over. Gorbachev's move was astute as he wanted a non-establishment figure to implement his new thinking in foreign policy. Gorbachev knew that the increasing defence burden was breaking the back of the Soviet Union and that his economic reforms would fail unless defence spending could be contained. Various other appointments were made including the transfer of Boris Yeltsin from being party leader in Sverdlovsk oblast, in the Urals, to Central Committee secretary for construction. This made him responsible for the construction industry throughout the Soviet Union.

PERESTROIKA

Academician Yury Yaremenko, an outstanding economist who died in 1996, devised the concept of resources in the Soviet economy. He divided them into third grade, second grade and first grade. All first grade resources went into the defence sector. Great skill was needed to make the Soviet economy more efficient because it rested on finding the right mix of resources. The gulf between the defence industries and the civilian economy was vast and unbridgeable in the short term. Waste was built into the system. The use of water, electricity, gas and heat was very wasteful as these services were not metered. The oil industry was also very wasteful of resources; it was common practice to flare or burn off the natural gas which was a byproduct of oil extraction. Too much water was mixed with oil in the pipelines. Contrary to common belief it was not the defence economy which was the most wasteful but the civilian economy. The highest quality products were in the defence sector with the rejection ratio sometimes almost 100 per cent. Defence rejects were fed into the civilian economy: poor quality became endemic. The primary reason for fires in flats in Moscow was exploding television sets. Gorbachev appreciated that the days of extensive growth were over: there were shortages of materials, labour and land. Labour productivity would now have to rise faster than investment. The name given to this mammoth task was perestroika or restructuring. This was to embrace all aspects of human endeavour, from steel making to primary school teaching. The goal was simple: utilise resources more efficiently – but how was this to be done?

Gorbachev had a limited grasp of Soviet economic reality. His career had been mainly in agriculture and he had not been responsible for large enterprises or a key industrial region of the country. He knew there were first, second and third grade resources but how did one change the mix to improve results? Various commissions, set up under Andropov, were given the task of making the system more efficient. However, they laboured under certain constraints, the most important one being that the rationale behind all reform was to strengthen the position of the communist ruling class, the nomenklatura, first and foremost the party elite.

Gorbachev thought the system was fine. It was like an engine which needed an overhaul. It would take Gorbachev two years before he realised that the system was not fine, that in fact the country was facing a systemic crisis. Abel Aganbegyan, one of Gorbachev's leading reform economists, concluded in 1988 that there had been no economic growth over the years 1981–85. The goal set for the Five Year Plan (1986–90) was for the machine-building sector to expand by 50–100 per cent, industrial production by 25 per cent, investment by 23.6 per cent and real (actual minus inflation) per capita income by 14 per cent. No one at the time pointed out that these goals were mutually incompatible. How could investment rise by almost a quarter while living standards also rose significantly? Most of the investment would go into machine-building which would only have a marginal impact on living standards. How were the various resources, first, second and third grade, to be juggled to improve efficiency without a sweeping price reform, one which would reflect the relative scarcity of goods? There was another burning issue – property. Was the solution to efficiency to transform state enterprises and farms into genuine cooperatives? Property proved such a hot potato that it was never really addressed under

Gorbachev. Price reform was also politically explosive with the result that the regime shied away from it.

Yaremenko was a pessimist when it came to perestroika. As far as he was concerned the main reason for the decline of the Soviet economy was the ability of ministries and agencies (especially the military) to escape from central planning control. They then followed their own interests and devoured resources. This led to a weakening of the communist party. Gorbachev's reforms promised greater autonomy and this was bound to end in disappointment. Yaremenko believed that the Soviet Union had to get out of the cold war if it were to survive. The world-class defence plants had to be converted to civilian production. This required good management from the centre. The transition to the market would take up to three generations. Yaremenko's writings had no impact because they were couched in technical economic language; as such they were incomprehensible to Gorbachev and the party elite.

Perestroika was long on promises and short on actual results. A story circulating in Minsk in 1986 summed up the public mood. Gorbachev, President Mitterrand of France and President Reagan meet and start discussing their problems. Mitterrand says he has nine mistresses and one is cheating on him but he can't work out which one. Reagan says that this is a minor problem compared to his. He has fifty guards and one of them is a KGB agent but he can't identify him. Gorbachev waves all this aside and says his problem is much more serious. He has a hundred ministers in his government and one of them is implementing perestroika but he doesn't know which one it is.

The new general secretary liked meeting people and travelling the country to preach his new gospel of perestroika. This was a welcome change from the previous leaders who only existed in virtual reality. Gorbachev was the first Soviet leader who took to television. He was a natural and was coached by Aleksandr Yakovlev (later to be called the father of glasnost) who had realised the potential of the TV image while being Soviet ambassador in Canada. Like all naturals Gorbachev was concerned about looking his best on TV. He went to the barber every day and spent much time deciding which tie went with which suit. On one occasion he visited a hospital and was shown healthy-looking patients sporting crew cuts. They were full of praise for the medical staff and the food but very vague about their ailments. It transpired that the KGB had turfed out the real patients and drafted in their own men! When the general secretary visited a worker's flat he found the kitchen table groaning under the weight of the delicacies. He went to Siberia and berated oil workers for their wastefulness. In the Soviet Union only 58 per cent of oil was refined whereas in the west it was about 80 per cent, and a cubic metre of timber only produced a fraction of the finished product expected in the west. Where Mikhail went Raisa was sure to go. She concerned herself with the TV coverage and objected to her husband being seen from the rear. As Yakovlev wryly remarked: 'Many people would be very pleased if the backs of their heads appeared on TV every day.'

Gorbachev continued Andropov's drive against alcohol. He was quickly dubbed the mineral water general secretary. A decree went out that the Soviet fishing fleet in the Pacific was to go dry. An inspection turned up the fact that there were 576 bottles of vodka on board but they were all for the second navigator's wedding! The development of viticulture was stunted. About 200,000 ha of vines were uprooted, particularly in Armenia. The loss to the Soviet exchequer was also severe. Foregone revenue in 1986 amounted to about $2 billion and $1.2 billion in 1987. Another $1.1 billion was lost due to lower wine production. In 1987, the legal production of alcohol dropped by over 50 per cent, while half a million persons were convicted for bootlegging. Samogon production skyrocketed. In 1987, about 180 million decilitres of hooch were produced, which works out at about six litres per man, woman and child in the Soviet Union. A wry joke was that Gorbachev's anti-alcohol campaign accelerated the collapse of the Soviet Union. People woke up from their drunken stupor and realised what a mess the country was in. They demanded a better style of life.

Alcoholism was also a personal tragedy for Gorbachev's own family. Raisa's younger brother, Evgeny, was an alcoholic and suffered bouts of depression after his wife left him in the mid-1970s. In 1985 he was given a larger flat in Voronezh but his condition deteriorated. Aware that he could prove an embarrassment to Gorbachev he was kept under close surveillance and eventually confined to a mental hospital. He is still there and has had no contact with his in-laws since 1992.

Radical economic reforms were promulgated in June and July 1987. The most significant was the law on the state enterprise. There were others on scientific-technical progress, financial mechanisms, prices, banking, branch ministries, republican agencies and social policy. Many ministries were abolished and the new legislation stated that ministries were to concentrate on long-term planning and technical innovation and leave enterprises to manage themselves. Gosplan lost half its staff. There were over 800 republican ministries and departments (responsible for activity only in their republics) and Gorbachev wanted to reduce their staffs also by a half. One of the goals was to increase the economic auto-nomy of the republics *vis-à-vis* the centre in Moscow. This was very good news for the local political and economic elites as they gained greater and greater control over their own territories. It was very bad news for economic efficiency as local enterprises acted in their own interests and ignored the national interest.

The law on the state enterprise provided for the election of directors and all management down to foremen, the election of works councils and a general assembly of all workers in an enterprise. What type of manager was elected? One who promised wage rises, safe jobs and increas-ing living standards. This law had momentous consequences for the Soviet Union and they were almost all negative. The raft of legislation passed in 1987 strengthened the trend towards regionalism and nationalism. Perestroika was now slipping away from the centre to the local level. Gorbachev did not realise that his reforms were strengthening the local ruling class and in so doing he was fast losing his ability to influence their behaviour positively.

Gorbachev's problem was that he knew what he did not want: the command-administrative system. But what should take its place? Capitalism? Of course not. A major problem was that he simply did not understand how a market economy functioned. He pleaded with the Americans for money as if dollars would magically transform a dying system into a vibrant economy. In December 1989, Nikolai Ryzhkov, the Prime Minister, presented to deputies a carefully worked-out tran-sition to market relations. There were two stages, each taking three years. Gavriil Popov ridiculed Ryzhkov's grasp of economics and told him that there were five fundamental laws which had to be introduced: on ownership, land, enterprises, economic independence of republics and local self-management. The problem was that Ryzhkov was talking about moving to a socialist market while Popov was advocating a cap-italist market.

Nevertheless Ryzhkov's group, headed by academician Leonid Abalkin, had many sensible ideas. Abalkin was much taken by the Japanese model of development and he and the government tried to establish a banking system which brought banks into close association with top industrial organisations (Hough 2001: 36–43). In 1987, USSR Gosbank was split into five specialised banks, corresponding to major sectors of the eco-nomy. In 1988–89, many commercial banks were founded to supplement the specialised banks. Some of these new banks serviced cooperatives and quickly became known as mafia banks. The largest branch bank was Avtobank, which serviced the automobile industry. Its director was the head of the finance department of the ministry for the automobile industry. As industry developed, these banks could become more like commercial banks in Japan or Germany. However they were not given the opportunity.

THE 500-DAY PROGRAMME

Gorbachev's lack of understanding of a market economy was shared by everyone else in the country. Market economists, such as Egor Gaidar, Gregory Yavlinsky and Boris Fedorov, preached the market with the religious zeal of converts. The only thing they lacked was doubt. They were brilliant mathematical economists and it was simple to prove that a command economy was inefficient and a market economy was efficient. Their teachers, academicians Shatalin, Abalkin and Petrakov, were wizards at simultaneous equations. The problem was that none of them had ever worked in industry or in a market economy.

How quickly should the country move to the market? The dapper, handsome Nikolai Ryzhkov, favoured the slow boat approach whereas the Shatalin–Yavlinsky group were for the big bang, which later became known as shock therapy. Gorbachev resorted to the old device, when in doubt set up a committee. The group set to work in a dacha outside Moscow, in August 1990. By 21 August the group came up with their panacea: the 500-day programme. Why 500? Think of a number between 1 and 10 and add two noughts! It had only symbolic importance as no government can move to a market economy in 18 months. The road to the market was signposted step by step. Privatisation and, of course, private property were of key significance. Gorbachev wanted a merger of the two approaches but this was not feasible; the gulf was too wide. The 500-day programme envisaged little state intervention whereas the other was heavily interventionist. In the former the Union government would be weak, in the latter it would be a strong, central force. On the crucial issue of taxation, the former proposed that republics collect taxes and transfer an agreed amount to the centre. In the latter the federal authorities would tax and collect the taxes themselves.

Yeltsin did not need to know much about economics to decide which version he favoured. The Russian government had participated in the drafting of the 500-day programme. The Russian Supreme Soviet adopted the radical programme in principle, in September 1990. The vote was quite startling: 213 for and one against. This underlined the fact that the communists had grasped that the programme gave them control of Russia. A tactic that Russia developed was to sign economic agreements with other republics without consulting the centre and try to wean away Union or centrally controlled enterprises and farms.

Privatisation at the local level was to be supervised by local soviets and the IMF and western governments objected to this. They also objected to the welfare social net which would cushion the effects of rapid change. Probably the most important reason why the plan never got off the ground was that the Bush administration was unwilling to commit funds to the Soviet Union during a recession in the United States.

GLASNOST

Glasnost became a top priority after the dreadful Chernobyl disaster in April 1986. The media handled it poorly, even putting it about in Kiev that there was no danger from radiation. At the same time the elite made off to more secure places. The public's view of the media was that its main task was to whitewash the regime whiter than white. A wit neatly summed it up. While watching a parade on Red Square, Napoleon sighs and says: 'Had I had tanks like those I would have won the battle of Waterloo.' Brezhnev comments: 'Had you had newspapers like ours no one would yet have found out that you lost the battle of Waterloo.'

Aleksandr Yakovlev was let loose to bring news alive. He appointed Vitaly Korotich editor of *Ogonek*, hitherto a run-of-the-mill magazine. Korotich soon made it spicy reading by publishing articles about the sins of the past, especially the Stalin era. However he was unconvinced of the real potential of glasnost, regarding it as tantamount to 'giving an old trollop a sponge bath, dressing her in clean clothes and assuming that this would restore her virginity'. Various other journals were taken over by new editors and ensured that the intelligentsia were on Gorbachev's side. Not every reader welcomed the changes. One old lady complained that she did not buy a newspaper to read bad news. She thought that Gorbachev's Soviet Union was going to the dogs.

In June 1986, the general secretary had a go at Gosplan (state planning commission) and the economic ministries. The next month he told newspaper editors that he was aware that party bosses around the country did not want glasnost. In Siberia, he was taken aback by the lack of concern of party officials for the population. A Moscow party boss advised his men to sit tight because in a few years everything would settle down.

Clearly the ruling class would not give up its privileges without a fight. In January 1987, Gorbachev went so far as to permit the cold draught of foreign criticism to waft over the country. The jamming of the BBC, Deutsche Welle and Voice of America ended. An even more formidable voice arrived in March 1987, Margaret Thatcher, the British Prime Minister. She demanded (Mrs Thatcher never asked) a live interview on Soviet TV. She used it to demolish her male interviewers and laid into Soviet violations of human right and Afghanistan. In the land of male chauvinism Soviet women hugged themselves with glee.

YELTSIN BREAKS WITH GORBACHEV

Gorbachev had inherited Viktor Grishin as party boss in Moscow. He was known as the Godfather and was so corrupt that he boasted to the press that he was unassailable. Gorbachev, an outsider, he was from Stavropol, brought in another outsider, Boris Yeltsin, from Sverdlovsk, to restructure Moscow. He was on to a hiding to nothing. The Moscow elites were past masters at cosmetic politics, saying they had implemented legislation but carrying on lining their own pockets. The tactic Yeltsin adopted was to transform himself into a populist. He was to be the voice of the ordinary man and woman. He went to work by trolleybus and metro (the underground), he took away officials' cars and sacked many of them. This made him a hero to Muscovites but a villain to the officials.

Yeltsin, a man of mood swings, became depressed by his inability to deal with the Moscow establishment. He requested Gorbachev, sunning himself on the Black Sea, to permit him to leave the Politburo and the Moscow job. Communication between two such strong personalities as Gorbachev and Yeltsin was never good at the best of times. They fell out in spectacular fashion. At a party plenum, on 21 October 1987, Yeltsin suddenly asked for the floor and reiterated his accusation that the party Secretariat was dragging its feet on perestroika. He also directly criticised Gorbachev and Raisa. This broke the taboo that there could not be any *ad hominem* criticisms of the leader, let alone his spouse. Gorbachev lost his temper and berated Yeltsin in Stalinist language. He then invited others to participate. The party wolves tore into Boris and his lame response was that Politburo members were not implementing perestroika and were not real supporters of the general secretary.

On 9 November Yeltsin was found covered in blood. Gorbachev read it as a suicide attempt using scissors to wound himself. Yeltsin lost his positions on the Politburo and in Moscow. On the latter occasion he had to come from his hospital bed to the meeting and propped up his head with his hands. In order not to give the impression that Yeltsin was being victimised he was made deputy chair of the state committee on construction with the rank of a government minister.

This was the parting of the ways for Gorbachev and Yeltsin. The two men were political heavyweights and also quite emotional with a highly developed sense of their own importance. Yeltsin was a strong supporter of perestroika out of conviction. However he also knew that he could not reach the top in the existing power structure. Perestroika had to blow it away to permit him to climb to the summit. Gorbachev transformed Yeltsin into an implacable enemy as it became clear that Moscow was not big enough for both of them. The battle for supremacy in Moscow began the day Gorbachev humiliated Yeltsin. Boris's sacking was to prove a fatal mistake. The tragedy for Gorbachev was that he needed Yeltsin more than Yeltsin needed him but he did not realise this.

THE 19TH PARTY CONFERENCE

When the draft proposals for the conference, to be held in June 1988, were published they caused a sensation. They announced the end of Soviet-style socialism and the advent of something akin to west European social democracy. This remarkable document proposed free, multi-candidate elections to soviets (local councils), secret ballots, freedom of the press, speech and assembly and promised legal protection for them. Social justice was to be a central plank of policy.

Gorbachev sensed that a conservative majority was forming against change. The best entertainment was saved until the last day, a no holds barred confrontation between Egor Ligachev, king of the conservatives, and Boris Yeltsin, the people's champion. Boris gave vent to his venom against the party and its privileges. He gave his version of the events of October 1987 when he had been sacked by the party. He sarcastically remarked that it was party custom to wait 50 years before rehabilitating a comrade. He wanted to be rehabilitated while he was still alive and kicking. Ligachev responded in kind. Everything Boris had done was wrong. He did not have a good word for his former Politburo colleague. Then, in a stentorian voice, he thundered: 'Boris, you are wrong'. He used the intimate second person singular *ty*, instead of the polite second person plural. This signalled condescension and was offensive. Ligachev could have been chastising his pet dog. Ligachev was especially stung by Yeltsin's accusations of party privileges. The only privilege he had enjoyed was to work his fingers to the bone. The delegates sided with Ligachev but the people sided with Yeltsin. Soon badges appeared with the inscription: 'Egor, you are wrong'.

Probably only Gorbachev could have got a conservative conference to agree to fundamental changes which removed the party from the management of the economy and accepted semi-free elections to the Congress of People's Deputies in 1989. He did it by splitting the opposition, making concessions which turned out to be less radical than they appeared and ruthlessly using his authority as party leader. He knew that the Politburo would do almost anything to avoid a public split.

THE CONGRESS OF PEOPLE'S DEPUTIES AND THE SUPREME SOVIET

Elections to the Congress took place on 26 March 1989 and were a watershed in Soviet politics. They were the first contested elections under Bolshevik rule. The congress was to have 2,250 deputies: 750 from social organisations; 750 representing territorial constituencies and 750 representing the nationalities. Those from the social organisations were indirectly elected, the rest directly. Of the social organisations, the party was to have 100 seats, the Academy of Sciences had seats allocated as did the trade unions and so on. Gorbachev decided that only 100 names were to appear on the party list. He feared that if there were more, say 200 names, all the reformers, like himself, would be defeated.

The Congress elected from its members a Supreme Soviet. It consisted of two houses, the Soviet of the Union and the Soviet of Nationalities, each with 271 members. This was to be the standing parliament which took over from the congress. The party managers were confident that they could handle nominations in such a way as to ensure that their men and women were elected. How did Yeltsin outfox them? He stood in Moscow in national territorial district one. There were ten on the ballot paper and a meeting was held to decide which two advanced to the election. The party had decided this would be Yury Brakov, manager of the ZIL car plant, and Georgy Grechko, a cosmonaut. However, Boris knew something the party bosses did not, Grechko planned to withdraw his nomination. He managed to persuade him to wait until the votes had been counted before doing this. So sure of itself was the party that it had arranged for the nomination meeting to be televised live on Moscow TV. Boris got a roasting from the party faithful but kept on smiling. When the votes were counted Brakov came first, Grechko second and despite all the odds Yeltsin third. Then Grechko dramatically announced he was withdrawing. Would the party declare a no contest and start again? It swallowed its pride and put Yeltsin on the ballot paper.

On 26 March, Yeltsin gained 89.4 per cent of the votes with an astonishing winning margin of over five million votes. It went straight into the Guinness Book of Records. There were some spectacular failures. The most sensational was Yury Solovev, a candidate member of the Politburo. He thought he had secured election simply by being the only name on the ballot paper. He forgot about the rule that a candidate is only elected if 50 per cent of voters choose him. That was the end of Solovev's political career. As a Russian observed, it takes quite a lot of talent to lose an election in which there is only one candidate. Many radicals who became household names were elected. These included Anatoly Sobchak, Nikolai Shmelev, the pro-market economist, and Oleg Bogomolov, another pro-reform economist. Bogomolov won in Moscow despite the party playing dirty tricks on him. After his victory he quipped that he had been unaware that it was such an advantage to stand against the party. Andrei Sakharov was elected as a member of the Academy of Sciences. Gavriil Popov, a radical economist and later to be elected mayor of Moscow, and Tatyana Zaslavskaya, a notable sociologist, were returned for social organisations. Another woman to make it was Galina Starovoitova, a specialist on ethnic minorities, and a leading light of the DemRossiya movement.

Gorbachev was elected speaker but would not permit any big name politician to oppose him. He was a wizard at backstage intrigues but he could not silence all his critics. Day after day (the congress ran from 25 May to 9 June) television viewers were served up live theatre. One delegate had the cheek to ask Gorbachev if a dacha was being built for him in the Crimea at state expense (it was). Unarmed demonstrators had been killed in Tbilisi, Georgia, on 9 April 1989. Andrei Sakharov criticised the role of the Soviet Army and caused a furore. Who had given the order to shoot? Gorbachev was in a no-win situation. His popularity began to slip. At the end of 1988, in a poll of leading politicians, he had scored 55 per cent with Yeltsin getting 4 per cent. It slipped in 1989 as a nobody could berate the party leader and get away with it.

Russia was allocated eleven seats in the Soviet of Nationalities. Boris Yeltsin was number twelve on the list. Aleksei Kazannik, a bearded lawyer from Siberia, saved the day by withdrawing. Pressure of business led to Gorbachev handing over the speaker's role to Anatoly Lukyanov, his deputy. Thus it turned out that Lukyanov was speaker during the attempted coup of August 1991.

There was one member who had charisma, one who saw himself as the people's champion, Boris Yeltsin. He became the natural leader of the radicals in and outside parliament. He was no intellectual but he had a gut instinct for politics. He loved one-to-ones with ordinary people and he could work an audience as well as Gorbachev. There was one burning issue the radicals had to resolve. Should they stay within the party and fight to reform it from within or leave and set up their own party? The average Russian's response would have been: 'Another party, God help us, isn't one bad enough?'. Hence, in July 1989, Yeltsin informed the Supreme Soviet that an Inter-Regional Group of communist deputies was being set up in parliament. How were the deputies to get their message across? They adopted the tactic which had proved brilliantly successful on previous occasions: the mass demonstration. These received coverage on television and hence helped to refute the conservatives' argument that the radicals had little public support.

A fundamental error in drafting amendments to the constitution to introduce the Congress of People's Deputies and the Supreme Soviet had not yet surfaced. This was the failure to understand the need to make a clear distinction between the legislature and the executive, in other words, the separation of powers. Under the new system, congress could issue orders to the government if passed by a two thirds majority. This was to have disastrous consequences for economic policy, first and foremost the battle against inflation. Congress, with little understanding of the role of money in an economy, often ordered the government to raise wages, pensions and increase investment in education, etc. Where was the money to come from? That was the government's problem. This fatal weakness was also transmitted to the Congress and Supreme Soviet of the Russian Federation. It was to lead to the tragic events of October 1993.

CONFLICT WITHIN THE PARTY

Over 400 party radicals met in June 1990 to form the CPSU Democratic Platform. Many of them were from the Inter-Regional Group of deputies. They favoured a multi-party system, the removal of article 6, democratic centralism and election of officials by secret ballot. They, like Yeltsin, believed it was better to stay in the party and work to transform it from within. However there were others, such as Gavriil Popov, who favoured splitting from the party if it did not become more democratic. Gorbachev began to weary of the party and his foreign travels had brought home to him the advantages of being an executive President. He was already a nominal President but wanted to emulate Bush and Mitterrand. Gorbachev sought Politburo approval for the establishment of a presidency on 19 January 1990. He was vigorously opposed by Egor Ligachev who argued that a presidency would undermine the party and its Politburo. Party discipline prevailed and the general secretary got his way. The Supreme Soviet's turn to debate the new institution came on 7 February and on 6 March it adopted, with an overwhelming majority, a law introducing the post of President. Gorbachev managed, almost by sleight of hand, to have a presidential system included in the new party programme to be presented to the 28th party congress, in July 1990.

FIRST PRESIDENT

He decided against being elected by the people, instead he was confirmed in office by the Congress of People's Deputies on 16 March. Even though he was the only person on the ballot paper he only secured 59.1 per cent. This was in marked contrast to his election as speaker of the Supreme Soviet, in May 1989, when 95.6 per cent of deputies had voted for him. He would most likely have won a popular ballot but he was a low risk politician when it came to top jobs. Also he would have needed to win in a majority of republics, eight out of fifteen. He would not have come top in Estonia, Latvia, Lithuania, Georgia and Azerbaijan, to start with. The decision not to go to the people weakened him and Boris Yeltsin, for one, made a lot of it. As part of the deal to make Gorbachev Soviet President, he agreed that all republics would have a President. The Soviet President nominated the Council of Ministers and submitted it for confirmation by parliament. A Presidential Council was to be established, full of the President's nominees. It can be seen as an ersatz Politburo. Also a Council of the Federation, representing the republics, was to come into being.

Hence Gorbachev chose a presidential system which owed more to French than American inspiration. Gorbachev's advisers counselled him against becoming involved in the running of the economy. Hence a Prime Minister was to be responsible for this. A major omission, perhaps a fatal mistake, was the absence of a strong central body to implement presidential decisions. Gradually, however, the presidential apparatus grew and it began to take over the party Central Committee apparatus and Politburo. Unfortunately for the President its ability to implement presidential decisions declined rapidly over time.

THE 28TH PARTY CONGRESS

The party did not split at the congress, in July 1990, and Gorbachev was re-elected general secretary. Egor Ligachev, who had done his utmost to be elected Gorbachev's deputy, failed and was sidelined. The new Politburo (it included one woman) was really new. Anyone with a state office, such as Nikolai Ryzhkov, the Prime Minister, was excluded. The lion of perestroika, Aleksandr Yakovlev, also departed. A major innovation was that each republican party leader was *ex officio* a member. The body which had ruled the Soviet Union since the late 1950s was now toothless. Yeltsin was nominated for the party Central Committee but declined since he was the speaker of the Russian parliament. Then he dropped his bombshell. He was resigning from the party. Gorbachev did not hide his pleasure at seeing the back of his arch-rival.

DESPERATE MEASURES

Public anger at Gorbachev boiled over at the parade in Red Square marking the anniversary of the October revolution on 7 November 1990. A man with a shotgun attempted to assassinate the President but his bullets went awry as he was seized. Many republican leaders, but not Yeltsin, encouraged Gorbachev to strengthen presidential power. On 18 November, he informed parliament that he was downgrading it. There would be a Vice-President. A Cabinet of Ministers would replace the Council of Ministers. The Council of the Federation would become a consultative body for centre-republican relations. The President was to nominate the head of government, to be called Prime Minister. Previously the government had been subordinate to parliament. The President would now have his own government. The language used was remarkable: the term used for Vice-President was *Vitse-Prezident*, not the usual Russian word for deputy or number two, *zamestitel*. The term for Prime Minister was *Premer Ministr* (the same as in French) and the deputy Prime Minister was *Vitse Premer Ministr* (*Vitse* was German and the rest French). This extraordinary array of neologisms was designed to achieve two objectives. One was to demonstrate that the world had changed and new terminology was needed to express the new ideas. The other permitted the President to define the new terms as he thought fit. It was a case of language means what I say it means. Yeltsin and the Russian parliament soon copied the new terminology.

On 24 November 1990 the draft Union treaty was published but, of course, it did not give the republics what they wanted. The draft spoke of joint control in key areas but the republics suspected that this meant central control. The two key republics were Russia and Ukraine. Leonid Kravchuk, speaker of the Ukrainian parliament and hence nominal head of state, informed the American ambassador that Ukraine would not sign a Union treaty until it had adopted a new constitution. This was expected in mid-1991, at the earliest. Yeltsin and Kravchuk then signed a bilateral treaty. Azerbaijan and Georgia were eyeing independence. Moldova was likely to follow Ukraine's lead. The Baltic republics wanted to escape Moscow's tutelage. That only left Belarus and Central Asia, the least developed parts of the Soviet Union. They felt they could not exist on their own and wanted to cleave close to Moscow.

Yeltsin and Kravchuk could now coordinate their tactics – negotiate with Gorbachev about a future federation or confederation but, in the end, they could overrule the Soviet President.

On 17 December 1990, at the opening of the 4th Congress of People's Deputies, a deputy rose to propose a vote of no confidence in Gorbachev. There were not enough votes in favour to place the motion on the agenda. Yeltsin and most of the democrats voted against the motion. There was an urgent need to clarify the rights of the legislative and executive branches but the President could not achieve a solution. This paralysed economic initiatives at a critical time. Inflation was rising fast as money was pumped into the economy and when Nikolai Ryzhkov suffered a massive heart attack on 25 December, Gorbachev moved to appoint his own Prime Minister, Valentin Pavlov, the minister of finance. Pavlov was unloved by the people, who applied the sobriquet 'hedgehog-swine' to him because of his crew-cut and corpulence. Ryzhkov had warned Gorbachev that Pavlov liked a tipple and was impulsive and easily swayed. Pavlov confided to the American ambassador that he set the black market rate for the dollar. The ministry of finance could get 40 rubles for the dollar at a time when the official rate was 5 rubles 60 kopeks. This was astonishing as trading in dollars on the black market was still, of course, a criminal offence. This revealed that Pavlov understood that existing retail prices were too low and he began freeing some prices. Some producers favoured allowing prices to rise but others opposed it. Those involved in retail trade were all in favour but heavy industry, for example, was strongly against. Ryzhkov had represented heavy industry. Pavlov knew that foreign credits were vital for survival. He asked the west for $24 billion but got nothing.

On 26 December, Gennady Yanaev became Vice-President but parliament was reluctant to endorse Gorbachev's choice. The President told them he wanted a man whom he could trust and that man was

Gennady Yanaev. He got his way but Yanaev was a poor choice, as later events were to demonstrate. Another voice which was becoming more influential was Anatoly Lukyanov, Gorbachev's choice as speaker of parliament. He worked closely with the Soyuz group dedicated to keeping the Union together. He was another comrade whom Gorbachev trusted explicitly. Again this was poor judgement.

A comrade who was feeling the pressure was Eduard Shevardnadze, the volatile Georgian who was foreign minister. He was savaged by deputies in parliament as the man who had 'lost' eastern Europe, who had permitted the unification of Germany, thus annulling Soviet gains in 1945, who had conceded too much to the American imperialists, who had deserted Saddam Hussein, a Soviet ally, in the Gulf War, and so on. In 1990, Marshal Akhromeev had informed Yuly Vorontsov, Soviet permanent representative at the UN, that the military 'one day will hang him [Shevardnadze]' for submitting to the United States.

RUSSIA AWAKES

Elections to the Russian Federation (RSFSR) Congress of People's Deputies took place in March and April 1990. The democrats, gathered under the umbrella of Democratic Russia (DemRossiya), did well but were still in the minority. They quickly revealed one of their greatest weaknesses, an inability to agree among themselves. Never the less DemRossiya won in major cities such as Moscow, Leningrad and Sverdlovsk (Yeltsin's base). Although over 400 had been elected, only 66 registered as DemRossiya deputies. Some of them were members of both the Soviet and Russian parliaments. It turned out that 86.7 per cent of deputies were party members but this was not all that significant because at that moment radicals had not yet left the party. Only 5.3 per cent of deputies were female.

When the Congress convened, a rough count revealed that the democrats were in a minority but only just. They made up about 40 per cent with the conservatives also having 40 per cent. The key to success in the Congress would be winning over the uncommitted occupying the middle ground. The post of speaker would be crucial. In order to succeed Yeltsin had to pose as the guardian of Russia to the middle of the road communist. Gorbachev had no intention of being neutral. He came out strongly in favour of Aleksandr Vlasov but he was a poor choice. He lacked eloquence and also dynamism. Gorbachev did all in his power to prevent Yeltsin succeeding because he knew that it would escalate their confrontation. 'I already knew that this man was by nature a destroyer', he later commented. On the third round of voting Yeltsin won by a wafer-thin majority. He stated that he would stand above all factions and parties and represent all the peoples of the Russian Federation (about 16 per cent of the population were non-ethnic Russians).

Yeltsin's election as speaker, which also made him head of the republic, provided him for the first time with a political base, independent of Gorbachev. As head of the largest republic in the Soviet Union he had considerable clout. However, Russia faced formidable problems in defining itself. Was Russia coterminous with the Soviet Union? This conflict between those who were termed 'empire-builders', those who believed Russia was the Soviet Union, and the 'nation-builders', that Russia was coterminous with the Russian Federation, was to tear DemRossiya apart. Another factor was that there were about 25 million ethnic Russians living outside the borders of Russia. Russia had no separate communist party, academy of sciences and ministry of culture. All other republics had. The Soviet Union administered Russia and in the era of sovereignty and autonomy this was insulting. Russian economists argued that Russia, with half the population of the Soviet Union, produced three quarters of the Soviet GDP. Russia was clearly being exploited by the other republics. If Russia gained control over its economy, Russians would be better off.

The first step was to claim sovereignty. After all the Baltic republics and Azerbaijan had already done so. The most important decision taken by the new Russian parliament was the declaration of sovereignty on 12 June 1990. This placed Russian Federation law above Soviet law. Russian institutions were to act in the republican interest and not to be subordinate to Soviet institutions. Vladimir Kryuchkov, head of the KGB, and one of the leaders of the abortive coup in August 1991, quickly perceived the import of this declaration. The 'decisive phase in the destruction of the Union began in the summer of 1990 after the RSFSR Congress of People's Deputies passed the Russian declaration of sovereignty and the primacy of Russian over Union laws'. Gorbachev also lamented this move. 'I am certain that had it not been for this fatal step, the Union could have been preserved.'

Gorbachev and Yeltsin held conflicting views on the new Union federation which would replace the Soviet Union. Gorbachev favoured strong central institutions but this implied weak republics. The republics countered by proposing a strong centre and strong republics. Yeltsin, on the other hand, proposed strong republics which would decide among themselves how much power to delegate to the centre. Gorbachev's model would make him a strong President but Yeltsin's model would turn him into a weak President. By October 1990 all republics had declared themselves sovereign or independent (but within the Union). This was necessary in order to negotiate a new federal state as equals. In the Russian Federation the Karelian autonomous republic declared sovereignty, in August 1990, swiftly followed by nine other autonomous republics. Many upgraded themselves from autonomous republic to a full republic within the Union. The sovereignty fever did not stop there and affected autonomous oblasts, within a krai in the Russian Federation. The reason for all this activity was very simple: money. The elites were attempting to lay their hands on the natural resources, economic assets, the right to keep taxes and even the ability to secede. Some of these regions were incredibly rich. Yakutia was flush with diamonds and oil, Krasnoyarsk krai had endless reserves of oil, natural gas and huge aluminium smelters.

Russian comrades kept up the pressure for their own communist party. 'Why should every other republic have a communist party and not Russia?' Gorbachev, of course, did not want a separate Russian party as it was certain to dilute his authority. By the spring of 1990 over 65 per cent of party members in the Russian Federation favoured a separate organisation. A conference of Russian communists was to convene on 19 June 1990, two weeks before the 28th party congress. Due to the lack of time to elect delegates it was decided to empower delegates from the Russian Federation who had been elected as delegates to the 28th Congress. The conference immediately decided to transform itself into the founding Congress of the Russian party. Conservative communists were in the majority and had already selected Ivan Polozkov, first secretary of the Krasnodar kraikom, as the new leader. Polozkov was frank about the deficiencies of perestroika. This alarmed Gorbachev and he proposed Ivan Kuptsov as leader. However the delegates ignored him and elected Polozkov. This was a stunning blow to Gorbachev. Later Gorbachev commented to Ligachev: 'Egor Kuzmich, you deify Lenin. I too have respect for Lenin . . . but Lenin was against the creation of a Russian party'. So why was the party set up? Ligachev was very blunt: 'Well, it was to get rid of you'.

Yeltsin pursued dual tactics in 1990, negotiating a new Union but also trying to break up the Union. This emerged from an astonishing conversation, in June 1990, between Ruslan Khasbulatov, Yeltsin's choice as speaker of the Russian parliament, and the US ambassador, Jack Matlock. The handsome Chechen informed Matlock that Russia would

ERA 55

soon be the successor state to the Soviet Union. The Union would be a loose confederation and would not need a constitution as it would not really be a state. There would be a brief Union treaty as the Union would have few powers. States would run their own economies with an agreed amount being transferred to the centre. Russia wanted to move to a market economy rapidly with privatisation a key objective. Abroad, Soviet embassies would gradually become Russian embassies. Russia was willing to assume the lion's share of Soviet hard currency debt, say 75 per cent. This scenario is remarkable close to what actually did happen and it is tempting to see it as Yeltsin's preferred option. However the key player besides Russia was Ukraine. If Moscow and Kiev decided on independence then the Union was doomed.

GORBACHEV ASSAILED

The militant miners called a warning strike for 1 March 1991 in Ukraine, mainly in the Donbass, with a mixed menu of economic and political demands. Karaganda miners in Kazakhstan joined in. Strikes in the Kuzbass, in western Siberia, and Vorkuta, in the Arctic north, gradually snowballed. By mid-March about one third of the pits were out and a half by 1 April. The Soviet government threatened to arrest the strikers but they ignored Moscow. Since Gorbachev's men could not resolve the crisis, Yeltsin stepped in. He travelled to the Kuzbass on 1 May 1991 and signed an agreement transferring all Russian mines to Russian jurisdiction and promising them economic independence. Yeltsin was the hero of the hour.

Gorbachev came up with the idea of a referendum on the future of the Union, hoping in this way to stem the tide of disintegration. The single question put to the voter had to be framed in such a way as to make it virtually impossible to say no. On 17 March 1991, 76 per cent of voters came out in favour of the Union. Some republics added a question. Russians were asked: do you favour a directly elected executive President? About 71 per cent were for the Union but almost as many for an executive President. The referendum turned out to be a boomerang. It helped Yeltsin more than Gorbachev and made negotiating a Union even more difficult.

A large rally was planned for Moscow on 28 March, the day the Russian Congress of People's Deputies was to vote on Yeltsin's competence as speaker. Gorbachev overreacted and subordinated the city of Moscow and Moscow oblast to the Soviet ministry of internal affairs and brought troops into Moscow. The Congress voted to annul Gorbachev's decree and demanded the withdrawal of the troops. When Gorbachev refused, Congress suspended business until the following day. The demonstration went off without any violence. Gorbachev had saved Yeltsin from possible defeat. Many communists voted for him, regarding Gorbachev's actions as an assault on Russia. There was an unexpected bonus for Yeltsin at the Congress: Aleksandr Rutskoi, an Afghan veteran, and later to be his Vice-President, formed the communists for democracy faction and brought these communists into Yeltsin's camp. Yeltsin achieved his most coveted prize on 4 April: direct presidential elections on 12 June. He then attended the Easter service, conducted by Patriarch Alexi II. This symbolised the reconciliation of temporal and spiritual power.

PRESIDENT YELTSIN

The law on the election of the Russian President and Vice-President stated that the position was for five years. Both had to suspend their membership of political parties and social organisations. The President could be removed for violating the Russian constitution by a two-thirds majority of all members of the Russian Congress of People's Deputies. The Constitutional Court, to be established, was to judge the legality of the decision. This proviso was to have momentous consequences for President Yeltsin and Russia during the next two years. The same rule applied to President Gorbachev, so it was not grasped how destabilising this arrangement could be in a hectic period of transition.

Yeltsin chose as his running mate Aleksandr Rutskoi, a handsome, dashing, mustachioed air force officer and Afghan war veteran. He knew little about politics but appeared to be a Yeltsin fan. He would also attract the military vote. Anyway the duties of the Vice-President were vague, as in the United States. Yeltsin hoped that the old American joke was true. John Schmidt had a meteoric rise and became Vice-President of the United States. Nothing was ever heard of him again. DemRossiya was very disappointed that one of their members was not on the ticket.

Yeltsin polled 57.3 per cent in the first round and hence was declared President. He did extremely well in the larger cities but poorly in the countryside, where the communists were still dominant. Nikolai Ryzhkov, recovered from his heart attack, came in a poor second with over 16 per cent. The real surprise was Vladimir Zhirinovsky, calling himself a liberal democrat, who polled over six million votes and over 7 per cent of the vote. He was almost as good a populist as Boris Yeltsin.

Yeltsin benefited from the fact that the electioneering period was very short, only five weeks after the decision by the Russian Congress. The opposition did not have enough time to mobilise. DemRossiya ran Yeltsin's campaign and he owed his success to their endeavors. He took the oath of office on 10 July 1991 on the Russian constitution and the Russian declaration of state sovereignty. He pronounced the beginning of a new era for Russia. The nation was reborn. He received the blessing of Patriarch Alexi II, the first time a Russian leader had been anointed since the coronation of Tsar Nicholas II in Moscow, in May 1896. Boris was twice blessed, by the people and the church. All Gorbachev could do was to watch and envy him.

THE ATTEMPTED COUP OF AUGUST 1991

Gorbachev finally agreed a draft Union treaty with Yeltsin and Nazarbaev at Novo-Ogarevo on 29 July. He announced on television that the formal signing ceremony would take place on 20 August. Yeltsin demanded that Pavlov, Kryuchkov, the head of the KGB, and Pugo, the minister of the interior, should be sacked. Gorbachev raised no objections. Naively they thought that they were in a bug-free environment but the KGB recorded every word. Astonishingly, Gorbachev decided to go off on holiday with his family to Foros, his new dacha in the Crimea, instead of preparing the country for the end of the Soviet Union.

On Sunday 18 August, just before 1700 hours, Gorbachev was surprised to be told that he had visitors. He was to sign the decree on the state of emergency. If he were not up to it, Yanaev could sign instead. Gorbachev refused to sign anything. Back in Moscow Pavlov and Yanaev had been hitting the bottle. Lukyanov was a bag of nerves. Finally they all signed order no. 1 of the state committee on the state of emergency. It was to last six months.

Just before 0530 hours on Sunday 19 August TASS (the official news agency) announced the state of emergency, that Yanaev was acting President as Gorbachev was ill and incapable of fulfilling his duties. All political parties and movements were suspended, all strikes and demonstrations banned and the independent media silenced. Yeltsin at his dacha at Arkhangelskoe, outside Moscow, was awakened by his daughter Tatyana early in the morning. He immediately telephoned Nazarbaev and Kravchuk but they would not commit themselves without further information. Yeltsin summoned politicians to his dacha and together they drafted an appeal to the Russian people. Mayor Anatoly Sobchak then left for Leningrad. Tatyana typed out the various versions. Then they decided to head for the White House, the seat of the Russian government. The KGB unit observing them let them pass without arresting them. They had no orders to arrest them. They made the White House by about 1000 hours through columns of tanks and military vehicles. Yeltsin went down to the Taman division, ordered them to take up position outside the building, and mounted one of their tanks. The resultant photograph became the most famous image of the time.

The plotters called a news conference and the Gorbachevs were able to watch it. Kryuchkov and Marshal Yazov, the minister of defence, judged it politic not to appear. Yanaev and the other made a poor impression. The acting President kept on drumming his fingers on the table. He could not think of anything convincing when asked about Gorbachev's specific ailment. Yeltsin had called a national strike and the Kuzbass miners came out. Pavlov ordered Yazov to arrest them. The minister did nothing as he thought the Prime Minister was drunk.

Communications were very important. The plotters attempted to control the dissemination of information but were outfoxed by an unknown computer network, Relcom-Demos, which had nodes throughout the Soviet Union. Within hours, a temporary node was set up in the Russian parliament, permitting President Yeltsin's denunciation of the coup and his appeal to the Russian people to be e-mailed across the country. Local journalists began circulating news reports throughout the network, many of which were reproduced in the local media uncensored by the central authorities. By evening, the Relcom-Demos network had become the major channel of communication between Moscow and the regions, linking all those opposed to the attempted coup.

Kryuchkov ordered the arrest of Yeltsin and the defenders on 20 August but no one would obey him. The failure of the KGB to arrest Yeltsin is still a subject of debate. An Alpha team was waiting at Chkalovskaya military airport to arrest him when he arrived from Almaty on 18 August; however, the plane was diverted to Vnukovo airport. Did Yeltsin have prior knowledge of the attempted coup? Why was an order not issued to arrest him at his dacha? On 21 August, at 1500 hours, Yazov ordered the troops back to barracks. Kryuchkov and a delegation went to Foros as did a Russian government delegation. The members of the emergency committee were arrested. Pavlov and Yanaev did not offer any resistance as they were blind drunk. Pugo was not to be found but it turned out that he and his wife had committed suicide. Another who departed was Marshal Akhromeev who left 50 rubles to pay his outstanding bill at the staff canteen. Then he hanged himself with his belt. An officer was expected to kill himself with his revolver but he had handed his in.

The coup failed because Gorbachev had transformed the political landscape. It was no longer possible for a hard man like Kryuchkov to bark orders and have them obeyed. The republics would not have given up their gains under Gorbachev without a fight. Another reason was that the plotters were incredibly inept. The military and the KGB were willing to shed Georgian, Azerbaijani, Lithuanian and Latvian blood but they balked at shedding Russian blood. Perhaps the main reason for the lack of success was the failure to arrest Yeltsin and his aides. That would have decapitated the protest movement. Kryuchkov had simply failed to comprehend the revolution which had occurred in the country. People had lost their fear of the party, the KGB and the authorities. There is yet another side to the story. Gorbachev claimed that the plotters isolated him at Foros. This is not accurate. He telephoned Arkady Volsky, chair of the scientific industrial union, in Moscow, twice during the time he was being held. Why did he not order the arrest of the plotters if the telephone lines were open?

YELTSIN TRIUMPHANT

The Gorbachevs returned to Moscow at 0200 hours on 22 August. They had left the Soviet Union but had returned to Russia. Gorbachev realised that the landscape had changed but did not grasp how much. He put his foot in it by saying that he believed that the party could be reformed and become the living force of perestroika. This was yesterday's language and Yeltsin was quick to drive this home. On 23 August, Yeltsin humiliated Gorbachev in front of the Russian parliament by placing the minutes of his government, on 19 August, before him and insisting that he read them aloud. It was a tale of betrayal. Only one minister had opposed the attempted coup. Yeltsin signed a decree suspending the activities of the party, banned *Pravda* and other party publications and sealed the party Secretariat building, turfing out unceremoniously any official who was there. Gorbachev protested but in vain. Yeltsin dominated Gorbachev and was exacting revenge for all the slights of the past. Gorbachev resigned as party general secretary on 25 August. Ivan Silaev, Russian Prime Minister, and Grigory Yavlinsky, his deputy, assumed responsibility for the Soviet economy.

Russia immediately recognised the independence of Estonia, Latvia and Lithuania. The USSR followed suit on 6 September. By the end of August, Ukraine (subject to a referendum on 1 December), Belarus,

Moldova, Azerbaijan, Kyrgyzstan and Uzbekistan had all declared independence. By the end of September, Georgia, Tajikistan and Armenia had followed suit. Turkmenistan waited until October when there was no other option. Hence the only two republics not to declare independence were Russia and Kazakhstan. The latter was in a delicate position as half its population were Slavs. Why were incumbent leaders so keen on independence? Apart from the Baltic republics and the Caucasus, most republics would have preferred to stay together. The reason appears to be that the communist leaders feared an upsurge of popular revolt, possibly spreading from Russia, which would sweep them away. If a democratic revolution did take place they would lose their wealth and possibly be put on trial. Just as in Russia, where Yeltsin the populist never intended the people to take power, the other leaders seized the initiative and claimed leadership of the nascent nationalist and democratic movements. They then ensured that a civil society which could redistribute wealth did not come into being.

On 6 November, Yeltsin assumed the office of Russian Prime Minister and appointed Gaidar head of the economic ministries. He took further revenge on the party on 6 November, the eve of the celebrations marking the October revolution, when he banned the CPSU and the Russian communist party. He had been drummed out of party life in October 1987, now he was drumming the party out of existence.

On 1 December, Ukraine voted for independence and Leonid Kravchuk was elected President. The Ukrainians decided they did not want to sign a Union treaty which had a central governing body. On 7 December, Yeltsin and Kravchuk arrived at Minsk, the capital of Belarus, and were immediately whisked off to Belovezh forest to meet their host, Stanislau Shushkevich. They invited Nazarbaev who was in Moscow. He agreed and then changed his mind. When he failed to turn up the three signed a joint declaration and an agreement establishing the Commonwealth of Independent States (CIS). The declaration stated that the agreement was open to all states. Yeltsin phoned Bush with the news and Shushkevich was asked to inform Gorbachev. Needless to say the President felt betrayed. Yeltsin briefed Gorbachev on 9 December arguing disingenuously that the agreement was to 'save what could be saved' of the Soviet Union. The treaty was quickly ratified by the respective parliaments.

Deputies from the three founding states were not to attend the Soviet Supreme Soviet or Congress of People's Deputies. This was the kiss of death because it deprived these institutions of a quorum. The Kazakhstan

Supreme Soviet declared independence on 16 December to permit the republic to negotiate as an equal with the other republics. On 17 December, the Russian Supreme Soviet took over from the Soviet Supreme Soviet in the Kremlin. The following day the Soviet parliament faced the harsh reality that it was dead. On 21 December, in Almaty, eleven states signed the CIS agreement. Only Estonia, Latvia, Lithuania and Georgia declined to attend. Georgia, however, later joined. Point five of the agreement was explicit: the Soviet Union and the Soviet presidency no longer existed. Gorbachev had much to carp about. There was no referendum on the ending of the Soviet Union. The Soviet Supreme Soviet should have met to dissolve formally the Soviet Union. Russia, Belarus and Ukraine claimed the right to terminate the Union as they had brought it into being. This was not quite true. There was a fourth founding member: the Transcaucasian Soviet Socialist Federated Republic (Azerbaijan, Armenia and Georgia). They were not invited to attend or comment.

Gorbachev formally resigned on 25 December 1991, addressing the nation and the world from his office in the Kremlin. The Soviet Union, in international law, formally disappeared on 31 December 1991.

NATIONALITIES

There were no serious nationality problems for Gorbachev until December 1986. In Kazakhstan Dinmukhamed Kunaev, the party ruler, was a natty dresser and cultivated the Brezhnev look, including the beetle eyebrows. He praised Brezhnev to the skies in public while privately building up his autocratic fiefdom at home. Both Kazakhs and Russians (about 40 per cent of the population) complained to the new man in the Kremlin about Kunaev's oriental ways. In return, Kunaev warned Gorbachev about troublemakers in the republic, especially Nursultan Nazarbaev, his Prime Minister. Kunaev suggested Nazarbaev be transferred to Moscow or even better, sent abroad to a Soviet embassy, preferably one as far away from Kazakhstan as possible. If Kunaev was Brezhnev's man then Gorbachev wanted his own man. He appointed an ethnic Russian, Gennady Kolbin, to run the republic in Moscow's interests. Kolbin even started learning Kazakh but his appointment was an affront to Kazakh pride. Gorbachev, in his memoirs, conceded that Kolbin's appointment had been a 'mistake'. It led to rioting in Alma Ata (now Almaty) and other Kazakh cities. What disturbed Moscow was that the targets of the rioting were ethnic Russians and Ukrainians. It was a racial conflict. Moscow responded by its tried and trusted method:

force. The centre was driving home a lesson: Moscow rules. Kolbin hung on until 1989 and then gave way to Nazarbaev. However Moscow learned a lesson. It was unwise to appoint a Russian or Ukrainian as party boss in a non-Russian republic.

Stalin deported many nationalities from the Caucasus in 1944 in an attempt to resolve the simmering ethnic conflicts there. They returned after 1956 except for the Crimean Tatars – Russians and Ukrainians had occupied their place in the sun. The first bloody confrontation under perestroika did not take place there but in the southern Caucasus. It was between the Muslim Azeris and the Orthodox Christian Armenians. They fought over Nagorno-Karabakh which was part of Azerbaijan but Armenians made up about 85 per cent of the population. On 27 February 1988, Azeris attacked Armenians in the Azerbaijani town of Sumgait, leaving 26 Armenians and six Azeris dead. Armenians began to leave Azerbaijan and the Armenian authorities began to force Azeris to move back to Azerbaijan.

Estonia, Latvia and Lithuania wanted to leave the Soviet Union. They had been annexed in 1940 and Moscow argued that they had joined voluntarily. On 23 August 1987, the 48th anniversary of the Molotov–Ribbentrop pact which had placed them within the Soviet zone of influence, the Balts decided to see how far glasnost could be stretched by demonstrating against the pact. Anti-Russian feeling was strongest in Estonia where the locals feared that Russians would soon form the majority of the population in the republic. In Latvia, the ethnic situation was not quite so serious but in Lithuania there was no threat. Popular fronts were set up to root for Gorbachev and perestroika but their long-term goal was independence. In Lithuania, the front was called Sajudis. The republican communist parties did not know how to cope with the rising tide of nationalism. Gorbachev was unaware of the gathering storm and, in 1992, conceded that it was only in the autumn of 1990 that he had realised the seriousness of the 'national question'.

The conflict between parliaments in the Baltic republics and the USSR Supreme Soviet escalated in late 1988 when the Lithuanian and Estonian parliaments passed legislation stating that their laws took precedence over Soviet laws. This 'war of laws', if not checked by Moscow, could make the Soviet Union ungovernable. The popular fronts won the elections to the republican parliaments in 1989 and this sealed the fate of the communist parties.

In early April 1989 the situation in Georgia became tense as new parties and movements demonstrated. On 7 April the party leader told

Moscow the situation was getting out of hand and requested that extra-ordinary measures be taken. Gorbachev, on his return from London on 7 April, was briefed and he asked Shevardnadze to fly to Tbilisi to assess the situation. The conflict was to be resolved by political means. During the night of 8–9 April troops charged the unarmed demonstrators, killing nineteen and injuring several hundred. Most of the dead were young women who had been asphyxiated by poison gas. Who had given the order to attack? Was it issued in Moscow or Tbilisi? To this day there is no clear answer. The tragedy did irreparable damage to ethnic relations in the Soviet Union, with most non-Russians believing that Gorbachev was responsible.

The truth about the Chernobyl disaster came out in 1989 and revealed that persons in the most seriously affected areas had been neither warned nor evacuated. Dosimeters, distributed to the population as part of civil defence, were collected by the authorities to prevent citizens from measuring radiation levels. When President Leonid Kravchuk was asked later when he had first decided on independence he replied: 'in 1989'. The full extent of the Stalinist atrocities had only become clear to him in that year. He concluded that only an independent Ukraine could prevent such crimes recurring in the future.

Things were moving fast in the Baltic republics. In December 1989, the communist party of Lithuania broke from the communist party of the Soviet Union and declared itself independent. When Gorbachev visited Lithuania, in January 1990, he received an elaborate welcome from Sajudis which appealed to its members to show due respect to the leader 'of a neighbouring country'. The following week Brazauskas, the independent party leader, was elected speaker of the Lithuanian Supreme Soviet. As such he was the nominal head of state. Brazauskas styled himself as President and prepared to meet another President – Gorbachev.

In December 1989, the Armenian Supreme Soviet annexed Nagorno-Karabakh. Azerbaijan responded by blockading the enclave. On 13 January 1990, the bloodiest riots of the Soviet era enveloped Baku, the Azerbaijani capital. Armenians were slaughtered wherever they could be found. The National Front took over and the communist party leader moved to Moscow. Moscow declared martial law and the troops moved into Baku. Over 200 were killed during the crackdown. This fuelled the Azeri desire to leave the Soviet Union.

Early on the morning of Sunday 13 January, Soviet troops, led by the crack KGB Alpha unit, attacked the radio and television centre in Vilnius. An attack on the parliament was expected but never came. The violence left thirteen dead and 165 injured. The violence was transmitted live to an appalled world by Lithuanian TV. Yeltsin seized his opportunity. He immediately flew to Tallinn, the capital of Estonia. This was possible because the air force commander in Tallinn was General Dzhokhar Dudaev, later to be President of Chechnya. Dudaev had refused permission for extra Soviet troops to land, thus ensuring there was no violence in Tallinn. Yeltsin met the leaders of the three Baltic republics. He called on all Russian (RSFSR) troops not to obey orders to act against 'legally established state bodies, and the peaceful civilian population which is defending its democratic achievements'. In other words, he was calling for mutiny. Yeltsin signed an agreement, by which Moscow recognised the sovereignty of the Baltic republics and agreed to base relations on international law. In other words, he was recognising them as sovereign states not as Soviet republics. He was fully aware that had the violence in Vilnius succeeded he would have been the next target. He was also trying to impress on Russian soldiers that their first loyalty was to him not President Gorbachev.

FOREIGN POLICY

Moscow always regarded Uncle Sam as the main enemy and Washington reciprocated. Russia was the big bad bear, quite un-European and hence quite uncivilised.

Gorbachev faced an uphill struggle with President Ronald Reagan who had once described the Soviet Union as the 'focus of evil in the modern world'. He soon changed his tune and the two leaders met in Geneva, in November 1985. Grim Grom Gromyko's face did not fit and the suave Eduard Shevardnadze became the acceptable face of Soviet foreign policy. Gorbachev talked about 'reasonable sufficiency' as the norm for the armed forces. Nobody could agree on what this meant – one of Mikhail's traits. The ideological strand was dropped from foreign policy and Gorbachev argued that security could not be achieved by military means. To be successful it had to be attained by political means and to enhance the security of all states. The Geneva meeting was a great success. Soon afterwards Gorbachev talked of a nuclear-free world. The new thinking in foreign policy removed the class approach and sketched out a superpower partnership to solve the problems of the world.

The next summit was in Reykjavik, Iceland, in October 1986. Gorbachev plugged away at his concept of a nuclear-free world but got nowhere. He then resorted to putting direct questions to Reagan. The President relied on cards to prompt him. He shuffled his cards but some of them fell on the floor. When he reassembled them they were out of order so he was lost for words. Never the less the two leaders agreed that nuclear weapons could be eliminated and came tantalisingly close to an agreement. When Margaret Thatcher visited Moscow, in March 1987, she reiterated her commitment to the nuclear deterrent, arguing that the Soviet goal was to take over the world. On other matters she was as sweet as honey. She praised perestroika and told Gorbachev that he was her favourite communist politician; he was the only one with whom she could have a decent argument.

Gorbachev's visit to America, in December 1987, was a watershed. He discovered the American public loved him and one can date Gorbymania from this trip. The best therapy for him after a domestic battering was to travel abroad to luxuriate in popular adulation. In February 1988, Gorbachev announced that the Soviet Union would withdraw its forces from Afghanistan. In June, President Reagan arrived for his last summit in Moscow, which went very well. In December 1988, Gorbachev announced at the United Nations that the Soviet Union would reduce its armed forces by 500,000 within two years without expecting the Americans to reciprocate. The incoming President, George Bush, thought that Reagan had been too quick to deal with Moscow. The White House spokesman referred to Gorbachev as a 'drugstore cowboy'. Bush, an indecisive man, finally met Gorbachev at Malta, in December 1989. The beginnings of an economic partnership were laid, something Gorbachev desperately needed. Gorbachev assured Bush: 'We do not regard you as an enemy any more'. Shevardnadze chipped in and stated that the superpowers had buried the Cold War 'at the bottom of the Mediterranean'.

Iraq's invasion of Kuwait on 1 August 1990 severely tested Soviet-American relations. Saddam Hussein was a good ally and there were Soviet troops in the country. Gorbachev really had no choice: he had to abandon Hussein as he needed American finance.

On 20 June 1991, Gavriil Popov, the newly elected mayor of Moscow, paid a courtesy call on the retiring American ambassador. After some polite generalities, Popov began scribbling something on a piece of paper. The message was dramatic: 'A coup is being organised to remove Gorbachev. We must get news to Boris Nikolaevich [Yeltsin was then in the US]'. The envoy wrote down: 'Who is behind it?' Pavlov, Kryuchkov, Yazov and Lukyanov. Since the room was bugged (the KGB were capable of bugging the US embassy) the information could not be transmitted orally. President George Bush telephoned Gorbachev and warned him of the plot. However, he decided it was politic not to name the conspirators. Gorbachev was very relaxed and thanked Bush for the information. He had been right to transmit it to him as a friend. What did Gorbachev do? He did nothing and left the plotters to try another time.

Bush arrived in Moscow in July 1991 for his fourth and last summit with Gorbachev. The growing stature of the republics led Gorbachev to invite Yeltsin and Nursultan Nazarbaev, the leader of Kazakhstan, to participate in a working lunch and to join the Soviet negotiating team for some sessions. Boris said he preferred to meet President Bush in his office, President to President. Yeltsin met Bush in the same office in the Kremlin that Gorbachev had used as speaker of the Soviet parliament. He kept Bush waiting ten minutes and the meeting lasted longer than scheduled. The Americans were not amused. At the official dinner, hosted by the Gorbachevs, Yeltsin sent his wife ahead and waited for Barbara Bush. He then tried to escort her to the top table as if he were the host.

EASTERN EUROPE

When Gorbachev met east European leaders at Chernenko's funeral he told them that henceforth force would not be used to solve political problems in the region. In Poland, the communists could not compete with Solidarity. In July 1989, the communists were defeated in elections and the way was open for the first real non-communist Prime Minister of Poland since 1944 to take office. Also in July, Gorbachev informed the Council of Europe in Strasbourg: 'Any interference in domestic affairs of any kind, any attempts to limit the sovereignty of states, both of friends and allies, no matter whose it is, is impermissible'. Gorbachev thought that this would provoke reform in eastern Europe but the party dinosaurs were not listening. In October 1989, in east Berlin, he warned that history punished those who are left behind. This helped remove the arch-dinosaur, Erich Honecker, but his successor, Egon Krenz, was a sorry apology for a communist leader. The fall of the Berlin Wall, on 9 November 1989, brought down communism in eastern Europe.

WORKERS

Workers were quick to understand the meaning of democratisation. It permitted them to organise and strike for better pay and conditions. The most radical were the miners. The first mass strikes under perestroika were by miners in the summer of 1989.

Russians developed great ingenuity in order to get round laws and regulations. A case in point were Moscow prostitutes. The flesh business was illegal but the ladies came up with a solution which beat the system. They paraded up and down Smolensk Square, opposite the ministry of foreign affairs and near some large hotels. The police did not intervene because the ladies had discovered that the boundaries of two police districts ran through the square. Each district left it to the other to intervene.

Women could improve their economic standing in other ways. One of these was to work for western embassies and companies. For some unfathomable reason there was one job a Soviet woman was not allowed to accept, that of nanny. Western students who wished to stay on in the Soviet Union after their exchange year found it very difficult to acquire a visa; however the KGB was willing to issue visas to nannies without a quiver. Hence foreign families in Moscow acquired the most academically highly qualified nannies in the world. But if the truth be told, they were more interested in Pushkin than in pushing a pram. Some of them were very religious. One took to leaving verses of scripture around the apartment. On one occasion the master of the house returned late after a night's carousing. In the morning, his spirits sank even further on reading the message he found in his slippers: Lord Jesus save me from Satan who lives in this apartment.

The state promoted dictatorships in areas far removed from ideology and politics. One of these was dentistry. There was no shortage of dentists but the average Russian had few natural teeth and the better off had a mouthful of golden teeth. This was strange in a country in which sugar consumption was lower than in the west. The reason was that a tooth dictator, Dr Anatoly Rybakov, ruled. He specialised in gums, not teeth. To him gums mattered and teeth did not. He stopped dentists using the long-lasting amalgam employed in fillings in the rest of the world. Instead they had to insert a cheap plastic which fell out after six months. For almost a quarter of a century he demoted or got rid of any dentist who disagreed with him. All protests and attempts to remove him failed because he was well connected with the ministry of health.

If healthy teeth were in short supply, humour was not. Someone coined a popular ditty:

> Sausage prices twice as high
> Where's the vodka for us to buy
> All we do is sit at home
> Watching Gorby drone and drone

Another caustic comment was: 'How do you translate perestroika into English?' 'Easy, science fiction.' A cartoon shows an enterprise director dictating a telegram to Moscow: 'We have successfully implemented perestroika. Please send further instructions'.

ENTERPRISE LEASING

There was one ray of economic sunshine however: enterprise leasing (Black et al. 2000: 57–9). This involved a contract between the state, as enterprise owner, and the enterprise management or its labour collective. The leasing contract gave the enterprise greater freedom of manoeuvre in investment and production management, increasing wages, retaining profits and the possibility in the future of purchasing the company from the state. All this was presaged on the enterprise making a profit which could be reinvested, used to increase wages and saved towards a future purchase of the company. The only finance which could be used to achieve a future buy-out was accumulated profit. This provided a powerful incentive to management to increase efficiency and not to waste profits through higher wages. Labour could monitor management and ensure that it was not paying itself high wages or siphoning off profits. If there was evidence of fraud they could be jailed. Privatisation was the goal for competent managers who would reap a greater reward than engaging in insider dealing. Tax would be levied on declared profits. Hidden profits could not be used later to buy out the company. This was the slow route to privatisation but it promised to be successful because the state would gradually garner greater experience in how to combat insider dealing and other scams. Leased companies could come together with commercial banks in their economic sector. Gradually a Japanese style industrial-financial group would emerge.

Enterprise leasing began in January 1990 based on a decree in April 1989 and a law in November 1989. It was an instant hit with management and workers. Most enterprises which chose leasing did well. In early 1992, there were about 9500 leased enterprises which were turning out 13 per cent of Russian industrial production and employing 8 per cent of the labour force. Chubais and his privatisation team then ended leasing. It is ironic that the expiring communist state came up with a better model of privatisation than the overconfident Gaidar-Chubais team and their western advisers.

WHY DID THE MILITARY ALLOW THE SOVIET UNION TO DISINTEGRATE?

The most powerful political interest group in the Soviet Union was the military and the military-industrial complex (VPK) (Nagy 2000: 85–7).

Why did the generals allow the country to fall apart. Their involvement in the attempted coup in August 1991 was half-hearted and on reflection they regretted getting entangled.

The productivity of capital in the Soviet Union began to decline in the 1960s. This meant that in order to achieve growth more capital per unit of increased output was necessary. A contributory factor was that labour productivity was falling.

President Reagan's decision to step up sharply defence spending forced the Soviet Union to do the same. However by the early 1980s Soviet growth was only about one per cent per annum despite greater rates of investment. In an underachieving economy the extra resources would have to come from squeezing consumption. However it was politically impossible to squeeze consumption below a certain level. The only solution was economic reform which provided the necessary incentives to stimulate growth. Unless this were done the Soviet Union would lose the Cold War. Hence the military favoured incentives which promised greater productivity. Gorbachev's first economic reforms which gave precedence to the machine building sector were welcomed. However political reforms led to greater and greater demands for increases in consumption. By 1989 things had got out of hand. The military reluctantly concluded that the command economy had had its day. They watched in dismay as it gradually wound down and brought the Soviet Union down with it.

A nagging question remains. It was clear to many of the nomenklatura that Gorbachev was leading the country to its doom but why did they not act? The most convincing answer is the dog-like obedience which had been drilled into them during their lives. The first commandment was always to obey party orders irrespective of what one might think of those orders. Great ingenuity was exhibited in getting round the orders but Moscow was always informed that the orders had been carried out.

The following example neatly illustrates this mentality (*The Independent*, 16 September 2000). In 1990, the nine ministers who ran the VKP became so concerned that they penned a collective letter to Gorbachev asking him to reconsider his economic policies. The problem was how to deliver the letter to Gorbachev. One of the ministers hung around Gorbachev's outer office for days but the general secretary had no time to see him. Eventually he became desperate and when Gorbachev made for the toilet he rushed after him. And so it happened that an extremely important letter was pushed into Gorbachev's hands while he was engaged in an intimate operation. He glanced at the letter and said the minister would receive a reply. (He never did.) On hearing this story, an astute Soviet observer suggested to one of the ministers a much more direct method of attracting Gorbachev's attention. 'Go to the headquarters of the general staff and phone Gorbachev from there. Tell him that all the VKP ministers are there together with the general staff and that you want to see him in twenty minutes. You will not have to wait twenty minutes, he will be with you in ten minutes.' On hearing this the minister blanched. He stuttered that such a thought had never entered his head. The industrialists were loyal to their President and would carry out any orders he gave. He probably thought he was listening to an agent provocateur. This episode underlines the fact that the ministers vis-à-vis the general secretary were like rabbits caught in a car's headlights. They preferred to fiddle while Moscow burnt. The thought of acting collectively in the interests of the country paralysed their will.

The VKP regarded President Yeltsin as a leader who could introduce the necessary reforms. Hence, initially, they did not oppose Gaidar and the young reformers. Once they realised that reforms were going wrong they joined the opposition. The disappearance of the general secretary ended their mental paralysis and they had no hesitation in sabotaging policies which they perceived inimical to their interests. However the VKP lost its commanding position under Yeltsin so officials and managers concentrated their energies on feathering their own nests.

GORBACHEV'S LEGACY

The oligarchs, the men who dominated the Russian economy under Yeltsin, emerged under Gorbachev. Their rise was a combination of three factors: money, influence and connections (Gustafson 1999: 22–6). Money is money and the more the better. Money buys influence and the more one has the more politicians and bureaucrats one can bribe in order to promote mutual enrichment. Once influence has reached a critical point one can establish connections with the key decision makers in the state. In Russia this means having personal contacts with the ruling family.

The Soviet Union was dominated by elites. One can call these clans. This is a tightly knit group and members build their relationships on trust. Clans can be political or economic or a combination of both. A Soviet example would be the team which Prime Minister Aleksei Kosygin put together and which moved up to the top with him. It could run to several hundred or even thousands of members. The Russian word for this group is *khvost* or tail. Here it is referred to as a clan. Soviet politicians, as they moved up, took their trusted associates, one is tempted to say retainers, with them. Someone like Gorbachev could have a 'tail' running into thousands, mainly from Stavropol krai, where he had been party leader. The same things applied to government ministers. The general rule was that the longer officials were in post the larger their clan became. Successful clans expand and embrace other groups and eventually clans. Clans are headed by clan chiefs. The most successful clan chiefs became oligarchs under Yeltsin. How did this process develop under Gorbachev?

The penetration of money set the whole process off. Wealth flowed steadily from state into private hands. The power of money made itself manifest as it began to function as a unit of political influence. Also the role of government began to change as the country moved from state to private ownership. These changes began fundamentally to alter values, social status and roles. The communist state had relegated money to a unit of account, in other words, money was passive, and planners decided preferences, not consumers. Of course, money was not always passive. In the black market money was active. The black market emerged to meet the demand for goods the official economy did not provide. As living standards rose so the unofficial economy grew. Having thousands of rubles did not guarantee that one's demands could be met. Something else was needed: influence. Another major factor was one's role and status in society. Those who had access to the subsidised nomenklatura stores could acquire goods at bargain basement prices. Active money changed lives. Soviet society was a mass society; the state paid little attention to the individual. Money permitted the individual to make personal choices which were not necessarily those the state would have preferred.

THE MAFIA

The term, *mafiya*, first appeared in the 1970s to describe corrupt communist party officials. Since the collapse of the Soviet Union it not only refers to officials but now encompasses those involved in organised crime and prominent businessmen, the oligarchs. Many of the mafiosi are not ethnically Russian and include other nationalities, Ukrainian, Georgian, Latvian, for example. However the mafiosi are predominantly Russian and have Russian and Israeli passports. This is because the mafia is dominated by Jews.

The Russian mafia went international in the 1970s when the Soviet Union, under pressure from the United States, began permitting Jews to emigrate. Moscow grasped the opportunity to rid itself of thousands of hard-core criminals, dumping vast numbers of undesirables on the United States, Israel and other western states (Friedman 2000: 13). Some of the toughest crooks formed loose associations while in prison and maintained these links after they left the gulag. The most ruthless of these associations are those that refer to themselves as *vory v zakone* (thieves observing their own law) who took an oath never to take a legal job, pay taxes, cooperate with the police or the state, except to mislead them. Some of them even wear a badge, a giant eagle with razor-sharp talons, tattooed on their chests. On their kneecaps they have tattoos revealing they would not bow to anyone. In a 1994 report, the FBI estimated there were up to 800 thieves observing their own law in Russia and abroad. Together with thousands of other legitimate Jewish immigrants, they settled in Brighton Beach in Brooklyn, New York. They then moved on to Miami and Los Angeles. In Europe they concentrated in Berlin, Cologne and Frankfurt-am-Main.

The collapse of the Berlin Wall, in 1989, provided global opportunities for the mafia. Drugs could be acquired in Thailand, smuggled into Singapore, shipped to Poland in TV tubes and then transported to America by couriers carrying small amounts on their bodies (Friedman 2000: 100–101). Semen Mogilevich has acquired star-status among mafia bosses (Friedman 2000: 237). It may not be an exaggeration to call him The Don of The Dons. Anyway, locals called him The Don with a Brain. He has set up a global communications network through secure satellite telephones, cellular clone phones, encrypted fax machines, e-mail systems and state-of-the-art computers, all run by highly qualified graduates. The centre has about three hundred employees. Most of them are related or tied in some way to Mogilevich. The organisation is divided into sections, such as arms smuggling or prostitution or according to geographical region. Fewer restrictions on travel and the great increase in world trade have enabled Mogilevich to establish a vast business empire consisting of legal and illegal companies. The objective is to penetrate national banking systems, stock exchanges and gain political influence.

Mogilevich was born in Ukraine but is a Russian citizen. He spent several years in a Soviet prison in the 1970s for illegal currency transactions and fraud. After release he made his first million dollars by defrauding fellow Jews who were emigrating. As they were not allowed to take their possessions with them he promised to sell their jewellery, works of art and other valuables and forward the money to them. He kept it himself. He set up in Budapest in the 1980s as Hungary was seen as a window to the west. Protected by a high-level police official he built up a criminal empire which included prostitution, extortion, drug and arms trafficking, art fraud and money laundering. (Under pressure from the United States, the senior police officer was sacked in 1988. Mogilevich then made himself scarce.) His organisation had two villas outside Prague which were used as punishment centres for those who had tried to cross The Don or had refused to pay extortion money. The methods used were extremely brutal and death was often the result.

Another mafia boss is Sergei Mikhailov who heads Solntsevo Brotherhood, in southern Moscow, possibly the largest of the Russian criminal organisations. It has, reputedly, two thousand members worldwide. It is divided into cells of ten to twelve members, each of which looks after banks and businesses in a certain area. It started as a series of sports clubs which under perestroika blossomed into a large criminal empire. A Swiss court acquitted him of money laundering charges, in December 1998, and he returned to Russia a hero. Even the Swiss courts could not nail him. Almost all top criminals have Israeli passports and Israel is a secure base for them. Several Russian mafia companies flourish in Israel and they contribute to the funding of political parties there. Any Jew has the right to Israeli citizenship and a passport. The only way a passport can be revoked is by demonstrating that citizenship was acquired by fraud. Sergei Mikhailov had his citizenship revoked in late 1999.

Another top hood was Otari Kvantrishvili, a Georgian wrestler who almost made the Soviet Olympic team and then became a coach in the famous Dinamo club. He was made chair of the Lev Yashin charitable foundation for the social rehabilitation of athletes in the late 1980s. Its purpose was to find jobs for athletes who were past it. They became Kvantrishvili's muscle men as he expanded his extortion empire. He also owned a company, the Twenty First Century, whose interests ranged from casinos to discotheques and car dealerships. His company also built many sports stadia and training centres. He became powerful enough to mediate disputes among the *vory* and to collect his cut from them (Klebnikov 2000: 19). (Kvantrishvili was murdered in Moscow, in April 1994, during the mafia war of 1993–94.)

Another is Iosif Kobzon, Leonid Brezhnev's favourite pop singer. He co-owned the Twenty First Century company with Kvantrishvili and also mediated disputes among the *vory*. He became a top fixer, a go-between, and handled anything from metals to arms. He became a member of the Russian Olympic Committee. He was even elected to the Russian Supreme Soviet in 1989 (and to the Duma in 1998) (Friedman 2000: 116). Kvantrishvili and Kobzon needed help against the invading

Chechen mafiosi in Moscow. Bribery secured the release of Vyacheslav Ivankov, a ruthless hit man, in February 1991. He was then let loose on the Chechens. So great was the carnage and the mayhem that Ivankov became an embarrassment to the *vory* and in early 1992 he was ordered out of Russia and told to go to America.

THE KGB AND THE MAFIA

The international department of the CPSU Central Committee was responsible for channelling funds to overseas communist parties and other useful groups. It became very skilled at using offshore tax havens, setting up dummy companies and laundering money. The KGB was normally given the task of implementing these wheezes. Dummy banks and companies were founded all over the world, especially in Cyprus, Greece, Portugal and Italy. Vast quantities were transferred to these institutions by Vneshekonombank, the Soviet foreign trade bank (Klebnikov 2000: 56). A typical scam was to transfer a large consignment of oil, minerals or timber to one of these companies at a very low price. The commodities were then sold on the world market and those involved pocketed the difference. The money, of course, stayed abroad and was invested there. When the economy began to collapse, the KGB performed the same function for the CPSU. Vast sums were invested in companies at home and abroad, beginning in 1990. The objective was to ensure that the Soviet nomenklatura retained its wealth in the stormy times to come. The source of the investment was to be hidden from the public and if suspicion were aroused the KGB could sell its stake and move on. Since the KGB's resources were not up to such a vast operation, it went into business with the mafia. The latter, until then, had specialised in vodka and other rackets. Now, with KGB money, they could set up banks and businesses (cooperatives). The most entrepreneurial communists were in the Komsomol, the young communist league. The Soviet Union's gold reserves were also plundered. About 1000 tonnes of gold were disposed of between 1989 and 1991. In November 1991, Viktor Gerashchenko, chair of the USSR State Bank, declared that all the gold had gone. Things were so desperate that Gorbachev and his entourage vamoosed after the Middle East peace conference, in November 1991, in Madrid, without paying their hotel bills. Soviet foreign trade reserves fell from $15 billion in 1985 to about $1 billion in 1991.

When the Soviet Union collapsed, the money belonged to those with access to it. Privatisation soaked up some of it but much was laundered abroad. Estimates of the money transferred abroad range from $150 billion to $250 billion (in March 2001 the Russian ministry of the interior estimated that Russians hold about $250 billion in western bank accounts). Such sums attracted gangsters and rogues like bees to a honey pot. No one knows how much of this fortune was embezzled and siphoned off. In 1992, the Russian government made an attempt to trace the missing billions but, predictably, with little success.

Until 1990 the mafiosi had been organised along neighbourhood, district and regional lines. They were often divided into ethnic units. The KGB provided the mafia with sophisticated communications, including computers and the latest high technology. An unholy troika gradually coalesced: the mafia, the nomenklatura, and current and former members of the government, military, and security services. They came into their own after the collapse of communism. The top mafiosi were the *vory v zakone* and one could administer a territory as large as Siberia. There would be a subordinate reporting to him in every city and town. A *vor* could be the boss of various mafia groups, head an association of gangs or lead a single gang (Friedman 2000: 113). Some *vory* might specialise in supplies, others in security. One estimate puts the number of criminal gangs in Russia in the mid-1980s at 9000 with 35,000 members. Nine main mafia organisations emerged controlling perhaps 40 per cent, perhaps 60 per cent of the economy. As one Russian banker remarked: 'In 1917 there was a Bolshevik revolution. In the late 1980s there was a mafia revolution. A businessman now has a three-way choice: pay the mafiosi, leave Russia or get a bullet in the head'. The most successful were the Chechens and their hallmark was extreme violence. They tried to push out the previously dominant Jewish, Georgian, Armenian, Russian and Ukrainian gangs. Shoot-outs and bloodletting were a commonplace occurrence.

THE CLAN CHIEFS EMERGE

Many of the spectacularly successful clan chiefs, those called oligarchs, were outsiders under Gorbachev (Freeland 2000: chapters 6 and 7). That is to say, they were not members of the communist nomenklatura or ruling class. The penetration of money in the economy gave these men their chance. This began a frenetic race to accumulate money as quickly as possible so as to buy influence and eventually connections. The goal of influence and connections was to make making money much easier. Here a clan chief is defined as someone who has made a million dollars by the end of 1991. An oligarch is someone who has accumulated over one billion dollars. There were no oligarchs in the communist period because the definition of an oligarch is someone who has high-level connections in the presidential administration and government. What is striking about the following men (so far there are no female clan chiefs or oligarchs) is that they emerged from the junior ranks of the system. They had the appetite for risk-taking which the older generation lacked.

Another irony is that the best training group for entrepreneurs turned out to be the Komsomol. In the 1970s, the Komsomol began to develop youth activities and dominated youth tourism both at home and abroad. It also organised summer work camps and this could involve bringing in the harvest or toiling on building sites. It organised dances, rock concerts and made television programmes. It was really into sport and owned many sports facilities and buildings. In the era of the scientific-technical revolution, so beloved of Brezhnev, it moved effortlessly into high technology. Whereas Yeltsin confiscated the central assets of the communist party and later returned some of the local facilities, the Komsomol escaped unscathed. One of the assets it retained was the Gossnab (state supply organisation) building which it had acquired in 1989 (this is now the Reforma institute). Even more valuable, it also acquired Gossnab stores throughout the Soviet Union. Later when privatisation arrived the former activists acquired the extensive property of the Komsomol for a song or even less. In 1991, the Komsomol promoted the association of young entrepreneurs and this enjoyed the patronage of Gavriil Popov, mayor of Moscow. The leaders of the association became the Moscow group and developed into leading businessmen.

Popov was so taken with Iosif Ordzhonikidze (grandson of Sergo Ordzhonikidze, one of the prominent early Bolsheviks until Stalin terminated him), responsible for supervising the Komsomol's business empire, that he made him deputy mayor of Moscow and responsible for land privatisation. In 2000, Ordzhonikidze was one of the most powerful members of Yury Luzhkov's Moscow administration. As such he was responsible for attracting foreign investment to the city and regulating the notoriously volatile hotel market. He was also involved in driving street traders off the streets and getting to grips with the illegal alcohol trade. On 19 December 2000, before it was light, his car was ambushed by gunmen who sprayed his armoured-plated Nissan with armour-piercing bullets, critically injuring him and killing his driver. Insiders linked the attack to his decision to support a British company's $100 million plan to build a motor-racing circuit, for Formula One racing, together with hotels, casino and a yacht club, in Nagatino, southern Moscow. This deal dealt a fatal blow to a competing $200 million project.

It was not only in Moscow that Komsomol activists proved successful businessmen. In Nizhny Novgorod, Sergei Kirienko, a future Prime Minister, acquired valuable skills during his activist days. Indeed one can claim that the Komsomol is the most important formative influence on many of the most successful Russian businessmen. Another startling irony is that the Komsomol was supposed to produce model communists but instead produced first-class capitalists. The Komsomol, far from defending communism in 1991, hastened its demise.

BORIS BEREZOVSKY

Born in January 1946, as the son of a Moscow rabbi, Boris was to prove himself the master at identifying those who could help him enrich himself. A gifted mathematician, he enrolled in the electronics and computer science faculty of the institute for forestry. However the institute did not concentrate on timber but on the Soviet space programme. On graduation he moved to the prestigious mechanics and mathematics department of Moscow State University. After receiving his candidate degree (PhD) he moved to the Soviet Academy of Sciences and spent over twenty years there researching decision-making theory. In 1983, he was awarded his DSc. At the Academy he became director of one of the laboratories of the institute of management which researched automation and computer systems for industry. He was elected a corresponding member of the Academy in 1991. As such he was a member of the Soviet and scientific elite. He was living proof that Jews could climb to the top of the ladder in the Soviet Union.

Short, balding, he speaks Russian with a Moscow Jewish accent. One of his special talents is to spot someone who can help him to make money. In other words, he is the master persuader. His message is disarmingly simple: 'I can make you rich'. He is unlike the other oligarchs in that his fortune encompasses a wide range of activities, cars, oil, banks and so on. His money-making career took off in the late 1980s when he visited the Avtovaz automobile works in Togliatti, the maker of the Lada, and presented a brilliantly simple business plan to Vladimir Kadannikov, the director. At the Academy he had helped to develop the automation systems at the plant. The proposal was to split car manufacture from sales. A joint venture would be set up with Logo System, an Italian company which had been working with Avtovaz to automate its production lines. The new venture was called Logovaz. Kadannikov was chair and Berezovsky general director. It soon forgot about automation and began to sell the cars and pocket the money. Avtovaz would carry on turning out the cars. It would be starved of finance, run up large debts and rely on the government to bail it out as it was too big to allow to collapse. Needless to say it would not be able to meet its tax bills.

Another wheeze to reduce the tax bill was to manufacture lots of cars with the same licence plate number. This understated output considerably and the extra cars could be sold by the daughter company. After all they did not officially exist. Another trick was transfer pricing. A company could be set up to supply inputs and inflated prices were charged. The main company then sold goods to this company at prices way below value. Management pocketed the difference. Daughter companies grew richer as the mother enterprise grew poorer. This tactic was widely deployed throughout the country under perestroika. Soviet managers were past masters at cooking the books and if a bureaucrat became too nosey he could be bought off. This revealed something very interesting about enterprise managers. Give them more freedom and they immediately used it to enrich themselves and defraud the state. Gorbachev naively believed that they would strive to make their enterprises more efficient and thereby make perestroika a resounding success.

By the time Mikhail Gorbachev had left the Kremlin, Boris was a millionaire, not a ruble millionaire but a dollar millionaire. Boris cultivated the new economic elite around Gaidar. In September 1991, Logovaz was granted a licence by the Russian ministry of foreign trade to export oil, aluminium and various strategic raw materials. Petr Aven, the minister of foreign trade, just happened to be an old acquaintance. Now Boris was in the big time. In 1992, according to official Russian statistics, Logovaz exported goods valued at over $1 billion.

MIKHAIL FRIDMAN

Born in 1964, in Lviv, in western Ukraine, into a city which had only become part of the Soviet Union in 1940, Fridman was a gifted mathematician and physicist. However he could not gain entry to the famous physical-technical institute in Moscow. He was also a Jew. He got into the institute of steel and alloys. He needed a part-time job to supplement his meagre student grant. Demand for theatre tickets exceeded supply. Students were wont to queue all night to acquire tickets which they then bartered for something else. Fridman brought order to chaos. Every university department had a head and each department was responsible for a different theatre. They met once a week to coordinate plans. Fridman had established his first monopoly. He also acquired valuable experience in negotiating barter deals. He traded in everything in demand from food to consumer goods. He also became acquainted with some of those who would later help him to set up and run the Alfa group with interests ranging from banking, oil, manufacturing to importing and exporting. On graduation he was assigned for three years to a factory in Ryazan oblast, the back of beyond. However his black market activities had bought him influence at the institute and instead he went to a steel plant outside Moscow.

Gorbachev legalised cooperatives in 1988 and this stimulated Fridman and his friends to go legal. They identified a market niche and rushed into it, from renting apartments to selling Siberian shawls and breeding white mice for laboratories. A big break was discovering an enterprise which had money but could not find a company to clean its windows. So the cooperative went into the window cleaning business. There were always hordes of hungry students willing to wipe any building clean. However central planning did not produce any window cleaning equipment so Fridman persuaded his own steel mill to do just this, to their mutual enrichment. With money rolling in the cooperative became more ambitious as it bought influence. It acquired the right to import western goods from cigarettes to computers and Xerox machines. This was hugely profitable and the cooperative eventually accumulated the wealth to acquire the most profitable piece of paper in the Soviet Union, a licence to export oil. This was immensely profitable as Soviet domestic prices were only a fraction of world oil prices. There was the added benefit of being paid in dollars. Most of the money stayed in western bank accounts. Fridman and his friends could enjoy a luxurious lifestyle when they went on holiday abroad. They were dollar millionaires by 1990. When Gorbachev spilled blood in Vilnius, they moved part of the business to Prague as an insurance policy.

MIKHAIL KHODORKOVSKY

Born in 1963, Khodorkovsky was a born engineer and graduated top of his year in chemistry from the Mendeleev institute in Moscow. He desired a posting to a defence plant and his ambition was to become a director of a prestigious enterprise. He was rejected almost certainly because, as a Jew, he was regarded as a high risk in a sensitive defence factory. While at the institute, in 1986, the party issued a decree permitting the formation of amateur groups and clubs. Khodorkovsky, deputy secretary of the institute's Komsomol, and some friends immediately set up a group. Shortly afterwards, the Komsomol was authorised to establish youth groups to foster scientific creativity. Khodorkovsky and his friends immediately transformed their group into a business whose main activity became importing foreign computers. A lucrative contract with one of the institutes of the Academy of Sciences provided the capital to expand the business.

Khodorkovsky became deputy secretary of the Komsomol in Frunze raion in Moscow after graduation. Had he been an ethnic Russian he would automatically have continued upwards and onwards in the communist party. Nevertheless the contacts he made and the imprimatur he acquired as a Komsomol activist were to prove very valuable. By 1987 he was director of the Komsomol youth scientific creativity groups with over 5000 under him working on over 500 contracts for state enterprises. This included writing computer programs and providing any service needed. In 1989, he faced a cash crisis when the government banned the paying of advances for contracts. Using his Komsomol contacts in the Moscow city government he raised the capital to establish a bank. The established banks turned him down so he had to display ingenuity in raising the capital. The authorised capital was originally 2.3 million rubles, paid in by an organisation headed by Khodorkovsky. However most shareholders only paid one third of the share price, the remainder being covered by bank credits. When the bank was founded in December 1988 its nominal capital was stated to be 5 million rubles. It was alleged in the early Yeltsin years that part of the capital had come from Komsomol funds. It was called the Menatep Commercial Innovation Bank for Scientific and Technical Progress. Menatep is an acronym from interbranch scientific-technical programmes. At first the bank provided a full range of services, including securities. Then the financial groups dealing with investments became a separate trading company, the Menatep-Invest Joint Stock Company. Commercial transactions became the responsibility of a separate trading company, Menatep Trading House Joint Stock Association.

In late 1990, Menatep Bank, after receiving permission from the USSR ministry of finance, offered for sale an additional 963,000 shares at 1000 rubles each. In late 1991, it was reregistered as a Russian bank although it had branch and affiliated offices in the states of the former Soviet Union. The group concentrated on importing computers and exporting raw materials. To do this it needed to acquire licences and here Khodorkovsky's contacts were of strategic importance. Menatep was a banker to the Komsomol and other state bodies. In late 1991, about 100 organisations made up the core of its business. A Menatep Moscow regional section was set up to cater for the requirements of several thousand small customers. Such Menatep clubs were to be found in Moscow, St Petersburg and the provinces. So high was its influence that Khodorkovsky was appointed an economic adviser to Ivan Silaev, prime minister of the Russian Federation, in 1990. This provided him with strategic government contacts.

VLADIMIR GUSINSKY

Born in Moscow, in 1952, Gusinsky's dream was to become a physicist but the physical-technical institute turned him down because he was a Jew. Instead he graduated in engineering from a less prestigious institute. Addicted to the theatre, and no mean actor himself, Gusinsky graduated in drama and began staging plays. Gorbachev changed his life. He organised festivals and theatrical events for the Komsomol. In 1986, the Komsomol asked him to organise the cultural activities for the Goodwill Games, funded by Ted Turner, the founder of CNN. This provided valuable contacts for Gusinsky and he and an American law firm set up a company called Most (bridge) to provide consulting services for US companies doing business in the Soviet Union (Klebnikov 2000: 149). In 1987, Gusinsky could not resist the thrill of trying his hand at being an entrepreneur. He drove a taxi, sold western jeans but a breakthrough was making and selling bracelets which supposedly warded off ill health. He then went into the construction business and met up with Yury Luzhkov, the mayor of Moscow. The bald, squat, dynamic Luzhkov, whose love of football tempts one to call him a tough Bobby Charlton, was the man to know as he was in charge of cooperatives (business) in Moscow. He began passing city construction work to Gusinsky's company. It found it easier than others to acquire property for redevelopment. To handle his finance he set up his own bank. Gusinsky's path to wealth was lined with Moscow city accounts. He sold Luzhkov the idea of transferring city accounts to a consortium of private banks headed by him. The great advantage of this was that Gusinsky now had liquid capital and could think big. Almost overnight he became a leading private banker.

VLADIMIR POTANIN

Born in 1961, as the son of a Soviet foreign trade official, Potanin spent part of his youth in New Zealand and Turkey. When he returned to Moscow he entered the state institute for international relations, an elite institute for sons of the elite. Very able, he proved a natural leader, be it playing sport or in the Komsomol. On graduation in 1983, he followed his father to the ministry of foreign trade. He advanced quickly and in 1989 was on the verge of being posted to Belgium or Canada. It dawned on him that leaving the Soviet Union at such a critical time could prove disastrous, so he stayed in Moscow and began thinking of going into business on his own account. Why not turn one of the state trade organisations connected to the ministry into a private company? He failed to persuade the bureaucrats to take the plunge and, instead, established his own cooperative, Interros. He imported computers and western consumer goods for other cooperatives. They did not have his contacts and knowledge of how the bureaucracy worked. However like all the other future oligarchs Potanin knew that the road to riches lay through banking. A chance encounter in March 1991 with a young banker coalesced into a partnership and they began recruiting talented young bankers from the state banks. Potanin used his nomenklatura contacts to sound out potential clients. He called his bank Oneksimbank, the unified export-import bank. Banking, as for so many others, was the passport to riches. There were about 1600 private banks in Russia in 1991.

ALEKSANDR SMOLENSKY

One of Boris Berezovsky's close business partners, he dabbled in the black market and went to prison several times before 1985. In 1988, he set up a successful building materials cooperative. His bank Stolichny was licensed in February 1989 with an authorised capital of 20 million rubles. There were 18 founding members, most of whom were Moscow cooperatives (Berezovsky was reputed to own 25 per cent). In 1990, Stolichny advanced $3 million to Alisa, a trading company specialising in building materials. The reason the credit was advanced was down to Artem Tarasov. Smolensky did a lot of business with Tarasov's trading company, Istok. In reality, Alisa was just a front for Tarasov and his shady business deals. It was headed by German Sterligov, a nephew of ex-KGB General Aleksandr Sterligov, well known for his pro-Stalinist utterances. (Klebnikov 2000: 85). (Alisa was closed down in 1992 and Tarasov was elected to the Duma in December 1993. As a deputy he had legal immunity from prosecution.) Stolichny was a founding member of various banks and the Moscow central stock exchange. It looked after Smolensky's business interests but made the breakthrough into servicing some Moscow city accounts. In 1991, the total turnover exceeded 20 billion rubles and profitability was put at 40 per cent. A major source of income was commission on currency accounts of customers and correspondent banks. A Jew, he maintained close links with Israel.

VLADIMIR VINOGRADOV

An ethnic Russian, Vinogradov graduated in 1979 from the Moscow institute of aviation and was then posted to Atommash, a company which
produced atomic power plants. He was active in the Komsomol organisation. In 1985–87 he was a postgraduate student at the Plekhanov
institute in Moscow and also worked as an economist for Promstroibank
and became senior economist in 1988. He then left the bank to set up
his own bank, Inkombank, in October 1988, with two friends in the
kitchen of his communal apartment. Some sources state that the initiative for the founding of the bank originated with V. Groshev, a banker.
The original staff were Groshev's students. Later the bank's headquarters were moved to the top room of a bar on the outskirts of Moscow.
They managed to attract nine shareholders including the Plekhanov institute, the association of aircraft manufacturers, Sokol, and the oil and
gas pipeline operator, Transneft. They then approached the Central Bank
for a loan of 10 million rubles. They got it but the official who had granted
it soon left the bank. From a small company employing 20 people and
an authorised capital of 10 million rubles it grew into a highly efficient
company with tens of millions of rubles in deposit accounts. In March
1991, it was decided to transform Inkombank into an open joint stock
company and in September 1991 it was registered in the Russian Central
Bank as such. In December 1991, it purchased a collection of 13 modern Russian paintings at an exhibition in Moscow for 1.6 million rubles
and had a budget of 5 million rubles for art. According to Vinogradov,
during the attempted putsch of August 1991 bank officials took bags of
cash, running into millions of rubles, to the beleaguered White House.
The money was a contribution to the defence fund.

VAGIT ALEKPEROV

An Azeri, he was born in 1950, in Baku, the capital of Azerbaijan. He
graduated from an oil institute and worked in the offshore oil industry
in Azerbaijan. He then moved to west Siberia. He quickly moved up as
an engineer and manager who solved oil production problems by taking risks. By 1983 he was head of a new oil company in Kogalym and
he transformed it into the fastest-growing oil producer in west Siberia.
It is today the core of the Lukoil organisation. By 1989 he was deputy
USSR minister of oil, and he was not yet 40 years old. He became first
deputy minister in 1990 and was in line to become the minister. He
went off to the west and asked BP to help him set up Lukoil. BP
thought that he had gone off his head. His negotiations were not well

received by conservatives in Moscow but the August 1991 attempted coup saved him from demotion. The minister was embroiled with the conspirators and Alekperov was left in charge of the ministry during the last months of the Soviet Union. He transferred the state's oil concerns to the state-owned Rosneft and placed his friend Aleksandr Putilov in charge. Two other associates became heads of the national oil companies in Kazakhstan and Turkmenistan. Alekperov and some of the brightest managers and engineers took over Lukoil, which had been registered as an integrated oil company with the Moscow city soviet in March 1991. In late 1991, he put together three Siberian oil producers, two refineries and a trading company and Lukoil was in business. As a non-Russian, he was an outsider in a fast-growing industry and he put together a team or clan of mainly non-Russians.

WHY DID THE SOVIET UNION DISAPPEAR?

- The major reason was Gorbachev's leadership. He was an extraordinarily skilful tactician when it came to manoeuvring in the upper echelons of the party bureaucracy. He was a genius at short-term tactical thinking. However as regards strategic thinking, long-term policies, he resembled Inspector Clouseau who was always full of bright ideas but was like a blunderbuss when he set about implementing them. This explains why Gorbachev set in motion events over which he lost control. Originally he had set out to improve economic performance, first and foremost labour productivity. When this did not achieve its goals he deduced that the responsibility for failure rested with the upper levels of the party bureaucracy. This led to radical political reform. There was no pressure from below for political reform. Hence Gorbachev attempted to run economic and political reform in parallel. This is something which history has shown elsewhere is extremely difficult to do successfully. At the 19th Party Conference, in 1988, Gorbachev effectively removed the party from the management of the economy. It had coordinated decision making at the local level. The local councils, soviets, were to take over from the party. This was a major misjudgement. The major function of local soviets had been to implement party and state orders. Now they were being expected to become involved in the formulation of policy. Had Gorbachev not set out to reform the unreformable he would still be there. His great tactical gifts would have ensured that he was not removed from office while the economy declined.

- The general secretary had a limited understanding of how the Soviet economy really functioned. The laws on the state enterprises, and cooperatives promoted asset stripping. Company directors were engineers not managers and had little inclination to promote efficiency in the western sense of the word, producing goods at lower prices. When the party was removed from economic management in 1988 there was no successor agency. In the confusion managers discovered they could rob the state. The rewards from asset stripping were greater than those being offered by Gorbachev's reforms.

■ Gorbachev believed that in order to ensure that perestroika succeeded, consumption had to increase. He did not understand that investment was the key to increased consumption in the medium term. The reform economists also failed to identify investment as a key success indicator. Gorbachev also neglected agricultural reform which would have saved hard currency and provided resources to purchase capital equipment abroad. Turning agriculture around was the quickest route to raising living standards.

■ The balance of trade turned against the Soviet Union. Oil prices fell and this contributed to a balance of trade deficit of $24.1 billion in 1990. In 1991 imports were cut to $68.2 billion from $120.7 billion in 1990.

■ A ruling class, the communist nomenklatura, had come into being. It consisted of party, state and industrial leaders. True, it did not actually own property but it disposed over state property. It ruled as if it owned the state. Corruption grew quite rapidly under Brezhnev. Permission was needed for almost any activity. (The Soviet joke was: why will the state never succeed in imposing birth control? The means of production are in private hands.) Shortages became endemic under Brezhnev and this led to the mushrooming of the black (illegal) and grey (semi-legal) economies. Gorbachev legalised cooperatives and permitted black economy money to be laundered into the legal economy. By 1991, there were 135,000 legally registered cooperatives. They accounted for 3 per cent of output but an astonishing 18.4 per cent of services. The real figures were probably higher. Many of the cooperatives or businesses were fronts for the laundering of money. Gorbachev also made it possible to found new commercial banks. Enterprises quickly set up their own banks. The foreign trade monopoly imposed by Lenin was relaxed and chosen enterprises could trade directly with capitalist countries.

■ The KGB which had been the party's eyes and ears succumbed to corruption. In the absence of the rule of law the KGB had imposed its own law. Remarkably the KGB was led by ascetics, such as Andropov and Kryuchkov, who were not interested in personal enrichment or sexual favours. However lower level personnel were quickly seduced by wealth. A major influence appears to have been the war in Afghanistan which destroyed many men's faith in the virtue of the communist system. New cooperatives and commercial banks could not function successfully without an agreement with the KGB. It also had the expertise in foreign commercial relations which was valuable to enterprises which were permitted to trade on their own account. This opened up limitless vistas for the enterprising. A case in point was East Germany where the military and the KGB did profitable business together. The KGB was involved, directly or indirectly, in every Soviet business involved with the west. The KGB and the party apparat transferred vast sums of money into western bank accounts in the late Gorbachev years. It is doubtful whether the Soviet President knew what was going on.

- One of the reasons for the failure of the August coup was that the communist nomenklatura had no fear of being dispossessed. The plotters merely wished to make the position of the ruling class more secure. They saw Yeltsin as a dangerous radical. His policies were leading to the break-up of the Soviet Union. However the vast majority of the nomenklatura were quite relaxed about the future. They had realised that communism was no longer viable in its traditional form. Their main concern was to become the ruling class of the successor system. In fact the communist nomenklatura became the capitalist nomenklatura.

- The people lost their fear of the party and the KGB about 1988 and economic decline made the average citizen bolder. The Komsomol had developed a business empire by the 1980s and Gorbachev's reforms saw it expand its money-making activities. Instead of promoting perestroika for Gorbachev it used perestroika to enrich itself.

- Gorbachev, like many other Russians, thought that the nationalities question had been solved and Soviet man and Soviet woman had come into being. He could not comprehend, for instance, why the Lithuanians wanted to leave the Soviet Union even though this would mean a drop in living standards.

- The conflict between Gorbachev and Yeltsin ensured that no Gorbachev-inspired post-Soviet federation could come into being. Yeltsin, a vain man and easily slighted, refused to work in tandem with Gorbachev.

- The republican leaders grasped very quickly that a market economy would give them control over the assets on their territory. They were seeking to become leading capitalists in their region. They were not interested in a competitive market economy, they wanted monopoly capitalism. In the new Union they favoured weak central control and taxation levels set by themselves.

■ Gorbachev was always thinking of the state and the wellbeing of the whole people whereas regional leaders were concerned about local interests. Was this irrational? No. The communist nomenklatura acted in a rational economic manner. In other words they acted in their own interests. They were responding to the incentives created by economic reform.

■ The Chinese example reveals that it is possible to move to a market economy without far-reaching political reform. Gorbachev made his task even more difficult by introducing political reform at a time when the economy was in decline.

■ The Soviet Union simply collapsed. There was no counter-elite which overthrew the communist ruling class. Hence there was no social revolution. The astute members of the communist nomenklatura simply became members of the new, capitalist nomenklatura. The capitalism which appeared was not liberal capitalism but state capitalism where the state was privatised in the interests of this new ruling class.

3

TSAR BORIS THE BRUISER: THE FIRST PRESIDENCY, 1991–96

THE YEARS 1985–91 WERE DOMINATED BY Mikhail Gorbachev but he bowed out a defeated man. Had he had his way Boris Yeltsin would never have moved into the Kremlin. The years 1991–99 were dominated by Boris Yeltsin but when he stepped down voluntarily, in December 1999, he was judged a failure. However, he was able to choose his successor, Vladimir Putin.

YELTSIN'S TEAM

August 1991 transformed Yeltsin's fortunes. Until then he had had to share power with Gorbachev and there was great uncertainty about the successor state to the Soviet Union. He had envisaged a long conflict with Gorbachev, possibly lasting three years. This would permit policies to be refined and an administrative system built up. In August 1991 power simply fell into his hands, like manna from heaven. He was totally unprepared and had no concept of how he should proceed. He did not have a team ready to take over. His supporters were a disparate group. They included some from his Sverdlovsk (Ekaterinburg) homeland, communists who had become disillusioned with Gorbachev, bureaucrats who sensed that Russia would increasingly control its own destiny, those who gambled that supporting Yeltsin would lead to faster promotion, such as Ruslan Khasbulatov, military figures such as Marshal Evgeny Shaposhnikov and General Pavel Grachev, who went over to Yeltsin during the attempted coup, others, such as General Aleksandr Rutskoi, who had thrown in their lot earlier in the year, Arkady Volsky, chair of the Russian Union of Industrialists and Entrepreneurs, who astutely appeared to be backing two horses, Gorbachev and Yeltsin. DemRossiya had contributed much to Yeltsin's election as Russian President and expected to taste the fruits of victory. It was a hodgepodge of conflicting policies. There were social democrats who wanted to see Russia move rapidly towards democracy and a social market economy. However there were also American-style or nomenklatura capitalists who wanted to get rich quick. Yeltsin skilfully supported the latter and in so doing greatly weakened DemRossiya. Most DemRossiya supporters were shocked to discover that Boris preferred a communist-style system of decision making. This involved various groups competing for influence around him and a very opaque decision-making process. This environment permitted Boris to act as tsar.

What did Boris Yeltsin do after his humiliation of Gorbachev in August? Did he engage in feverish activity to build the new Russia? No, he simply went on holiday and came back to Moscow in October. There were rumours that he had suffered a slight heart attack in September but his lack of dynamic involvement is astonishing. It proved to be typical of his behaviour. After expending great amounts of energy to resolve a crisis he was wont to repair to the Black Sea or his dacha outside Moscow. It began to emerge that he took decisions based on gut instinct. He was not a rational, calculating leader.

Politics between August 1991 and the summer of 1993 was dominated by one topic: economic reform. Yeltsin relied on two groups of advisers whom he had known for many years in Ekaterinburg (Hough 2001: 131–6). They had radically different views on economics and the independence of Russia. One group, headed by Gennady Burbulis, a professor of Marxism–Leninism, advocated rapid economic reform and Russian independence. The other, led by Oleg Lobov and Yury Petrov, party officials under Yeltsin in Ekaterinburg, favoured an industrial policy and a Japanese or South Korean approach to development (the state identifies the key sectors and concentrates resources in them; export-led growth is crucial).

Burbulis, who had been Yeltsin's main political adviser during the June 1991 presidential campaign, had many supporters in DemRossiya and several non-economic Russian ministries. As such his group lacked economic expertise. He allied himself to the young reformers, led by Egor Gaidar and Aleksandr Shokhin. Gaidar came from a famous family and

had the finest command of Russian among the elite. He was no outsider, he was a member of the communist nomenklatura. He had
headed the economics section of *Kommunist*, the party's own journal.

The Gaidar team began drafting an economic programme in a dacha
outside Moscow. They regarded the defence sector as the only part of
manufacturing industry which was competitive on the world market.
However they did not wish to promote arms sales as this was incompatible with a closer relationship with the west. This was indispensable
if integration in the world economy was to be achieved. The funds for
the modernisation of Russian industry would come from the export of
oil, gas and raw materials. The manufacturing sector should be exposed
to the cold winds of international competition and this would force it
to contract to become more efficient. Fuel prices should be set at world
levels to force economies. This would make more available for export.
Gaidar was taken by Mancur Olson's view that it is better to destroy
old institutions and let new ones take their place. One is irresistibly
reminded of the Russian nineteenth-century anarchist, Mikhail Bakunin,
who preached the destruction of the existing in order to create a better
world. The team accepted that the programme amounted to deindustrialisation and huge unemployment. Workers could move into the services
sector which was woefully underdeveloped. Cold, merciless economics.

Oleg Lobov had risen through the defence industry, then moved into
the party apparatus and eventually became first deputy Russian Prime
Minister. Yury Petrov had also started in the defence sector then moved
into party work, ending up in the party Central Committee apparatus
in Moscow. He returned to Ekaterinburg to succeed Yeltsin as party leader
when Boris moved to Moscow as part of Gorbachev's team. When Yeltsin
fell out with Gorbachev in 1987 Petrov was packed off to Cuba as ambassador. Yeltsin appointed him head of the presidential administration in
August 1991. Gregory Yavlinsky was also brought aboard.

Almost all those concerned with the economy in the Russian government supported the Lobov–Petrov group. It wanted to protect industry
and to ease it gently into the world economy. There was considerable
physical and human capital and it should not be destroyed. It favoured
insider privatisation. Tariffs were needed to protect manufacturing until
it became competitive internationally. Russia could begin by exporting
low quality goods, following in the footsteps of China and the east Asian
tigers. Foreign direct investment was critically important and foreigners
would also be protected by tariffs. The other republics supplied vital
raw materials and other inputs. Hence it was important that Russia

remained within a Soviet successor state. A single economic space should be retained.

The two scenarios had far-reaching consequences for the future of Russia and the Soviet Union. The Burbulis-Gaidar team thought the retention of the Soviet Union would hold back Russia's march to the market. Breaking the links with the republics did not matter as Russian industry would be exposed to the winds of international competition. Burbulis instructed the Gaidar group to work out a programme based on the assumption that a commonwealth would not come into being. It was to be a blueprint for Russian economic independence. This did not please Washington. It made it clear, in October 1991, that an inter-republican economic agreement was a precondition for large amounts of aid. Yeltsin then pretended that his goal was an economic union. Russia and seven other republics immediately signed an economic treaty. However the resignation of most economic ministers from the Russian government made it clear that Burbulis–Gaidar had won and Lobov–Petrov had lost.

An intriguing question remains. Had Gorbachev resigned as Soviet President after the attempted coup, would Russia have chosen inde-pendence? The Lobov–Petrov programme would have suited Russia much better. However Washington wanted monetarism, tight bud-getary discipline and a rapid move to the market. Aid depended on these. Was the Burbulis–Gaidar programme chosen on political or economic grounds? One is tempted to say political as it achieved two goals: the destruction of the Soviet Union and western aid.

Yeltsin's first government was in place before the attempted coup. Ivan Silaev, a bureaucrat, was Prime Minister. Andrei Kozyrev was foreign minister. He was a professional diplomat and had not played a leading role in any political grouping. Before August, anticipating trouble, Yeltsin dispatched to Ekaterinburg a group of Russian officials, headed by Oleg Lobov, his former party subordinate in Sverdlovsk oblast, and then first deputy Prime Minister. Their task was to manage the Russian economy and maintain the 'effective functioning of the key state struc-tures'. Kozyrev was dispatched to Paris to proclaim a Russian govern-ment in exile, if necessary. DemRossiya was not invited to the top table. Galina Starovoitova, a specialist on nationalities, and Sergei Stankevich did not become ministers but were invited to serve in an advisory capa-city. As is well known, advisers' counsel can be ignored.

On 28 October Yeltsin presented his economic programme to the Russian Supreme Soviet. Buried in it was a short paragraph which spelled out short therapy in the republic. He chose 6 November 1991, the eve of the anniversary of the Bolshevik revolution, to announce his new government. Boris decided to be his own Prime Minister. According to his memoirs, this was to avoid having to present Burbulis to parliament as his nominee. He was certain to be rejected. Gaidar became deputy Prime Minister, responsible for the whole economy, and was also minister of the economy and finance. Gennady Burbulis and Aleksandr Shokhin became deputy Prime Ministers. On 15 November, Yeltsin decreed that all Soviet institutions on Russian territory had become subordinate to Russia. A mistake was made by the government when it did not object to the Russian Central Bank being subordinate to the Russian parliament. This was to cost it dear over the next two years.

Russia was different to Poland, Czechoslovakia and Hungary, for example. There was no counter-elite waiting to step into the shoes of the departing communists. Russia, like the other countries, did have radical market economists, but the implementers of policy were missing. Many second-level communists quickly grasped the opportunity for advancement. Ideology was not a problem. They assimilated the reform rhetoric of the dissidents and sounded like the real thing. This was to be a hallmark of the Yeltsin elites. They assimilated the democratic rhetoric of DemRossiya while pursuing a ruthless drive towards wealth redistribution in their own interests.

Although Burbulis–Gaidar had won, they were only one of three centres of power around Yeltsin (Shevtsova 1999: 18). There was the government which, along traditional Tsarist and Soviet lines, was only responsible for the economy. Then there was the State Council, headed by the firebrand Gennady Burbulis, the leader of the radical camp, and then the presidential administration, led by Yury Petrov. Hence from the beginning the various institutions competed for influence. Yeltsin rejected the idea of forming his own political party and wanted to be above all factions. He also juggled the various circles of power so that no single one became dominant. The downside of this was that Yeltsin did not put together a cohesive team which could forge policy to reform Russia. To the western mind this was inefficient but it was normal in Soviet and Russian politics. There was one major difference. Under the communists there had been competition for influence but an enforced unanimity once policy had been decided. There had also to be complete loyalty towards the boss. Yeltsin retained the latter but encouraged competition among his associates. There was no concept of cabinet responsibility. Any official could contradict any other official in public. Politics was personalised and power was personalised.

It took Yeltsin about a year, 1992, to put in place his own executive. The failure of economic reform in 1992 and 1993 was due to the policies adopted by the Yeltsin team. However this could not be admitted and a scapegoat had to be found. It turned out to be parliament. All the economic ills were ascribed to its obstruction of the government's policies. High inflation was due to the printing of money by the Central Bank which was subordinate to parliament. Reality was different. Parliament had only limited control over the economy. Key decisions were taken by the Yeltsin team and this involved providing off-budget subsidies and credits to enterprises and regions. There was the official budget which went through parliament and pleased the IMF and the unofficial budget which was only known to Yeltsin insiders. Emission of money by the Central Bank was supervised by the ministry of finance. Yeltsin's own executive was in place but, of course, it did not act in unison. Gaidar was balanced by Petrov in the presidential administration. Yeltsin needed Gaidar to get western loans but he also needed Petrov to ensure that industry was not devastated by shock therapy. Hence from the beginning the old and new nomenklaturas coexisted side by side.

Power in developed states resembles a barrel but in Russia it was a pyramid. All power flowed from the top. It was overlooked that there was another institution which, according to the Russian constitution of 1978 as amended, was the supreme organ in the state. This was the Congress of People's Deputies, the outer parliament, and the Supreme Soviet, the inner, permanent parliament. The Congress voluntarily, in late 1991, granted Yeltsin the power to appoint the heads of local executive agencies and also the right to override any existing legislation and to reorganise the government as he saw fit. He could rule as an autocrat until December 1992. When the economy did not respond to shock therapy, the immanent conflict between the two bodies claiming supreme power, parliament and the presidency, burst into the open. The President deliberately exacerbated relations with parliament to disguise his lack of economic success.

Economic decline sharpened the conflict between Burbulis, the radical, and Petrov, the conservative (Shevtsova 1999: 53). As befits a former professor of Marxism–Leninism Burbulis was certain he knew the answer to every question. If in doubt, become more radical. Yeltsin practised his own version of checks and balances: he sided with Burbulis on some issues and with Petrov on others. He was also wont to disappear from time to time and left Burbulis in charge. The latter was good at invective and polemic and had a natural gift for making enemies. He also began to irritate the President and Boris sacked him in April 1992. The President was easily slighted and had a high opinion of his own importance. Familiarity was something that Yeltsin strongly objected to. Burbulis seems to have overstepped some invisible mark and Boris ruthlessly culled him. He became a state secretary but Yeltsin sacrificed him in December 1992 as part of a deal with parliament.

Another problem was Aleksandr Rutskoi, the Vice-President. He thought he was Yeltsin's first deputy. However the President regarded the position as purely ceremonial, the American position. Rutskoi's pride was hurt and he refused to accept this. He set out to transform the vice-presidency into a real job. He decided he did not like shock therapy. Yeltsin gave him a real job: he put him in charge of agriculture. This was intended as the kiss of death in Russian politics. There was a joke about agriculture. There are only two men who understand Russian agriculture: one is dead and the other is mad. Rutskoi carried on regardless and gradually raised his political profile. The new dissidents, the communists and the nationalists, began to think of him as a possible leader.

DemRossiya was united by only one thing: dislike of communism. Once communism had passed away the democrats fell out. DemRossiya was an umbrella organisation and needed a strong leader to keep it together. Yeltsin could have played this role but refused to do so. He wanted to continue as a communist apparatchik, cutting deals which benefited him. Many DemRossiya members defected and went off on their own. One of them was the dandy, Sergei Baburin, from Novosibirsk, who moved to the nationalist right and became leader of the Russian National Union. The nationalists regarded shock therapy as the rape of Russia and found willing allies in the communists. A red-brown coalition was taking shape and in September 1992 they formed a Front for National Salvation. Among the leaders were Sergei Baburin, Gennady Zyuganov and General Albert Makashov. Arkady Volsky, representing red industrial directors, saw his opportunity. He founded a centre party to occupy the gap between the left and the right. Shock therapy did not create a nationalist opposition. It was already there. It had developed under Gorbachev and bitterly opposed perestroika. It was natural that it would also oppose Gaidar's policies.

The government was always short of money because it could not collect enough tax. Why was this? Western advisers and the Gaidar team both advocated a free trade policy and the privatisation of the export industries, alcohol and foreign trade companies. Yeltsin deliberately ignored these potentially very lucrative sources of government revenue.

He even permitted some organisations to import duty-free alcohol and cigarettes. Hence the government threw away billions of dollars of revenue every year. This was one of the most egregious mistakes of the Yeltsin administration. The oligarchs were the main beneficiaries.

Many democrats left parliament to take up positions in the executive. One of these was Sergei Shakhrai, who was chair of the committee on legislation. In all, over 100 deputies eventually left to accept positions in the executive. Those who held full-time positions in the Supreme Soviet had to resign from them when they moved into the executive. They were usually replaced by opponents of radical reform. On 15 March 1992, Khasbulatov, as speaker, demanded the dismissal of the Gaidar team. Ministers rarely appeared in the White House, the seat of parliament, and when they did they showed little respect for the deputies. More skilful management of parliament would have avoided the violent confrontations which developed. In other ways Yeltsin was more successful. A key tactic deployed was to offer government jobs and positions to his critics. Co-optation gradually thinned the ranks of the effective opposition.

CONFRONTATION IN THE CONGRESS OF PEOPLE'S DEPUTIES

The sixth Congress (6–21 April 1992) marked a turning point in Yeltsin's relations with parliament. It began to develop into a counterweight to the President, seizing on the lack of success of economic reform. The speaker, the handsome, formidably fluent Ruslan Khasbulatov (cognate with Hizbollah), exacerbated relations with the President quite deliberately. In an effect to deflect criticism, the President, on 2 April, removed Egor Gaidar as finance minister and downgraded Gennady Burbulis from deputy Prime Minister to state secretary. The deputies sensed that Yeltsin was on the defensive and became more obstreperous. They demanded the resignation of Gaidar and his team. In the middle of the debate, Gaidar and his team announced they were ready to resign and dramatically walked out of the chamber. The deputies were nonplussed as they had no contingency plan for this eventuality. They feared that Yeltsin might dissolve parliament and declare a state of emergency. It turned out that Gaidar had neither consulted Burbulis nor Yeltsin about his démarche.

Yeltsin reached a compromise with Sergei Filatov, deputy speaker, by which Congress agreed that the government should continue with economic reform but with modifications. For the first time it was clear that the President no longer had a two thirds majority in parliament to pass a resolution dissolving it and introducing a new constitution. About 200 deputies had moved from the democratic camp to the communists and nationalists. In addition to those moving into the executive others had been appointed the President's regional representatives or heads of administration (governors).

Yeltsin accepted a Congress proposal to replace the ministry of industry with five new institutions: a state committee for industrial policy and state committees for the defence, metallurgy, machinery and energy industries. They were headed by industrialists. In return, Congress passed amendments to the constitution which strengthened the presidency. One of the new deputy Prime Ministers was Georgy Khizha, who became responsible for the military-industrial complex and problems associated with its transformation to civilian use on 20 May (he lasted less than a year in office and then left Russian politics). On 30 May, Viktor Chernomyrdin became deputy Prime Minister responsible for fuel and energy. On 2 June, Vladimir Shumeiko joined the government (he stayed in office for about 18 months but remained at the top until January 1996).

On 3 June 1992, the President signed a decree setting up the Security Council. Yury Skokov was appointed secretary. He was from the military-industrial complex. This body gradually assumed considerable influence as it brought together the power ministries, the ministries of internal affairs, defence and security.

THE CIVIC UNION APPEARS

Had the communists and nationalists been able to unite, Yeltsin's problems would have been compounded. However he knew that the two main groups opposing his reforms could only agree on one thing: they were against the rapid drive to the market. Khasbulatov might have become the leader of the opposition but he was regarded by most of them as too moderate. Then there was the military. General Aleksandr Lebed, commander of the 14th army in the self-proclaimed Transdniester republic (part of Moldova), began calling for law and order. He quickly acquired a profile as an honest officer who put society not himself first.

On 21 May the Civic Union coalition came into being. It welded together Arkady Volsky, representing the red directors, Nikolai Travkin, who had been a keen Yeltsin supporter but had moved to the right because he favoured keeping the Soviet Union in some form and had become quite a nationalist, and General Aleksandr Rutskoi who was still Vice-President (Shevtsova 1999: 50). Various other groups also came aboard. Behind the rhetoric, Civic Union represented the old nomenklatura. Its task was to force concessions out of the new nomenklatura. If Yeltsin could be removed there was a possibility that the old nomenklatura could seize the property of the new nomenklatura. The nomenklaturists had no social base, voters saw them for what they were, bosses. A major problem for the Civic Union and other groups was that citizens were becoming disillusioned with politics. They regarded the wranglings in Moscow with disgust. The President's popularity began to slide. An opinion poll, in July 1992, registered only 24 per cent who were totally satisfied with him. Rutskoi for the first time scored higher, 28 per cent, than the President. DemRossiya suffered quite a slide in popularity.

By the summer of 1992 many interest groups were clearly discernible. There were the financial-industrial group, the raw materials and natural resources group, the fuel and energy group, the agrarian group, the military-industrial complex and the regions. They lobbied hard and rewarded the officials who granted them concessions. For instance, enterprises' debts to the state were written off. Foreign trade was still regulated. Licences to export commodities, such as oil, timber, gas and ore, were very lucrative. They were also lucrative for the officials who granted them.

Yeltsin had promised the sixth Congress that he would step down as Prime Minister. On 15 June he appointed Gaidar acting Prime Minister. This was to avoid having to present him to parliament for approval, something he was unlikely to achieve.

Yeltsin's closest associates became frustrated by his lack of leadership and took things into their own hands on 16 October 1992. Anatoly Chubais, responsible for privatisation, Andrei Kozyrev, Gennady Burbulis and Mikhail Poltoranin, minister for information, held a press conference for foreign journalists and waxed eloquent about the danger of a communist coup d'état. This was to be a constant theme and was preparing the ground for the dissolution of parliament. It could be followed by a state of emergency and a presidential dictatorship.

THE PRESIDENT AND THE 7TH CONGRESS

Yeltsin's special powers were due to end in December 1992. In anticipation of the 7th Congress (1–14 December 1992) he became unusually conciliatory. He was ready for dialogue and even criticised Gaidar and his reforms. He began discussions with Civic Union, creating an impression that a change in economic policy was being planned. He dismissed some economic ministers, including Petr Aven, minister for foreign trade, a close associate of Gaidar. Andrei Kozyrev, the foreign minister, a particular butt of nationalist and communist criticism for his pro-western orientation, stayed in office. The President needed him to create a favourable image in the west so as to secure financial aid. Then he said goodbye to Gennady Burbulis and Mikhail Poltoranin.

Just before the Congress opened the Supreme Soviet passed legislation subordinating the government to parliament. How would the President react to this challenge? The Congress had the necessary two thirds majority to amend the constitution. The Prime Minister and key ministers were to be approved by Congress. The right to reorganise the government was passed to the Supreme Soviet. The procedure for impeaching the President was agreed. Yeltsin met the Congress halfway: if Gaidar were confirmed in office, he would submit the heads of the power ministries (interior, military and security) and the minister of foreign affairs to the Supreme Soviet for approval. Congress spurned this offer. The President went back to his dacha very depressed; he locked himself in his bathhouse and may have become suicidal. He was coaxed out. Suddenly a member of the family suggested he go to the people and ask them if they wanted him or Congress. This fired his imagination and he spent most of the night working on his speech.

On 10 December, Yeltsin launched a vigorous attack on Congress and accused it of planning a 'creeping coup'. The goal of Congress leaders was to become the absolute rulers of Russia. He wanted the confrontation to be resolved by a referendum. Then he attempted to cow Congress. He declared that he could not work with parliament and called on his supporters to leave with him. A large enough number would have left Congress without a quorum. However, very few followed him. This crass misjudgement was shown live on television. To compound Yeltsin's defeat the procurator general and the power ministers declared before Congress they would abide by the existing constitution. Tension was mounting and there was a danger that the opposing groups could clash on the streets. In stepped Valery Zorkin, chair of the constitutional court, to mediate. The eloquent lawyer brought Yeltsin and Khasbulatov together.

It was agreed that a national referendum on a new Russian constitution would be held on 11 April 1993. Congress was not to make any more amendments to the constitution. The Supreme Soviet would draft the new constitution and if it and the President could not agree (virtually certain) then the public would decide by referendum. Congress was to propose five names for Prime Minister and the President was to choose one of the top three and submit him for congressional approval. Yury Skokov (Yeltsin had promised him the premiership before the Congress) got most votes, followed by Viktor Chernomyrdin. Then came Egor Gaidar. Yeltsin could have nominated Gaidar but knew that he would be rejected. Gaidar was suspicious of Skokov and saw him as a representative of the military-industrial complex. So Egor proposed Viktor Chernomyrdin and Yeltsin agreed. His background was in the gas industry so he knew the industrial sector well. If Gaidar was the best speaker of Russian among the elite, Chernomyrdin was one of the worst. Taciturn because he could not put into words what he thought, he gave the impression of being stolid and reliable. When stuck for a word he simply invented one. No wonder the Russian purists pulled out their hair. Congress took him to its bosom. It thought that one of its own had taken over from the despised Gaidar. It was to be disappointed as Viktor soon developed an appetite for market economics.

Chernomyrdin was the opposite of Gaidar in other ways. Chernomyrdin was a manager and saw government as management. The silver-tongued Moscow intellectuals thought that Chernomyrdin was dim. They overlooked the fact that he had already fashioned Russia's largest company, Gazprom, and would soon be worth a few billion dollars himself. Whereas Chernomyrdin was always aware of the human factor, Gaidar and his team all but ignored it. The Gaidarites believed they could live with Chernomyrdin since he would be keen to promote the export-oriented sectors.

Yeltsin displayed his old skill in applying checks and balances to the new Prime Minister. He installed Boris Fedorov, a keen advocate of rapid economic reform and more self-confident than Gaidar, if that were possible, as deputy Prime Minister and minister of finance. Fedorov epitomised the young radicals; they were always right and never wrong. This confirmed the age-old verity: absolute certainty is always based on absolute ignorance. One of the reasons for their enthusiasm for the market was that they possessed the skills to flourish in it. Yeltsin replaced Yury Petrov as head of the presidential administration with Sergei Filatov, Khasbulatov's deputy in parliament. Filatov had been keen to leave parliament as he had developed a visceral dislike of the cunning Chechen.

CONFLICT RESUMES

Voices inside and outside parliament were quickly raised against the referendum. It was divisive and could exacerbate existing tensions. Regions could add a question about independence (as had happened to Gorbachev's referendum on 17 March 1991). Early elections troubled many deputies. In a period of rapid change they enjoyed great privileges as members of parliament. They did not want to be voted out. Democrats were also concerned lest a new parliament come to an agreement with the President which was not favourable to democratic change. Yeltsin proposed various deals to parliament which would have transferred some of his prerogatives to it, if it agreed to the referendum. However, much of this manoeuvring appeared to be tactical. Yeltsin and his team had been discussing ways of dissolving parliament since the beginning of 1992 and had drawn up plans for a state of emergency. He would arrest the deputies if they impeached him. He had even taken soundings in western capitals about their reaction if he took extraordinary measures. His behaviour revealed that he thought he had their acquiescence.

Parliament thought that the tide of public opinion was flowing in its direction and convened an extraordinary 8th Congress (10–13 March 1993). Congress was opened by Khasbulatov who sharply criticised the President and accused him of acting unconstitutionally. It voted to strip the President of the extraordinary powers granted him at the 5th Congress in late 1991. He could no longer issue decrees with the force of law, appoint regional administrative heads and choose ministers without the approval of parliament. Congress cancelled the April referendum. Yeltsin made some concessions. He signed a decree conferring cabinet rank on Viktor Gerashchenko, chair of the Russian Central Bank, and three other officials. These new ministers were to be subordinate, in the first instance, to parliament. Congress rejected Yeltsin's proposal to hold a referendum on 25 April to resolve the conflict between the legislature and the executive and on private land ownership. This underlined the fact that the President no longer had a majority for any important issue in Congress. The main reason for this was that the deputies who occupied the middle ground – called the swamp – between his supporters and opponents had deserted him. Yeltsin stalked out of Congress and vowed never to return.

ON THE OFFENSIVE

The President, on national television, on 20 March 1993, announced that he was introducing a special regime and the referendum of 25 April would go ahead. Parliament could no longer block his decrees. Everyone watched television that night to see and hear the reaction. Deputies were, of course, outraged. Rutskoi talked a lot without saying much, but came out against the decree. Valery Zorkin, the chair of the constitutional court, was expected to be cautious. However he surprised everyone by declaring Yeltsin's démarche unconstitutional. So did the procurator general, the chief law official, Valentin Stepankov. Not all the President's men supported him, notably Yury Skokov, head of the security council. Chernomyrdin, the Prime Minister, and the heads of the power ministries commented extensively but avoided committing themselves one way or the other. On 21 March, everyone rushed out to buy *Izvestiya* or other newspapers so as to read the decree. It was not there. The constitutional court went ahead regardless and declared the President's move unconstitutional. Eventually the President prevailed on the Prime Minister and key ministers to appear on television where Chernomyrdin read out a message of support. The body language of the group was revealing: they were unhappy with the decree.

The initiative illustrated Yeltsin's decision-making style. Come up with an idea, announce it and expect the government and other supporters to fall in line. There was no decision-making process, no consultation and no attempt to build up support beforehand. There was no telling what Boris would come out with next. When the decree was published a few days later the offending phrase 'special regime' was missing. Those who wanted to put a gloss on the President's behaviour claimed that it was a trial balloon to gauge support for a full-scale state of emergency. Some of his opponents damaged their reputations. The main loser was Valery Zorkin who forgot that in Russian law a decree has no validity until published.

With tension mounting the 9th Congress convened (26–29 March 1993). It was opened by a biting speech, full of contempt for the President, by Khasbulatov. Yeltsin appealed for a compromise but this was rejected contemptuously. Congress clearly believed that it had the votes to impeach the President. Yeltsin then did what he always did when forced into a corner: cut a deal. He reached an agreement with Khasbulatov. He abandoned the referendum and agreed early elections to the presidency and parliament in November 1993. Khasbulatov agreed to dismiss Congress and support the formation of a new bicameral legislature. All groups in Congress were furious. The democrats, independents, communists and nationalists were appalled by the cutting of a deal behind their backs. Votes of no confidence were tabled against Yeltsin and Khasbulatov. In order to impeach the President, the first step in dismissing him, two thirds of the deputies had to support the motion. Khasbulatov confidently told a television reporter that the vote was in the bag. It was not and fell 72 votes short of the required 689. Clearly quite a few deputies had changed their minds influenced by the appeal by the Yeltsin camp not to impeach the President and plunge the country into a constitutional crisis and possibly into civil war. Khasbulatov did better but 339 deputies voted against him, about one third. This was a rap over the knuckles for the abrasive Chechen. He was subordinate to Congress and had to remember this.

Both Congress and the President had to retreat. Congress agreed to the referendum but tried to phrase it in such a way as to make it impossible for the President to win. There were to be four questions: (1) Do you trust the President of the Russian Federation, Boris Yeltsin? (2) Do you approve of the socio-economic policies carried out by the President of the Russian Federation? (3) Do you consider it necessary to hold early elections for the presidency of the Russian Federation? (4) Do you consider it necessary to hold early elections of the People's Deputies of the Russian Federation? Congress decided that, in order to win, the President had to obtain 50 per cent of the electorate, not those who turned out on the day. Yeltsin appealed to the constitutional court. It reached a judgment of Solomon. It ruled the President only needed a majority of those who voted on two issues: confidence in him and on socio-economic policy. He would need the support of half the electorate to convene new presidential and parliamentary elections. Had he been impeached the President had a contingency plan to dissolve parliament, using force if necessary.

On 15 April 1993, Yeltsin appointed Oleg Lobov deputy Prime Minister and minister of the economy. The President appeared to be taking Congress's views on the economy into account. Lobov had not changed his views since losing to Burbulis-Gaidar. His new target was Boris Fedorov. Lobov thought that Chernomyrdin would support him against the radical Fedorov. Instead the Prime Minister sided with Fedorov against Lobov. No convincing explanation has been advanced to explain Chernomyrdin's sharp change of course.

25 April turned out to be a red letter day for the President. The voter turnout was surprisingly high, 64.5 per cent, and 58.7 per cent expressed confidence in Yeltsin and an astonishing 53 per cent in his socio-economic policies (was this number inflated by returning officers?); 49.5 per cent favoured early presidential elections and 67.2 per cent early parliamentary elections. Measured against the level set by the

constitutional court, 31.7 per cent of the total electorate voted for early presidential and 43.1 per cent for early parliamentary elections. It was a great but flawed victory for the President, a 'second presidential election two years after the first', to quote his words. If one considers the 37 million who did not vote then he had minority support in the country. The President's policies did not receive a majority in over half of Russian republics and in many regions. Given the dire social and economic situation many voters must have voted for the President as the lesser of two evils.

When deputy Prime Minister Georgy Khizha and Yury Skokov, head of the security council, resigned in May, reformers expected a new government bereft of representatives of the military-industrial complex. Instead Oleg Soskovets, an ex-Soviet minister for metallurgy, was also made a deputy Prime Minister. Once again Yeltsin had decided on a balance between the traditionalists and radicals in his cabinet. All the time Aleksandr Rutskoi was growing more popular with voters and the President's team began to regard him as the most dangerous political opponent. A new constitution was needed which would abolish the post of Vice-President.

TOWARDS A NEW CONSTITUTION

The draft Yeltsin constitution was published on 30 April and on 20 May Yeltsin signed a decree convening a constitutional assembly. Each of the republics and other regions were to send four delegates. Fifty of the largest trade unions, 15 major religious denominations and 10 creative associations (journalists, actors, etc.) were summoned. All the major parties and movements were invited. Over 100 organisations were to be represented. The President, before 692 delegates, opened the assembly on 5 June. Over 10,000 communists and nationalists demonstrated outside against the assembly. Yeltsin invited delegates to discuss the presidential and Supreme Soviet draft constitutions. They were, of course, incompatible. The former aimed at a presidential republic, the latter a parliamentary republic. The President made it clear that the days of the soviets were over. They had to go. Khasbulatov immediately went on the attack but was booed and catcalled and left the assembly, together with over 50 supporters, in a huff. Next day he proposed that if there were no agreement between the President and parliament all constitutional drafts should be put to the people, in a referendum.

On 7 June most of those, but not Khasbulatov, who had walked out returned after Yeltsin appealed to them to attend. A major problem was relations between the centre and the republics and other regions. The republics had gained considerable economic concessions and wished to keep them. Regions in which Russians dominated tried to raise their status to that of the republics. There was a proposal that the Russian regions should be grouped together in guberniyas, the pre-1917 territorial divisions. Sverdlovsk oblast voted to form a Urals republic. Eduard Rossel, governor of Ekaterinburg, was an enthusiastic supporter. Needless to say the stronger the regions and republics the weaker the centre and President would become. There was a danger that Russia could move from being a federation and become a confederation. Then on 13 July a draft constitution which satisfied the President was passed. Now Boris could force a showdown with Congress.

In mid-summer, the Supreme Soviet passed a state budget which envisaged a deficit of some 25 per cent of GDP. It had greatly increased spending, especially on pensions and defence, and had completely rewritten the government's draft. Boris Fedorov, minister of finance, threw it out. Privatisation was another bone of contention. All small businesses were to be privatised by 1 August 1993 and the list of enterprises excluded from privatisation considerably shortened. The Supreme Soviet suspended the decree and voted to transfer responsibility for privatisation from the state property committee, headed by deputy Prime Minister Anatoly Chubais, to the whole cabinet. In July, parliament voted to reassert Russian sovereignty over Sebastopol, a Ukrainian port on the Crimea. It also nullified an agreement between Presidents Yeltsin and Kravchuk of Ukraine on the division of the Black Sea fleet. This was the first time that the Supreme Soviet had ventured into foreign affairs, hitherto the monopoly of the President. Legislation was also passed restricting the activities of foreign banks and foreign religious organisations in Russia.

Both the speaker and the presidium of the Supreme Soviet had the right to issue decrees and directives with the force of law. In the first six months of 1993, Khasbulatov issued over 630 and the presidium even more. The war of laws was worse than under Gorbachev. The President vetoed most legislation passed by the Supreme Soviet and issued his own. In the first seven months of 1993, the President signed over 1150 decrees. The Supreme Soviet tried to outbid the President for the support of the regions and was attempting, in reality, to become a parallel executive. This caused endless confusion in the regions. Deputies also looked after their own interests. They passed legislation privatising their own offices and apartments in central Moscow. This was one aspect of privatisation which they did not object to. There was another tactic which the Supreme Soviet pursued. The procuracy was subordinate to parliament and so it was used to harass members of Yeltsin's government. Criminal investigations were launched against, for example, Mikhail Poltoranin, the head of the committee on information, and Vladimir Shumeiko, a deputy Prime Minister.

THE FINAL THRUST

The President's whereabouts were always a matter for speculation. He was physically in decline and his health became an issue of debate. On one occasion, President Clinton spent several days trying to locate him. He was informed that the President was in a place without a telephone. He returned to Moscow in early July not looking his best. A conference of democrats called for action and the President confirmed that if parliament did not agree to early elections he would act. Yeltsin disliked reading official memoranda. When Oleg Lobov, at the end of August, proposed more state management of the economy he agreed. When the radicals got to him he changed his mind.

He began his offensive on 1 September when he temporarily suspended Vice-President Aleksandr Rutskoi on the flimsy accusation of corruption. Two weeks later Yeltsin declared he would agree to early presidential elections if parliament agreed to early parliamentary elections. Parliament ignored him. Then, on 16 September, the President brought Egor Gaidar back into government as first deputy Prime Minister and minister of economics, ousting Lobov (he was made secretary of the Security Council). This appears to have been connected with promised IMF and World Bank loans. President Clinton made it clear he was on Boris's side. He could now act. In his memoirs he states that he wrote and signed, in longhand, a decree dissolving parliament but he did not tell a soul and locked it away in a drawer. Various ministers, including Prime Minister Chernomyrdin, tried to get Yeltsin to change his mind about confrontation. Gaidar did his best to get an audience but failed. Hence the President was as much to blame as parliament for the bloodletting which was to come.

On 21 September 1993, presidential decree no. 1400 dissolved Congress and the Supreme Soviet and set new elections to a bicameral legislature (Federal Assembly consisting of a Duma with 450 members and a Council of the Federation with two representatives from each of Russia's 89 republics and other regions) on 11–12 December 1993 (Shevtsova 1999: 83). The Duma was to have 450 members, half elected on the first-past-the-post principle and half on the basis of party lists (in order to qualify for seats parties had to obtain at least 5 per cent of the total vote). DemRossiya was delighted. It praised Yeltsin for breaking the 'vicious circle of the power struggle'. The nationalist newspaper *Den* called Yeltsin an 'outlaw'. Democrats were called *dermokraty*, from the Russian word *dermo* meaning shit.

An extraordinary session of Congress was convened but only 638 deputies turned up. Those who opposed the coup were expelled. In an all-night session it swore in Aleksandr Rutskoi as President, dismissed the power ministers, Grachev (defence), Golushko (security), and Erin (internal affairs), and appointed its own. Now Russia had two Presidents, two ministers of defence, two ministers of security and two ministers of internal affairs. This was dual power with a vengeance. Weapons were handed out to those who were willing to defend the White House. An extraordinary 10th Congress was hastily called. Parliament was going to fight. The President had miscalculated. The original plan had been to occupy the White House on a Sunday when it would be almost empty. There was no contingency plan to cope with armed opposition.

This time Chernomyrdin and the government sided immediately with Yeltsin, gravely disappointing the White House. International approval was instant based on the assumption that the crisis would be resolved without violence. Everyone knew that the President was acting unconstitutionally but ignored this.

The President offered those deputies who left peacefully generous benefits, including their most prized possessions, their Moscow apartments, but most stayed. On 28 September, the White House was blockaded by police and ministry of internal affairs forces. Those who wanted to leave could do so but no one was permitted to enter. Electricity, water, phones and the appurtenances of modern life were cut off. The deputies thought they would win as they judged the military and most provincial leaders to be on their side. This was a fatal mistake. The military did not wish to spill the blood of Russians. August 1991 had made them wary of becoming embroiled in political struggles. Also they wanted to be on the winning side. Civilian support was also weak. Moscow and St Petersburg city councils, among his strongest supporters in 1991, now refused to back him.

On 30 September, the Kremlin accepted the Orthodox Church's offer of mediation. They reached agreement the next day. Water, electricity and the phones were switched on and hordes of reporters entered the White House to interview the 200 or so deputies still there. There were also about 500 armed defenders. However the deputies voted to reject the compromise; they would not hand over their weapons. Rutskoi and Khasbulatov appeared intent on destroying any hopes of a deal. They called the President a drunkard and talked of his creation of a 'political concentration camp in the middle of Moscow'.

The first violent confrontation took place on 2 October in the square opposite the ministry of foreign affairs. A pitched battle between demonstrators and militia ensued. By the evening one militiaman was dead and 24 injured. Yeltsin and his staff went off to their dachas outside Moscow. On 3 October demonstrators broke through cordons (although there were perhaps 15,000 OMON (Special Police) and other units) and reached the White House. The crows waved banners, inscribed 'Hang Yeltsin', 'Judas Yeltsin' and 'Rutskoi is President'. Rutskoi was jubilant. 'We have won', he shouted. 'It's time to finish off the fascist dictator Yeltsin. The Kremlin will be taken today', Khasbulatov told deputies. The crowd made for the Moscow mayor's office (next to the White House) and smashed their way in using trucks. The militiamen did not put up a fight. The next target was Ostankino, the television centre. If they took it they could broadcast the success of their revolution and demand that the population obeyed them. Inside *spetsnaz* (special forces) fired back. As the battle raged Yeltsin arrived back in the Kremlin from his dacha on the evening of 3 October. He immediately demanded of General Pavel Grachev, the minister of defence: 'Where are the troops?' Grachev said they were on their way and repeated this every time the President enquired. In reality, there were no troops as they had refused to move. The President went to the ministry of defence himself and harangued his generals. They would not move. Eventually, one of the President's own security staff proposed that ten tanks be placed in front of the White House. Grachev would not act without a written order from the President. He got it. Most of the work organising the armed attack on the opposition was carried out by Aleksandr Korzhakov, head of the presidential guard. Even he could not get some of the elite groups of the guard to act.

Egor Gaidar was appalled by the inactivity of the President and his men to rally the support of the population. So he went on television and called for all supporters to come on to the streets and defend the new order. Many others followed, including famous names from the theatre. The President sat in his office and watched television. Gaidar spoke to the crowd outside the Moscow city soviet building on Tverskaya Street and the road from there to the Kremlin was packed with supporters. Gaidar was roundly reproached for his initiative. On the radio, journalists accused him of irresponsibly putting many civilian lives at risk. Fighting was the responsibility of the militia and the military. However the pro-Yeltsin demonstrators were heavily armed. They broke into the Moscow city soviet and chased the deputies out. They then chanted that the city soviet had been disbanded. Mayor Luzhkov confirmed this on 5 October. Yeltsin then disbanded the Moscow oblast soviet, arguing it was a remnant of the Soviet era.

The President declared a state of emergency in Moscow at 0400 hours on 4 October. Over 1000 troops from elite divisions were in front of the White House by 0700 hours. However they disobeyed an order to shoot. Only when a White House sniper killed a soldier did they go on the offensive (the soldier was mysteriously shot in the back). The tanks began shelling the building about 0930 hours but the shooting dragged on. The reason for this was that after each burst there was a lull while the troops called on the defenders to surrender. The top four floors of the White House were quickly set on fire. Attempts were made through-out the day to bring the bloodletting to an end but it was 1745 hours before Rutskoi and Khasbulatov came out and were shipped off to the Lefortovo prison. Snipers continued firing during the night. The Kremlin stated that 20 soldiers had been killed taking the White House and 40 defenders were found dead inside. At least 20 had been killed in Ostankino. Other sources put the number of dead at over 170 with about 1000 injured. No deputy had been killed. That evening Yeltsin was given an envelope. Inside was Khasbulatov's clay pipe. He took it out and then flung it against a wall smashing it into pieces. He had destroyed his main enemy.

There is another version of these events (Shevtsova 1999: 88–90; Knight 1996: 76–7; Reddaway and Glinski 2001: 423; Medvedev 2000: 120–23). The President's men deliberately allowed the crowd to break through the cordon outside the White House and acted amateurishly in defence of the mayor's office and Ostankino. From midday on 3 October there were helicopters flying around the White House and thousands of troops. Suddenly they were all withdrawn. The armoured vehicles also withdrew. On the square in front of the White House trucks were left unattended with keys in the ignition. Towards evening all police in central Moscow disappeared, even those on traffic duty. This gave the impression to the opposition that taking power would be easy. At Ostankino, broadcasting ceased on the orders of Chernomyrdin. There were other TV stations nearby belonging to the ministries of defence, communications and emergency situations. They offered their services but no one took up their offer. The only TV news available was the government news channel which carried a printed message stating that the station had been seized by an armed mob. This was completely untrue.

Once the demonstrators had used violence, the authorities could justify bloodletting by saying they had acted in self-defence. Yeltsin wanted to destroy the opposition and they fell into his trap. What about Gaidar and the democrats who rallied to Yeltsin's side? They really did believe that a coup was under way. They were simply not privy to the subterfuge. The President was very slow to react because he was waiting for the decisive moment to strike. Rutskoi played into his hands by calling for an assault on the Kremlin. Had he called on his supporters to barricade the White House, Yeltsin, almost certainly, would not have attacked. He would have been forced to reach an agreement with Rutskoi and the others. Aleksei Kazannik, the procurator general, after he had resigned, criticised the Yeltsin administration for not having negotiated seriously with the Supreme Soviet leaders. This could mean that the storming of the White House had been, in legal terms, a crime. Kazannik argued that the attack could only be justified legally if negotiations had irretrievably broken down.

There were important lessons to emerge from the violence. Yeltsin was willing to spill blood to achieve his goal of untrammelled power. He suffered from depression from time to time but he came back to life if a fight were in prospect. He decided he could not work with Congress after his confrontation in December 1992. He then set out to destroy it and devoted nine months to the task.

It was a very Russian, even Bolshevik confrontation. Armed struggle was the natural way of resolving the impasse. The battle in the White House had not been between the President and mainstream communists for power (the communists in the White House were on the far left). Gennady Zyuganov, leader of the communist party of the Russian Federation, made sure he was on holiday when the fighting started and stayed well away until everything was over. Ivan Rybkin, head of the Agrarian Party of Russia, the communists' sister party in the countryside, moved in and out of the White House until he saw that violence was imminent. Then he made himself scarce. The communists were not interested in taking over Russia. They were only interested in sharing power. They were no longer a revolutionary force. Their leaders were more concerned about personal wealth than wealth redistribution. Rybkin was to collaborate closely with Yeltsin as speaker of the first Duma. The President's men liked to talk of the communists preparing for revolution but this language of confrontation alienated most people, especially the intellectuals. The government had to find some scapegoats for the mess the country was in. One can view the confrontation with parliament as a refusal by Yeltsin to agree to a more equitable redistribution of state assets. The democratic majority in parliament wanted a fairer society. The President could cut deals with communist deputies who were managers but he strongly objected to those who used populist slogans against him. They were a threat as long as the economy was in decline. They had to be destroyed. They could not be co-opted so they had to be swept away.

THE SPOILS OF VICTORY

Yeltsin wanted the normalisation of politics as quickly as possible. Only the far left communist and nationalist parties and their press were banned. For instance, the communist party of the Russian Federation and Rutskoi's People's Party of Free Russia were free to participate in the 12 December elections to the Duma (Rutskoi was in jail). The last thing the President wanted was a martyr with a cause. However the People's Party did not make it to the starting line. In all, 13 parties and movements qualified for the elections, having collected the requisite 100,000 signatures.

Many westerners expected the government to set up its own coalition party and present electors with a clear choice: us or them. The natural leader would have been Yeltsin. However, as before, he decided to remain above politics. Government ministers could not agree so they set up their own parties. Egor Gaidar set up the Russia's Choice bloc. This was a smart move. In Russian the word for elections is the plural of the word for choice. Sergei Shakhrai and Aleksandr Shokhin together founded the Party of Russian Unity and Accord (PRES). Prime Minister Chernomyrdin decided to throw in his lot with them. Aleksandr Zaveryukha, the minister of agriculture, joined the Agrarian Party of Russia (APR) which was full of the countryside's ex-communist nomenklatura. To put it mildly, this caused fissures within the government. Other ministers and their deputies got themselves on to party lists. If their bloc got over five per cent of the total vote they would have a seat in the Duma as half of the 450 deputies would be elected by proportional representation. The electoral law had been drafted to bring into being large centrist coalition groups, along the lines of the parties in the United States and Great Britain, for instance. The main reason why this did not occur may have been the realisation that power did not rest with parliament but with the President. Another reason for the proliferation of small parties may have been the Yeltsin camp's realisation that these would split the vote many ways. Yeltsin's men may even have financed or helped to finance some of the smaller parties.

Presidents, governors and heads of the legislature of the 89 subjects were granted *ex officio* membership of the upper house, the Council of the Federation. So the members of the executive would become members of the legislature. They would have an interest in passing laws which benefited themselves. Also members of parliament enjoyed immunity from criminal prosecution. In practice, they could be as corrupt as they desired. Here was a ruling class looking after itself.

The President was not concerned about corruption, he was concerned about the draft constitution. Guided by Sergei Shakhrai, it went through several drafts. It was published for discussion on 10 November 1993. It was not a presidential system but a superpresidential system. The President was akin to a Tsar. He is head of state and guarantor of the constitution and elected for four years, as in the United States. He appoints the Prime Minister and he in turn selects the government. Only the Prime Minister has to be confirmed by the Duma. If parliament rejects the President's nominee three times he may dissolve it but not during the first twelve months of its term. If the Duma passes a vote of no confidence in the government twice within a period of three months the President may either dismiss the government or dissolve the Duma. The lower house does have some power. Besides confirming the Prime Minister in office it does the same with the chair of the Russian Central Bank. The state budget has also to be approved by it. This permits the Duma to haggle with the government over expenditure. Legislation passed by the Duma and the Council of the Federation is forwarded to the President for signing. If he refuses and the two houses, by at least a two thirds majority vote, return it, he must sign and promulgate it. It is virtually impossible to remove the President. Amendments to the constitution are extremely difficult to achieve as the President must approve them. The constitution rejected the principle of the division of powers. It conferred on the President enormous legislative, executive and judicial powers. What would happen if the President were incapable of exercising his enormous power? Given his failing health this question was bound to be raised. There was an article which stipulated that he was to resign if he could no longer perform his duties. There was no indication who would decide when he became incompetent. In reality, he was often incapable but his assistants stated that he was reading state papers. This was palpably untrue but there was no constitutional redress.

Changes were made after the October events. Among the losers were the republics and other regions. In previous drafts they had been accorded many more powers. The change of mind had occurred after so many of them had supported parliament against the President. However the Council of the Federation increased its powers. As it turned out the Council gave the President far fewer headaches than the Duma. The main reason for this was that Moscow had money and privileges to disburse. The constitution bore all the hallmarks of being put together to ensure that the October events never recurred. It introduced a constitutional dictatorship. For instance, the constitutional court only made an appearance in 1995. The constitution contained hidden dangers for the future.

The election campaign was enlivened by the clown prince of Russian politics, Vladimir Zhirinovsky. Called Mad Vlad by some, he was an unashamed populist. He was already known because he had tilted at the Russian presidency in 1991. Critics called his party, the Liberal Democratic Party of Russia (LDPR), neither liberal nor democratic nor a party. He promised every woman a man and everyone free vodka. How could he fail to win votes? He was also anti-Semitic and pilloried the new business elite, catching well the public mood. He championed law and order and promised to shoot criminals. Again this touched a public nerve. He was the most skilful campaigner on television (Gaidar was hopeless) and a master of the outlandish remark. He knew how to capture the sound-bite. His researchers discovered what the public wanted and he promised them it. Another contender was Yabloko, a liberal coalition headed by Grigory Yavlinsky. It was a strident critic of Gaidar's economics and wanted more state regulation. The LDPR and Yabloko had something in common. They were headed by men with enormous egos. Women of Russia also appeared, a brave attempt to rally women around a political cause. They met considerable resistance among educated women who did not wish to be associated with a purely feminine party.

THE CONSTITUTION AND THE FIRST DUMA

The Yeltsin camp were confident that they would get about a third of the votes in the first Duma elections on 12 December (Shevtsova 1999: 91–9). They had a splendid television studio which showed the results live as they came in. The mood changed very quickly as the first results from the Far East and Siberia were digested. The real victors were Zhirinovsky followed by the communists and the agrarians. Suddenly a (political) fault developed in the technology and the live results ceased coming in.

In order for the constitution to be adopted at least 50 per cent of the electorate had to turn out and over 50 per cent had to vote for the constitution. If they did not then the Duma elections were invalid. Officially 53.2 per cent of the electorate cast their votes, 58.4 per cent voted for the constitution and 41.6 per cent against. This revealed that only about 30 per cent of the electorate had affirmed the constitution. Voters rejected the constitution in 24 of the 88 subjects (Chechnya did not participate) of the federation, including eight of the 20 republics. In 17 of the 88 subjects, the referendum was invalid because less than 50 per cent of voters participated. The above suggests that it was a minor miracle that the constitution was approved. In fact it was not approved. The report of the Central Electoral Commission was never published and may no longer exist. There was the mysterious disappearance of seven million ballot papers. One can assume that they were all against the constitution. Perhaps it was all to the good that there was fraud. Without it Russia would not have had a constitution or a parliament. This does not bear thinking about. However it set a dolorous pattern. Electoral fraud was to become the norm in Russian politics.

Russia's Choice turned out not to be Russia's choice (Table 3.1). Gaidar's bloc only received 15.5 per cent of the total vote. The split in the government meant that votes were spread over several pro-reform parties. Those who were unhappy with Gaidar's reforms voted for Yavlinsky's Yabloko bloc, 7.9 per cent, and Shakhrai's Party of Russian Unity and Accord, 6.8 per cent. Hence about 30 per cent of voters supported the rapid move to the market. These results, however, could not obscure the fact that the government had been soundly defeated. The real victor, a stunning surprise, was Vladimir Zhirinovsky. His LDPR picked up 22.8 per cent of the total vote, better than any other party. This catapulted Zhirinovsky into prominence and made him a leading politician overnight.

Yeltsin was surprised but had the consolation that the original four-year term for the Duma had been cut to two. The reason for this was Duma elections would be a sounding board for the presidential elections. Surely in two years' time his allies would have greater support. However, if 1993 was bad 1995 was worse. The President had been wise not to identify with any of the parties. Many of those who voted for the constitution deserted the pro-reform parties. The communists and agrarians were strongly against the constitution but Zhirinovsky was in favour. He wanted to be a strong President. Zhirinovsky talked of making Russia great again and attacked radical economic reform and the communists. Could the LDPR become a third force between Yeltsin and the communists? He owed his rise, in part, to help from the Yeltsin camp. He was given a lot of air time and used it skilfully. The television companies, in their defence, argued that they had been told to make money so they sold air time to the highest bidders. Russia's Choice demonised Zhirinovsky, warning voters that he represented neo-fascism. This scared the children but not the adults. If Gaidar had watched television he would have known that many viewers love horror movies. The Yeltsin camp was pleased that Zhirinovsky would take votes from the communists. He now also spoke for the nationalists and this scuppered Rutskoi's chances of toppling Yeltsin.

THE FEDERAL ASSEMBLY

Parliament consisted of a lower house, the Duma, an upper house, Council of the Federation (also referred to as the Senate and its members as senators). The upper house was unelected, like the US Senate in the nineteenth century. The deputies had to leave the White House (it was renovated by a Turkish company and became the seat of the Russian government) and move to central Moscow. Ivan Rybkin, of the Agrarian Party, was elected speaker of the Duma. He was a moderate and a compromise candidate. The liberals and democrats could not command anything like a majority and only the LDPR wanted Zhirinovsky as speaker. Rybkin was to prove himself an excellent chair of parliament. Gradually he moved towards Yeltsin and mediated many of the sharp conflicts between the Duma and the President. Some began to see him as a future Prime Minister as it was clear that he had become the President's man. Vladimir Shumeiko, first deputy Prime Minister, was elected speaker of the Council of the Federation.

One of the first acts of the Duma infuriated Yeltsin. It granted an amnesty to the plotters in August 1991 and the leaders of the October 1993 events. The President proposed a deal. Drop the investigation into the October 1993 events and he would sign the amnesty bill. The deputies agreed. When the procurator general, Aleksei Kazannik, received the text of the legislation he prepared to release the prisoners. The President put Kazannik under great pressure by proposing that the amnesty be delayed a while or even indefinitely. However the state's main law officer refused and resigned in protest. On 26 February 1994, 74 were released from Lefortovo prison. The crowd outside chanted: 'Rutskoi – President!'. Kazannik, a democrat of the first hour, was disgusted by Kremlin politics. Afterwards he did not join Gaidar's party but that of Svyatoslav Fedorov, the eye surgeon, a Yeltsin critic. Even more damaging he revealed that Yeltsin had pressured him in October 1993 to investigate the armed clash and charge the arrested with serious crimes, after which they would be sentenced to death in two- or three-day trials (Reddaway and Glinski 2001: 461).

Neither the President nor the Duma was content with the constitution but gradually learned to work within it. Over the two years of the Duma's term 461 legislative acts were passed and of these 282 were signed by Yeltsin and were promulgated. These included amendments to the constitution affecting the constitutional court, arbitration courts and referenda. The Duma confirmed the members of the constitutional court (which was now solidly pro-President), the procurator general and two of the three chairs of the Russian Central Bank (the exception was Tamara Paramanova, acting chair from October 1994–November 1995). However the voting record of the first Duma revealed that over half the deputies usually voted against legislation proposed by the government. There were about 200 deputies who were adamantly anti-Yeltsin and only 188 who could be relied upon to support his initiatives.

The results of the elections heralded the end of the Gaidar era. Yeltsin, ever sensitive to the shifting mood of the country, decided that radical economic reform was no longer politically attractive. The Gaidar group had failed to weld together an interest group which embraced the old and new elites. They had not put down roots in industry and finance. Gaidar departed on 16 January 1994 and Boris Fedorov, the minister of finance, on 26 January. Ella Pamfilova, the minister for social welfare, also went. However one of the radicals, Anatoly Chubais, stayed. He had political skills which the others lacked. He had struck up a relationship with Viktor Chernomyrdin, the Prime Minister. Chubais was to prove one of the great survivors of Russian politics. Others such as Aleksandr Shokhin and Sergei Shakhrai, who had been close to the radicals, gradually distanced themselves from them and stayed in government. The appointment of Gaidar in September 1993, just before the bloody events of October, and his dismissal in January 1994, led to speculation that Yeltsin had used the radical economist as a fig leaf to cover up the unconstitutionality of his actions. With Gaidar in government the west would forgive Boris.

In the upper house only 48 senators could be classified as pro-Yeltsin reformers with 58 who were clearly opposed. The others (there were technically 178 senators in all but the two from Chechnya never sat in the chamber) were described as independents. With Shumeiko as speaker there was little likelihood of confrontation. However the tactic adopted by the Council of the Federation was to haggle with the President in order to gain maximum concessions before accepting his proposals. On the first vote they rejected the President's candidate for the post of procurator general, chair of the Central Bank and nominees for the constitutional court. In the end they voted them through.

THE PRESIDENT'S LIFE-STYLE

After the exertions of the December elections the President again played the magician: he disappeared. He repaired to his dacha-sanatorium at Barvikha, outside Moscow. He was almost always in a foul mood. In February-March 1994, he was away from the Kremlin for about five weeks. He had changed completely compared to two years previously. Then he had been a workhorse, staying in the Kremlin until late evening, usually working Saturdays and even sometimes on a Sunday. Now he was physically and mentally a shadow of his former self. Meeting after meeting was cancelled. His malaise may have set in after his dismissal by Gorbachev in 1987. However the excitement of the following years caused the adrenalin to flow. Now he suffered from depression and insomnia. He was wont to wake in the early hours and get up because he could not go back to sleep. Gaidar had another explanation. The 'sin of bloodshed' had stained his soul. Others remarked that the bloody events of October haunted him. Yeltsin admitted that he suffered despair and grief at the sight of the poor and dying in Moscow. He was the father of the nation and he was responsible.

Always a bibber, Yeltsin gradually began to drink to excess (Aron 2000: 573–6). This may have been because of depression or insomnia in the hope of getting some sleep. He would indulge at lunch, in the afternoon and evening. He had a special favourite, green vodka spiced with herbs. This meant that he was well lubricated when meeting high-ranking foreign guests. The whole world was treated to a piece of theatre on 31 August 1994, in Berlin. Yeltsin was there to mark the departure of the last Russian troops from Germany. Tipsy, he grabbed the conductor's baton and began to conduct the police band. He was out of tune but the band stayed in tune. He finished by singing Kalinka, a Russian folk tune. In his memoirs (2000), he sheepishly conceded that he had been up all night drinking with Pavel Grachev, the minister of defence. His closest advisers wrote him a letter asking him to behave with more dignity. This infuriated him. On another occasion President

Clinton saved the day by laughing loudly until Boris had regained some composure. The drinking allowed some negative traits of Yeltsin's character to surface too often. He could be imperious, insulting, mocking and grossly insensitive to the feelings of others. His subordinates felt the sharpness of his tongue on many occasions. Some days it was best to avoid the President.

If there was a semblance of a decision-making process before this, it now disappeared. It was replaced by ad hoc decisions. Yeltsin delighted in the trappings of power and loved the opulence of the Kremlin. He hired and fired with gay abandon. Given his inability to concentrate for long periods those wielding influence were those close to the ailing Tsar. This promoted intrigue and mutual suspicion among the Yeltsin entourage. The government was headed by ministers who had run the Soviet economy, for instance, Viktor Chernomyrdin (gas), Oleg Soskovets (metallurgy) and Vladimir Shumeiko (instrument-making). Oleg Lobov, secretary of the Security Council, (engineering), fitted in well. Yeltsin felt comfortable with these men. The other type which surrounded Yeltsin was young, ambitious and with little technical or administrative expertise. Gaidar called them nincompoops (*nedoumki*) (Aron 2000: 576). The President liked their company, they were intellectually undemanding, and like a Roman emperor he hosted huge dinners with generous libations almost every day. The bathhouse or sauna was also a part of this lifestyle. Good living soon showed on Yeltsin's waistline. If he was a big man before he was now a bigger man.

There was an inner circle consisting of Aleksandr Korzhakov, head of the presidential guard and much more besides, Mikhail Barsukov, head of Kremlin security, Viktor Erin, minister of internal affairs, Pavel Borodin, head of the administration of affairs, Oleg Soskovets, Pavel Grachev, minister of defence, and Shamil Tarpishchev, the President's personal tennis coach, at least as long as he played tennis. Members of the inner circle benefited from special economic concessions granted by the President. It is striking that none of the liberals or radical reformers was a member of the inner circle. They were in the outer circle and found access to the President almost always blocked. All this led to erratic policy making. On one occasion the President issued a decree on Russian military bases abroad; one was to be in Latvia. This caused a diplomatic furore and was explained away as a technical error. It testified to the lack of expertise displayed by some of the President's advisers.

The effects of the plane crash in Spain, in May 1988, when he was saved from paralysis by the skill of a Spanish surgeon, became more and more burdensome. The difficult spinal operation had left its mark and he suffered much back pain. He had to drag slightly his right leg. Spinal nerves also became inflamed and were extremely painful. He also suffered from heart disease or ischaemia. In simple language this was blockage of the coronary arteries. It caused chest pain and other maladies. Yeltsin took painkillers chased down by alcohol. Heart attacks inevitably followed. He suffered one in July 1995 and was unable to leave the plane to meet the Irish Prime Minister at Shannon airport on 30 September, thereby causing great embarrassment. He suffered another heart attack in October. Afterwards he found it difficult to walk and sit. Eventually he underwent a quintuple heart by-pass operation.

POLITICAL REACTIONS

The first Chechen war, December 1994–August 1996, caused many democrats to come out against Yeltsin (Shevtsova 1999: 116–18). However some like Boris Fedorov, a former minister of finance, and Vladimir Lukin, a former Russian ambassador in Washington and later chair of the Duma foreign affairs committee, backed the use of force. They argued that the interests of the Russian state were paramount. The President received almost unanimous support from the radical nationalists. Zhirinovsky was always on side at critical moments.

War in Chechnya increased the burdens of office. Yeltsin gave the impression of finding it all too much. He was irascible, stubborn and seemed incapable of taking much advice. His health continued to fail. In Kazakhstan, in February 1995, he had to be supported on both sides. Increasingly he avoided meetings and people.

The war in Chechnya was unpopular in the Russian republics. It signalled that the Kremlin intended to claw back some of the power which had devolved to the regions. In January 1995, in Cheboksary, the capital of Udmurtia, several republican leaders met to mobilise opposition to the war. The Chechens were Muslims as were most of the republics. Some Islamic leaders opposed the fighting. Little came of this as most regions needed to stay on good relations with Moscow due to the economic benefits they could reap. Ingushetia and Dagestan did not wish to become embroiled in hostilities although the Chechens were attempting to widen the war. Stavropol krai supported military intervention partly because the lawlessness there had negative economic effects on it. Trains had been held up and robbed and cattle and sheep rustling was a problem. There were benefits for Georgia. Russian control would cut off Chechen aid to the separatists in Abkhazia. Ukraine seized the opportunity to dampen the Republic of Crimea's hopes for independence and the office of President of the Republic was abolished.

BUDENNOVSK

On 15 June 1995 about a hundred Chechen fighters bribed their way through Russian controls and seized a hospital in Budennovsk, a town in Stavropol krai, which borders on Chechnya. They took over a thousand people hostage. Their leader, Shamil Basaev, had a reputation as a daring front commander. He demanded the immediate withdrawal of Russian troops from Chechnya and the recognition of Chechen independence. Yeltsin was not fazed and left for a G7 (seven leading industrial countries) summit in Halifax, Canada. He approved military action to free the hostages but the operation went badly wrong. It resulted in large losses of life, especially among the hospital patients. Viktor Chernomyrdin, in charge while the President was away, began negotiating with the rebels. He caved in to Basaev and agreed that the Chechens would have safe passage back to their homeland. There would be an immediate ceasefire in Chechnya and peace talks would begin. Basaev's actions ensured that the sympathy that some Russians felt for the Chechens was now dissipated.

THE DUMA TESTS THE PRESIDENT'S POWER

The mishandling of the Budennovsk crisis was seized upon by the communists in the Duma to begin the process of impeaching the President. This was the first direct challenge to the President since the events of October 1993. On 21 June 1995, the communists mustered 172 votes but they needed 300 or two thirds for an impeachment motion to be carried. On 22 June, a motion of no confidence in the government was passed by 241 votes (it needed a simple majority or 226 votes) to 70. According to the constitution, a second vote of no confidence in the government would force the President to dismiss the government and appoint a new Prime Minister or dissolve the Duma. Yeltsin and Chernomyrdin counterattacked. The President warned parliament that he would not accept the government's resignation. This implied he would dissolve the Duma. The Prime Minister demanded that parliament proceed to a second vote of no confidence immediately. Most deputies wanted to keep their job and the perks which went with it. The President wanted to keep his Prime Minister. The two sides compromised. Parliament was to have a greater say in the drafting of the 1996 budget. The President asked the Duma to refrain from attempting to

amend the constitution and to avoid direct confrontations with the government. In return the deputies wanted the power ministers removed.
On 29 June, Yeltsin sacked Sergei Stepashin, director of the federal counter-
intelligence service, and reluctantly Viktor Erin, minister of internal affairs.
Against all the odds he left Pavel Grachev, the minister of defence, in
office. Grachev was unpopular with the military and hence a weak
minister. That type of minister suited Yeltsin. Both sides revealed mod-
eration at a time of crisis and therefore defused the most serious situation since October 1993. The stress told on the President and he fell
seriously ill and disappeared from public view. To calm the situation he
signed a decree setting 17 December 1995 as the date for the next Duma
elections. Electioneering could now begin. Everyone was aware that the
Duma elections were a mere prelude to the main elections, that of a
Russian President in June 1996. Would Boris be alive then or if so would
he be able to run? That was the question.

NEGOTIATING A PEACE

Peace negotiations could have been conducted by the two Presidents,
Yeltsin and Dudaev. However Dudaev was a 'bandit' and one could not
reach agreement with a bandit. The Chechens wanted independence but
perhaps that could be regarded as a long-term objective. The short-term
objective could be the withdrawal of most Russian forces, new elections
in Chechnya and autonomy inside the republic. On the Chechen side
there was little disagreement on objectives. This was not the case on
the Russian side. There were three main points of view: Chechnya could
be granted independence, it could be reintegrated into the Russian
Federation by force, or it could be granted a status somewhere between
integration and independence. In the latter case, in the very important
realm of foreign affairs, it would have considerable autonomy. The
military and the politicians in Russia were split. The military wanted to
keep Chechnya in the Russian Federation for strategic reasons. Many
politicians were willing to grant Chechnya greater autonomy. Option
three above would have been the best solution but the military would
not hear of it. The negotiators came up with various formulations
but it was clear that there were powerful forces in Chechnya and Russia
which did not want the crisis resolved. The war was a source of wealth
for groups on both sides. A military but not a political agreement was
signed in late July 1995. Chechen opponents of the agreement ensured
that it failed. They blew up General Anatoly Romanov, commander of
Russian troops in Chechnya, on 6 October 1995. Prospects for peace
were also blown away.

The new commander of Russian forces in Chechnya turned out to be General Vyacheslav Tikhomirov. The Chechens did not wait for a Russian offensive but struck at Kizlyar, in neighbouring Dagestan, on 9 January 1996. About two hundred Chechens, commanded by Dudaev's son-in-law, Salman Raduev, repeating the same tactics as at Budennovsk, seized about 3000 hostages at a hospital and maternity home. The Chechens took some hostages with them on their way back to Chechnya. However the Russians surrounded and attacked them with bombers, missiles and artillery at Pervomaiskoe, near the border. Despite being completely outnumbered many of the Chechens made it back home, including Raduev. Again many hostages perished. The man put in charge of resolving the Kizlyar crisis was Mikhail Barsukov, head of federal security service (FSB). He had no experience of field operations. Yeltsin went on television and demonstrated how the Chechens would be defeated by 38 snipers. Many viewers concluded that the President was living on a different planet.

Yeltsin desperately searched for a way out of the Chechen war as he feared that it could cost him the election. He would not meet Dudaev face to face. Yeltsin declared that hostilities would cease on 31 March and that Russian forces would begin withdrawing. His military ignored him. Then on 21 April Dudaev was killed by a missile. Yeltsin immediately invited his successor, Zelimkhan Yandarbiev, to Moscow for negotiations. They quickly reached a consensus and in Nazran, the capital of Ingushetia, in August 1996, an agreement was signed which envisaged the withdrawal of Russian forces from Chechnya. It had been easy to reach agreement as the Russians had decided to capitulate.

THE DUMA ELECTIONS OF DECEMBER 1995

There was only one political party which had a pan-Russian organisation and support, the communist party of the Russian Federation (KPRF). Most new parties were like butterflies, they fluttered for a season and then disappeared. One of the high-profile casualties was DemRossiya. It could not collect the necessary number of signatures to take part in the election and faded away.

Russia's Choice, headed by Egor Gaidar, lost members and influence rapidly. The President had distanced himself from the radical economics of his former darling boy. Even though he was no longer in government many voters still blamed him for the economic mess Russia was in. Yabloko, led by Grigory Yavlinsky, was establishing itself as the mainstream liberal party which favoured a less bumpy road to the market.

It appealed to many middle-class voters because it consistently criticised Yeltsin's policies. Gaidar, going down, wanted an alliance with Yabloko, going up. Yavlinsky declined as he had no intention of joining any coalition – even with parties on the way up. He did not want to confuse the voters since he wanted them to vote for him and no one else.

A new coalition on the nationalist right was the Congress of Russian Communities (KOR). Two of its leaders were old hands at Russian politics: Yury Skokov and Sergei Glazev. The latter was an excellent economist but had come to see shock therapy as tantamount to the genocide of the Russian people. As minister for international economic relations, he had been the only minister to resign in protest in October 1993. On their own, Skokov and Glazev would have remained political also-rans but they pulled off a major coup. They managed to bring Aleksandr Lebed on board and thereby transformed the movement. Lebed had quit the army and appeared in Moscow, in June 1995. Everyone wanted to meet him. He did not pretend to be a democrat and his economic ideas were fed to him by Glazev. He praised Augusto Pinochet, the Chilean dictator. Was he the Russian Pinochet? His Russian nationalism did not go down very well among Russian Muslims. However non-ethnic Russians only made up about 16 per cent of the electorate.

Ambitious politicians in Russia had to form their own parties. This was to enhance their profile as possible future Presidents. Leaders of parties received funds from the budget to campaign and appear on television. The best chance of being elected was to stand as party leader in a single member constituency. The other possibility was to be on a party list but in order to obtain seats a party needed to secure at least five per cent of the total vote. This was too risky for an aspiring politician. A flood of small parties and blocs emerged. Boris Fedorov, the former minister of finance, Svyatoslav Fedorov, the eye surgeon, Irina Khakamada, the half-Japanese businesswoman, and Ivan Rybkin, the speaker of the first Duma, headed their own grouping. Ella Pamfilova, minister of health, joined two others and formed the Pamfilova–Gurov–Lysenko bloc. These politicians concentrated their efforts in their single member constituencies and left the national stage to others. Yeltsin had an interest in fragmenting the political rainbow. They could all be offered sweeteners, if elected to the Duma.

Opinion polls made it clear that the favourites were the communist party (KPRF). It had the votes of the over 50s, old age pensioners, those who were used to voting communist and those who wanted to preserve Russia from Americanisation. It appealed to the losers since 1991 and Russia was full of them. It decided to compete directly with its former ally, the Agrarian Party, in the countryside. Its leader, Gennady Zyuganov, steered the party to the right. It became traditionalist, conservative and nationalist. The extremists on the left were pushed out. It no longer saw itself as the vanguard of the proletariat. Zyuganov, called disrespectfully potato face by some critics, learnt quickly the language of democratic politics and how to say different things to different audiences. He became a natty dresser, looking like a business executive in his Saville Row suit and expensive shoes. Everyone in Moscow, Russian and foreigner, wanted to meet him. The new civilised, parliament-loving KPRF could be trusted with power, or so he said. He promised everyone more. Higher pensions, salaries, wages, secure jobs, a better health service and so on. Who was going to pay for all these goodies? Gennady would find the money. People wanted to believe this economic cloud-cuckooland could become reality. The Russian Orthodox Church was the bearer of Russian culture and should be supported. Communists could now go to church with a good conscience. Despite its strong support base the party never took on Yeltsin directly. It always shied away from a fight at the last moment. The leadership appears to have concluded that Yeltsin would not give up power voluntarily. It would have to be taken from him by force and that could mean civil war. The communists had no stomach for such a conflict.

It had not escaped the President's attention that many developed countries had two party systems. In April 1995, he suggested to Viktor Chernomyrdin that he form a centre-right bloc and Ivan Rybkin, a centre-left bloc. This would split the opposition vote and attract more voters to the party of power. This latter expression meant those parties, groups and movements which exercised power around Yeltsin. Again the President deemed it politic not to set up a presidential party. If Chernomyrdin failed he could dismiss him as Prime Minister. Our Home is Russia (NDR) was launched on 27 May and many ministers joined and quickly began organising the new party during working hours. NDR set out to win support in the regions. The latter seized on the opportunity to do a deal: pay us subsidies and we will vote for you.

Critics had some fun with the party's symbol. It was a roof (*krysha*) but this was also the mafia word for protection. The NDR was the nation's protector. NDR attracted some high-profile politicians such as Yury Luzhkov, mayor of Moscow. The latter had a nose which unerringly sensed in which direction the political wind was blowing. Well, almost always. A major problem for Chernomyrdin was that big names such as Egor Gaidar and Grigory Yavlinsky refused to join the NDR bloc.

The centre-left bloc, headed by Ivan Rybkin, was launched on 22 June but foundered very quickly. It was given the impossible task of fashioning a centre-left grouping which, if it dominated the Duma, would be friendly towards Yeltsin. It was to attract communists and others on the left but the centre-left, by definition, opposed the President. If Russia were to develop into a two-party system, the opposition had to oppose the government and present itself as a viable alternative. Rybkin soon gave up and formed his own bloc.

Evidence of how hard NDR would find it to win in the provinces was provided by the election of the governor of Ekaterinburg (Sverdlovsk), Yeltsin's home city, in August 1995. The contest was between Eduard Rossel, whom Yeltsin had removed in 1994 after he had proclaimed the Urals Republic, and the sitting governor, Aleksei Strakhov (NDR). Rossel won because he represented local interests and Strakhov was seen as Moscow's man. Yeltsin quickly reacted. At a press conference, in September, he brutally stated that NDR would only win 8–12 per cent of the national vote in the Duma elections. This undercut his main political ally. He also criticised the government's performance. What was his objective? Was Chernomyrdin getting too big for his boots and, given his own ill health, ready to take over? At the press conference he lashed out at the west and warned against NATO expansion eastwards. This was the language of the nationalists. Later he went off to New York to celebrate the 50th anniversary of the United Nations and to meet President Bill Clinton. This time he left his anti-western rhetoric in Moscow. The Bill and Boris show rolled on. Boris now spoke two languages: hard-line Russian nationalism for home consumption and measured words abroad for foreign consumption. The west knew at the end of the day that Boris would side with it. His objective in criticising Chernomyrdin and the west at home may have been to demonstrate that he was still capable of being a hands-on President.

The American trip almost killed him. On 26 October he lost consciousness and had to be taken to a clinic by helicopter. His heart condition had worsened. There was feverish speculation about whether the President was alive or dead. According to the constitution, the Prime Minister was acting President. On 30 October, Chernomyrdin announced that, with the President's agreement, besides his government duties, he would be supervising the activities of the power ministries (defence, internal affairs, security) and foreign affairs. The presidential administration was stung to the quick. The following day, Mikhail Krasnov stated that the Prime Minister could not carry out functions which were not part of the government's remit. Pavel Grachev announced that the military would, as before, only take orders from the President. Yeltsin's officials were not going to permit Chernomyrdin to take over the President's mantle. On 3 November, a tired and ill President appeared on television. On 4 November, the presidential administration announced that the power ministries and foreign affairs were to remain subordinate to the President. It appeared that the battle for succession was under way with a vengeance. Chernomyrdin had obviously decided not to bid for power and hence retreated when challenged. Astonishingly, Yeltsin recovered in December and appeared to have all his faculties.

The most flamboyant politician turned out once again to be Vladimir Zhirinovsky. He knew how to attract attention: express politics in sexual metaphors. He called the Lenin era, rape, the Stalin period, homosexuality, the Khrushchev years, masturbation, the Brezhnev years, group sex, and the present era, impotence. He declared that the period of impotence was over and that orgasm had begun. Hedonism would take on a new meaning in Vlad's Russia.

To qualify a party or bloc had to collect 200,000 signatures. This was a simple task for the larger parties but the smaller groups lacked the necessary organisation. The old adage that necessity is the mother of invention turned out to be true. The beer lovers' party handed out free beer to those willing to sign. Who was going to check signatures reeking of beer? Enterprising individuals collected signatures for a fee. In all, 43 parties or blocs qualified for the elections. This suited the government as it split the vote many ways. There was a potential danger however. With so many small parties there was a risk that only one or two parties would pass the five per cent threshold. They would qualify for the 225 seats awarded according to party lists. They could also be opposition parties. There was talk of changing the electoral law to abolish the minimum threshold but nothing came of it.

THE ELECTION RESULTS

The turnout was a respectable 64.4 per cent, higher than in December 1993. The winner, as expected, was the KPRF, with 34.9 per cent of Duma seats (Table 3.2). Our Home is Russia came in second, with 12.2 per cent of deputies. It was followed by the LDPR (it had been confidently predicted that its support would collapse) and Yabloko. Only these parties crossed the five per cent threshold; 50.5 per cent of voters chose these four parties. Thus 49.5 per cent wasted their party list votes as their parties did not cross the five per cent barrier. One of the parties to fail was

Russia's Democratic Choice, the new name for Gaidar's party. The biggest surprise of all was the poor showing of Lebed's Congress of Russian Communities (however, Lebed was elected as a deputy for Tula). Another surprising failure was Women of Russia. They had often supported the establishment during the first Duma and were punished by the voters for this. A striking factor was the number of independents. In some cases they were communists who had tactically stood as independents. Was there evidence of electoral fraud? Does water run off a duck's back? Of course, there was. It was evident in the results of the party lists votes.

The Duma was dominated by the four parties which obtained party list seats: the KPFR, the NDR, the LDPR and Yabloko. The chairs and membership of Duma committees were allocated according to the strength of Duma groups. The communists placed some of their members in other groups, thus enhancing their influence. This applied particularly to the Agrarian group, and Power to the People group, headed by the nationalist Sergei Baburin and Nikolai Ryzhkov, once Gorbachev's Prime Minister. Independents formed Russia's regions' group. According to one analyst, reformers obtained 43 per cent of the vote in 1993 but only 38.2 per cent in 1995. The opposition polled 42.8 per cent in 1993 but 52.8 per cent in 1995. The behaviour of this Duma, as that of the previous one, was to be counter-intuitive or not what a westerner would expect. There was no clear distinction between government and opposition. Sometimes the LDPR and KPRF voted to save the government. This reveals that deals were cut behind the scenes. Anything was possible if the money was right.

Elections were also held in Chechnya. NDR came out top in the federal elections and the pro-Moscow Doku Zavgaev won in Chechnya. Russian soldiers also voted in the Chechen elections and it appeared all 40,000 chose Zavgaev. He was declared the winner with 93 per cent, a result which no Chechen believed. He was Moscow's President of Chechnya and as such rejected by Chechens.

It was imperative that a moderate be elected speaker of the new Duma and Chernomyrdin's NDR tried its best to ensure that Ivan Rybkin continued as speaker. Zhirinovsky's LDPR agreed to support Rybkin but the wheeling and dealing was unsuccessful and Gennady Seleznev, a moderate communist, was elected. In the upper house, the Council of the Federation, there was no need to haggle as there was one strong candidate, Egor Stroev, governor of Orel oblast. Stroev, a former communist, now supported NDR but remained on good relations with the communists. Hence he was a good negotiating partner for the Yeltsin administration.

In early 1996, Egor Gaidar finally broke with Yeltsin and he called on the President not to run for re-election. Policy differences and opposition to the war in Chechnya had finally led to the break. Another prominent democrat, Sergei Kovalev, the prominent human rights activist, was exasperated by the conduct of the war in Chechnya and sharply criticised the President. He also lamented the fact that the decision-making process had become more secretive and opaque than in the old Politburo. The democrats scouted around for an alternative to Yeltsin and hit on Chernomyrdin. Gaidar actually called on the Prime Minister to declare his candidacy, much to Chernomyrdin's embarrassment. In response, the Prime Minister sang the praises of Yeltsin and declared that only the President should run. He could not risk being seen as disloyal to Yeltsin. In fact Chernomyrdin collected the necessary signatures to run but like any smart politician he declared he would not run. He was just not one of nature's risk takers. Eventually the democrats could not find any winning alternative to the President and reluctantly backed him. Neither Yeltsin nor Chernomyrdin wanted to be seen to be close to Gaidar and the democrats since this would lose them votes. Hence the democrats had to support Yeltsin without any hope of influencing his policies.

THE PRESIDENTIAL RACE

With the Duma elections over the real race, to the Kremlin, could now begin (Shevtsova 2000: chapter 7). Yeltsin needed to do something dramatic to revive his sagging fortunes. On 31 December 1995, he appeared in public for the first time since October. He walked in the Kremlin gardens and chatted to some people who just happened to be there. He asked them if he should run again for the presidency. Handpicked, they were enthusiastically in favour. He thanked them for their support and told them that soon all Russia's problems would be solved and the country would begin to flourish. He gave the impression of actually believing in this dreamland.

In January 1996, Yeltsin was behind all the leading candidates: Gennady Zyuganov, Grigory Yavlinsky, Vladimir Zhirinovsky and Aleksandr Lebed. Zyuganov was to hold the leading position in the opinion polls almost to the elections. The President's supporters needed a fallback candidate who could replace Yeltsin and win.

The President's populist instincts soon showed. He dumped his most unpopular ministers. First to go was Andrei Kozyrev, the foreign minister, who was perceived as the Americans' pet poodle. In came Evgeny

Primakov, head of counter-intelligence (FSK). No one could accuse him of being Washington's pet poodle, indeed he was a Rottweiler where the Americans were concerned. His critics thought he was too tame towards Saddam Hussein. Primakov was an Arabist and highly intelligent. Indeed he was so subtle with words that it was normally difficult to work out what he was driving at. This demonstrated that he was a brilliant diplomat. The difference between Kozyrev and Primakov was that everyone would respect Evgeny. Anyone who could outfox him would be very smart indeed.

On 15 January, Yeltsin parted company with Sergei Filatov, one of the few in the administration who had not put his own personal interests ahead of those of the country. A decent man and friend of the democrats, he had been hounded out of the Supreme Soviet by Khasbulatov. He was replaced, as head of the presidential administration, by Nikolai Egorov, deputy Prime Minister and a former minister of nationalities. He was known for advocating the use of force in the north Caucasus. Egorov had no original ideas on the Chechen crisis but the President saw him as capable of mobilising electoral support in the regions.

On 16 January, the most hated man in the government, Anatoly Chubais, was sent on his way. Known as Gospodin Privatizatsiya (Mr Privatisation) or rather Mr Theft (*Prikhvatizatsiya*) he was blamed for the emergence of business clans which the average Russian saw as mafia groups. The red-headed economist was more of a Bolshevik than a democrat. The Prime Minister Viktor Chernomyrdin was also expected to be shown the door but his special relationship with US Vice-President Al Gore was one reason for keeping him. Russia needed American money. The man who would have replaced him, Oleg Soskovets, did not have Chernomyrdin's US contacts.

The President needed a campaign team and it was naturally headed by the most influential man in the Kremlin, next to the President, Aleksandr Korzhakov. His confidante Mikhail Barsukov and the rapidly rising Oleg Soskovets were the other main members. They were a formidable team. Soskovets was probably still chair of the commission on inter-enterprise debt, taking day-to-day decisions which affected enterprises and regions. Such a man could not be ignored. Korzhakov earned his sobriquet of Sasha the knife by threatening opponents, especially the communists, in very direct language.

The magnitude of the task became clear in February 1996, at the World Economic Forum, in Davos, Switzerland, when Russia's captains of industry were shocked by the behaviour of western bankers, businessmen and politicians. They fawned over Gennady Zyuganov as though he were on his way to the Kremlin. It was not only westerners who had picked Zyuganov as the winner. When the Russian group arrived at Zurich airport, the ambassador could only take one politician with him in the official car to Davos. He picked Zyuganov. Even George Soros, the legendary financier who had made two billion dollars in 1992 by betting on a devaluation of the British pound, was sure that moon-faced Gennady would take over. Boris Nemtsov talked about giving Zyuganov a crash course in market economics. After a few days of this Anatoly Chubais had had enough. He arranged a press conference and castigated westerners for their gullibility. 'There are two Zyuganovs', he bellowed, 'one for domestic and the other for foreign consumption'. He prophesied civil war if the communist leader won. Communist party literature declared that Zyuganov would nationalise property which had been privatised.

Gusinsky was impressed as was Berezovsky. The two barons were at daggers drawn but they realised that Chubais was the only man who could save their empires. From a media point of view it was a brilliant move. Gusinsky's NTV [independent television] and Berezovsky's ORT [Russian public television] dominated Russian television news. (ORT was set up in November 1994 when Channel 1 was privatised. Berezovsky and associates obtained 49 per cent and the Russian government 51 per cent. This was to ensure that the government continued to subsidise the company. Berezovsky never regarded it as a vehicle to make money, merely influence public opinion.) They then brought Mikhail Khodorkovsky and Vladimir Vinogradov on board. Back in Moscow, Vladimir Potanin, Aleksandr Smolensky, Mikhail Fridman and Petr Aven were added to the group of conspirators. It was to be the first and last time the oligarchs worked together to achieve a political goal. The seven oligarchs (Vinogradov was only a candidate member) were dubbed the Group of Seven after the G7, the seven leading world economies. They were after all the seven richest men in Russia. They were also known as the seven wise men, the *semibankirshchina*, the times of the seven bankers, and by other sobriquets which are unprintable. Some of them could not stomach Chubais but in the hour of need everything is forgotten. He was the only one with the guts, some would say the balls, to take on Zyuganov and win. Some of Chubais's St Petersburg team were doubtful about working with the tainted oligarchs. Chubais brooked no opposition. He was given $2.9 million in rubles, half salary, half campaign costs. The money was an interest-free loan extended by Smolensky's Stolichny Bank, in which Berezovsky had a 25 per cent stake, to a private foundation, the centre for the defence of private property. The money was immediately invested in government bonds at 100 per cent annual interest and the profits paid into Chubais's private bank account.

With Chubais on board, the oligarchs had to sell their plan to the Tsar. This would be tough as Boris was happy with the Korzhakov team. Yeltsin made the point that things were going well and Chubais had the effrontery to contradict him to his face. Everyone waited for him to explode. After thinking for a few minutes Yeltsin calmly said they might have a point. The man who tipped the scales was Yury Luzhkov. The arch-enemy of Chubais and Berezovsky decided that the situation was so desperate that he would put old enmities aside. He advised the President to appoint Chubais as campaign manager. The Tsar arrived at one of his usual solutions. Chubais's team could go ahead but the Korzhakov team would remain. The two could slug it out for influence. As one politician said they were like two bears and Russia was only big enough for one.

The Chubais team was joined by Viktor Ilyushin, assistant to the President, Igor Malashenko, director of Gusinsky's Most-Media and NTV, Sergei Zverev, also from Most, Vasily Shakhnovsky, Luzhkov's right-hand man, and Tatyana Dyachenko, the President's daughter who had developed an appetite for politics. Reportedly, at one of its meetings someone asked how much it would cost to bribe every regional electoral official to falsify the returns. One estimate was $600 million. It was decided to spend the money on advertising. Berezovsky masterminded the 'letter of the 13', in April 1996, in which he, other oligarchs and others appealed for a compromise between the supporters of President Yeltsin and those of Zyuganov. What kind of compromise? Berezovsky said it should include 'sharing real executive power with the opposition'. This would involve the setting up of certain temporary structures during the present complicated transitional period. In other words, a state of emergency and no elections.

THE ELECTORAL CAMPAIGN

Yeltsin launched his campaign in his home town, Ekaterinburg, in February 1996. He tried to be his old self but he could no longer cope with large public meetings. However he could still play the populist. He stumped around the city and wanted to hear what was wrong. He would put it right. One director asked for billions of rubles to upgrade his factory. 'OK, you've got it', was the instant reply. He promised that all unpaid wages would be paid. (Back in Moscow he promised compensation to investors who had suffered losses as a result of bankruptcies and pyramid schemes.) Eventually his promises added up to about one fifth of the 1996 budget. There was no way the government could extend such largesse except by printing money and thereby stoking up inflation. This did not bother the President who after all was only concerned about being re-elected.

He was following a classic electoral strategy. Since he was perceived to be the father of radical economic reform which had failed, he had to move to the centre. He had to appear to be a moderate and to be occupying the middle ground. Zyuganov was not flexible enough to counter this. In elections it is not objective truth which is important. It all depends on what electors believe. Another key element in Yeltsin's electoral victory was the absence of an attractive alternative candidate to Yeltsin and Zyuganov – a centrist who could also attract left-wing votes. The Yeltsin camp made sure that no one emerged to play this role by ruthless organisational measures. Potential candidates were starved of media coverage and campaign contributors were threatened with a visit from the tax police.

In August 1996, after the election, the President, by presidential decree, quietly rescinded 50 decrees promising tax exemptions and government largesse. Not surprisingly, the number of presidential decrees reached a peak in 1996 when there were 458. In 1994, there had only been 202. Numbers declined after 1996 and, in 1999, there were only 144.

Promises were deemed insufficient to raise morale so a host of entertainers accompanied him wherever he went. He also added matchmaking to the entertainment. He visited a sweets factory and was struck by the beauty of the girls who turned out to be unmarried. He decided to arrange with a military college, full of bachelors, up the road, introductions so that in no time all the girls would be married! Many were not taken in and saw it for what it was, a show.

Gennady Zyuganov, the communist candidate, was not President so he could not promise instant gratification. Predictably privatisation had to be reversed and Chubais brought to account. Banks did not benefit society, they only enriched bankers. The press should not be permitted to conceal its sources and radical democrats should be investigated by the security services. This was music to the ears of the Chubais re-election team. Chubais could argue that the communists would prevent everyone from having more than one job. They would take away the newly won freedoms and the KGB would rule again. The communists could be relied upon to provide enough copy to hang themselves. However in order to win, Zyuganov needed support from some of the winners since 1991. Hence he had to choose his words carefully. He avoided terms such as socialism and communism – both discredited under Gorbachev – and chose traditional Russian concepts such as collectivism, community and people's power. The party had abandoned revolutionary violence to achieve power. Zyuganov spoke much of the Russian idea which appeared to mean simply that Russia was unique. Russia, Ukraine and Belarus should unite to promote a common Slav identity. Since he believed that a state cannot live without an ideology, he proposed the ideology of 'official government patriotism'. Western consumerism was regarded as a cancer which could kill Russia. Another target was western democracy which was a screen behind which the real masters of the west operated. These were the manipulators of the financial markets – the Jewish diaspora. An extension of this was Zyuganov's belief that there was a world conspiracy whose aim was to suborn Russia and all other countries. The ideologists of 'one-worldism are themselves convinced of the imminent arrival of a Messiah who will establish on earth the laws of the perfect religion and be the founder of a "golden age" for all humanity under the rule of a single worldwide supergovernment' (*Pravda Rossii*, 13 April 1995). In secular language, this appears to be the second coming of Christ. Jesus, after all, was a Jew. This nightmare haunts Zyuganov but he does not oblige other members of his party to share it. In the new communist party faith is optional.

Zyuganov could not afford to antagonise the economic barons so negotiations got under way in private. In public he criticised them so as to appeal to the little men and women but behind the scenes he courted them. It was up to the Chubais team to demonstrate that Gennady was a wolf masquerading as a moderate. Yeltsin was first class at presenting Zyuganov as the devil incarnate. One of the slogans deployed was 'Zyug Heil!' (a play on the Nazi slogan of Sieg Heil! or hail the victory!). Zyuganov's tone was measured but some of his fellow leaders were not so disciplined. They publicised their thirst for revenge. Then the IMF promised billions of dollars. The message was clear. Yeltsin as President meant more and more money for Russia.

In order to be registered for the elections a candidate needed to collect at least a million signatures. However it was possible to do this and not be registered. This happened to Artem Tarasov. Having collected a million signatures he informed Berezovsky that he was going to run. Oligarch Boris told him he was not. He collected over 1.3 million signatures and presented them to the electoral commission. The commission checked the signatures in two days and ruled that almost 500,000 signatures were not valid. So he was not registered. The reason for this was that Tarasov would have been campaigning on the same platform as Yeltsin. Berezovsky and Chubais wanted to ensure that no one competed with the President on this terrain. Had Tarasov been a communist they would have helped him to collect the signatures because he would have been taking votes away from Zyuganov. They were very pleased when Gorbachev declared himself a candidate. Lebed presented another type of problem. Korzhakov offered the general command of the airborne troops if he did not run. Chubais and Berezovsky did not agree. They saw Lebed as taking votes from Zyuganov, not Yeltsin. In late April there was an agreement to aid Lebed in the closing weeks of the campaign. Oligarch Boris provided the funds. Yeltsin denied that there was an agreement with Lebed but it was obvious that there was. Lebed was the only presidential candidate who did not criticise the President. He also suddenly appeared in well-cut suits and his wife in pretty dresses. His economic programme became coherent overnight.

The communists and their allies in the Duma presented Yeltsin with a gift on 15 March 1996. They passed a bill annulling the Belovezh Forest agreement which had dissolved the Soviet Union in December 1991. Constitutionally this did not affect the agreement. It needed a majority in the Council of the Federation and the President's signature to annul the treaty. However the circumstances had been created to declare a state of emergency. The President could claim that the communists and their allies were now planning a coup. Would the communists call on the armed forces to invade the Commonwealth of Independent States and the Baltic States so as to restore the Soviet Union?

THE PLANNED COUP

The Korzhakov election team saw this as a golden opportunity to postpone the presidential elections. The President instructed them to prepare the dissolution of the Duma, the postponement of the elections and the banning of the KPRF. Laws were drafted ready for Yeltsin's signature. Korzhakov had learnt from the mistakes Yeltsin's supporters had made in October 1993. On Sunday 17 March, a bomb scare ensured that deputies and staff left quickly. Troops then sealed off the parliament. Yeltsin told Anatoly Kulikov, the MVD chief, that he wanted another two years to sort things out. Kulikov told the President he needed time to think it over and would report back at 1700 hours. Kulikov saw the procurator general Yury Skuratov and the chair of the constitutional court,

Vladimir Tumanov, in order to discuss the legality of the President's behaviour. They discovered that Yeltsin had told each of them that the other had agreed to the planned coup. This was a lie, a big lie. At 1700 hours, Kulikov, Skuratov and Tumanov saw the President together. Yeltsin's response to Kulikov was abrupt: 'Minister, I'm dissatisfied with you. The decree is coming. Go and carry it out'. Then Kulikov found out that neither Chernomyrdin nor Petr Grachev, the defence minister, knew anything about what was afoot. At 0600 hours, on 18 March, Yeltsin met selected ministers and singled out Kulikov for some rough language. They then learned that the plan was to arrest the members of the KPRF central committee. The MVD had 16,000 men but needed another 12,000. The Duma would be dissolved since the President reiterated that he needed 'two more years'. However, at 0800 hours, the Duma reopened. He had given in to Kulikov and the others (Reddaway and Glinski 2001: 512–13). However Chubais, who had also argued against the démarche, could not be certain that the President would not go ahead with his unconstitutional act.He decided there was only one man on earth who could ensure that Boris did not blunder: President Bill Clinton. Egor Gaidar was chosen to talk to the US ambassador and present the delicate invitation. In the event Clinton did not need to phone but it was an extraordinary situation. Fortunately for the Chubais team neither the news about the planned coup nor the request for Bill Clinton to intervene became public knowledge at the time. The whole episode was very revealing. It demonstrated that if the President felt he was certain to lose the elections he would postpone them. He would not give up power.

CAMPAIGNING CHUBAIS STYLE

The Chubais team ruthlessly exploited their near monopoly of television, radio and the print media. They engaged in character assassination at every turn and every clairvoyant, soothsayer and astrologist in Russia, it appeared, was on the Kremlin payroll to predict that a Yeltsin victory was foretold in the stars. The governors and local media were also roped in. Opposition candidates found that the best venues in the provinces had already been booked and that their campaigns were largely ignored in the local press. Journalists were misinformed about the time Zyuganov would speak and the press carried sensational revelations about the communists' economic programme. They were all forgeries but there were so many of them that it was impossible for the communists to rebut them successfully. In case any electors failed to watch the political programmes anti-communist films were served up to underline the horrors that awaited everyone if Zyuganov won. It was a very dirty election campaign and this revealed that Yeltsin would have lost had a western-style campaign been permitted. It also demonstrated that morality had died in the minds of the Chubais team. Huge amounts of money were paid out in bribes to journalists, radio and TV companies. They were willing to do anything to protect the interests of the Tsar. In serving him they were serving themselves. They stood to lose too much if the President changed. They were true Bolsheviks – the end justifies the means – a sobering thought in the supposedly new, democratic Russia.

In order to cut some of the ground from under the communists, Yeltsin proposed a union of Russia and Belarus. This was an astute move as it gave the impression that Russia might merge with other states, voluntarily, of course. There was another bonus. If Yeltsin proved unelectable it could be used to postpone the election. A referendum could be called and after that a President of the new union elected.

Aleksandr Lebed began changing his critical attitude to the Chechen war. Now he asked why the bandit and terrorist Dudaev should be permitted to dictate to Russia. A year earlier he had refused to permit any of his troops to participate in the attack on Chechnya. To him Chechnya was a lost cause and should be abandoned. In May, the President's team agreed with Lebed that he would recommend that his supporters switch to Yeltsin in the second round. They could vote for Lebed in the first round. Only the top two out of the ten candidates would proceed to the run-off. As it was virtually certain that Lebed would not come top or second his supporters would be looking for guidance as to whom to support in the second round. What did Yeltsin offer Lebed? The precise details were only negotiated after the first round which would be a barometer of Lebed's popularity. Lebed was made secretary of the Security Council and adviser to the President on security affairs. Lebed overlooked the fact that advisers to the President were ten a penny or rather ten a kopek. Lebed wanted to be the President's deputy but Yeltsin had had bad experiences of deputies. Lebed thought he would be able to appoint his men to military and security positions. Yeltsin proved himself a wily negotiator and Lebed a very naïve one.

Some of the other candidates went to extraordinary lengths to attract public attention, Vladimir Bryntsalov, a flashy new Russian and a vodka and pharmaceutical tycoon, displayed some of his assets in television advertisements. His opulent office floor was covered by a Persian rug, costing $2500 a square metre. Nearby was a Rodin white marble sculpture of a man and a woman locked in a passionate embrace. It had been brought back by the Red Army from Germany to Moscow in 1945 as war booty. One of his most valuable assets was his wife. She revealed a Marilyn Monroe cleavage and an exquisitely sculptured bum to viewers. Presumably she was only courting the male vote.

In the last two weeks of the campaign it became clear that the Chubais team had successfully manipulated public opinion. Many would vote for Boris as the lesser of two evils. Evgeny Kiselev, NTV's star interviewer – the Jeremy Paxman of Russian television – made his contribution. Whereas he had been critical of the President from time to time, during the run-in he had only honeyed words to utter.

In January 1996, opinion polls gave Yeltsin 8 per cent of the vote but in the first round he scored 35.3 per cent. It was one of the most remarkable political comebacks of modern times. Zyuganov was just over 3 per cent behind (he was not running as a communist leader but as head of the bloc of national-patriotic forces of Russia) (Table 3.3). The major surprise was the surge in popularity of Lebed who sensationally achieved 14.5 per cent. It was clear that most of the nationalist vote had gone to the general at the expense of Vladimir Zhirinovsky. Yavlinsky, expected to take third place, was pushed down into fourth. The best of the also rans was Svyatoslav Fedorov, the eye surgeon, who almost got one per cent. Then came Mikhail Gorbachev, who proved he was yesterday's man, with 0.5 per cent. The turnout was higher than expected. Voting took place on the same day as the Russia–Germany match in the 1996 European football championships and the team harboured fears that the fans would not bother to vote. They did.

Aleksandr Lebed was appointed secretary of the Security Council on 18 June and moved immediately to remove his old adversary Grachev. The minister of defence put his troops on alert but it availed him nothing. The President had to part with him.

KORZHAKOV'S FINAL GAMBLE

The battle between the Korzhakov and Chubais teams now reached a climax. On 19 June, two associates of Chubais, Arkady Evstafev and Sergei Lisovsky, were detained by Korzhakov's security forces as they were leaving the White House, the seat of the Russian government. They were carrying a cardboard box containing $538,000. The reason for this was that the election slush fund was kept in a very secure place, a White House safe. The night before, Korzhakov's men had broken into the safe which was in the deputy finance minister's office. They found about $1.5 million in cash and payment receipts which revealed that campaign funds were being channelled to offshore accounts. The money was transferred by leading Russian banks but only a portion returned to Russia. The campaign team kept the difference (Klebnikov 2000: 240).

Chubais immediately realised that Korzhakov was planning to force the President to cancel the second round of the elections and declare a government of national unity. If that happened, Chubais, Berezovsky and the others would be out of business, perhaps even dead. They met in Berezovsky's Logovaz club in an alarmed state. Yeltsin was asleep so they asked Tatyana to intervene. She and Valentin Yumashev, later to head the presidential administration, arrived by car. She then phoned Korzhakov and ordered him to release the detainees. He refused. The only recourse left was to drive to her father's dacha, wake him and brief him. The President phoned Korzhakov and asked him what was going on. He got a soothing reply that everything was under control and that he could go back to sleep. Korzhakov was threatening the arrested associates and was trying to get damaging compromising material (*kompromat*) on Chubais and Chernomyrdin from them. So confident was Korzhakov that he went to bed.

In the early hours of 20 June the oligarchs went on a media offensive. Evgeny Kiselev gravely informed viewers that there was an emergency. Korzhakov had launched an attempted coup. Chubais needed someone to go on television and lambaste Korzhakov and Barsukov. There was no point in Chubais doing it, he was the most hated man in Russia. The oligarchs were also in the league of the damned. There was only one man who had the authority to do it: Aleksandr Lebed. Chubais phoned him and briefed him. He drove to his office and, to the waiting TV cameras, hit all the right buttons. He warned that any rebellion would be crushed and crushed ruthlessly. There would be no mercy for those who wanted to return the country to bloody strife. The TV blitz unnerved the guards and they released the associates without consulting Korzhakov.

When Yeltsin arrived at the Kremlin he summoned Korzhakov. He thought that the meeting had gone well. The media campaign had irritated the President but that had been initiated by Chubais and the others. Then Boris saw Chernomyrdin and Lebed. As ever the President announced a compromise. Korzhakov would pay for having provoked a media scandal but he would remain as head of the presidential guard. This did not suit Chubais. Before seeing Yeltsin, he reported that

Malashenko and he had called a press conference for later that day. Chubais needed his formidable presentational skills to convince the President to break with Korzhakov and his friends. The key argument was that it was in Boris's best interests. He would win the election with the Chubais team. The Korzhakov team would prevent the election and provoke bloodshed. Then the President revealed his ruthless streak. He sacked Korzhakov (his presidential security service was also disbanded), Barsukov and Soskovets without so much as a thank you. However there was another side to Yeltsin, he could change his mind immediately. In order to ensure that Korzhakov did not bounce back, Chubais was melodramatic at the press conference. He declared triumphantly that the President had hammered the final nail into the coffin containing the illusion of a military coup against the Russian state. The winners had been playing a game more serious than poker and blood had been at stake. He warned the losers that if they tried to use force they would be crushed with a wag of General Lebed's little finger. (This was a risky statement to make. After all Stalin had declared that he would crush Tito, the Yugoslav leader, expelled from the Cominform in June 1948, with a wag of his little finger. Tito outlived Stalin by 27 years and died in his bed still Yugoslav leader.) Chubais did not present any evidence to back up his story and the question of what the assistants were planning to do with more than half a million dollars was left unmentioned. It was a classic case of a palace coup or rather a Kremlin coup. Later it emerged that the Chubais case against Korzhakov was a lie from beginning to end. There was a downside to Korzhakov's dismissal. He had played an important role in keeping Yeltsin in power. When the President needed some dirty deed to be done he turned to Korzhakov. He was Sasha the enforcer as he had dirt on everyone. He was feared across Russia, with reason. His like would never be seen again during the Yeltsin era.

The whole episode demonstrated that clans could use armed men for their own ends. There were an estimated 15 to 24 armed forces in Russia ranging from the army to the presidential guard. There were between three and four million men under arms. These do not include the many private security guards employed by banks and other businesses. In other words no one knows exactly how many are under arms. Politicians fought among themselves to gain control over them. A modern state needs to exercise strict control over the instruments of power. In Russia it was clear that the instruments of power were being privatised. Would this distasteful episode cost Yeltsin the election? Had Zyuganov been a Machiavelli he might have cut a deal with the disgraced team on the principle that the end justifies the means. Also there were many on the left, including the intelligentsia, looking for a candidate to represent them. All the evidence revealed that Zyuganov was a very poor tactician. Yeltsin was lucky that Zyuganov had learnt little from his hero, the master tactician Lenin.

The conflict was too much for the President's health. He collapsed and disappeared from view. Various ingenious reasons for his stay at Barvikha were offered but many feared that Boris was finished. The President had pursued a punishing schedule before the first round, marching and dancing around Russia. His body was bound sooner or later to rebel against the constant intake of drugs. Fortunately, he was capable of voting in the second round. He appeared partially paralysed and his face was immobile and puffy. Amazingly, many voters in the regions were unaware that he was unwell. Vasily Shakhnovsky put it nicely: 'Had it been necessary, a mummy would have been elected.'

Yeltsin won easily in the second round (Table 3.4). In some regions, such as Dagestan, Zyuganov's vote dropped. It turned out that the President's team had warned the regions that if a majority did not support the President they would lose subsidies or have electricity or energy cut off. In some regions, such as Tatarstan, the results were rigged. Despite all this Zyuganov was happy to concede defeat. Clearly he did not relish the task of ruling Russia at a time of economic collapse. Most voters would have preferred an alternative but faced with the stark choice of a lame duck President or an untried communist who revealed no appetite for power, they chose stability. Younger voters favoured Yeltsin overwhelmingly. Among voters under 25 years, 80 per cent chose Yeltsin and only 20 per cent Zyuganov.

The presidential election was a small step on the road to democracy. Elections were becoming a part of democratic life and it would be more difficult in the future to postpone elections. However the real test would come when the incumbent President lost an election. Many communists assumed that had Yeltsin lost he would have refused to step down. They were right. The result reflected Russian political culture. Many people could not vote against the existing powers. Yeltsin, sharply anti-communist in his rhetoric, benefited from the communist tradition of confirming those in power. There was also the view that elections changed nothing. The ruling class continued in power.

With Yeltsin physically incapable of ruling, his supporters fought over the spoils of victory. Chernomyrdin was to continue as Prime Minister and the communists informed him they would support his nomination in the Duma. They were looking ahead to the day when Russia would need a new President. The heir apparent was now Viktor Chernomyrdin. Deals could be done with the verbally constipated Prime Minister. On decisive questions he never appeared capable of making up his mind. He might even be drafted on to the communists' team. Here again the communists were poor judges of character. Chernomyrdin, incoherent though he may often have been, was a quick learner and became a power broker in his own right.

The other victor was Anatoly Chubais. He was named head of the presidential administration, replacing Nikolai Egorov. He had made a quick comeback. In January 1996, the President had sacked the prince of privatisation and swore he would never return to power. This was just another example of electioneering. Perhaps the key to Chubais's success was his association with Tatyana Dyachenko who soon joined Anatoly's team. Chubais was a good choice for Yeltsin. Since he was so unpopular among the electorate he could never replace the President. Hence he was dependent on Yeltsin. Also he was the only top economist with political and administrative skills. In fact he was the only top manager the Yeltsin camp had. Tatyana was well on the way to founding a family dynasty. The family quickly became an expression in Russian politics. Its critics used the term in its Italian meaning, a mafia family.

The oligarchs were exultant as they had now crossed the bridge from economic to political influence. They agreed that Potanin should enter government, as deputy Prime Minister, on their behalf. He was given a golden hello by the government. He won tax breaks and other concessions worth over a billion dollars for his new company Norilsk Nickel (this helped the new management to achieve growth and to pay off wage arrears to workers by January 1998). Part of his task was to reform the system of private banks managing government accounts. He shortened the list but, of course, Oneksimbank was still on it. There was one dissenting voice, that of Gusinsky, to Potanin joining the government. He suspected that Potanin would not be even-handed but would feather his own nest. He was very prescient. They regarded Chubais as their man around the President but he did not see it that way. He told them that he was independent and would treat everyone equally. This did not sound very Russian. The tradition was that when a clan got near the Tsar it helped itself to anything it could lay its hands on. Inevitably another clan would displace it eventually so there was no time to lose. Chubais wanted to break with this tradition. The conflict between Potanin and Chubais, between the old and new tradition, was to have momentous consequences and cost Russia dear.

Lebed also saw himself as one of the victors. He was not modest about his ambition to be one of the top dogs. The Yeltsin team quickly set up the Defence Council to counterbalance the Security Council, now that Lebed was its secretary. General Igor Rodionov, who will always be remembered as the commanding officer of the Tbilisi massacre, was made minister of defence. Lebed's influence appeared to be growing.

He also offered a radical alternative to the IMF-dominated policy of Chubais and Chernomyrdin. On 29 June he published his economic blueprint which had been penned by Sergei Glazev. It advocated price controls in the public sector, government planning and financial support for science and technology and protection for Russian producers. Reliance on the IMF and global markets was undermining Russia's security, claimed the document. It bore some of the hallmarks of the east Asian economic model with state guidance of the transition to the market. An economic security directorate was set up in the Security Council, headed by Glazev. This was a direct challenge to Chubais and his commitments to the IMF.

4

TSAR BORIS THE BOOZER: THE SECOND PRESIDENCY, 1996–99

VIKTOR CHERNOMYRDIN WAS EASILY CONFIRMED AS Prime Minister by the Duma. He was on good terms with the communists and the alternative, from their point of view, Anatoly Chubais, did not bear thinking about. Chernomyrdin represented the major monopolies, oil, gas, electricity and transport. Chubais, head of the presidential administration, competed with the Prime Minister for influence over the economy. Chubais had allies in Vladimir Potanin, first deputy Prime Minister, and head of Oneksimbank, Aleksandr Livshits, deputy Prime Minister, and Evgeny Yasin, minister of economics. Chubais and his allies wanted the government to regulate the market but not manage it. If Chernomyrdin spoke for the energy and transport lobby, Chubais and his allies represented the finance lobby. The other major player was Aleksandr Lebed whose self-confidence was growing by the day. This three-way split suited the President as it ensured that no interest group dominated policy making.

The doctors worked a miracle and Yeltsin managed to get through his inauguration on 7 August 1996. However he walked stiffly, took the oath of office haltingly and gave the impression that he was only half-alive. It was clear that he was President but that he did not rule. According to the constitution the Prime Minister acts when the President is incapacitated or out of the country. However it soon transpired that the person who was acting President was Anatoly Chubais. He and Tatyana Dyachenko controlled access to the President and were his conduit of information. All documents which were passed to the President were vetted by Chubais. He could intervene in all matters of state and began to place his men in important posts. It was uncertain whether the President or the Chubais-Dyachenko team was taking the decisions.

LEBED FRAMED

Lebed did the impossible in the Caucasus and negotiated an end to the war in Chechnya. It meant de facto independence for the rebel republic. This did not please many in Moscow. One reason for sending him to the Caucasus was the hope that he would sink in the Chechen mire. He was much too big for his boots and surely he could not come out of the war with honour. When he triumphantly returned to the Russian capital Yeltsin would not see him. Politicians of all hues, from Chubais to Zyuganov, accused him of humiliating Russia. However, in early September, the President approved the agreement. The regime had no other choice. It insisted, as before, that Chechnya was a constituent part of the Russian Federation.

Lebed was now on a roll and the continued absence of Yeltsin from public view emboldened him. Lebed called on the President to hand over power to Chernomyrdin. The alternative was for Chubais to rule and that did not suit Lebed. He talked about military unrest and the country being ready to explode. All he needed now was Boris to expire. His popularity would have swept Chubais and Chernomyrdin aside and he would have become Russia's de Gaulle.

On 10 September, the Kremlin revealed that Yeltsin was suffering from heart disease and needed bypass surgery. Power was delegated to Chernomyrdin but the nuclear briefcase, with the codes, remained at the President's bedside. Hence responsibility for supervising the power ministries, which was the duty of the secretary of the Security Council, had now temporarily passed to the Prime Minister. The right to supervise the top appointments in the military was transferred to Yury Baturin. Lebed now did not enjoy any real power. In Brussels, NATO generals greeted Lebed as if he were already President.

Korzhakov struck up a tactical alliance with Lebed. He was to support Korzhakov in his bid to win Lebed's Duma seat in Tula. Korzhakov frightened the Kremlin by claiming he knew about intrigues, secret meetings and the like and knew how those in power had climbed up the slippery pole of success. The Kremlin hit back and accused Korzhakov of being involved in shady deals which had netted him millions. This rubbed off on to Lebed and cost him the support of much of the independent media. However the Kremlin was in a panic. It decided to frame Lebed. On 16 October, in a desperate move, General Anatoly Kulikov, the minister of the interior, a bitter personal rival, accused Lebed of preparing a creeping coup d'état (Shevtsova 1999: 201). Lebed intended to take power with the support of 1500 Chechen gunmen and a Russian legion. The latter was not in existence as it was only a suggestion to combat civil unrest. According to Kulikov, the reason why Lebed had requested the following week off was to prepare his coup. Lebed replied sarcastically that he was taking a holiday because he did not like warm beer. The accusations were patently absurd.

On the night of 16–17 October, inter-city communications were cut. The President dismissed Lebed the next day, rejecting a plea by Lebed for a personal meeting to set the record straight. One of the reasons for sacking him was that opinion polls demonstrated that he was the most trusted politician in Russia. As tension rose military units patrolled the streets of Moscow. There was no public protest and the military did not come out in Lebed's support. Lebed had no doubt about who had engineered his downfall: Anatoly Chubais. The latter saw Glazev's economic programme as a dangerous challenge to his and the oligarchs' continued domination of the Russian economy. Lebed bitterly commented that the Security Council was just like a Potemkin village, all show and no substance. He knew the establishment was against him and had only expected to stay in power two months but had survived for four. The writing was on the wall on the second day when he had asked for a telephone for his private office. He was informed he could not have one as it was too expensive. He simply lacked the political skills necessary for success in the Kremlin. He had gambled that Yeltsin would die quickly and present him with a golden opportunity to succeed him. He lost. Nevertheless, despite being expelled from the Kremlin elite, Lebed could still have become President had elections been held shortly afterwards. The longer Yeltsin clung to power the less likely it was that Lebed would achieve his goal.

Ivan Rybkin, speaker in the first Duma, replaced Lebed as secretary of the Security Council. The former communist was a peacemaker and had no direct links to the military. The man named deputy secretary caused a sensation. It was Boris Berezovsky, one of the seven business barons who had bankrolled Yeltsin's re-election. He was the second of the group to attain high office. The first was Vladimir Potanin who was first deputy Prime Minister. Oligarch Boris was to be in charge of the economic regeneration of Chechnya. Berezovsky once famously quipped that the most profitable business was politics. Here was lucrative evidence that this was so. Federal finances would be channelled through Berezovsky's companies. His detractors, who were legion and ranged from defeated business rivals to anti-Semites, saw him as Don Boris, the mafia boss. *Forbes* magazine went so far as to describe him as the Godfather of the Kremlin, in December 1996, and suggested that he was behind the high-profile murder of the managing director of ORT, Vladislav Listev.

YELTSIN REASSERTS HIMSELF

On 5 November, Yeltsin underwent a quintuple bypass operation. It was performed by a Russian Tatar surgeon as the President had declined to leave the country for surgery. He wanted to underline his faith in Russian medicine. There was also the point that had he left Russia for Germany or the US he might have returned a private citizen. While recuperating in the clinic a Chechen delegation, headed by Aslan Maskhadov, arrived in Moscow to see Viktor Chernomyrdin. They signed an agreement which saw the last Russian troops leaving Chechnya. This was not popular in Russia but the regime had concluded that it could not risk further conflict in Chechnya as long as the President was incapacitated in hospital.

Just before New Year Yeltsin dragged himself back to the Kremlin and spoke to the nation on the radio. He was not presentable enough to appear on television. He had a sorry tale to tell. The country was in a mess. Pensions and wages were months in arrears, taxes were not being collected and theft was widespread. Everything would improve in 1997 but few believed him. After all, would he still be alive at the end of 1997? In early January he was struck down by pneumonia. Even his allies began talking about interim arrangements until the President's term of office was up. Chubais fashioned various scenarios, all guaranteed to protect his own power. The constitution stated that the President was to stand down if ill health prevented him from carrying out his duties. It did not say, however, who was to decide that the President was incapable of carrying on. The presidential spokesman reported from time to time that the President was looking at papers. This fiction would hopefully head off a concerted bid to remove him. The fevered speculation about Yeltsin's health fuelled the belief that Boris was on his last legs. There was no shortage of contenders for his crown. Gennady Zyuganov and Aleksandr Lebed were the front runners but Yury Luzhkov, the mayor of Moscow, and Grigory Yavlinsky, were challenging strongly. Chubais and Chernomyrdin were nowhere.

Yeltsin amazed everyone by reappearing in the Kremlin and giving the impression that he had regained some of his old vigour. His opinion poll rating was down to 16 per cent with the economic situation a major reason for his unpopularity. The clans were fighting over his legacy and the national interest did not enter into their calculations. The financial elite was enriching itself by lending to the government at very high rates of interest. The less tax that was collected the more money the government needed. The more it borrowed the richer the bankers became. Yeltsin's usual tactic to demonstrate that he was in charge was to sack some ministers. One of those to go was Vladimir Potanin but presumably he had concluded that he could make more money dealing with government rather than being in government.

Anatoly Chubais came in as first deputy Prime Minister on 7 March 1997 (and as minister of finance on 11 March) and on 17 March Boris Nemtsov, from Nizhny Novgorod, became the second first deputy Prime Minister. These two intended to launch a new round of shock therapy (officially it was billed as the second liberal revolution). Gaidar tactically remained outside government, but acted as the key economic adviser (he boasted about his role several times in the press). Feelers were put out to co-opt the two best-known opposition economists, Sergei Glazev and Grigory Yavlinsky, but they refused to take the bait.

Nemtsov, partly Jewish, handsome, young and the darling of the press because of his willingness to provide good copy, took over responsibility for reforming the public utilities (he was expected to increase rents, for instance, but not in Moscow because the wheeler-dealer mayor, Yury Luzhkov, had obtained exemption from Yeltsin personally), including breaking up the natural monopolies, especially in the energy sector. He was also to deal with wage arrears and to fight corruption. He was reluctant to leave Nizhny Novgorod and it took a seven-hour car journey to Nizhny by Tatyana to convince him to take the job. However his portfolio was designed to make him almost everyone's enemy. His chances of success were limited as he had no personal staff. Just like Lebed before him he would have to navigate the shark-infested waters of the Kremlin without a map.

Nemtsov was not starry eyed about the task confronting him. He told a journalist that there were two models of the market economy in Russia. There was the 'government-monopolistic, mafia-corrupt model'. The other was 'democratic capitalism'. The former was 'being realised on a grand scale in Russia'. The President agreed with this analysis and was determined to steer the country from 'bandit capitalism' to 'people's capitalism'. Why did Nemtsov take on the task? He believed in a strong Tsar and thought that top-down administrative reform could sort out the natural monopolies and corruption.

There were other good omens. Some of the roving bandits had concluded that they would be more successful in a regulated market and a stable state. If the cost of operating partly illegally (paying bribes to government officials, etc.) exceeded the taxes and benefits saved then it was rational to go over to operating fully legally. Nemtsov was their man. He said that the interest groups were getting tired of lobbying the government. They wanted an even playing field in which the rules, clear and simply expressed, were the same for everyone. The problem for Nemtsov was that a larger group of roving bandits had lost their fear of a communist restoration and therefore did not see why they should not continue exploiting the state. Evidence of this surfaced, in July 1997, when one clan declared war on another. Various newspapers quoted from a leaked letter from the Central Bank to Chernomyrdin. It implicated an Oneksimbank affiliate in the embezzlement of $237 million due to the government from the sale of MiG-29 fighters to India. Another bank, also closely linked to Oneksimbank, had stolen $275 million en route to the Moscow oblast administration. Oneksimbank counterattacked and muttered about shady deals involving banks close to Chernomyrdin. The case was dropped. Nevertheless Nemtsov and Chubais were able to chalk up some successes in the summer of 1997. More tax was collected, government procurement policies were revised and a beginning was made to reform Gazprom.

Nemtsov also made some money out of being first deputy Prime Minister. An autobiography, *A Provincial,* was rushed out. He received an advance of $90,000 from Sergei Lisovsky, close to Chubais and Berezovsky. Only 25,000 copies were printed and sold for under a dollar a copy. Government ministers had now to declare their annual earnings and net worth. Chernomyrdin put his 1996 earnings at $8000 and his assets at $46,000. *Le Monde* did some quick calculations and came up with assets of $5 billion. *Izvestiya* was unwise enough to reprint this and the Prime Minister was so furious he launched a war for control of the newspaper. The eventual winner was Oneksimbank.

Valentin Yumashev, a journalist, replaced Chubais as head of the presidential administration. He had originally been brought into the Kremlin by Korzhakov to write Yeltsin's memoirs. After Korzhakov was sacked, Anatoly became Yumashev's patron. Evgeny Yasin, the former minister of economics, stayed in the government as minister without portfolio and responsible for long-term strategic planning. The new minister of economics, Yury Urison, was also a liberal economist. Among those who were shown the Kremlin door, on 23 May, was General Igor Rodionov, defence minister and Lebed's buddy. The new minister was General Igor Sergeev, commander of the strategic rocket forces. The balance of power in the government had moved in favour of Chubais and away from Chernomyrdin.

Nemtsov made himself immediately popular with the public by obliging federal officials to give up their Mercedes and BMWs and travel in Russian Volgas. These cars are made in Nizhny Novgorod! However most officials ridiculed this order and carried on as before. The Volgas tended to break down and Nemtsov was once stranded in a Moscow street after his Volga overheated and broke down. The same applied to Boris Yeltsin's ZIL. There was an unintended consequence of this move. Some officials were able to acquire the foreign motors at knock-down prices. Nemtsov had no client network so was doomed to fail unless he was skilful enough to build one up rapidly. He did not. He was nicknamed Kindersurpriz (a child's surprise), the name of a popular egg-shape chocolate, but also slang for an illegitimate child. He admitted later that he made egregious mistakes and achieved very little. However he does have a sense of humour. He was wont to tell his favourite joke: Ivan is going on a business trip to Paris; his wife asks him to buy her a sexy French bra. 'Buy you one, my dear, but you have no breasts! What is the point?' 'Well', she replies, 'I buy your briefs.'

A government dominated by Chubais was not popular with the Duma. It also needed to collect much more tax and to cut back on government borrowing. The drive to collect more tax was targeted at small and medium businesses as the large ones were wily at protecting themselves. The bankers favoured a large budget deficit and the sale of government assets to boost revenue. Chubais spoke of the need for the state to assert itself and to play a more active regulatory role in the economy. Yabloko, a liberal party, was scathing. It repeatedly called on Chernomyrdin to resign as he was seen to be in cahoots with the energy lobby. The weakness of the Chubais group was that it had no roots in society. Businesses did not want to pay taxes. Its financial backers did not favour tight monetary and fiscal discipline. The bankers also favoured inflation and a weak currency (they borrowed rubles from the Central Bank, changed them into dollars and paid their debts in depreciating rubles). What was good for the bankers was not good for Russia. The ruling class did not favour a competitive market economy. In the regions the elites wanted to act in their own economic and political interests. This

involved the centre permitting them to keep a high proportion of collected taxes (federal taxes were collected by federal agents). A reform-
minded government in Moscow thus discovered that it was as difficult
to implement reforms (which by definition went against the wishes of
powerful interest groups) as under Khrushchev or Gorbachev.

The new reform-minded government conformed to a clear trend. In late
1991 the radical, market-oriented government, dominated by Egor Gaidar,
promised to restructure the Russian economy and ensure growth. It failed
and Viktor Chernomyrdin was brought in as Prime Minister. He was loyal
to the President but only used traditional methods to promote economic
growth. When Yeltsin decided to confront the Supreme Soviet in September 1993 he brought back Gaidar to try again to stimulate growth.
He was dropped in January 1994. Chernomyrdin could not kickstart
the economy so in came Chubais in November 1994 in a desperate
attempt to halt the remorseless decline of the economy. After the bad
Duma election results of December 1995 Chubais had to go as it was
clear that his continued presence in the government would harm
Yeltsin's chances of re-election. Chernomyrdin could not turn the
economy round after the President's re-election, even with the assistance
of Vladimir Potanin and his team, so back came Chubais and his team
in March 1997. The significance of the March revolution was that
Yeltsin lost Korzhakov and his men with whom he had felt most at
home. These men had provided a link with the past. In government he
preferred conservative loyalists such as Chernomyrdin. However lack of
economic success forced him to turn to economic radicals such as
Gaidar and Chubais. When they failed he then reverted to those with
experience of the Soviet economy, the only alternative he had.

THE BANKING WAR

It was inevitable that the Davos group of seven leading bankers would
come to blows sooner or later (Freeland 2000: chapter 12). What had
obliged them to pool their differences, the fear that Yeltsin would not
be reelected, no longer obtained. Now they could challenge one
another to be top dog. Political influence was of key importance in
this struggle. Vladimir Potanin, the former first deputy Prime Minister,
had strengthened his position. His bank, Oneksimbank, had secured
the account of the state customs committee and had gained control of
the newspapers *Izvestiya* and *Komsomolskaya Pravda*. It also controlled
Russian television (RTR). Here was evidence that Potanin was close to
Chubais.

Boris Berezovsky, and Vladimir Gusinsky, of Media-Most, believed that it was their turn to acquire more state assets at bargain basement prices. The assets in question (25 per cent of the equity) were Svyazinvest, the state telephone and telecommunications monopoly, a potentially enormously profitable undertaking which would confer control over the media. Instead Chubais conducted a real auction, at least on the surface, and Potanin's group paid $1.75 billion dollars for Svyazinvest, in July 1997. In reality, Chubais had decided that Potanin would get Svyazinvest and Valentin Yumashev, the head of the presidential administration, had acquired Yeltsin's consent.

Potanin was being greedy. Gusinsky was convinced that there was an unwritten agreement that he would obtain Svyazinvest since he had lost out in the original loans for shares bonanza and his media group had played an important role in ensuring that Yeltsin was re-elected. A key factor in Potanin's success in raising this money was his alliance with George Soros, the Hungarian American financier, who put up about $1 billion of the money. The other oligarchs were united against Potanin. Gusinsky and Fridman proposed that the auction be annulled on a technicality and that they be permitted to acquire the Svyazinvest shares for $1.88 billion. Chubais would not budge. This was a fateful decision as it set in train a banking war and the oligarchs also turned on the young reformers. It proved destructive for both parties.

Before and after the auction Potanin and Berezovsky–Gusinsky traded insults through their media outlets. One could predict that *Izvestiya* and *Komsomolskaya Pravda* would laud the deal and attack Berezovsky and Gusinsky and that *Nezavisimaya Gazeta* would attack it and blacken the reputations of Potanin, Soros, Chubais and Nemtsov. One of the prizes which Gusinsky had bagged after the defeat of Korzhakov had been permission for NTV to broadcast twenty-four hours a day. Berezovsky had ORT. The Russian media had ceased to be independent and was being used as a mouthpiece for different business groups.

Potanin scored another success in August. He obtained, by auction, 38 per cent of the shares of Norilsk Nickel. He had already acquired these from the state in the loans for shares scheme but they had only been held in trust. He was now buying them outright. Understandably, Berezovsky was furious. He accused Potanin of 'economic totalitarianism' and of attempting to 'monopolise not only economic but political power' (Reddaway and Glinski 2001: 561).

On 15 September, Yeltsin acted and called a meeting with six of the seven members of the Davos group (the only one missing was Berezovsky because he was a member of the government). The President tried to get the financial oligarchs to settle their differences. Chubais and Nemtsov wanted him to fire Berezovsky as deputy secretary of the Security Council but he refused. He was not going to take sides in the banking war but chose to act as referee. He demonstrated that he still retained some of his old infighting skills.

YELTSIN AND THE OCTOBER COMPROMISE

The President's physical frailty fuelled the ambitions of his adversaries. They were already looking ahead to the presidential elections, in June 2000. The Russian constitution stated that an incumbent President could only be re-elected once. However Yeltsin had been elected in June 1991 under the Soviet Russian constitution. Did this permit him to run again in June 2000? There was just no agreement. The President tried to scotch rumours and stated he would not run again in 2000. It was time for him to step down and be replaced by a 'young, dynamic democrat'. But was this his final word? Would he change his mind on the morrow?

Anyway, hardly anyone believed that Boris would be alive and kicking in June 2000. The President adopted his usual tactic. If weak, attack. He accused the Duma of failing to do its job and hinted at dissolution. The upper house, the Council of the Federation, was more responsible (he could not dissolve it). The Chubais team wanted a leaner and meaner budget for 1998, new tax legislation and less state spending on welfare. The communists, predictably, feigned to be horrified and Yabloko, as usual, lambasted the government. The communists wanted more welfare not less. Yabloko wanted more rapid progress towards a liberal market economy. On 9 October, the Duma rejected the draft budget which had to go through four readings. It began preparing a motion of no confidence in the government. Yabloko would not cooperate with the communists in the no confidence vote. Grigory Yavlinsky could not give voters the impression that he was the lackey of the communists. It was also clear that the communists were split. The moderates were afraid that if the Duma provoked Yeltsin into dismissing Chernomyrdin, the next Prime Minister could be Chubais or Nemtsov. If new Duma elections were called Aleksandr Lebed would do well as would Yury Luzhkov, a rising star and mayor of Moscow. Who would gain and who would lose if the incumbents played their political cards incorrectly?

On 15 October, the Council of the Federation called on the President, the government and the two houses of parliament to search for a solution. The President appealed to Duma members not to place him in a difficult position. He would have to act if the Duma passed two votes of no confidence in the government within three months. On 21 October, the President met the main Duma factions and reached a compromise. The tax legislation would be withdrawn. Other concessions he made to the communists included regular meetings of the Council of Four (the President, Prime Minister and speakers of both houses of parliament), round table meetings of the leaders of the Duma factions and the President or Prime Minister, and on occasion members of the Council of the Federation and representatives of social organisations, such as the trade unions, the housing crisis was to be addressed and a commission of government and parliament was to be established to consider changes to the law on government. The Duma was to be given two hours per week on Russian Television (RTR) and two hours on state-controlled radio. The 1998 budget would provide funding for a parliamentary newspaper. On 22 October, Zyuganov announced that the communists were withdrawing their no confidence motion and were satisfied with the compromise. However if the Council of Four and round table talks proved mere talking shops the communists reserved the right to place the motion of no confidence back on the agenda. The Council of Four convened sporadically in late 1997 and during spring 1998 and debated several contentious issues, such as a land code, on which it almost reached agreement, candidates for government positions, and constitutional reform.

The compromise underlined emerging trends in Russian politics. The communists, despite their hard rhetoric in public, were willing to defuse the situation. The moderate wing of the party, under Zyuganov, did not want to force premature parliamentary elections or change the government. Instead of strengthening the institution of parliament the communists chose to discuss policy in extra-parliamentary bodies. This accelerated the trend towards backstage decision making and made politics less transparent. The communists were willing to play along with Yeltsin who did not want parliament to acquire a stronger role in policy making. Overall it appeared that the communists had decided they did not want to come to power. They were aware of how difficult it was to rule Russia and did not want the task.

The compromise also signalled that the President's attitude to the communists had changed. He was willing to make concessions to them and perhaps even to have leading communists in the government (there had been several Agrarian Party and KPRF members in government). This disappointed the democrats and liberal economists and indicated that

Yeltsin was moving away from them. Radical economic legislation could now not pass through the Duma as the communists, in effect, would have a veto. The executive and the legislature would cease to confront one another and try to reach agreement. The Yeltsin camp wanted a run off with Zyuganov in 2000.

BEREZOVSKY GOES

On 5 November, the President shocked the political establishment by dismissing Boris Berezovsky as deputy secretary of the Security Council. The oligarch was blamed for the murder, on 18 August, of Mikhail Manevich, deputy governor of St Petersburg, head of its state property committee, a prominent member of the city's Jewish community and an important member of the Chubais clan. Berezovsky had very good relations with Chernomyrdin and was close to the Yeltsin family, especially Tatyana Dyachenko. He had previously tried to get rid of Chubais and Nemtsov. Now the roles were reversed. 'Russia is moving away from oligarchical capitalism', trumpeted Anatoly. How had they done it? On 4 November, Chubais and Nemtsov had turned up at Yeltsin's dacha and convinced him that Oligarch Boris had to go. They chose a day on which Chernomyrdin was away and Tatyana otherwise engaged. They also slipped around Valentin Yumashev, head of the presidential administration and the President's doorkeeper. It was a classic thrust by Chubais. He had previously deployed it with success against Korzhakov. Unilaterally he was breaking the fragile peace which had obtained since the Svyazinvest fracas. But two could play at that game.

THE BOOK SCANDAL

On 18 August 1997, an article in Gusinsky's *Novaya Gazeta* claimed that Alfred Kokh, deputy Prime Minister and head of the state privatisation committee (GKI) until 13 August, had accepted an advance of $100,000 from a Swiss accountancy firm to write a book about privatisation. The real target was Vladimir Potanin as the Swiss company had close links to Oneksimbank. The oligarchs were regarded by the public as corrupt but not the young reformers. Chubais and they had made much of the fact that their job was to clean up Russia. Suddenly one of them had been caught accepting money. It was presumed that the money had come from Potanin and was for services rendered during the privatisation process.

Chubais was fiercely protective of his clan and berated those who attacked Kokh, claiming that Russia should be grateful for the services rendered by Kokh. He made no mention of the $100,000. On 12 November, Gusinsky struck back. One of his radio stations reported a scoop: five young reformers, all members of the Chubais clan, had received advance royalties for a book on economic reform. Each of the 'authors', Chubais, Maksim Boiko, deputy Prime Minister and chair of the state property committee (GKI), Petr Mostovoi, chair of the federal bankruptcy committee, Alfred Kokh, former GKI chair and Aleksandr Kazakov, deputy head of the presidential administration, had received $90,000. The book's publisher, *Segodnya Press*, was mainly owned by Oneksimbank. Even more damning was the news that this had been paid before the Svyazinvest auction. Here was evidence that Potanin had bribed Chubais to ensure that he won the auction.

The President was furious. He demanded a written explanation of the $450,000 advance. He sacked Kazakov on the spot. Chubais, fighting for his political life, conceded that the advance had been too high. The next day, Boiko and Mostovoi were dumped. The Kremlin revealed that Chubais had been told that his behaviour was intolerable. He offered to resign but a shorn Chubais was of use to Yeltsin as Russia's door to the west. Washington had seen Chubais and his men as the 'dream team'. Now most of them had gone and its leader, Chubais, was soon removed as minister of finance. Worse still, it went to Mikhail Zadornov, of Yabloko, and a persistent critic of Chubais. Chubais remained as deputy Prime Minister but it was mainly ceremonial as he had no ministry under his control. Nemtsov was fired as minister of fuel and energy – but he stayed as deputy Prime Minister – and was replaced by Sergei Kirienko.

It was all Anatoly's fault. His arrogance had led him to assume that he could walk on water. He thought he did not need the support of the President's family. What is astonishing is that Chubais and his men signed a contract as a front for receiving a bribe. Why not ask for the money in a brown envelope and pay it into a Swiss bank account? Or even better – why not ask for the money to be transferred to their Swiss bank accounts? The Swiss never tell. Perhaps Potanin wanted evidence of the deal so as to ensure Chubais kept his side of the bargain. The 'authors' received $450,000 to secure an asset valued at $1.75 billion. This is so cheap that one presumes that other bribes, as yet undetected, were also paid. It is ironical that a mere $90,000 brought down Chubais. This was small change to a man who was used to making millions. It underlines the truth that the richer one becomes the less important money becomes. One ceases to take elementary precautions. The scandal also ended the myth of the incorruptible young reformers in the west. Anatoly was no longer Mr Clean.

Another who began to feel the winds of change was Boris Nemtsov. As the blue-eyed boy of Russian politics, he had been close to Chubais. Potanin had cultivated him and he had spent weekends at Luzhki, Oneksimbank's hedonistic watering hole just outside Moscow. Girls were part of the service and they were paid to take off their clothes. A video camera showed Nemtsov and Oneksimbank bankers lounging at a swimming pool watching young things disrobe. It appeared on television, of course, and titillated the public. It revealed that oligarchs could obtain compromising footage on each other without much trouble. They had no scruples against using it to advance their position. Relations between the two Borises began to cool. Nemtsov was no longer seen as a possible future President.

Chubais's fall was predictable since Yeltsin was physically weak and incapable of running the country on a daily basis. The President had to ensure that none of his appointees became so strong as to pose a challenge to his own power. When they appeared to be out in front they had to be brought down. First it was Gaidar, then Burbulis and then Chubais. On the security side this also applied to Korzhakov and Barsukov. Chernomyrdin was also a potential threat but he lacked the decisiveness and appetite for risk taking that characterised Chubais. The Prime Minister, however, was used to blocking the Chubais clan's attempt to take over the whole economy. The President had to ensure a balance between the two. Yeltsin gained but Russia lost.

Why did the Chubais clan lose? After all Chernomyrdin had amassed quite a fortune and had accounts in various western banks. Other ministers mixed public and private business. Yeltsin was notorious for turning a blind eye to an official's minor or major peccadilloes if he remained loyal to the President. The book scandal was a factor but not the main cause. The Chubais clan were young, very self-confident, convinced they had all the solutions to Russia's economic ills – solutions could always be mathematically expressed and were insensitive to the interests of others. They lacked political skills. The basic rule of politics is not to offend everyone at the same time. Pick your opponents off one at a time.

Chubais's boys were a new breed. They were technocrats and had not emerged from the old nomenklatura. Hence they had no base there. They wanted to increase taxation so as to strengthen the role of government but this was not in the interests of the new economic clans. The government needed to cut social expenditure. Rents for housing were much too low as were gas, electricity and water prices. Fiscal tightening suggested that all these prices be raised. This was very unpopular with the population who knew that price rises would further depress their living standards. Arguably domestic oil and gas prices were too low but it would be politically inadvisable to increase them at the same time as other prices.

The Chubais team would have liked to break up the oil and gas monopolies but Chernomyrdin stood in the way. They continued to underpay tax. The Svyazinvest deal split the bankers and ensured that the Chubais clan would receive a hammering in their media. Clan interests were so ensconced by the mid-1990s that Chubais could make little headway. It had become accepted that bureaucrats could enrich themselves at the state's expense. The distinction between public and private interests had been blurred. Chubais's privatisation of property had also led to the privatisation of the state, an unintended consequence. An official's position was an opportunity to make money.

Chubais's war with Berezovsky led to his falling out with Tatyana Dyachenko and Valentin Yumashev, the head of the presidential administration. As they were the President's doorkeepers this was a suicidal move. He might have weathered the storm had his promises to solve Russia's economic crisis had any substance but the continuing non-payment of wages, the downward spiral of production and social discontent weakened his position. The only thing he was good at was getting money from the west – but only a minority fed at that trough. Another who was delighted to see the back of Anatoly was Yury Luzhkov. War was the natural state of things between the Chubais and Luzhkov clans. The truce to ensure the re-election of Yeltsin had been the exception.

YELTSIN REVITALISED

In the autumn of 1997 Yeltsin got his energy back. He travelled a lot. He visited western Europe, China, met the Japanese Prime Minister in Krasnoyarsk, Siberia, and promised to sign a peace treaty with Japan by 2000 which would lay to rest the conflict over ownership of the Kurile islands. In December, he appeared in the Duma and asked the deputies to pass the 1998 budget. They did, to everyone's astonishment. Even the communists voted in favour. Yabloko as usual voted against. Later the same month, in Sweden, the strain began to tell. He confused Sweden and Finland and thought Germany and Japan were nuclear powers. One of his strengths was impromptu remarks. They now caused embarrassment. He began to compare himself with Peter the Great and even said he was Tsar Boris I. He should have said Boris II since Boris Godunov had been Russian Tsar from 1598–1605. He was confused and confused others. When he returned to Moscow he took to his bed.

CHERNOMYRDIN GOES

On 23 March 1998, the President dismissed Chernomyrdin, Chubais and deputy Prime Minister Anatoly Kulikov (Shevtsova 2000: 238–40; Freeland 2000: 288). The decision to dismiss the top ministers had been taken in the utmost secrecy and astonished observers as well as the public. Chernomyrdin was being released to prepare the presidential elections in 2000. This did not please the former Prime Minister who retorted that if he were to prepare an election campaign it would be his own. Yeltsin had decided that Chernomyrdin was too given to compromise and would lose the presidential election (Yeltsin 2000: 108). 'All these years he had stood behind me as an exceptionally decent, conscientious and devoted person. Still he had to go.'

Who was going to succeed him? Boris himself was to assume the post temporarily. However this was unconstitutional. Presumably no other candidate had been approached for fear that the sacking of Chernomyrdin could leak out and permit him to prepare his defences. This revealed how strong the President perceived Chernomyrdin to be. Even more revealing, Boris announced that economic policy would remain the same. Previously the President had balanced Chernomyrdin and Chubais. Of late, however, they had struck up an understanding. So both had to go. Since Tatyana and Yumashev had fallen out with Chubais they were unlikely to trust him as Prime Minister. After all, the Prime Minister acted as President when Boris was indisposed.

What had precipitated the sacking? The government was not solving the economic and social problems of the country but this had not brought it down. A plan had been mooted to seize company assets in case of non-payment of taxes but Chernomyrdin pulled out at the last moment. This was damning evidence that he was not willing to confront the roving bandits. However there may also have been a foreign policy dimension. Chernomyrdin had developed a close relationship with US Vice-President Al Gore. Their March 1998 meeting in the United States was dubbed the meeting of the future Presidents. This was like a red rag to a bull for Boris. Then Chernomyrdin went off to Odessa to talk to the Presidents of Ukraine and Moldova without informing Boris. Many in Moscow at the time assumed Boris was being very subtle and was displaying his talents as a master politician. It turned out that he was merely protecting his own back. The first task was to decapitate the government. Then think of the next move.

ENTER KIRIENKO

The next move was to announce that Sergei Kirienko was to be proposed as Prime Minister (Shevtsova 1999: 240–52; Freeland 2000: 289–309). This astonished everyone and the usual refrain was: 'Kiri-who?' The dapper, diffident, bespectacled 35-year-old was understandably bemused when he was presented to the nation. He had come up through the Komsomol, had been in banking and had headed an oil company in Nizhny Novgorod. Boris Nemtsov had brought him to Moscow when he had become deputy Prime Minister. Kirienko was partly Jewish and spoke clearly and crisply, a great improvement on Chernomyrdin. From Yeltsin's point of view he was an excellent choice. He was an outsider and therefore had no political or economic base in Moscow. He therefore lacked the vitally important client network. This made him dependent on the President and his circle. The downside was his inexperience. He had been minister of fuel and energy but had only occupied the post for four months before getting the call. The Duma listened to him and refused to endorse him as Prime Minister twice. The communists saw him as weak and wanted posts in his government. Yabloko did not think he was up to the job and was merely Boris's lapdog. It was time for the President to issue a few threats. If the Duma rejected Kirienko a third time it would be dissolved. There was also a carrot. Accommodation and other problems of a deputy's life would be addressed but only after the vote. The message was clear. Vote for Sergei and live better. It was an outrageous bribe but it worked. Only 25 deputies voted against Kirienko on the third vote. He was duly appointed on 24 April 1998. Clearly the deputies had no desire to give up their ever improving lifestyle in Moscow.

The President had no intention of giving the new Prime Minister and his technocrats a free hand. He made Boris Berezovsky acting secretary of the Commonwealth of Independent States (CIS). This enhanced oligarch Boris's business prospects. On 5 May, Chubais was elected chair of the Unified Energy Systems of Russia, responsible for the generation and distribution of electricity throughout the land. This meant all the oligarchs would have to deal with him and the war between him and Berezovsky would continue. This was all part of the President's plan to ensure that no single interest group became too dominant.

Kirienko chose Boris Nemtsov, Oleg Sysuev and Viktor Khristenko as his deputy Prime Ministers. They were all from the provinces and hence outsiders and had little experience of the Moscow political and economic machine. Kirienko's writ was to manage the economy. Evgeny Primakov remained as minister of foreign affairs, Igor Sergeev as minister of defence and Sergei Stepashin as minister of internal affairs. They were, as before, directly subordinate to the President.

Kirienko and his technocrats faced a Herculean task. In the Duma things became more difficult. Chernomyrdin was head of the Our Home is Russia (NDR) faction which had always been loyal to the President. Now it was alienated from Yeltsin. Chubais would hardly work to strengthen Kirienko's authority. The promotion of Berezovsky revealed that the President's family were dependent on him as he was its financial manager. Kirienko and Nemtsov were associated with Vladimir Potanin and the latter was no friend of oligarch Boris. Chernomyrdin would represent the energy lobby and make change difficult. Also officials in the ministry of fuel and energy had direct links to Gazprom and various oil companies. Russia's ruling class was fragmented and there was little likelihood that they would agree on a successor to Yeltsin. This was to the President's benefit. At a time when democratic institutions needed to be strengthened, power was being used to divide and rule. The President paid a price for this situation. He had turned his back on DemRossiya and had no political base. He had little support in the bureaucracy. His strength was that the constitution allowed him to dismiss governments at his whim and to cow parliament when he so desired. If there had been social unrest the military could not have been relied upon. Russia was stable but was the President risking instability to maintain his power?

Kirienko was an economic cold shower after the warm optimism of Chernomyrdin and Chubais. He starkly presented the seriousness of the crisis. Mindful of the upcoming presidential elections Yeltsin was pressing for more social expenditure. Clearly Russia was approaching breaking point. The Moscow stock market was in a panic. Inevitably the ruble came under growing pressure and the Central Bank increased interest rates from 30 per cent to 150 per cent (Freeland 2000: 291). This was very bad news for a government which borrowed heavily to cover its budget deficit. The alternative, devaluing the ruble, was regarded as a worse option. There was a way out. Obtain huge credits from the International Monetary Fund (IMF) and other western financial institutions. Anatoly Chubais was dispatched to Washington to paint a picture of the horrendous consequences of not bailing out Russia. A big bad dictator would come to power and threaten the United States with nuclear weapons.

In late May, the IMF, nudged by the White House, agreed to a $10 billion loan over three years. Russia was caught in the maelstrom of the global financial crisis. Brazil and South Korea were major holders of Russian short-term bonds and were selling. The Central Bank supported the ruble and ran down its hard currency reserves, now $12 billion or about half of the year before. It was fast running out of rubles to redeem its short-term state bonds (GKOs and OFZs). The decision to replace the experienced Chernomyrdin with the inexperienced Kirienko was looking foolhardy. The problem was that the President and his men had no idea how to stem the tide. They just repeated the old mantras about increasing tax collection and cutting government expenditure.

When the water temperature is right sharks appear. The sharks in question were the politicians and economic barons sensing blood, the President was fast reaching a position where no one would defend him. Boris Berezovsky and Vladimir Gusinsky, members of the famous seven who had funded his re-election in 1996, now demanded that he declare he would not run again. A State Council, consisting of leading politicians, should run the country until the next elections. Sergei Shakhrai, a long-term ally, declared his support for Yury Luzhkov, mayor of Moscow, as the next President. Some of the economic barons suggested a consultative council to help the government but most people assumed this was to help themselves. Even the Our Home is Russia faction in the Duma talked of the constitution being amended to strengthen parliament and weaken the President. Miners from Siberia camped in front of the White House and banged their helmets on the ground to underline their frustration at not being paid. There were rumours that the military might stage a coup. However, as one wit remarked, the military were as likely to launch a successful coup as Boris was to climb Everest.

Chubais came up with the goods (Freeland 2000: 297). On 13 July, knowing that the IMF, the World Bank and Japan would provide credits amounting to $22 billion, the President went to the Duma and ate humble pie. He promised there would be no coup, no dissolution of the Duma, no amendment of the constitution. All he was asking was for the deputies to approve the government's stabilisation programme. It had been drafted by the IMF and others. Why had the IMF suddenly agreed to lend Russia over double what it had previously requested? The man behind the volte face was President Bill Clinton. He wanted to bail out his friend Boris. The Bill and Boris show still had some mileage in it. The $22 billion was to cover short-term government debt, especially GKOs and OFZs, held by western banks, estimated at $16 billion. So the IMF and the others were providing billions which would be transferred to Moscow and then be returned to western banks.

The Duma passed some tax legislation but rejected increasing personal taxation. The President overruled it by issuing his own decrees. This contravened the constitution which states that tax legislation has to be approved by the Duma and the Council of the Federation. The IMF tut-tutted and cut the first tranche from $5.6 billion to $4.8 billion. Lukoil and other large companies were not impressed; they would have preferred a ruble devaluation. The rationale behind this was that the stabilisation package obliged them to pay more tax. They earned most of their money from exports and hence the weakened ruble would not hurt them unduly.

RUSSIA DEVALUES AND DEFAULTS

Sergei Kirienko, Sergei Dubinin, chair of the Central Bank, Mikhail Zadornov, minister of finance, Anatoly Chubais and Egor Gaidar reached a momentous decision. The foreigners would pay to rescue Russia. On 17 August, the government announced that the ruble was to float between 6 and 9 rubles 50 kopeks, the servicing of international debt would be suspended for 90 days, trading in government bonds was suspended and non-residents' currency transactions were restricted. In simple language this meant that Russia was bankrupt but the fiction had to be maintained that it was still viable. It was too large a country to collapse. The timing of the démarche was crucial. It could only be implemented after the $4.8 billion loan had been received. Insiders cashed in their government bonds, exchanged the rubles for dollars at about 6 rubles to the dollar and transferred the money to their offshore bank accounts. When the $4.8 billion had been spent it was time to devalue and default. So Russia's financial edifice turned out to be a house of cards. It was the pyramid scheme of all pyramid schemes. There was some irony in the fact that the main architects of the glittering façade, Egor Gaidar and Anatoly Chubais, were the wolves who blew it down.

Chubais openly admitted that he had conned the IMF and the west out of about $20 billion. He brazenly claimed that there had been an understanding that Russia had had no other option. A more experienced Prime Minister might have devalued first and then defaulted later. Such a mountain of bad news all at once triggered financial panic. Yeltsin and his advisers do not seem to have anticipated this. The Kirienko government lost credibility at home and abroad. Sergei offered to resign but Boris told him to sort out the mess. This was rather unfair since no one in Russia had any idea how to do this.

Russia made two crucial mistakes and thereby made a bad situation worse. It should have devalued earlier and it should have contacted its foreign

Yeltsin and the Pyramids. The three pyramids are: IMF debts; wages and pensions arrears; government bonds. The wry comment is that Yeltsin's economic policies were all pyramid schemes. Created by Igor Revyakin.

creditors before devaluing and defaulting. Why did it not devalue earlier? The main reason may have been that certain roving bandits, especially the bankers, needed breathing time to transfer their assets off-shore. Some Russian banks were making fortunes in the existing business climate. They borrowed heavily abroad at interest rates which were much lower than in Russia and ran no exchange rate risk as the ruble rate was fixed. They bought short-term government bonds with the money and made handsome profits. A devalued ruble could make this business unprofitable. An overvalued ruble was also of great value to those engaged in capital flight. They knew how serious the financial situation was (apparently they were much better informed than Kirienko). They also needed the government to order banks not to pay their foreign debts, including forward contracts. They obtained both. They were also able to exchange their government bonds for dollars and move that money offshore. The government should have consulted the IMF and other foreign creditors to discuss restructuring Russia's repayments and debts. However, according to Boris Fedorov, the IMF delegation in Moscow was apprised of what Kirienko was about to do and remained calm and not

One miner to another: 'And there is light at the end of the tunnel!' A wry comment on the endless promises made by Yeltsin about a better tomorrow. Created by Igor Revyakin.

unduly concerned. Fedorov, it goes without saying, opposed the freezing of government bond debt and was alarmed by the whole package.

The government's ham-fisted behaviour exacerbated the crisis but did not surprise the average Russian. He or she was used to the government reneging on its debts and promises. This had started with the commodity debt which had been run up by Gorbachev's government in 1990–91. In return for financing the budgetary deficit citizens were promised goodies such as VCRs, cars, fridges, and so on. The only Russian citizens who ever got any money back were a select few, insiders of course. Then their savings were wiped out by the inflation of 1992. The promised compensation never arrived. In 1998 their savings were wiped out again. Why should they have any faith in the market economy?

ENTER CHERNOMYRDIN

Kirienko did not have to wait long for the executioner's axe to fall. On 23 August, the President dismissed him and proposed Chernomyrdin as his replacement. The next day, Boris appeared on television to promote the former Prime Minister's abilities. An experienced hand was needed on the tiller. What had been promised to Chernomyrdin to entice him to take on the thankless task of running the economy? Some Kremlin observers say that Boris told him he would be the official candidate in the presidential elections in 2000. Now it was over to the Duma and it had seven days to decide.

Duma deputies and indeed everyone wanted to know why the President had sacked a Prime Minister he had raised up and praised to the heavens less than five months before. After all the main architect of the financial collapse had been the previous government, headed by Chernomyrdin. Why should Chernomyrdin do any better second time round? Some saw the hand of Berezovsky behind Kirienko's demise. The increasingly difficult economic situation meant that many banks and companies could not meet their debt repayments to foreign banks. Here was an opportunity for the government to place them in receivership and fatally weaken the oligarchs. Instead the oligarchs struck back and toppled the government. The moratorium on foreign debt payment provided them with a breathing space. Why did the President side with the bankers? The reason may have been that the plan of Kirienko and Nemtsov to allow the large banks to fail might have brought down Berezovsky. He managed the Yeltsin family portfolio and this would also be affected. Since the President's health was fragile he might have to resign at a moment's notice. In order for him to go, he needed a Prime Minister who could guarantee him and his family freedom from arrest and financial sequestration. If the oligarchs failed a new financial elite might emerge which owed the President nothing. It was safer to protect the economic barons and sacrifice domestic and foreign investors. Chernomyrdin was a desperate choice but he was now the Yeltsin family's best hope of avoiding political and financial disaster.

The ruble went into free fall and everyone tried either to exchange their rubles for dollars or buy something. The supply of dollars soon ran out and Russians resigned themselves to losing their savings – again. The many who had dollar accounts tried to withdraw their savings but, of course, the banks did not have sufficient dollars to meet demand. The beleaguered President was expected to resign but on 28 August he finally addressed the nation on television. He declared he would stay until his term of office expired but no one believed him. His performance was as shaky as the economy. The communists in the Duma saw their chance of reducing the powers of the President. Political and economic agreements were drafted and the weak President caved in. Chernomyrdin was confident that he would be approved, possibly on the first ballot.

Shortly before the first vote, Gennady Zyuganov, on television, declared that the communists had decided against signing the political agreement. Yavlinsky weighed in with his usual condemnation of the government. He believed the whole edifice would collapse to permit him and his team to take over. It was Chernomyrdin, not Kirienko, who was the architect of the financial crisis. Zhirinovsky declared that his faction would vote against Chernomyrdin. The former Prime Minister's chances of being confirmed had vanished. Why had such a startling reversal of fortune occurred? After all Chernomyrdin had always enjoyed a cosy relationship with the Duma, especially with the communist faction. It appeared that the main reason was that deputies knew that they were voting for the future President. In the past, the ex-Prime Minister had been clearly subordinate to Yeltsin but was now clearly taking over from the President. Chernomyrdin made matters worse by trying to intimidate the deputies. He clearly lacked the political skills which might have rescued his position.

On 31 August, the Duma rejected Chernomyrdin's nomination by 251 votes to 94 (he needed 226 to be approved as Prime Minister). On 1 September, the ruble fell to 22 rubles to the dollar, less than a third of its value a month earlier. Foreign companies were reluctant to grant their Russian customers credit and basic goods were running out in the shops. Yeltsin thought he could cow the Duma once again but this time it did not work. Chernomyrdin won over the Council of the Federation but this did him little good as it was the lower house, the Duma, which would decide. On 7 September, the Duma rejected Chernomyrdin by 273 votes to 138 (this time Zhirinovsky voted for the nomination) in the second ballot. Would Yeltsin propose him again and call the Duma's bluff? Communist deputies warned that they would start impeachment proceedings, thereby making it impossible to dissolve the parliament. The President's support base began to fracture with some favouring Yury Luzhkov, the Moscow mayor, as Prime Minister.

Out of the blue, Grigory Yavlinsky proposed Evgeny Primakov, the seasoned foreign minister. Primakov was attractive because apparently he had no presidential ambitions. After threshing around for a few days in a vain attempt to find a more suitable candidate, the President conceded defeat and nominated Primakov on 10 September. One of those who had turned him down was Yury Maslyukov. The KPRF had instructed him to take the job but Maslyukov revealed his independent streak by declining to follow party instructions. The following day, the Duma confirmed Primakov as Prime Minister by 317 votes to 63. This dramatic margin indicated that the new head of government was regarded as someone who would side with parliament rather than the President. He was perceived as left wing, the first left-wing Prime Minister of the post-communist era. As foreign minister he had clashed repeatedly with America and was a doughty defender of Russia's national interest. His successor as foreign minister was Igor Ivanov, a deputy minister of foreign affairs since 1993 and a specialist on Spain.

The acid test was how Primakov would manage the economy. He was no friend of market experimentation and viewed the liberals as responsible for the mess Russia was in. He recruited Yury Maslyukov, former head of Gosplan, and Viktor Gerashchenko, who returned to his post of chair of the Central Bank. Maslyukov was not such an outrageous appointment as might appear on first glance because Sergei Kirienko had also chosen him for his team. Maslyukov's attractiveness was that he was a technician with a detailed knowledge of the military-industrial complex. Primakov's goal was stabilisation after the shocks of the previous month. In order to achieve this the government had to intervene and regulate the economy. Primakov sought social peace. This implied paying back wages and improving social and medical care. Here he was caught between the devil and the deep blue sea: he would have to print money to do this but that, in turn, would increase inflation and the ruble would weaken. He needed to impose tight fiscal discipline and cut government expenditure, and some banks and companies would have to go to the wall. Liberal economists forecast Russia's suicide but, amazingly, the country did not collapse. Primakov's consensus-building style gradually won more and more support. Here was a pragmatist who favoured policies that worked.

Primakov needed to strengthen the centre at the expense of the regions since this was the main way to increase tax collection. However the governors had developed an appetite for greater authority which had been whetted by the weakness of Moscow. If Primakov took on this powerful interest group it could undermine the fragile stability the country was enjoying. There were other interest groups the Prime Minister would have to deal with if he were to attempt to strengthen his power. This included the powerful oil and gas lobby. Would he take on the economic barons? The 1999 budget surprised many of his critics by cutting government expenditure to the bone. However the IMF was not impressed and thought it did not go far enough – the IMF regarded bringing down inflation as the primary task and it was worth paying any social price to achieve this. Primakov knew that this would antagonise parliament. He strove to reach an agreement with the Duma which would have resulted in parliament affording the government its support in return for the President permitting the Duma and government to function without presidential intervention; but no agreement could be reached and this initiative foundered, in April 1999.

Primakov began the first real crackdown on organised crime since the fall of communism. Among those caught in the net were Boris Berezovsky. Tatyana Dyachenko had ended her relationship with Berezovsky in 1998 amid lurid rumours about her financial dealings with Boris. In late 1998, US authorities began examining a money laundering operation, perhaps involving $7 billion. The main bank involved was the Bank of New York. In February 1999, the authorities raided Sibneft and other companies in which Boris was involved. Atoll, his intelligence gathering network, was closed down. ORT ceased to receive government subsidies. Swiss prosecutors began investigating fraud and money laundering by top Russian officials. One case that stood out was Mabetex, linked to Pavel Borodin. They also raided Forus and other Berezovsky companies and froze their bank accounts. He was refused entry to Switzerland. On 2 April 1999, Berezovsky was sacked as executive secretary of the Commonwealth of Independent States.

In March 1999, Primakov took a hard line against the NATO bombing of Serbia and relations with the west cooled. Yeltsin felt insecure on two fronts: on foreign policy and the dangerous investigations into corruption in high places in the Kremlin. Primakov was not willing to give Yeltsin and his family the cast-iron guarantees against prosecution and the protection of their assets that the President wanted.

Primakov was beginning to look like presidential material. This was enhanced by his repeated assurances he would not run. He became the most trusted man in Russia. He began acting independently of the President but, then, this was not difficult as Boris was becoming Boris the Phantom President. Primakov was sacked on 12 May 1999. The timing was opportune. It came a few days before the Duma was to vote on impeaching the President. Some deputies thought better of impeaching the President in such a tense situation. The motion failed.

ENTER STEPASHIN

Sergei Stepashin was appointed Prime Minister on 19 May 1999. In his memoirs, Yeltsin (2000: 276) states he really wanted to appoint Vladimir Putin but this was not possible because it 'was too early'. His next choice was Nikolai Aksenenko, head of the railways. He was Berezovsky's suggestion. In stepped Chubais and he ensured that Stepashin got the nomination. The latter thought it wise to define his true identity: 'I am not General Pinochet', he declared in the Duma, 'My name is Stepashin.' This was an attempt to dispel rumours that he intended to copy the Chilean dictator's methods to turn the economy round. Stepashin was trusted by Yeltsin and had proved in the past that he was not squeamish about using force on behalf of the President. Stepashin had developed a reputation for putting the state's interests ahead of those of democracy. He was a *Realpolitiker*; the interests of the state, which meant Yeltsin's family, came first. Would he be strong enough to protect the President and the family after Boris left office? One way to ensure this would be to become the next President. His first task was to ensure that the pro-Yeltsin forces, the party of power, did well in the Duma elections in December 1999. This appeared a Herculean task as during the summer of 1999 Primakov was the public's favourite to take over from Yeltsin. Stepashin did not make much headway in improving the prospects of the party of power in the forthcoming elections.

When Shamil Basaev and Emir Khattab, with over 2000 men, invaded Avaristan, in Dagestan, on 2 August 1999, Stepashin was not afraid to use force to expel them. The fighters wanted to establish an Islamic Dagestan and this could not be countenanced. However Stepashin was not afforded the opportunity of completing the operation against the insurgents because he was dismissed as Prime Minister on 8 August 1999. Stepashin at first refused to go but Aleksandr Voloshin, head of the presidential administration, informed him that his dismissal was a *fait accompli*. There was a feeling that Stepashin was weak and this was reinforced after his dismissal when he commented that Russia 'could well lose Dagestan'. There are rumours that the Russians colluded with Basaev over the invasion of Avaristan; they apparently needed a pretext to attack the Wahhabim villages in Avaristan and with Basaev and Khattab ensconced there they had it.

After his removal Stepashin claimed that he had been dismissed because he 'could not be bought'. This may have been a reference to a leaked memorandum, dated 26 June, which advocated wreaking havoc in Moscow and mentioned another document which proposed igniting a war between mafia clans. Under this cover, kidnappings of prominent businessmen could be carried out. The objective was to discredit Luzhkov, declare a state of emergency and cancel elections. Pavel Krasheninnikov, the minister of justice, was sacked on 17 August. He maintained that he was removed because he had not been able to find legal reasons for banning the KPRF and preventing Luzhkov's Fatherland movement registering for the Duma elections (Reddaway and Glinski 2001: 611).

ENTER PUTIN

The man chosen to succeed Stepashin was a fast rising star, Vladimir Putin. Anatoly Chubais strained every nerve to prevent the appointment. As head of the FSB Putin was already involved in Dagestan. Yeltsin, who liked to think of himself as the Tsar, surprised many by announcing that he regarded Putin as his heir; this made Putin the Tsarevich. Observers regarded the anointing of Putin as the kiss of death. He was little known and hence his approval rating was in single digits.

The Chechen conflict reached the Russian capital on 31 August when a bomb exploded in Manezh Square, near the Kremlin, killing one and injuring 41. About midnight on 8–9 September another explosion demolished a nine-storey apartment block in south east Moscow, killing 94 and injuring over 200. On 13 September, an eight-storey apartment block was demolished, killing 60 and injuring 13. Moscow was not the only city to suffer terrorist attacks, with others occurring in the south. On 4 September, a car bomb exploded outside an apartment block inhabited by military personnel in Buinaksk, Dagestan, killing 64. On 16 September, an explosion in an apartment block in Volgodonsk killed 17 and injured 47. Who was responsible for this bloodletting? Chechens, Dagestanis, even the FSB and the GRU, military intelligence, were suggested. Those who were addicted to conspiracy theories pointed to the beginning of the election campaign, the invasion of Avaristan and the nomination of Putin as Prime Minister all coinciding. Yeltsin was regarded as a weak, disappearing President. Only a popular war could resurrect the family's fortunes. Sowing death and destruction among Muscovite civilians would raise the political temperature and lead to demands for the Chechen threat to be dealt with once and for all. Russians needed a strong man. He was already in place, Vladimir Putin. Is there any truth in all this? Why should the Chechens, who denied any responsibility, provoke the Russians in this way? Surely they knew that savage retribution would follow. Khattab pointed the finger at the Dagestanis. Were extremists responsible? But how could they acquire the necessary bombs and plant them without being discovered? This at a time when every Muscovite was looking anxiously over his shoulder to see if any swarthy north Caucasian was nearby. Whatever the truth Putin was a lucky man. He was presented with a golden opportunity to demonstrate that he was a strong man capable of defending Russia.

THE NEW DUMA

Elections to the new Duma took place on 19 December 1999 (Table 4.1). The winner was the communist party with 26 per cent of the vote and

113 seats, followed by Edinstvo which had supported Putin. In the party list vote, the communists polled 24.3 per cent, Edinstvo, 23.3 per cent, OVR (Fatherland-All Russia), which was headed by Yury Luzhkov and Evgeny Primakov, obtained 13.3 per cent, the Union of Right Forces, 8.5 per cent, the Zhirinovsky bloc, 6.4 per cent and Yabloko, 5.9 per cent.

How substantial was electoral fraud, given that it is part of Russian politics? This affects mainly the party list results. Various insiders put the actual communist party list vote at around 33 per cent, that of Edinstvo at about 15 per cent, OVR at perhaps 25 per cent, Yabloko at around 14 per cent, SPS at around 3 per cent and the Zhirinovsky bloc at about 5 per cent. The Duma did not investigate these claims. The average Russian voter remained apathetic.

Just over a third of the deputies were members of the previous Duma, including 77 who had served in the first Duma. This was the same as in the previous Duma. Some new members have served in local legislatures and this means that 220 of the deputies have had legislative experience. There is a group of another 70 who have served in executive positions at the local level, have been ministers and deputy ministers at the local and federal level and regional and municipal officials. This Duma is unique in having all previous federal Prime Ministers as deputies. Nikolai Ryzhkov, Gorbachev's Prime Minister until 1990, is also a deputy. Indeed of the Prime Ministers since 1985 only Valentin Pavlov and Ivan Silaev are not members. There are ten trade union members. Among the deputies are 23 former secretaries of party committees, 35 secretaries of raion and city party committees, and 22 secretaries of oblast and republican party committees. There are 35 former Komsomol secretaries and two who used to work in the Komsomol central committee. The business lobby is composed of about 80 deputies. The energy lobby is well represented. Evgeny Khramov (Onako), Roman Abramovich (Sibneft), Dmitry Savelev (ex-president, Transneft), Viktor Chernomyrdin (chair, board of directors, Gazprom), four representatives of Yukos, and one each from Tyumen oil company, Surgutneftegaz, Slavneft and Rosneft were elected. This is the first time that such a strong oil lobby has appeared in the Duma. Six of the wealthiest Russians are now in the Duma: Boris Berezovsky (third on the list), Viktor Chernomyrdin (16th), Vladimir Bryntsalov (19th), Roman Abramovich (21st), Iosif Kobzon (22nd) and Mikhail Gutserev (36th). Only one of the top 50 financiers, Boris Berezovsky, became a deputy. However Berezovsky resigned his mandate in July 2000, saying he was leaving the Duma to fashion an opposition party to Putin.

Sixteen new deputies used to be rectors of universities or institutes or professors. Three new deputies were previously unemployed and three are drawing their pension. Almost a third of the deputies are under 45 (90 are under 40) and almost a half between 45 and 55. All but four have some form of higher education. Only 34 of the deputies are female compared to 46 in the previous Duma. There are six heroes of the Soviet Union, four heroes of socialist labour and three heroes of Russia among the deputies. The heroes of Russia are Evgeny Zelenov, for the evacuation of Russian diplomats from besieged Kabul, Aleksandr Karelin, for his sporting prowess, and Elena Kondakova, for going into space.

The communists won most single member seats, 46, but this was short of the December 1995 results, 58. They were strongest in the traditionally red belt regions. Here the anti-Semitism of Zyuganov went down well. He regarded globalisation as a conspiracy, fuelled by Jewish expansionism. The traditional allies of the communists, the agrarians, deserted them in this election but only one agrarian was elected. OVR did well in Moscow (Yury Luzhkov, the mayor, headed the party and it obtained nine of the 15 single member seats in the capital), Tatarstan (run by President Mintimer Shaimiev, co-founder of the party, returned three OVR candidates out of five in the republic), and Bashkortostan, three out of six. Edinstvo, as a new movement, did poorly in single member constituencies but obtained 23.3 per cent of the party-list vote. Vladimir Putin did not associate himself too closely with it but it was clear that it supported him. Communists failed to win a seat in Moscow city and St Petersburg.

In the 1995 Duma elections over 40 per cent of the votes went to parties which did not cross the 5 per cent threshold but in this election it was only 17 per cent. In 1999, only six of the 26 parties and movements cleared the 5 per cent hurdle. The main beneficiary of this mature approach was Edinstvo.

Putin moved quickly to secure a majority in the new Duma. Even with OVR and several other parties, Edinstvo could not muster 226 votes. The simple way of securing a majority was to strike a tactical alliance with the KPRF. This was done on 18 January 2000 and Edinstvo and the communists split most of the Duma committees between them. Gennady Seleznev stayed on as speaker. Sixty-six of the independents came over to Edinstvo and formed the people's deputy group in the Duma. OVR deputies came over as well. Soon Edinstvo could fashion a two-thirds majority in parliament for essential legislation (this was needed to override Council of the Federation opposition).

THE TSAR DEPARTS

The good showing of Edinstvo and the growing popularity of Putin made it possible for Tsar Boris to make his last, momentous decision. He had several factors to consider. He could only go when he was assured his nominee would succeed him. Also he needed his successor to grant him legal immunity from prosecution for any of the crimes committed in his name while in office. He needed too to ensure there would be no sequestration of the wealth, at home and abroad, which the family had accumulated over the years. Putin agreed to these conditions. An early departure meant that there would have to be presidential elections within 90 days. This would give Putin a head start.

There is another way of looking at Boris's departure. He did not go, he was pushed. The turning point was his inability to get the Duma to confirm Viktor Chernomyrdin as Prime Minister after the sacking of Sergei Kirienko. A group had formed and it eventually ensured that Evgeny Primakov became Prime Minister. In office, he began to consolidate his position and build up a coalition which would eventually take over the presidency of Russia. When Sergei Stepashin succeeded Primakov as Prime Minister, the MVD rejoiced. The police believed that they were on the road to supreme power in Russia as Stepashin now appeared the likely establishment candidate. These hopes were dashed when Vladimir Putin took over. Stepashin's record was reasonable and he would have used force in Chechnya to keep the federation together. However he was not given the opportunity to do so. There are those who believe that the Chechen incursion into Dagestan had been masterminded by the Primakov clan. The goal was to create a situation which would allow Putin to play the strong leader and the defender of Russia's interests. The good showing of Edinstvo in the December 1999 Duma elections (aided by a little electoral fraud) permitted the Primakov clan to bring forward the presidential elections. It was a neat solution. Yeltsin would bow out on the last day of the 20th century and Vladimir Putin would be the millennium Tsar. Had he wanted, Primakov could almost certainly have become President himself. His tactics during the presidential election campaign were quite astute. He formed an alliance with Yury Luzhkov, the mayor of Moscow, and in this way blunted the mayor's chances. Gusinsky, of Media-Most, supported Primakov and Luzhkov. Berezovsky supported Putin. By the end of 2000, both media barons were in exile. Primakov is satisfied to remain Putin's key adviser and undertakes various missions for him. Instead of saying the Putin clan is taking over Russia it would be more exact to say the Primakov–Putin clan.

So, on 31 December 1999, President Yeltsin stunned Russia with his New Year's message on television. Everyone had expected a Santa Claus act but instead he announced that he was stepping down immediately and wanted Vladimir Putin to succeed him. He asked to be excused for failing to make the dreams of the population in 1991 reality. 'I ask you to forgive me for having failed to fulfil the dreams of those who believed that it would be possible to jump from the grey, stagnating, totalitarian past to a bright, rich and civilised future in one go . . . I am leaving. I have done all I can.' To Putin, he simply said: 'Take care of Russia.'

In his New Year's message, acting President Vladimir Putin was brutally frank about the position of Russia and the tasks which confronted everyone. Russia's GDP had almost halved during the 1990s and was only a tenth of that of the US and a fifth of that of China. After the August 1998 crisis per capita GDP dropped to about $3500 or about a fifth of the G7 states' average. The structure of the Russian economy has changed drastically with fuel and energy, power engineering and ferrous and non-ferrous metallurgy dominating. They account for about 15 per cent of the GDP, 50 per cent of industrial output and 70 per cent of exports. Labour productivity in electricity generation and raw materials output is about world average but in other sectors it is under 24 per cent of the American level. One of the reasons for low productivity is the age of the capital stock. Over 70 per cent of Russian machinery is over ten years old, twice the level of advanced countries. Only about 5 per cent of Russian enterprises engage in research and development whereas the top 300 transnational companies devoted about $240 billion to R & D in 1998. Russia has been pushed out of the market for science-intensive consumer goods. Russia now has 1 per cent of the global market whereas the US has 36 per cent and Japan 30 per cent. Real incomes of the Russian population are now less than 10 per cent of the American.

Who is to blame? The communist party: the Russian people has had to pay an 'outrageous price' for the Bolshevik experiment. Russia has had its fill of revolution, cataclysms and radical reforms. The experience of the 1990s demonstrates that Russia cannot be renewed by experimenting with 'abstract models and schemes taken from foreign textbooks'. Every country, Russia included, has to seek its own way of renewal. Russia does not need to revert to an official state ideology. However Russia as a nation needs patriotism, national pride and dignity. Otherwise the Russian nation will not be capable of great achievements. Russia will not become the United States or Britain Mark II in which liberal values have deep historical roots. Russians regard a strong state as the guarantor of order and the initiator and main driving force of change.

5

THE TSAR'S COURT:
THE PRESIDENTIAL
ADMINISTRATION,
THE SECURITY COUNCIL
AND THE GOVERNMENT

THE PRESIDENTIAL ADMINISTRATION IN SOME WAYS resembles the old
Politburo. It was a decision-making and supervisory body and left the
implementation of policy to others, such as the government. The government would take orders from the presidential administration and run
the economy. Security would be concentrated in the Security Council.
However it did not always work like this. Since the President could
not be dependent on the military in emergencies he needed his own
presidential or Kremlin guard. This would be part of the presidential
administration. Under the communists, parliament or the Supreme
Soviet had been consultative (until 1989). Yeltsin wanted this to continue. However parliament had had a taste of decision making after 1989
and wanted to expand its influence. The inability of the President to
enforce his will on parliament and often on government led to the
strengthening of his personal staff. It gradually duplicated all the governmental ministries and became a shadow government. It also duplicated the other institutions of state. When the constitution of 1993 was
drafted Yeltsin was careful not to include his personal administration
in it. The head of the presidential administration became one of the
most influential officials in the state.

As Yeltsin's health gave way the role of the administration assumed greater significance. It was important that the Prime Minister, who became acting President when the President was abroad or indisposed, only continued to run the economy. The presidential administration had to ensure that the nuclear black box containing the codes did not pass from its hands. It was the symbol of power in Russia.

Gorbachev's failure to restructure institutions in the light of the presidency affected Russia as it inherited the same confused system. Yeltsin lost his built-in majority in the Supreme Soviet in April 1992. From then on it openly opposed shock therapy and advocated greater state management of the economy. The President countered by enlarging government to a point where several hundred officials had the title of minister. The larger the corps of government ministers the less likely they were to govern efficiently. A presidium of the Council of Ministers, just as in Soviet times, emerged. The key ministers were to be found there and most of them were Yeltsin's men.

The December 1993 Duma elections did not produce a parliament which would do the President's bidding. Various agencies were set up to link the legislative and executive branches. These formed part of his personal staff. The President had always been skilled at co-opting his opponents. In 1994, the speakers of both houses of parliament were appointed to important presidential bodies such as the Security Council and the council for cadre policy. Here he was fortunate that Ivan Rybkin, the Agrarian speaker of the Duma, was conciliatory and cautious by nature. The speaker of the upper house was a Yeltsin man. One of the benefits of this policy was that when the war in Chechnya broke out in December 1994 the parliamentary leaders were involved in Security Council decisions.

Ministries in the late Soviet era had become fiefdoms for respective interest groups. This carried over into the Yeltsin era. Gaidar complained that the first priority of ministries was to defend and expand their sphere of interest. Inevitably this resulted in fierce conflicts with other ministries. No one, not even the President, could mediate these turf battles. There was no concept of collective responsibility. Ministers criticised one another in public. They ran to the media and enlisted the support of opinion makers in battles with other ministers. They divided the Kremlin against itself. Discretion, decorum, loyalty, were virtues almost absent. There were exceptions, of course, one of them being Sergei Filatov. This is all the more astonishing, given the practice of the Soviet era when officials had observed tight discipline and bureaucratic loyalty. Russia revealed itself a land of extremes. It went from the tight-lipped communist official to the open-mouthed Yeltsin official overnight.

The usual tactic of a ruler in such a situation is to blur departmental boundaries. The more overlapping the better for the leader. This was a key reason for the inefficiency of the Yeltsin administration. After 1993, it was exacerbated by the President's failing health. By 1995, there were several thousand officials in the presidential administration. They duplicated over 1100 officials attached to the Prime Minister and deputy Prime Ministers. Each official attempted to enlarge his own staff and a measure of his influence was the increasing size of his staff. They were rewarded with dachas, cars and the good life. No wonder spending on the state bureaucracy increased from 0.23 per cent of GDP in 1992 to 0.58 per cent in 1994. Another reason for the bloated administration was that there were hordes of officials who became redundant when the Soviet Union collapsed in 1991. They were all keen to find a trough to feed in. It was also important in the volatile situation of the early and mid-1990s to give these empty hands work to do. Otherwise the opposition might recruit them. Those who were at the trough had something to lose if Yeltsin lost.

THE DEVELOPMENT OF THE ADMINISTRATION

The communist system was hierarchical and power flowed from the top down. The effectiveness of the vertical structure was due to the skills of the party Central Committee Secretariat. It supervised the implementation of Politburo decisions. If there was a dispute between two ministries it could intervene and impose a solution. In 1991 all this collapsed. The only model Yeltsin had was the communist one. He knew how it functioned and there were hordes of officials looking for employment. There was no time to think about alternative administrative structures or to train new officials. The President's first tasks were to build up the Russian state and implement radical economic reform. How was he to do this with officials who had no experience of such matters and were often opposed to the policy?

The presidential administration (Huskey 1999: 45–74) (Table 5.1) was deeply split over reform. Yeltsin himself was strongly opposed to the communist system and wished to introduce changes which would ensure the communists never returned to power. These views were shared by Gennady Burbulis who became the President's most influential policy adviser. Egor Gaidar became the tsar of the new economy, Andrei Kozyrev became the west's best friend in the Kremlin but lacked

Gorbachev's charisma in foreign affairs and Sergei Shakhrai set about building a new legal order.

The radicals were all outsiders, lacking knowledge of the machinery of government and security affairs. Opposing them, one can call them traditionalists or slow reformers, were officials such as Yury Petrov, the first head of the presidential administration. He saw the young reformers as wild children let loose in a sweet shop. Yeltsin gave him the task of reining them in. Oleg Lobov fitted the same mould.

Yeltsin deployed his usual skills and played one group off against the other. The President sacked his staff in line with tactical political considerations. He would sacrifice officials if it gained him advantage in parliament or the regions. On balance, the radicals fared better than the traditionalists. However when it came to key decisions on security, radicals could be sidelined. Sergei Filatov, head of the presidential administration, was only informed about the dissolution of parliament shortly before it happened, in September 1993. Yury Baturin, the President's security adviser, was excluded from the meeting which decided to launch the war in Chechnya, in December 1994. He had warned the President of the political and military dangers of such a policy.

The conservatives were much better at politics than the radicals. They had grown up in the apparatus and were used to striking tactical alliances. Many of the radicals shared a Bolshevik propensity. To underline his authority the boss shouted at his subordinates and treated them as if their brain had gone missing. Gaidar and Filatov were exceptions to this. Those who fitted the Bolshevik pattern included Gennady Burbulis and Sergei Pashin, a young legal reformer. Their shortcomings underlined the small pool of talent the radicals could draw upon. The President was often peremptory with his staff and could be biting in his contempt. As he was a man of moods it was wiser to enquire about his condition before attempting to see him. His aversion to paperwork increased over time and he could be very short tempered if asked for a decision on an important matter.

His absences permitted his staff to promote their own empires and many of them did not see the chief for long spells. It suited the President that there was no accepted decision-making process. Decisions were made ad hoc, if at all. Hence the influence of his closest associates was crucial. They passed on requests for favours. They could be for tax exemption, funds for some worthy project, measures to deal with crime, more staff and so on. Everyone knew the President liked playing Santa Claus. Never mind the bill the ministry of finance had to pick it up. He was a very generous man but then he was not giving away his own money. One presumes that those who promoted these requests also got a success fee. This was a great system, if you were in the money. It was good for those involved but bad for Russia.

The chancellery managed the paperwork which landed on the President's desk. Yeltsin placed a tick on those he agreed with and an exclamation against those that had to go back for further consideration. Presidential decrees received the official stamp of the chancellery of the President and thereby were promulgated as laws.

The counsellors' service was the smallest in terms of numbers but one of the most important in terms of influence. Its head from 1992 onwards was Viktor Ilyushin, who had the title of chief adviser. The service provided advisers in all key policy areas. Each counsellor had his own staff, personally recruited. Only Ilyushin saw the President daily, that is when he was around. He was also responsible for recommending new advisers. Yeltsin knew Ilyushin very well. He had spent 15 years with Yeltsin when he was party leader in Ekaterinburg and came to Moscow with him in 1985. He was always at Yeltsin's side at critical moments, for instance in the White House during the attempted coup. He helped him draft decrees and speeches. Yury Baturin, counsellor for both security and legal affairs from 1993–95, had served Gorbachev but his wide-ranging abilities impressed Yeltsin. He had graduated in physics, law and journalism. Aleksandr Livshits, an Academy of Sciences economist, was an economic adviser in the apparatus and then became counsellor for economics, in November 1994. He later became minister of finance. As the President had an aversion to paperwork he expected his counsellors to decide what was most important for him to see. There was a group which drafted the state of the union address which the 1993 constitution required the President to deliver each year. It was an expensive exercise. By 1998 it was costing $3.5 million to draft. The money went on dachas, food, consultants and equipment. After all the body had to be cosseted if the mind was going to come up with the telling phrase. Often the counsellors acted as the President's spokesperson.

The administration of affairs or the main property department was of key importance. It was originally established, in July 1991, as a property management division in the presidential administration. After the October 1993 events it acquired the functions of managing the properties of all federal agencies, including payment of salaries of Duma deputies and court judges and officials. On 2 August 1995, President Yeltsin signed a decree including it in the list of federal entities of the executive and it acquired a new statute. On 1 April 1993, Pavel Borodin took over as act-ing head of the main property department. He had a staff of about 350 directly subordinate to him. Five years later its property portfolio had increased tenfold to reach about $600 billion. In 1998, Borodin claimed that the department had an annual income of 'at least $2.5 billion'.

Stories circulated that the way that Pavel had endeared himself to President Yeltsin was by demonstrating his brilliant skill at making Siberian dumplings. He discovered that the way to the President's heart was through his stomach.

In 1994, the department spent about half of the $1 billion budget of the presidential administration. The money was used to pay salaries, the President received about $5000 in 1995, for instance. It is responsible for managing 3 million square metres of floor space in office buildings in Moscow, including the Kremlin, the White House, the buildings of the State Duma and the Council of the Federation. It pays and looks after the needs of about 12,000 leading Russian officials. It has a fleet of 3000 cars for official state use. The department is even responsible for putting flowers and mineral water on tables.

Borodin personally supervised the refurbishment of the White House after the depredations of October 1993. Other projects in which he was closely involved were the Senate building in the Kremlin, where President Putin's apartments are located. He also oversaw the restora-tion of the Grand Kremlin Palace. One of the companies involved was the Swiss-registered Mabetex. It became the source of many accusations of corruption against Borodin.

The department plays a very special role in the lives of Russian officials. It makes clothing, shoes, boots, provides medicine and constructs apartments for the elite; it also looked after Yeltsin's health. Since state salaries are low, officials rely on the administration for all the goodies which make life comfortable. Allocation of apartments, dachas, cars and telephones was centralised and distributed by the department in consultation with the President. Becoming a favourite is materially rewarding. This was a direct extension of the Soviet practice. The party Central Committee Secretariat had had its own administration of affairs and had even acquired its own enterprises in order to be independent of other bodies. Hence the party built up its own business empire. Yeltsin just followed suit. By 1995, his administration owned 75 enterprises; it also had many hotels and dachas and rented them out for a consider-ation when not in use. It has its own medical establishments. It owns the Rossiya airline which carries top state officials. It also owns property in 78 foreign states. In 1995, the business empire employed over 30,000 persons. By 2000, one estimate put the number of employees at home and abroad at around 100,000.

When President Putin became acting President, he swiftly removed Pavel Borodin as head of the property department. He was appointed state secretary of the Union of Russia and Belarus, a not very important post.

The lack of resources from the budget forced every other state institution to go into business. Hence in Russia it became normal for state agencies to engage in private business. A branch of the Academy of Sciences could let its basement to a restaurant group. This ensured that its staff got wholesome meals at subsidised prices and the institute had enough money to pay staff salaries when the state failed to pay on time. Government ministries and other state bodies tried to maximise their private business income as it gave them more independence vis-à-vis their superiors. It also made it easier to recruit staff. The administration was of great use to the President when parliament cut his grant. The administration's own factories were granted special privileges, such as export licences and no duty on imports.

The second most lucrative branch of the apparatus is the centre for presidential programmes. Its budget was almost $500 million in 1994. It disbursed largesse to state and private agencies not connected with the presidential administration. For instance, it funded festivals in Moscow and book prizes. It also supplemented the state budget when natural disasters occurred. Any money left over was invested in private enterprises.

Agencies grew up in an ad hoc manner from 1991 onwards and in early 1993 the presidential administration was set up to group them all together under one roof. There were so many disparate functions that neither a vertical hierarchy nor a horizontal jurisdiction emerged. Agencies had differing access to the President and the presidential administration can be seen as a loose confederation of interests. By 1995, there were 43 bureaux and over 2000 staff. After Filatov was sacked, in January 1996, a purge of the administration did take place with about one quarter of the staff going. They did not suffer hardship as they were found other niches.

The presidential administration had its own secretariat consisting of Filatov's own personal apparatus and deputies. He controlled the budget and staffing level of each agency. Some agencies were strong enough to escape his control. The administration of affairs, the property department, soon broke loose from his administration and gained autonomy within the presidential apparatus. Filatov was a democrat but did not enjoy close relations with Yeltsin.

Among the agencies set up was the general department which liaised between the presidential apparatus and the government. A department of the same name performed the same function within the communist party Secretariat. Another twin was the cadres administration. Its task was to build up files on personnel who could fill key political and administrative positions. It served as the most important source of information for the council on cadre policy.

The gathering and dissemination of information received high priority. The presidential administration inherited a huge library of books and periodicals from the communist era. One of its tasks was to provide summaries of the views published in the domestic and foreign press. It also inherited the communist party archives, a vast storehouse of material which could be used for political as well as academic purposes. For instance, compromising material was published before the 1996 presidential elections in the struggle with Gennady Zyuganov. The presidential administration also inherited an important newspaper, *Rossiiskie Vesti,* which was published in Moscow and eleven provincial cities. It could be used to promote the President, especially at election time. There was also a publishing house.

Liaison with the press was the responsibility of the press service, headed by Anatoly Krasikov, and the office of the press secretary, Vyacheslav Kostikov, the latter being also a member of the counsellors' service. When Krasikov and Kostikov were both sacked, in May 1995, the two offices were combined into the federal press service. It was added to the presidential administration. Another competitor for the personal apparatus was Mikhail Poltoranin who became minister for the press in the early heady days of the Yeltsin era. The President dropped him, in April 1992, to placate the Supreme Soviet but moved him sideways to head the new federal information service. When he was sacked, in late 1993, the federal information service disappeared with him.

Most economists were employed in the group of experts, headed by Aleksandr Livshits, the expert-analytical centre and the analytical centre for socio-economic policy. In May 1994, the three agencies were fused in an analytical centre, headed by Evgeny Yasin, a future minister of economics. More economists were to be found in the finance and budget administration which monitored state budgets and supervised the ministry of finance and other economic agencies. In early 1993, plans were laid to establish a bloc of presidential parties in parliament. This was soon abandoned but parties and groups in the Duma were cultivated and also in society to boost support for the President. One of the groups targeted were the Cossacks, with some success.

The administration for work with territories was responsible for relations with the 89 subjects of the Russian Federation. It was the intermediary between the President and the regions. Its head, Nikolai Medvedev, believed that some ethnic territories should be afforded special privileges and this was reflected in the numerous treaties signed with the subjects. This caused friction with ethnically Russian areas. The administration often duplicated the work of the ministry of nationalities and this was a further source of conflict.

Much of the activity of the presidential administration concerned legal matters. One important area was dealing with citizens' letters. It was not unusual for the President to receive over one million letters a day, all complaining about officials and the courts. Many came to petition the President personally, an old Tsarist and communist tradition. In 1994, over 33,000 came to Moscow to submit their petitions. The government could also be petitioned in person.

The two most important legal agencies were the state and legal administration and the monitoring administration. The state and legal administration was established on 7 December 1991 to advise the President on legal matters and to promote a single legal space in Russia. The promoter and first head of the administration was Sergei Shakhrai who used it as a stepping stone to greater political influence. He built it up as an empire and it retained its importance after Shakhrai left in the middle of 1992. It became the key centre for considering legislative initiatives and thereby influenced policy. The monitoring commission performed the same functions as the party control commission, even occupying the same premises. It was the largest commission in terms of staff. Its task was simply to ensure that officials carried out their duties and were loyal; its favourite tactic was to raid ministries and agencies and carry out immediate inspections. It also considered citizens' complaints about the malfeasance of officials and reports from inspectors in ministries and agencies.

THE PRESIDENTIAL ADMINISTRATION DURING THE SECOND PRESIDENCY

Chubais quickly set about reforming the administration when he took over in order to maximise his influence over policy (Huskey 1999: 87–97).

By October 1996, it was in place and Chubais then managed to get the President to sign a decree giving him control over all parts of the apparatus, including the counsellors' service. The only exception was the Security Council. Chubais formed a team consisting of a first deputy and six deputy heads of the presidential administration. Each official was responsible for a specific policy area. The first deputy head was Aleksandr Kazakov, who had been with Chubais in the State Property Committee (GKI) (responsible for privatisation). Maksim Boiko, a deputy head responsible for relations with parties and civic associations had also spent time in the GKI. Three other deputy heads came from St Petersburg, Chubais's home town. They were Yury Yarov, Aleksei Kudrin and Evgeny Sevostyanov. The last was a former general who had had experience in the security services and was responsible for personnel policy.

This arrangement only lasted until March 1997 when Chubais returned to government as first deputy Prime Minister responsible for economic reform. He also became minister for finance. Chubais was also to be acting Prime Minister when Viktor Chernomyrdin was away. Some of Chubais's team went with him into government and others made the reverse journey into the presidential administration. For instance, Aleksandr Livshits, first deputy Prime Minister and minister of finance, became the head of a new economics administration. Who would replace Chubais as head of the presidential administration? Anatoly did not want a heavyweight economist who could challenge his authority. The choice fell on Valentin Yumashev, a 39-year-old journalist. He had acted as ghost writer of the President's two autobiographies and as such had developed close relations with the Yeltsin family and its clan over the years 1989–94. He had also a top position in the magazine, *Ogonek*, owned by Boris Berezovsky. In this way he entered Boris's web. Aleksandr Korzhakov saw Yumashev as scruffy, unkempt and unconcerned about his appearance. Chubais brought Yumashev into the re-election team in the spring of 1996 and he became an adviser to the President on the press after July 1996. Yumashev had also established good relations with Tatyana Dyachenko, something which an ambitious man had to do.

Yumashev continued Chubais's drive to strengthen the presidential administration. When Viktor Ilyushin became a first deputy Prime Minister, in August 1996, he was not replaced as head of the counsellors' service. Over the period March 1997 to June 1998, most of the counsellors departed but were not replaced.

One of those recruited to the administration was Vladimir Putin. According to his biography he became unemployed after Anatoly

Sobchak failed to be elected governor in 1996. He had been working for Sobchak since 1990 after returning from East Germany. He states that he did the rounds of the St Petersburgers in top posts in Moscow. Almost all of them owed their positions to Chubais. Suddenly, in August 1996, he landed a top job. He was appointed deputy head of the administration of affairs, under Pavel Borodin. In 1997, Putin became head of the monitoring administration, as befitted someone whose career had been in the KGB. It collected files on officials' corruption. He progressed rapidly and in 1998 became one of the two first deputy heads of the presidential administration under Yumashev. He was responsible for Russia's regions and travelled the country getting to know the governors. In July 1998, Putin left the apparatus to become head of the federal security service (FSB).

There was much resentment at the size of the presidential administration, indeed of the number of bureaucrats and ministers. The Duma, the IMF and the unpaid kept up a cacophony of protest and the President was eventually forced to downsize. The counsellors' service was a casualty and Yumashev may have fired about two hundred in all. However these officials were not thrown on to the streets. They simply moved sideways to a different trough. Sometimes a new trough was created just for them. For example, Georgy Satarov, the counsellor for political matters, was made head of a new think tank funded by Pavel Borodin's office. Apparently when Nikolai Egorov was fired as head of the presidential administration, in July 1996, Boris asked him: 'What government post would you like?' At the top it was the circulation of elites. Once in the nomenklatura meant always in the nomenklatura. This did not apply lower down where junior staff were thrown on the scrap heap. This was because they had not risen to a position which qualified for membership of the nomenklatura.

Whereas under Chubais the presidential administration had concentrated on policy formation, under Yumashev it began to concentrate on selling the President. Over half of Yumashev's staff were specialists in information and communications. They were spin doctors, to use modern parlance. One of the deputy heads and presidential press secretary was Sergei Yastrzhembsky, a lawyer, former diplomat and journalist. Tatyana Dyachenko officially joined the presidential administration as her father's 'image maker'. Clearly packaging the President was becoming a problem. The only way to solve it was to recruit more and more personnel.

Besides selling the President, Yumashev devoted more time to monitoring the regions. The first gubernatorial elections in Russia, in late 1996, were of great significance for centre-regional relations. Directly elected governors had a power base to strengthen local control over state assets. The presidential administration's support of certain candidates did not have the desired effect. Few pro-Moscow governors were elected. This led the President to attempt to strengthen the role of presidential representatives in the regions. They were to monitor the implementation of federal laws and decrees at the regional level. The administration for the coordination of the activity of presidential representatives in the regions, in the presidential administration, was given extra responsibility.

In foreign affairs the presidential administration expanded its role. In late 1996, a foreign policy administration, headed by Aleksandr Manzhosin, was set up. However it was Sergei Yastrzhembsky who took a much higher profile in foreign affairs as befits someone who had been head of the ministry of foreign affairs' press service from 1992–93 and Russian ambassador to Slovakia from 1993–96. He organised the President's foreign itinerary and was even seen as a future foreign minister. As such he was competing directly with Evgeny Primakov, the then minister of foreign affairs. When Primakov became Prime Minister he wasted no time in firing Yastrzhembsky. The latter had been pushing for Yury Luzhkov to become Prime Minister rather than Primakov. Yastrzhembsky, not surprisingly, moved into Luzhkov's personal apparatus. He later returned to the Yeltsin entourage. Yumashev was also sacked. Nikolai Bordyuzha, a former KGB officer, deputy head of FAPSI and director of Russian border troops, became head of the presidential administration, in December 1998. Three months earlier he had become secretary of the Security Council. This confirmed a developing trend. As the President became more and more feeble he was increasingly surrounded by men with expertise in security affairs. The reformers and the journalists were pushed aside as the President's family and their advisers frantically looked for someone to succeed Boris. It had to be someone who could guarantee them safety from prosecution and the protection of their formidable assets. Bordyuzha turned out to be a disappointment and was sacked from both his posts, in March 1999. Aleksandr Voloshin took over as head of the presidential administration.

A major function of the presidential administration was to organise off-budget subsidies to enterprises and regions. It acted as a protector of Russian industry. It liaised with the Central Bank and ministries of finance and the economy. The oligarchs lobbied in the presidential administration to further their own interests. They also tried to place their nominees in key positions in the presidential administration.

THE SECURITY COUNCIL

The origins of the Security Council go back to the Russian Security Council which was set up soon after Yeltsin was elected President in June 1991 (Huskey 1999: 74–80) (Table 5.2). It was conceived as a consultative body parallel to the government. Yeltsin dissolved the Security Council along with various other institutions when he became Prime Minister, in November 1991. The law on state security of 5 March 1992 recreated the Security Council. It was to be chaired by the President and to have four other permanent members. A law of 4 April 1992 identified seven main functions for the Security Council including drafting policy and determining the main tasks facing the President. In April 1992, the 6th Congress of People's Deputies obliged Yeltsin to give up his portfolio as Prime Minister and other close associates, such as Gennady Burbulis, also departed. This led the President to expand the Security Council's remit to include drafting an annual programme for executive bodies and drafting decisions.

The Security Council in many ways resembles the National Security Council in the US. Both have a permanent staff and a group of senior politicians who gather from time to time to debate policy. The Security Council has permanent members with voting rights, the President, the Prime Minister, the secretary of the Security Council, the ministers of defence, foreign affairs and director of the domestic intelligence (FSB). Then there are other members with a consultative voice, the ministers of the interior, finance, justice and so on. Other officials such as Viktor Ilyushin and Yury Baturin normally attended meetings which took place about once a month. The Security Council has many specialised commissions ranging over a very wide area.

Yury Skokov, the first secretary of the Security Council, was a seasoned bureaucrat from the military-industrial complex. He was also politically ambitious. One plan was to position the Security Council between the President and the power (men with arms) ministries. This could mean the Security Council giving orders to the power ministries and not merely monitoring them. He proposed, for instance, that the General Staff be removed from the ministry of defence and made subordinate to the Security Council. Another move was to establish a super-ministry of security; Sergei Shakhrai had also toyed with the idea, but such a ministry had previously existed under Beria. The Constitutional Court ruled it unconstitutional. Skokov was not be outdone. A presidential decree of 7 July 1992 further expanded the reach of the Security Council. It could now issue orders to heads of ministries and local authorities. It was also to supervise the implementation of its decisions. On 8 October 1992, a commission, headed by Aleksandr Rutskoi, was set up to combat crime and corruption and added to the Security Council. Then, on 23 October, the secretariat of the council of heads of republics was allocated to it. In December 1992, a commission to coordinate foreign policy was set up in the Security Council and chaired by its secretary. Skokov even tried to set up regional security councils subordinate to Moscow.

The Security Council was beginning to take on the form of the old Politburo and this was sure to encounter resistance from politicians who wished to enlarge their autonomy. Primary among these was Pavel Grachev, the minister of defence, Viktor Erin, minister of internal affairs, and Andrei Kozyrev, minister of foreign affairs. Then there were the economic reformers such as Egor Gaidar and Anatoly Chubais who did not want a presidential institution clipping their wings. All these officials were aware that the Security Council, being subordinate to the President, was not subject to parliamentary scrutiny. Not surprisingly, the power ministries, especially, would have liked to see the Security Council dissolved. Skokov had another adversary nearer to home. Sergei Filatov, head of the presidential administration, was excluded from the Security Council and set out to restrict its influence. In early 1993, Filatov succeeded in moving some of the functions of the Security Council to his administration. Some of the staff of the Security Council were officials from other ministries, especially the ministry of defence. They served on a rotation basis but their primary loyalty was to their own ministry.

When it became clear that he could not transform the Security Council into a Politburo, Skokov began looking elsewhere for political advancement. He even saw himself as a successor to Egor Gaidar as Prime Minister. On 10 May 1993, he was sacked as secretary of the Security Council and began gradually to sever his close links to Yeltsin. The President, however, after the disappointing Duma elections, brought him back in early 1994 as co-chair of the council on cadre policy. The other co-chair was Sergei Filatov and that guaranteed frosty relations. Skokov's appointment was another example of Boris's practice of providing a watchdog to restrict the ambitions of his staff. Later Skokov moved completely into the opposition and formed the Congress of Russian Communities, a mixture of red directors and nationalists. Its greatest coup was to attract Aleksandr Lebed to its ranks in the December 1995 Duma elections. Its failure to cross the 5 per cent threshold for party lists surprised many observers. This confined Skokov to the political wilderness.

The President's choice as Skokov's successor was Marshal Evgeny Shaposhnikov who had stood by him in August 1991. However this did not meet with approval and eventually Oleg Lobov took over in September 1993. He had left the ministry of economics under a cloud after proposing greater state intervention in the economy. The Security Council was mentioned in the December 1993 constitution. The 'President forms and heads the Security Council' is not very revealing. Yeltsin saw Lobov as his man and relied on him to keep it in order. The Security Council now tended to concentrate on domestic affairs and played only a minor role in foreign policy. Kozyrev, the foreign minister, was added to the membership, in January 1994, but was immediately criticised by Grachev, the defence minister. The opportunity for the Security Council to become a new Politburo had passed. Such an arrangement did not suit Boris who did not favour one institution dominating all others. Lobov was charged, in June 1994, with combating crime and corruption which was becoming a major problem.

The Security Council came into its own in December 1994 as the body which launched the war against Chechnya. Yeltsin only allowed discussion after the vote for military action had been taken. The Security Council was split with several members, such as Evgeny Primakov, director of the foreign intelligence service (SVR), Vladimir Shumeiko, speaker of the Council of the Federation, and Yury Kalmykov, the minister of justice, opposing the action. Kalmykov felt so strongly that he resigned.

The Security Council became a war cabinet during hostilities. Grachev had unwisely promised the President that the military would deal with the Chechens in a matter of days. The reputation of the Russian military and the President suffered as the war dragged on. In August 1995, Lobov was made the President's representative in Chechnya.

The hostage taking at Budennovsk, in September 1995, was humiliating. An interim peace treaty was signed with Maskhadov, in May 1996, but the Russian military would not accept defeat. Lobov had failed ignominiously and was replaced on 18 June 1996 by Aleksandr Lebed. There had been another reason for sacking him. He was named by Aum Shinrikyo, the cult which tried to kill thousands in the Tokyo underground, in 1995. The blueprints of the deadly sarin gas they used, they claimed, had been provided by Lobov for a bribe of $100,000. He was also accused of providing military training for Aum members at a secret army base in central Russia. He denied all these charges. General Lebed demanded and got the dismissal of Yury Baturin as Yeltsin's security adviser. Afterwards Baturin went on to higher things. He became an astronaut on the Russian MIR station.

In October 1996, Ivan Rybkin, who had been speaker of the first Duma, became secretary of the Security Council. This signalled the arrival of a consensus-seeker and a stark contrast to Aleksandr Lebed. Rybkin was not an empire-builder and preferred to consolidate existing structures. As a result the Security Council became less prominent in national affairs. He gave way, in March 1998, to Andrei Kokoshin, who was the leading civilian specialist in military affairs. He had been the first civilian first deputy minister of defence and accordingly much concerned with military reform and doctrine. He had no political base. Chechnya was a troublesome problem for the Security Council and there was the ever-present need to bring Russian military doctrine up to date. In September 1998, Kokoshin was replaced as secretary by Sergei Ivanov.

OTHER SECURITY AGENCIES

One of the most powerful and secretive agencies of the presidential administration is the federal agency for government communications and information (FAPSI) (Huskey 1999: 71–2). This was the new name for the twelfth administration of the KGB. Its writ ran from the security of information, the black box for nuclear weapons, domestic phone tapping and encryption. If it wanted to listen in to a conversation it just went ahead and did not seek court permission. It was responsible for the state telephone service, the *vertushka*. The number of telephones on an official's desk was a clear indication of his seniority; each telephone was only connected to one other person. FAPSI bugged the offices and homes of leading politicians and it was standard practice, for example, for presidential counsellors to exchange notes when they wanted to communicate something sensitive; they assumed, probably correctly, that 'big ears' was listening. Under its first director, General Starovoitov, FAPSI built up a vast database in its main administration for information resources. Most of its large staff were military officers with the relevant technical expertise.

In December 1998, Starovoitov was suddenly sacked and replaced by General Vladislav Sherstyuk. His stay was short as he was replaced, in May 1999, by Vladimir Matyukhin. He had been a deputy director since 1993. At present there are about 80,000 staff and if communications troops are added this brings the total to about 120,000 men and women. An important function of FAPSI is to hack into western communications and computer systems, especially those of the security forces.

Another key institution dealing with security was the main guard directorate (GUO) headed by General Mikhail Barsukov. Its task was to guard state buildings and important state personnel. The elite Alpha and Vympel units were part of this force. It also inherited from the KGB former party property and nature reserves which had been used for the recreation of the ruling class. In a time of financial stringency, these assets were used to make money. Barsukov thought up a great wheeze in 1994. He asked Pavel Borodin, head of the administration of affairs, for several billion rubles to maintain existing wildlife and introduce some new species! At least he was imaginative in his request! Had he received the resources few believe the wildlife would have benefited.

The most controversial agency was the presidential security service (SBP), headed by former KGB General Aleksandr Korzhakov. Unlike the other security agencies it did not owe its birth to the KGB. Instead, Boris set it up specially for his long time friend. Korzhakov had been Yeltsin's security guard when he had been party boss in Sverdlovsk oblast; he followed Yeltsin to Moscow when Boris was recruited by Mikhail Gorbachev. When his boss was sacked Korzhakov decided to stay with him. He was in the White House during the attempted August coup.

Boris was very indulgent to his friend and allowed him to build up his own empire. Eventually he had over 1500 armed men under his command. He even had aides who doubled as the presidential photographer and the presidential chef. In July 1995, he managed to bring Barsukov's GUO under his supervision. Korzhakov was no ordinary policeman. His ambitions reached into every nook and cranny of Russian life. In order to have his own sources of information he set up an analytical centre which had specialists in political, economic and social policy. The centre was headed by General Georgy Rogozin who had spent part of his career in military intelligence. Again he was no ordinary general. He had a great interest in telepathy and the abnormal – he was clearly in his element in the Kremlin – and sought to help the President to sleep better. His bed was aligned on a north–south axis. The general also introduced a faith healer who promised Boris eternal life. The President could be hoodwinked but not to that extent.

According to Korzhakov, the President told him and Mikhail Barsukov to take Vladimir Gusinsky down a peg, having been irked by persistent criticism in Gusinsky's media. Then there was the stingingly accurate reporting on the Chechen war. More irritatingly, wife Naina and daughter Tatyana had complained to him on numerous occasions that their cars had been held up at road blocks to allow Gusinsky's entourage through. Yury Luzhkov and Gusinsky had struck up a relationship and the Moscow mayor was even thinking of running for the Kremlin. This alarmed the Yeltsin camp and Korzhakov warned

Luzhkov twice to break with Gusinsky. Korzhakov's deputy asked Gusinsky for some compromising material (kompromat) on Luzhkov – his bank accounts, for instance. Gusinsky stonewalled.

The next day, 2 December 1994, three cars, one of them the personal car of Barsukov, full of heavily armed masked men, followed Gusinsky from his dacha to his Media-Most office in Moscow. His security staff identified the pursuers as Korzhakov's men. A very nervous Gusinsky decided to make use of his security contacts and informed Evgeny Savostyanov, Moscow head of the FSK [later the FSB], that there were armed men outside his office which was a stone's throw from the White House. When the FSK officers arrived a fight broke out. One of Korzhakov's men was flattened by a right cross from an FSK female. Suddenly one of the FSK men recognised one of the others. The FSK apologised and left with their tails between their legs. Gusinsky, fearing retribution from Korzhakov, called Russian and foreign journalists to the scene. Korzhakov sent more men and they beat up the Media-Most guards. The press witnessed the violence and understood that this was a clan fight. Korzhakov managed to get Viktor Erin, the MVD head, to send militiamen to arrest the beaten-up guards but they were released soon afterwards. The presence of the press may have saved Gusinsky's life. 'I am on a goose chase', Korzhakov commented the following day. This was a play on Gusinsky's name: *gus* means goose in Russian. Gusinsky feared for his family's safety and sent them to London; on 18 December 1994, he decided it was more advisable to join them and they took up residence in Chelsea. Gusinsky had had to leave town even though he had probably the largest private security service in Moscow. Estimated at over a thousand, it was headed by General Filip Bobkov, a former deputy head of the KGB. Replete with former KGB officers, it was skilled at providing intelligence on political and business rivals. When Korzhakov fell from grace Gusinsky moved back.

Even though he had not got his goose, Korzhakov went from strength to strength. He even instructed Chernomyrdin how to negotiate a multi-million dollar loan from the World Bank. He was one of the first, in April 1996, to call for postponement of presidential elections as he feared the consequences of defeat for Yeltsin. In June 1996, Chubais managed to frame Korzhakov and the President removed him together with Barsukov and Soskovets.

OTHER ADVISORY AGENCIES

Yeltsin inherited from Gorbachev a presidential council, its members being mainly reformers and scholars, but the President consulted it little (Huskey 1999: 81). Several members resigned over the Chechen war and soon afterwards it was dissolved. There was a host of commissions, ranging from relations with religious groups, women to demography. Handled correctly or rather incorrectly a commission could enrich its members. One of the prime examples was the commission for physical culture and sport, headed by Boris's tennis coach, Shamil Tarpishchev. He managed to get the national sports foundation a national monopoly for the import of alcohol and tobacco into Russia duty free. Ostensibly this was to finance the training of Russian sportsmen and women. *Izvestiya* calculated that the import of vodka duty free was costing the government alone $200 million dollars a month in 1995.

One commission which caused Boris endless headaches was that on human rights, headed by the veteran campaigner Sergei Kovalev. It had been under the Supreme Soviet but when it was dissolved, in late 1993, the commission migrated to the President's personal apparatus. He was a constant critic of the corruption of the regime and the war in Chechnya. He resigned in early 1996. Human rights' monitoring then again became the responsibility of parliament.

GOVERNMENT

To say that the function of government in Russia is to run the economy would be too simple. Nothing as simple as that is true about Russia. The government in Russia is different from its counterparts in the west (Huskey 1999: chapter 4). The President chooses his Prime Minister and parliament confirms him in office. This is to underline that the Prime Minister is the President's man and not the choice of parliament. Government ministers are chosen by the Prime Minister in consultation with the President but they are not confirmed in office by parliament. Hence the President can sack and appoint ministers as he thinks fit. Whereas the personal staff of a British Prime Minister may be less than two hundred officials, the Russian Prime Minister has over a thousand to help him. One of the reasons for not following the US model and dispensing with the Prime Minister was that Yeltsin saw himself as above-party and hence as the President of all the people. This led him to reject the notion of a presidential party which he would head. Also he did not want to be responsible for day-to-day administration of the state. In a period of great change he wanted to detach himself from responsibility for failure. If things went badly he could blame his officials and when necessary sack them. Members of the government may not sit in parliament or local assemblies. Here Russia follows the French practice.

The government is made up of ministries and state committees and the number varies from time to time. In the late 1980s there were over one hundred ministries and state committees. There were periodic reorganisations aimed at reducing the number and making the system more efficient. These reforms were more apparent than real. If a ministry were abolished its duties and staff were transferred to another ministry where it became a department. At a later date the ministry could reappear. Soviet ministries never had the full complement of staff so that when they were ordered to downsize they could do so by eliminating those positions which were not filled. This bureaucratic practice was carried over into the Yeltsin era. The President ordered the downsizing of the government and personnel and it was carried out. In reality very little changed. For instance, in 1992 the ministries of finance and economics were merged but shortly afterwards reappeared as separate ministries. The same applied to the ministries of foreign affairs and foreign economic relations. The practice of cabinet or collective responsibility has not developed in Russia. This is because the Prime Minister has never been the top official in the state.

Yeltsin found that he had a small pool of competent pro-reform ministers to choose from. Democrats were often academics or political activists with little technical and managerial expertise. The communist practice had been to promote from within a ministry and this led to the accumulation of considerable expertise; the drawback was that the minister had little grasp of other areas of government policy.

Until the 1993 constitution parliament had the power to appoint ministers and also the chair of the Central Bank. Yeltsin, in order to appoint the reform economic ministers he favoured had to concede more conservative appointments in less sensitive areas. In the first Duma there was an anti-Yeltsin majority so the President had to haggle to reduce tension. It became the practice to appoint an Agrarian Party member as minister of agriculture. Hence the same government could have ministers who favoured private ownership of land and those who did not. The minister for agriculture represented the agrarian lobby and its task was to secure the highest possible subsidies for the rural sector. In technical ministries it was normal to appoint a minister from within the ministry. Attempts were made in the immediate post-1992 period to break up the gas and oil monopolies but Yeltsin succumbed to intense pressure by the energy lobby. Their men took over. Democratic ministers were no match for the bureaucratic apparatus and found that their writ did not extend far in their ministries. Officials, inherited from the communist period, were very skilled at blocking initiatives.

Concessions wrung out of Yeltsin by parliament in 1992 saw several industrial ministers join the government. Their loyalty was to their own constituencies and not to the Prime Minister, parliament or the President.
Throughout the Yeltsin era both he and the Prime Minister often vented
their frustration on ministers who neglected to implement government
policy. One tactic was for a minister to send a deputy and avoid personal responsibility. This was so widespread among economic ministers
that Chernomyrdin actually requested a written explanation for non-
appearance. Another problem for the Prime Minister is that he does not
deal directly with ministers. There is a layer of first deputy and deputy
Prime Ministers who are responsible for a sector of the economy. One
of these may also be a minister. Hence a first deputy Prime Minister
can also be minister of finance. The loyalties of these first deputies and
deputies vary from official to official. When Anatoly Chubais was in government his first loyalty was to the President. When Viktor Ilyushin joined
the government, in 1996, he likewise looked to the President. It was
common for the Prime Minister and minister of economics to have
differing views on economics. Some deputy Prime Ministers represented
industrial lobbies and placed these ahead of loyalty to the Prime Minister.
In 1997, there were nine first deputy and deputy Prime Ministers.
Coordinating policy and implementing it became virtually impossible
– just getting them together was quite a feat of organisation. There was
a presidium of key ministers but it does not appear to have been very
effective.

First and deputy Prime Ministers have their own support staff but these
are quite modest, from twenty to fifty officials. The main government
bureaucracy is the secretariat which has over twenty departments, each
with up to fifty officials, but, in addition, many technical and support
staff. The divisions of the secretariat mirror those in the presidential
administration: finance, legal, relations with regions, justice and so on.
In economic affairs the two institutions do not shadow one another.
Whereas in the presidential administration there is one main economic
section, in the government secretariat there are several which represent
the various sectors of the economy: transport, construction, the defence
industry, for example. This practice was inherited from the Soviet
government.

The government secretariat is at the disposal of the first and deputy Prime
Ministers in supervising the ministries under their aegis. However these
ministers come and go so the primary loyalty of the secretariat is to its
head. He is appointed by the Prime Minister and prepares the agenda
of government and presidium meetings. From early 1993 to late 1995,

Vladimir Kvasov was head of the secretariat. He had worked for about a decade with Chernomyrdin in the gas industry. He was succeeded by Vladimir Babichev who also came from the gas industry. The head of the secretariat can influence which topics are discussed and which documents are enclosed with the agenda. This promotes tension between him and the various first and deputy Prime Ministers. When Chubais rejoined the government, in March 1997, he was determined to turf Babichev out. However Chernomyrdin refused to sacrifice his man and a compromise was worked out. Chubais's man, Sergei Vasilev, was made Babichev's deputy. Primakov brought in Admiral Yury Zubakov as head of the secretariat. In 1989 Zubakov began working for Primakov who was then speaker of the Soviet of the Union. Zubakov graduated from the KGB higher school.

The number of civil servants employed by the federal agencies and local administrations has grown inexorably. In 1994, 1,004,000 officials were employed but this had risen to 1,133,000 in 1999. This does not include those working in the ministry of defence, ministry of internal affairs and other law enforcement and state security departments. In 1994, 514,500 persons were employed in regional and local administrations but this number grew to 593,700 in 1999; this at a time when the declared policy of the Russian government was to reduce the number of officials. The normal procedure when numbers have to be reduced at the centre is to find them a niche at the local level. In fact there are more officials at the local level than are recorded in the statistics. This is because many shell companies have been set up by local administrations and those supposedly employed in them are on the payroll. An opinion poll in 1999 found that 30 per cent of businessmen regularly bribe local officials to expedite affairs. About 500,000 officials were recruited according to the civil service law. Each had to have a university degree. However about 150,000 of them did not, with another 10,000 not having even completed secondary school.

Argumenty i Fakty (no. 23, 2000) expands on the above, giving the total number of officials or civil servants, in 1985, as 1,204,000 rising to 1,602,000 in 1990. Gorbachev clearly lost the battle to cut back on bureaucrats. In 1995, the number had increased to 1,893,000 and, in 1998, to 2,777,000. This represents a truly phenomenal 70 per cent increase over the years 1990–98.

This massive executive branch was a terrible burden during a period of economic decline. The transition to a market economy was an excuse to increase the number of officials. Apparently the number of civil servants in the Russian ministry of agriculture in 1992 was over two thousand, two and a half times the number of the USSR ministry of agriculture. One of the attractions of the ministry of agriculture was that it had one of the best subsidised restaurants in Moscow! After all, if the ministry of agriculture could not procure choice food who could? One wheeze to find new jobs for old functionaries was to set up committees to supervise the transition to a market economy. For instance, Yury Petrov, in 1992, became head of a state investment fund which had a budget of $100 million of venture capital to invest in promising companies. By 1995, the government had set up over sixty such agencies, with appropriate budgets, to assist fledgling entrepreneurs. Strange to relate, government inspectors could not identify one company which had benefited from government largesse. Needless to say the budgets had been spent!

Many ministers were in the government but were not subordinate to the Prime Minister. These were mainly the power ministries. They were defence, emergency situations, internal affairs, foreign affairs, border troops, counterintelligence (FSK), protection, railway troops, federal security service (FSB) and government communications (FAPSI). They were answerable directly to the President. Gaidar called them presidential ministers. However they were subject to the government in one important area, finance. Their budgets were allocated by the government. This underlines the fact that the key ministry is finance. All funds flow through the ministry and new projects have to be assessed by it. Its officials are an elite and are paid accordingly. The ministry of finance is responsible for the whole of Russia as is the ministry of economics. The latter emerged from the collapse of the Soviet Union unscathed. Originally it was the state planning commission (Gosplan) but, in 1991, it was renamed the ministry for forecasting. Under Yeltsin it became the ministry for economics. An important new economic committee was the state property committee, GKI [*goskomimushchestvo*] (now a ministry), which was set up to provide a vehicle for privatisation. It was Chubais's base and he recruited like-minded economists. This was in marked contrast to the ministries of finance and the economy which had a thin layer of radicals at the top and a thick layer of traditional officials.

There are various government committees and they can become so influential that they can circumvent the Prime Minister on certain issues. One of these is the committee for operational questions, which in 1999, was chaired by Nikolai Aksenenko. An influential member of the insider Yeltsin group, called the family, he rose to be first deputy Prime Minister and was even seen as a future Prime Minister. However he was later demoted to the post of minister of railways but still chaired the committee. He was even able to act over Vladimir Putin's head. During a visit by Putin to New Zealand, in September 1999, Aksenenko replaced the head of Transneft, the monopoly operator of Russia's oil pipelines. The sitting boss was evicted by armed police and replaced by, reportedly, an associate of Roman Abramovich, who, in turn, is associated with Boris Berezovsky. When questioned about the incident the Prime Minister just shrugged his shoulders. Aksenenko remained minister of railways in President Putin's first government, appointed in May 2000.

6

COLONELS AND SPIES: DEFENCE, INTERNAL AFFAIRS AND THE SECURITY FORCES

THE MILITARY

IN AUGUST 1991, MARSHAL EVGENY SHAPOSHNIKOV, commander of the Soviet air force, was rewarded for his opposition to the attempted coup by being named Soviet minister of defence. Gorbachev made the announcement but the choice had been made by Yeltsin. Shaposhnikov swore an oath of loyalty to President Gorbachev. Shaposhnikov had been one of the only two high-ranking officers, the other being Pavel Grachev, openly to oppose the move by Kryuchkov and the others. They had included Dmitry Yazov, Soviet minister of defence. Shaposhnikov committed treason by refusing to obey the orders of his superior in August. He again committed treason, in December 1991, when he countersigned the Minsk agreement ending the Soviet Union. By this act he signed the Soviet armed forces into oblivion. His reward was to be named commander in chief of Commonwealth of Independent States (CIS) joint forces. Yeltsin had chosen well. Shaposhnikov was to prove quite incapable intellectually of coping with the momentous changes which were under way. Just what were the CIS forces? Were they to be Russia's armed forces masquerading under an international name? What use would Russia make of these soldiers in the other states of the former Soviet Union? Shaposhnikov did not know. What he did know was that he wanted to sack many officers in the ministry of defence and in the high command. One of the first to go was Vladimir Lobov, chief of the general staff, and intellectually vastly superior to Shaposhnikov. He was replaced by General Viktor Samsonov, commander of the Leningrad military district. Samsonov had ignored orders from the coup plotters to impose martial law in Leningrad and had struck a deal with Anatoly Sobchak to keep the troops in their barracks. Samsonov was not as intellectually imposing as Lobov and was more democratically minded. The pill had to be sweetened for senior military officers who were no longer needed. There were also those whose loyalty had to be bought. The simple solution was to give them dachas in the hope that they would not join any conspiracy.

Yeltsin did not want to begin setting up a separate Russian army and saw the CIS forces as a useful short-term solution. Over 80 per cent of officers were Russian and this fact disturbed many of the newly independent states. They harboured suspicions that these forces could be used to advance Russian interests. Russia did not want other states to establish their own armed forces. However Ukraine, Azerbaijan and Moldova declared immediately that this was precisely their objective. Only the Central Asian states supported Russia since they lacked the resources to set up their own forces and it provided them with security on the cheap.

Russian hopes lasted until May 1992, when a meeting was arranged in Tashkent to flesh out the bones of the military organisation. Ukraine and Moldova did not turn up and Azerbaijan and Armenia were battling it out in Nagorno-Karabakh. The joint forces were still born and it was clear that all states would have to set up their own forces. The joint forces' command still had a useful function: to supervise the destruction and transfer of nuclear weapons. There were four nuclear states: Russia, Ukraine, Belarus and Kazakhstan. The joint forces met again, in July, at Tashkent and agreed on peacekeeping forces but by then the Russians had already set up their own ministry of defence. This new institution competed with Shaposhnikov and it proved stronger. Russia was concerned about national forces whereas Shaposhnikov thought in terms of multi-national forces. On 15 June 1993, the joint command was phased out and replaced by a council of CIS defence ministers. Shaposhnikov, who had risked all for Yeltsin twice, was redundant. Boris wanted him as secretary of the Security Council but he was pushed out of this job as well, in August 1993. The joint command did have a useful legacy. It gradually transformed itself into a forum for CIS leaders to discuss political, economic and security matters.

THE RUSSIAN MINISTRY OF DEFENCE

When the ministry of defence was set up, in May 1992, formed mainly from the Soviet ministry of defence, Yeltsin cast around for another Shaposhnikov to be his minister of defence. Suggestions ranged from seasoned soldiers to Galina Starovoitova, a specialist on ethnic relations, and Andrei Kokoshin, the leading civilian specialist on arms control and military doctrine. No decision could be taken and Yeltsin declared himself his own minister of defence. On 7 May, he ordered the establishment of a Russian army with himself as commander in chief. On 18 May, he chose General Pavel Grachev as his minister of defence. He had been commander of the Soviet paratroop forces and was a brave, young officer. From Yeltsin's point of view he had another priceless asset: he possessed no political base. Indeed he was to prove himself a very poor politician. What he was good at, indeed he became a past master, was corruption. Under his leadership, or rather lack of leadership, the military descended into petty and grand thieving. Grachev just laid his hands on what he wanted (of course, he always paid a nominal sum) as did almost all his officers. Morale plummeted and the great Russian military became a ragtag army. This suited Boris very well since such an organisation was incapable of seizing power in Russia. He knew his minister of defence would always do his bidding.

Andrei Kokoshin became first deputy minister of defence and set out to reform the army and turn part of the bloated military industry over to civilian use. The military ganged up on him and he achieved little. Grachev immediately brought in his own men. They had all seen service in Afghanistan. Grachev himself had earned the title Hero of the Soviet Union – no mean feat – for his five years there as commander of paratroop forces. This brotherhood was known as the *afgantsy*. One of the first deputy ministers of defence was General Boris Gromov, the last Soviet soldier to leave Afghanistan in 1989. One of Gromov's previous jobs had been deputy Soviet minister of the interior. Boris Pugo, the hardline minister, picked him, in December 1990. Gromov was no angel.

The Soviet military had concluded that the country could no longer support a military force of over four million. Glasnost had resulted in a decline of respect for the military as abuses such as *dedovshchina* (bullying by older soldiers of conscripts) were exposed. Two thirds of soldiers were conscripts and the military call-up became more and more unpopular under Gorbachev. The role of the military in the Tbilisi massacre, in Baku and Vilnius and in the unsuccessful coup promoted the view that the military should stay out of politics. A professional army

The NCO sees these conscripts as lambs for slaughtering. They see him as the devil incarnate. Created by Igor Revyakin.

was another goal. The Conventional Forces in Europe treaty (CFE), signed in Paris, on 19 November 1990, was ratified by the Russian Supreme Soviet, on 8 July 1992. It stated that the Russian army and navy had to contract from 2.8 million to 2.1 million by 1995. The Russian ministry of defence went further and pointed to 1.5 million as the target by the end of 1995. In 1998, the Russian armed forces were to be reduced from the existing 2.3 million to 1.8 million in 2000 (Table 6.1).

The law on defence, in September 1992, imposed strict control over the military. It, in turn, promised to maintain Russia's position as a great power.

RUSSIAN MILITARY DOCTRINE

Armed forces require a military doctrine to act as a compass in a rapidly changing world. Gorbachev's new military doctrine, in 1990, spoke of defensive defence and reasonable sufficiency. In 1992, the Russian ministry of defence presented its new doctrine and it was, on paper, more aggressive than Gorbachev's. It proposed that the CIS be kept as a military alliance with Russian security needs taking precedence (this was quite similar to the old Warsaw Pact); a threat could emanate from anywhere and this required Russia to maintain large, mobile, forces outside its borders; a nuclear first strike was advisable under certain circumstances (Gorbachev had committed the Soviet Union to no first use); the military not only had the right but the duty to defend Russians living outside Russia; the unstable nature of the CIS meant that low intensity operations (limited military operations, anti-guerrilla campaigns) had to be envisaged. If the military played up the threats from abroad, the President played them down. He assured everyone who would listen that Russia did not consider any state or coalition of states its enemy. Russia would promote the emergence of friendly states on its borders. In December 1992, the Security Council passed the ministry's draft and emphasised the future role of the military in anti-guerrilla conflicts and the protection of Russia's borders. All this led to a rethink about the downsizing of the military. Grachev began talking about 2.1 million being the target, not 1.5 million. The tasks of the military now ranged from low intensity conflict to conventional warfare from eastern Europe to the Pacific and from the Arctic to Transcaucasia. The decision was taken to divide the military into elite mobile forces and strategic reserves. The mobile forces were further subdivided into immediate rapid reaction forces (paratroops and marines reaching their target in 24 hours) and rapid deployment forces to arrive a further 48 hours later. The mobile forces consisted of various brigades which could be brought together quickly from different parts of the country (Bowker and Cameron 2000: Chapter 12; Sakwa 1993: chapter 15).

In February 1993 the actual strength of the armed forces was 1.8 million plus 1.7 million civilian personnel. In January 1996, it was 1.5 million plus 600,000 civilian personnel. In November 2000, the actual strength was 1.2 million and a target of 850,000 was set for 2003. In 2001 this was amended to 1 million by 2006.

RETREAT

The most painful retreat for the Soviet Army was abandoning the German Democratic Republic (GDR). Mikhail Gorbachev and the German chancellor Helmut Kohl did a deal which provided compensation for the withdrawal. Over the period 1989–91 West Germany provided over $33 billion in aid but almost all or perhaps all was embezzled. Part of the compensation fund was to build accommodation for the returnees. There were 375,000 troops, in October 1990, when Germany reunified and they were known as the western group of forces. After unification (October 1990) officers and NCOs were paid in Deutschmarks and suddenly discovered the temptations of capitalism. Units began to buy up German goods and ship them to Russia for resale. An astute officer could become rich in one or two years. Ordinary soldiers sold everything they stood up in. They also sold on petrol, diesel and anything the Germans would buy. Not surprisingly many tried to desert and stay in Germany but the Germans were keen they return to Russia. Tales abounded of officers offering rocket launchers and armoured vehicles to passers-by. MiG fighter planes could also be acquired. The commander of the western group of forces, General Matvei Burlakov, acquired a legendary reputation for selling off anything that belonged to the Russian state. Such behaviour could not have continued had it not been for collusion with the ministry of defence in Moscow. General Pavel Grachev and the top officials enriched themselves rapidly as they realised that this was a once-in-a-lifetime opportunity. Burlakov presented Grachev's son with a Mercedes as a wedding present and the press began calling Grachev, Pasha Mercedes. There were plenty of takers for the equipment. Libya and Iraq were very keen and Moscow supplied tanks to both Serbia and Croatia during the Yugoslav civil war.

All good things come to an end and Russians troops finally left on 31 August 1994, in a grand ceremony in Berlin. The occasion was made memorable by President Yeltsin seizing the baton from the conductor of a German band and engaging in ex tempore conducting himself. Boris also gave a rendering of Kalinka and an exhibition of Russian folk dancing. It was a mournful day for many Russians who had regarded occupying East Germany as their prize for winning the war.

The Russians retreated not only from Germany but from the rest of eastern Europe and parts of the former Soviet Union. By June 1991, they had left Hungary and Czechoslovakia and, in October 1992, most were out of Poland as well. Withdrawing from the Baltic States was another matter. It was a strategically important region and there was nowhere for the troops to go if they returned to Russia. In late 1991, there were about 25,000 troops in Estonia, 60,000 in Latvia and 40,000 in Lithuania. As the Russians prevaricated, the number of troops declined as conscripts completed their national service. At the end of 1992 there were still about 50,000 troops in the region. The good offices of the US were used by the Baltic governments and eventually this pressure paid off. On 31 August

1994, the last Russian troops left Lithuania and closed a chapter in the region which had begun in 1940.

Most officers and their families lived in miserable circumstances on their return from abroad. Ordinary soldiers were even worse off. This led to a rapid decline in discipline and military equipment was 'privatised' and sold off. Deserters formed armed bands and became hit men for mafia groups. Officers with technical skills left for the private sector. Moscow was aware that leaving Azerbaijan, Armenia and Georgia would undermine Russian security in the south with unpredictable consequences. Nevertheless the ill feeling engendered by the Tbilisi and Baku massacres heightened demands for the Russians to go home. Troops left Azerbaijan and Nagorno-Karabakh but they also left their matériel which, in turn, fuelled the war over Nagorno-Karabakh (an estimated 35,000 had died in the conflict by 2001). The situation in Georgia was more complex as Abkhazia and South Ossetia wished to secede and join the Russian Federation. Civil war in Georgia made it easier for the Russians to stay. In 1997, the Russians had a headquarters in Tbilisi and four major military bases in Georgia. In Abkhazia, there was a Russian contingent under CIS aegis. There was one base in Armenia but none in Azerbaijan. Russian forces stayed on in Tajikistan after the civil war began. The concern that the Taliban, who controlled over 80 per cent of Afghanistan, would attempt to invade Tajikistan and other states in Central Asia led to a CIS peace-keeping force being based in the republic. In 1997, a Russian brigade remained in Moldova and a joint Russian-Moldovan peace-keeping force has been deployed since July 1992. In the Balkans, Russian troops have contributed to peace-keeping in Croatia, Bosnia and Kosovo. One of the advantages of the union of Russia and Belarus for the Russian military is that troops and equipment can be based there. Belarus borders on Poland which is now a NATO member.

TRANSDNIESTRIA

One of the lessons Yeltsin learned during the defence of the White House, in August 1991, was the significance of airborne troops. Soviet army units could become part of the armed forces of the new republics but this did not apply to airborne troops. They were of strategic significance and therefore had to remain under CIS command. Lebed had gone over to Yeltsin's side outside the White House and was appointed the Russian representative in negotiations over the future of airborne units. He was part of the ministry of defence team which had to negotiate with each new republic. The republics regarded everything on their territory as belonging to them. After all Yeltsin had encouraged them to take as much sovereignty as they wanted. For Lebed the most difficult negotiations were in Chisinau, the capital of Moldova.

Grachev, the corruptible, and Lebed, the incorruptible, naturally did not see eye to eye. Lebed thought that an officer's dignity should not be besmirched by engaging in commercial dealings. When Lebed failed to become commander of airborne troops, Grachev had to find another position for him away from Moscow. He was becoming too popular with the military command. Moldova presented such an opportunity. Russians and Gagauz felt threatened by Moldovan nationalism and, in August 1991, declared their regions independent of Moldova. The Russians, on the eastern bank of the Dniester, established the Dniester Moldovan republic.

Fighting began and the Russian 14th army gradually became enmeshed in the conflict. It became apparent that the 14th army might suffer defeat, but even more catastrophic was the possibility that huge arms dumps would fall into the hands of the Moldovans. Grachev may have thought that sending Lebed to Moldova was like throwing him into an Irish bog. Lebed immediately launched a ferocious artillery barrage on the advancing Moldovan forces. This broke their will to advance and the way was open for negotiations. He began to act independently and addressed Yeltsin over the head of Grachev. He negotiated a ceasefire on his terms, in July 1992, and Yeltsin was pleased. This was the first occasion that Russians in the new republics, or near abroad, had been defended by Russian arms. It suited Boris that Grachev and Lebed were behaving like fighting cocks. Lebed began thinking of a political career and stood for election to the supreme soviet of Transdniestria in the autumn of 1992. He won easily. However he soon discovered that politics can be a dirty business and this disillusioned him.

Transdniestria sent some men to participate in the attack on the White House, in October 1993, and Lebed was disgusted when participation in the conflict was denied in parliament. He resigned his mandate as a deputy. He was also appalled by the corruption of the local President and his government. They began to campaign for Lebed's removal. In August 1994, Grachev thought he had hit on the solution. He downgraded the 14th army to a division which meant it could be commanded by a more junior officer than Lebed. The general was on leave but did not return immediately. He made for Rostov on Don and was feted by the local Cossack units. The message was clear. When he returned to Transdnietsria he declared that war was possibly imminent and that withdrawing or downsizing the 14th army would be irresponsible. Grachev drew back and changed tack. He offered Grachev the command of Russian troops in Tajikistan but the general declined.

After returning from Germany, General Burlakov was made a deputy minister of defence. This infuriated Lebed who stated he would not allow Burlakov to inspect his troops. 'We do not welcome thieves here', he declared. Grachev eventually had to let Burlakov go, in November 1994, because of the relentless press campaign against him. Lebed cheekily said that Grachev should resign as well in order to protect the honour of the army. On 17 October 1994, an investigative journalist, Dmitry Kholodov, was killed by a bomb in a package of documents he was examining. He had specialised in corruption in the western group of forces. It was assumed that the military were behind the killing. Corruption had now escalated into murder.

THE FIRST CHECHEN WAR, 1994–96

President Dzhokhar Dudaev, from late 1991 until the outbreak of the first Chechen war in December 1994, ruled by provoking confrontation. The economy was in ruins and unemployment was over 50 per cent. Robber clans appropriated some of what was produced and Dudaev's people the rest. Dudaev had been loyal to Yeltsin – he was the airforce commander in Estonia which made it possible for the Russian President to land there after the killings in Vilnius, in January 1991. Why did Yeltsin not invite Dudaev to discuss the future of Russian–Chechen relations?

A 'party of war' began to emerge in Moscow. This consisted of Aleksandr Korzhakov, Mikhail Barsukov, Sergei Stepashin, director of the federal counter-intelligence service (FSK) (later to be the FSB), Viktor Erin, minister of internal affairs, and Nikolai Egorov, Yeltsin's special representative in Chechnya, and a Cossack who favoured strong Russian control in the north Caucasus (Grachev, *Trud*, 15 March 2001, identified him as the first to suggest sending troops to Chechnya). They pursued their own private and institutional interests. Grachev, the minister of defence, was aware that the general staff thought that a Chechen campaign would be difficult. Russia had two options: either use force or accept de facto independence for Chechnya. On the academic side, in the Academy of Sciences, the advice was that military force in the Caucasus would fail. At the Security Council meeting which decided on intervention, Grachev opposed the deployment of troops in winter, recommending they be sent in spring; thereupon Chernomyrdin accused him of

MAP 2: The Caucasus Region.

cowardice and demanded he be sacked. After the meeting Yeltsin gave Grachev ten days to prepare a plan for sending troops.

Russia provided the Chechen opposition with troops and matériel but Dudaev's forces always proved too strong. Some Russian officials thought of a successful, little war. It might do the trick in time for the Duma elections in December 1995 and the presidential elections in June 1996.

There was another lobby which needed a war: the general staff. The military budget was being cut remorselessly and the only way to reverse this trend was a short, successful war. The military and the other power ministries managed to ensure that a meeting on 25 August 1994, chaired by Sergei Filatov, took the decision to remove Dudaev by force. This overturned a statement by Filatov earlier in the month that force would not be used in Chechnya. The military were aware that Dudaev was well armed. After all they had sold him the weapons in a series of unofficial deals.

Dudaev's forces captured Russian military officers and men during an attempted coup on 26 November 1994. The plan had been for the units to take Grozny, set up a pro-Russian government and then invite Russian troops into Chechnya. Yeltsin demanded, in an ultimatum on 28 November, that Dudaev disband his forces. Then he decreed that the Chechens had to lay down their arms by 15 December. This diktat rallied all Chechens around Dudaev. Chechens could fight one another but when the main enemy Russia appeared they united against it. Dudaev for the first time became the Chechen national leader. General Grachev came out with the remark that Grozny, the Chechen capital, could be taken by one airborne assault regiment in two hours.

Air strikes against targets in Chechnya began on 2 December, revealing that Yeltsin had already decided on war. The war began on 11 December 1994 and ended on 31 August 1996. It resulted in the first military defeat of the new Russia. This was extremely painful for Moscow. Egorov, earlier in 1994, when told of the difficulties which might result from armed action, asked: 'Are you saying our tanks cannot beat a load of shepherds?' He clearly did not accept, nor indeed did any of the members of the party of war, that the answer could be yes. A major factor, not then clear, was that the once feared Soviet Army had just about disintegrated.

From the planning stage many senior military officers did not wish to become involved in Chechnya. They remembered Baku, Tbilisi and Vilnius and wished to stay out of political-military operations. They argued that the military were responsible for the external security of the Russian Federation. The ministry of internal affairs, which had its own troops, and other domestic agencies were responsible for security within the Russian Federation. Colonel General Eduard Vorobev, first deputy commander of ground forces, chose to resign rather than become involved in the coming bloodbath. Meticulous military preparations, the hallmark of the Soviet Army, were absent. Troops were not trained in urban or mountain warfare. There was no effective overall commander. Each service attempted to control its own men and to ensure that as few of them died as possible. The Chechens were quickly seen as almost superhuman. Aerial assault followed by artillery bombardment was necessary before infantry would advance.

On the day the assault was launched the President performed one of his disappearing acts. He went to hospital for a minor nose operation.

This was an ominous sign that the President was attempting to evade responsibility for the war.

At 0700 hours on 11 December 1994, about 40,000 troops began moving towards Chechnya. The goal was to surround Grozny. However the troops were soon caught up in civilian traffic on their way to market. The locals sat down in front of the tanks. It soon emerged that the Russian commanders had no contingency plans to cope with civilian protests. The advance had been launched in the middle of winter; many young drivers could not keep their vehicles on the icy roads. By the time they got to Grozny there were about 15,000 Chechen fighters waiting for them. A major offensive was launched on 31 December 1994 but at least 2000 Russian troops died. There were stories of starving dogs eating decomposing bodies in the streets.

The Russian public turned violently against the war. The presidential palace was only taken on 19 January 1995 and Grozny, as late as 22 February 1995, was declared cleared of Chechen fighters. During the period 11 December 1994 to 1 December 1995, the Russians lost 2034 dead and 7172 wounded (Blandy 1996: 12). The main reason for such high casualties was lack of combat readiness. Sergei Stepashin's FSK recruited mercenaries from prisons and penal institutions. Those who volunteered were promised shorter sentences. The mercenaries were absolutely ruthless and did not distinguish between Chechen fighters and civilians. Chechens treated captured Russians as prisoners of war but they simply shot mercenaries on the spot.

The Chechens scored six military victories: (1) the rout of columns advancing on Grozny in December 1994–January 1995; (2) the seizure by Basaev of the hospital in Budennovsk in June 1995; (3) a similar operation by Salman Raduev in Kizlyar and the breakout from the siege of Pervomaiskoe in January 1996; (4) the ambush and rout of a column of the 245 motor rifle regiment in April 1996; (5) the storming of Grozny in March 1996; and (6) the storming of Grozny in August 1996 (Blandy 1996: 22).

The taking of Grozny was the main objective. The pacification of the countryside and the elimination of 'bandit' or guerrilla formations were the others. Villages were bombed if guerrillas were suspected of being harboured there, irrespective of civilian casualties. A ceasefire was arranged in the summer of 1995 but bitter fighting broke out again in December 1995 as the war entered its decisive phase. The Russians achieved their objective of killing Dudaev, in April 1996, in a rocket attack on a village just outside Grozny. Apparently he was on a mobile phone speaking to King Hassan of Morocco who was acting as a peace negotiator. A Russian fighter locked on to the signal and fired rockets, instantly killing him. It was ironic that he was killed while discussing peace. Zelimkhan Yanderbiev was appointed to succeed him.

There were three main factors which made it extremely difficult for the Russians to win. Firstly, the Russians pursued a dual policy of force and the promise of negotiations. The military were never given free rein to pursue the war. Secondly the Chechens, when facing defeat, diverted attention by attacking soft targets outside Chechnya: Budennovsk in Stavropol krai, and Kizlyar and Pervomaiskoe in Dagestan. Thirdly, and perhaps most important of all, the war was not popular at home, especially among mothers whose young sons were being sent to their deaths. In sharp contrast to the second Chechen war, Moscow never convinced a majority of Russians that the war was necessary.

On 6 July 1996, General Vyacheslav Tikhomirov issued an ultimatum. He demanded that the Chechens surrender and referred to Zelimkhan Yanderbiev, the Chechen leader, as a bandit. The man behind the decision was Aleksandr Lebed, secretary of the Security Council. He was aiming for a quick kill. However Russian forces were not strong enough and fierce fighting spread to Grozny. In August, over 1500 persons were killed and many more injured. The Russians threatened to bomb the Chechen capital to the ground but at the last moment Lebed called off the assault. On 10 August, he became the President's representative in Chechnya and, on 14 August, was commander of all federal forces there. He ignored the President's order to take Grozny and began to pursue his own agenda. He removed Doku Zavgaev, Yeltsin's puppet, from the negotiations and began dealing directly with the Chechen military. On 31 August, he signed an agreement with Aslan Maskhadov, the Chechen chief of staff, in Khasavyurt. Federal troops were to leave and the vexed problem of Chechen independence was glossed over by leaving the decision to a referendum in five years' time. Lebed thought that the war had cost about 80,000 lives and 240,000 wounded. It was the costliest since 1945. A wit wryly concluded that the Russian army was so incompetent that it could not even invade Russia.

INTERBELLUM

The Russian military regarded the Khasavyurt accords as the starting point for the return of Chechnya to the Russian Federation. President Maskhadov needed to satisfy the aspirations of a majority of the Chechen population. However he had also to contain the ambitions of an extreme minority who wanted to take the war further. The latter group included Islamic states and organisations supporting Chechnya which were willing to ignore the wishes of the almost 60 per cent of the Chechen people as expressed in the election of Aslan Maskhadov as President on 27 January 1997. Such was the damage to Grozny that only one building was deemed completely safe for the inauguration of President Maskhadov in February 1997. Moscow prevaricated so long after the Khasavyurt accords that it made it virtually impossible for moderate views to prevail in Chechnya. On every occasion the two Presidents who had signed the treaty of 12 May 1997 were scheduled to meet, some violence occurred. This led to President Yeltsin's advisers recommending that the meeting be postponed. There were those in Moscow who believed that the longer Moscow held back the weaker Maskhadov's position would become. His level-headed leadership represented the greatest threat to Russia's ambitions to bring Chechnya back into the Federation. Maskhadov's authority over the various fighting bands diminished over time. There are persistent rumours that Boris Berezovsky had discussions with Shamil Basaev and Movladi Udugov, the goal being to encourage Chechen warlords, in association with Islamic extremists, to invade neighbouring Dagestan. Berezovsky is said to have been acting in association with the FSB and to have paid Basaev one million dollars.

THE SECOND CHECHEN WAR, 1999–

Early in the morning of 2 August 1999, groups of Chechen fighters crossed the border with Dagestan and entered the village of Agvali, in Tsumadinsky raion, to establish Islamic order there. The local militia and villagers forced them to retreat and they took over three other villages. This was followed by Chechen and Islamic fundamentalist fighters, numbering about 2000, led by Shamil Basaev and the Saudi Arabian Emir el Khattab, occupying more villages on 7 and 8 August (Blandy 2000: 4). The area invaded was Avaristan, the land of the Avars. The primary objective was to establish an Islamic republic and the secondary objective was to overthrow the Dagestani government in Makhachkala.

Sergei Stepashin was removed and Vladimir Putin became Prime Minister on 9 August. This changed the situation completely. One of his first innovations was to order the formation of a single data bank on terrorism. Russia established a monopoly over information and restricted journalists to certain areas. The Russians were very concerned to restrict the flow of weapons and funds to the Chechens. They identified three main channels. External Islamic sources ranging from Usama bin Laden to the fifty or so pro-Islamic organisations in the US. Then there are the Russian banks which pay protection money to Chechens, the trade in oil and various illegal rackets. Finally there is drug dealing and income from hostage taking and counterfeit currency. Altogether the Russian ministry of internal affairs calculated that the fighters may have acquired about $4 billion in 1998.

An important move to improve efficiency was the transfer of operations from the ministry of internal affairs to the ministry of defence, on 17 August 1999. The fighters were forced back into Chechnya. Then the bombing of border Chechen villages began and this was extended to Grozny. Also economic targets, such as dams and reservoirs, were also targeted in an attempt to destroy the infrastructure of Chechnya. This operation appeared to have been influenced by the NATO bombing of Serbia. Troops began to encircle Chechnya and the war led to over 200,000 refugees crossing into Ingushetia. All able-bodied males remained in Chechnya. By the middle of December, Grozny had been encircled after the occupation of Gudermes, Argun and other towns and villages. Russian airborne troops had occupied the southern border with Georgia in an effort to cut off supplies to the fighters. The Russian ground troops changed their tactics. They avoided pitched battles and hand to hand combat and concentrated on using overwhelming fire power to destroy enemy groups.

They demonstrated that they had learnt some lessons from the debacle of the first Chechen war. One of the things which had changed was that the Transcaucasian Group of Forces was disbanded, in March 1997, and replaced by the Group of Russian Forces (Transcaucasus). It was subordinated to the North Caucasus military district, with headquarters in Rostov on Don. Various intelligence directorates were moved from Tbilisi, Georgia, also to Rostov on Don. Considerable military matériel was moved from bases in Georgia in line with agreements between Georgia and Russia.

The overwhelming military superiority of the Russian troops gradually ground the Chechens down and they retreated into the southern hills. The war became one of attrition with the Chechens killing about twenty Russians a week. They specialised in ambushing Russian convoys. In late 2000, the Russian military admitted casualties of about 2700 dead and 9000 wounded. Soldiers' rights groups say that the real numbers are about double these. The hopeless position of the Russian military is neatly summed up by one soldier: 'We cannot stay and we cannot leave'.

Why did Russia intervene a second time in Chechnya? The first intervention was a total failure and this rankled with Yeltsin. The President never forgot a humiliation. The most important reason may have been the upcoming Duma elections, in December 1999, and the presidential elections, in June 2000.

In June 2000, Putin signed a decree establishing direct rule from Moscow and this, in effect, means presidential rule. The next step was to put in place a local administration, staffed by Chechens loyal to Moscow. On 12 June 2000, Akhmed Kadyrov was appointed head of the Chechen provisional administration. The Russian military leadership has stated that it intends to station permanently about 25,000 troops in Chechnya. This ensures that the guerrilla war will continue.

HEALTH, DRUG ABUSE AND AIDS IN THE MILITARY

About one Russian citizen in five suffers from cancer in one form or other (Field and Twigg 2000: 272), hence the number of soldiers with cardiovascular diseases and malignant tumours is increasing. Those suffering from tuberculosis have doubled since the mid-1990s. Psychiatric disorders have jumped 30 per cent among soldiers and 19 per cent among officers in the period 1996–98. In 1998, suicides accounted for an astonishing 27 per cent of all military fatalities. Most suicides are among conscripts.

One estimate is that drug abuse in society increased two and a half times between 1993 and 1998. Over the last decade the number of drug-related deaths has grown twelve-fold. Those between 18 and 25 years comprise about 80 per cent of drug addicts and this is the group which is conscripted. Drug abuse has taken over from alcoholic abuse as the primary social problem especially among children. The military state that they do not conscript drug addicts but they do take young men with needle marks on their arms. The increase in drug addiction has led to the growth of Aids (acquired immune deficiency syndrome), the main cause being the sharing of contaminated needles. So far the military do not admit that they have any personnel with Aids. They do admit that there are some who have tested HIV (human immunodeficiency virus) positive. The policy is to discharge a person when Aids manifests itself.

Living standards for military personnel have deteriorated to such an extent that the military are chronically short of young officers, especially those

This conscript is so dumb or stoned that he is using a sign saying mines for shovelling snow! Created by Igor Revyakin.

with technical skills. Officers and men moonlight in order to feed their families. In 1995, a retired Russian admiral gave a group of Latin American drug barons a tour of a secret naval base. The drug barons were looking for a submarine to smuggle cocaine from Mexico to the beaches of California. The admiral was keen to help, at a price. The deal never went through because it ended up in a US court case. According to the court the admiral had offered the drug barons a range of vessels costing from $20 million to $75 million.

Some officers are members of mafia gangs. In 1997, about 18,000 officers were charged with criminal offences. A common practice is to use conscripts to build one's dacha but some officers are more entrepreneurial. They build several dachas and sell them. Building materials are stolen. When soldiers become drug addicts they have to steal to pay for their habit. Crimes by these men have been growing by leaps and bounds.

The diet is poor and there have been cases where soldiers have died of malnutrition. It is now common practice for towns with ships or submarines named after them to supply goods for the sailors on a regular basis. For instance, a group of Bryansk city councillors visited 'their' submarine which was part of the Northern Fleet in 1997 and were shocked to discover how poor conditions for the sailors were. The Bryansk was armed with 16 ballistic missiles but the submarine did not have the money to buy potatoes. Within months the city of Bryansk was donating potatoes, vegetables and furniture, even a VCR and videos for their sailors to watch at sea. Not surprisingly, in 2000, about 70 per cent of the navy's ships needed major repairs.

Only three per cent of the intake during the first quarter of 1998 had completed any form of higher education. Most had not even completed primary school. The general level of education of the military has declined and it appears that they only get the less able because the more able avoid conscription. This is reflected in their physical condition. A 1997 report found that only about 40 per cent of recruits are capable of performing the most modest level of physical training for soldiers. This is partly due to the fact that 11.5 per cent are underweight. About half the boys finish secondary school with a serious ailment. About one conscript in four requires constant medical supervision and 28 per cent show signs of being mentally retarded. Only half of Russian children can now be classified as normal in their mental development. The main reason for this is poor nutrition. The incidence of mental illness among children has increased by 150 per cent over the last ten years. In April 2001, there were six million adults and children registered as mentally ill but those suffering from mental disorders was put at 30 per cent of the population or almost 50 million.

NUCLEAR ARMS

There were four nuclear successor states: Russia, Belarus, Ukraine and Kazakhstan. The US and they agreed that nuclear weapons should come under a single power, Russia. The Almaty meeting in December 1991 established the CIS but also a unified command. This meant that Marshal Shaposhnikov and President Yeltsin were the guardians of the nuclear briefcase. This lasted until the CIS joint command was dissolved in June 1993; Yeltsin then assumed sole control.

At Almaty, Ukraine and Belarus agreed to sign the non-proliferation treaty as non-nuclear states. Only Kazakhstan had doubts about agreeing the withdrawal of nuclear weapons from its territory. Ukraine later changed its mind about going non-nuclear. By July 1992 all tactical nuclear weapons had been transferred to Russia but Kazakhstan and Ukraine were reluctant to transfer strategic nuclear weapons. They were aware that nuclear weapons are a symbol of sovereignty and were one of the few bargaining chips they had in discussions with Russia. Ukraine, by 1993, had effectively classified itself as a nuclear power but would go non-nuclear when it had negotiated suitable binding guarantees on security with Russia and the west. Kazakhstan also would go non-nuclear but not for at least 15 years. It was mindful of the fact that its neighbour China and Pakistan were nuclear powers. Nevertheless Ukraine and Kazakhstan finally signed the non-proliferation treaty in December 1994. Belarus had no doubts and returned all nuclear weapons to Russia.

Russia inherited about 27,000 nuclear warheads and many other nuclear devices. The vast majority had been based in Russia. There were over a thousand missiles, including almost all the intercontinental ballistic missiles, in Russia, 176 in Ukraine, 54 in Belarus and 104 in Kazakhstan. All Soviet nuclear submarines were in Russian ports. In the later Gorbachev era nuclear weapons had been withdrawn from the Baltic republics and Transcaucasia. Russia renamed its Strategic Rocket Forces the Strategic Deterrence Forces.

The Duma ratified the Start 1 treaty, in November 1992, and began the long process of ratifying Start 2. This was only achieved in 2000. The number of warheads was to be cut by Russia and America to 3000–3500 by 1 January 2003. Altogether about 21,000 strategic warheads were to be scrapped.

MILITARY REFORM AND DOCTRINE

Military reform is based on the goals of the country, the perceived threats to its national security and ways to combat them. The goals of the state are formulated in a national security concept. This in turn serves as the basis for a military doctrine which is the blueprint for reform of the armed forces. Military doctrine includes, among other things, identifying the sources of military danger and threats, the state's use of the armed forces, the firing of nuclear weapons, the economic and social tasks involved in maintaining national security and guidelines for restructuring.

General Pavel 'Pasha' Grachev was minister of defence from May 1992 to June 1996. He was incompetent, corrupt but loyal to Yeltsin. General Lebed's nominee General Igor Rodionov succeeded Grachev. Rodionov was not corrupt and was keen to get on with military reform. In order

The military is so hard up that it uses a tin of sprats to make up the gun. Created by Igor Revyakin.

to do this he needed to work closely with the secretary of the Security Council. However as part of Yeltsin's strategy to reduce Lebed's influence as secretary of the Security Council, a Council of Defence was established with many of the functions of the Security Council. Yury Baturin was appointed its head. Rodionov had a low opinion of Baturin's grasp of military realities.

The President did not support his minister of defence's proposals for military reform. He turned a deaf ear to any proposal which entailed increasing the military budget. Rodionov was driven to issue, from time to time, dire warnings about the collapse of the armed forces if more funding was not forthcoming. Rodionov was sacked, in May 1997, having achieved little. The new minister was General [now Marshal] Igor Sergeev, formerly commander of the strategic deterrence forces. The new secretary of the Security Council was Andrei Kokoshin, a civilian and the only person to have a grasp of defence economics. With Lebed gone the Council of Defence was merged with the Security Council. The new chief of the general staff was General Anatoly Kvashnin. Could this new triumvirate kick-start military reform?

A start was made, in December 1997, when a presidential decree adopted a new national security concept. It identified the threats facing Russia and how they should be dealt with. The greatest threat was the state of the Russian economy which in turn promoted criminality, the decline of the scientific and technical base, an increase in regionalism which stimulated non-Russian nationalism and the disintegration of traditional Russian cultural values. The external threat required the maintenance of strong nuclear forces (this implied dropping the no first use principle). Conventional forces had to be reduced and mobile forces expanded. On the positive side, various structural changes were under way. The five branches of the armed forces had been reduced to four: the strategic deterrence forces, the air force, the ground forces, the navy. Each of the eight military districts would have one or two divisions and air support to deal with local problems and wars. Military personnel was to be reduced from 1.7 million to 1.2 million (of which 400,000 would be ground forces). Only the border guards, ministry of internal affairs, railway troops and FAPSI will be able to recruit conscripts. The defence budget was not to exceed 3.5 per cent of GDP. In fact, the defence budget, in 1997, was officially 3.83 per cent of GDP but the ministry of defence only received 2.71 per cent of GDP.

As regards equipment the present Russian army is a shadow of its Soviet predecessor. Only about 40 per cent of tanks and vehicles can be classified as modern and this drops to 2 per cent of helicopters. Military procurement is very low. About 60 per cent of ICBMs are past their guaranteed life and the situation with other nuclear weapons is even more bleak. Only a few Topol-Ms, the new ICBM, are being delivered annually. The attempt to professionalise the military through short-term contracts has failed (the goal was 50 per cent by 2000). The army is top heavy with senior and middle level officers but very short of young officers. Those who are technically competent leave for civilian life. Another major reason is that over 100,000 officers' families have no apartments.

A new draft military doctrine appeared in November 1999. It lamented the fact that things had changed for the worse since the previous military doctrine of 1993. There are two mutually exclusive tendencies in the world at present: a unipolar world (the United States is not mentioned by name) and the resolution of major problems by force, and a multipolar world based on the equal rights of states under international law. It is implied that NATO (again not mentioned directly) and some other states are inherently hostile towards Russia. However it is not recognised that Russia's economic weakness is the main reason for its loss of influence. The military balance has swung decisively against it. The main domestic threat emanates from the north Caucasus and Central Asia. However the term 'world war' has been dropped. The doctrine speaks of allies (but does not define the term) and partners (but does define the term). The doctrine strengthens the role of the President as commander-in-chief of the nation's armed forces. Putin is certainly more at ease with the military than Yeltsin.

Russia has to confront the fact that NATO has expanded into eastern Europe (Poland, the Czech Republic and Hungary). The US and others are modernising their militaries and Russia's economic decline makes this unrealistic at present. This makes Russia a second-rate military power. NATO intervention in Serbia, in 1999, contravened the UN rule that intervention is only legitimate when sanctioned by the UN Security Council. NATO has said that it could not stand aloof if war broke out in the Caucasus. Does this mean that it could intervene against Russian interests? There is a widespread Russian belief that the west has pursued a policy of diminishing Russian power. Russia's conventional weakness forces it to rely on nuclear weapons to deter aggression. Military gloom is the result of economic gloom. In 1999, Russian GDP was only slightly larger than that of Mexico and on the UN human development index it ranked 58th alongside Surinam.

INTERNAL AFFAIRS

The Russian ministry of internal affairs (MVD), the police or militia, is responsible for law and order. The head of the Soviet ministry of internal affairs, Boris Pugo, was one of those involved in the attempted coup of August 1991. Yeltsin chose Viktor Barannikov to succeed Pugo and also made him head of the Russian ministry of internal affairs. It was vital for Yeltsin to secure the loyalty of the instruments of coercion. In December 1991, Yeltsin amalgamated the ministries of security and internal affairs into a super-ministry but this did not go down well with democrats. They remembered that the last head of this super-ministry had been Lavrenty Beria. Many objected to the concentration of so much power in one ministry at a time of momentous change. The constitutional court ruled, in January 1992, that it was unconstitutional. Viktor Erin, previously first deputy to Barannikov, was appointed Russian minister of internal affairs. He had been one of the drafters of the decree on the super-ministry and had a reputation of being very loyal to Yeltsin. His appointment was not popular with many middle and lower ranking officers who regarded him as less able than the outgoing minister, Andrei Dunaev, who now became Erin's first deputy.

The MVD was quite incapable of dealing with mushrooming crime in Moscow and elsewhere. One of the main sources was inside the Russian government and state agencies. This had developed under Brezhnev and many mafia bosses before 1991 were top party and state officials. According to one MVD officer, in 1991, one third of the mafia's profits were used to bribe MVD officers. Yeltsin sacked Barannikov, in July 1993, for his alleged involvement in scandals. One involved a three-day shopping spree in Switzerland by the wives of Barannikov and the first deputy minister of internal affairs, Dunaev. They were the guests of Seabeco, a Canadian-Swiss company with whom Barannikov had relations. The girls ran up a $300,000 bill and were fined $2000 for excess luggage – they had 20 cases – but this too was paid by Seabeco (Yeltsin 1994: 327–36).

The President's relations with the military were not always smooth and this was potentially dangerous because the conflict with parliament was escalating in the summer of 1993. Suddenly the MVD became more important to Yeltsin. Erin began to enjoy presidential favours. The press saw Erin as loyal but mediocre and ready to carry out any order. In August, Erin had the use of the presidential dacha in Sochi. In September, Yeltsin and he visited the Dzerzhinsky division, the elite, special-purpose troops trained to counter internal disorder, stationed near Moscow. On 1 October, Erin was promoted to army general. Presumably Erin had promised that his men would do their duty in the imminent conflict with parliament. There were reports that senior MVD officers did not support Yeltsin's dissolution of parliament. Erin called the Dzerzhinsky division and OMON units (troops of special designation) into Moscow to reinforce the regular militia of which there were over 100,000 in Moscow alone.

When violence erupted on 3 October the militia was quite incapable of dealing with it. Indeed there were reports that about 200 men defected to the politicians in the White House. At Ostankino, there were OMON units and about 500 internal troops but they did nothing to prevent the storming of the TV centre. The ministry of security, which was responsible for suppressing mass violence, kept its head down and did little to help the MVD. The final assault on the White House was carried out by defence and MVD troops. The White House defenders knew that the military and police were divided on the use of force and this dragged out the conflict. The MVD suffered most losses. Erin was made a hero of the Russian Federation for his efforts. When a new Russian military doctrine was revealed, in November 1993, it authorised the use of army personnel to suppress civil unrest. This provided the President with greater freedom of action. He used these powers for the first time in Chechnya the following year.

The strong showing of Vladimir Zhirinovsky's liberal democrats and the poor showing of the Russia's Choice bloc in the Duma elections, in December 1993, led Yeltsin to change tack on domestic security. Rampant crime and corruption had to be tackled and the MVD was not up to the job. Many MVD officers were linked to organised crime and others took bribes to augment their meagre wages (Anatoly Kulikov, MVD head from 1995–98, thought that about 90 per cent of his officers took bribes). In January 1994, the federal counterintelligence service (FSK) became the leading agency charged with fighting crime, corruption and terrorism. In November 1994, the President restored the investigative apparatus which included special FSK subdivisions to counter crime. The director of the FSK, Sergei Stepashin, knew the MVD well. He had taught at the MVD higher political school until 1990. Also he had served as a political commissar in MVD units in various hot spots, all in ethnically non-Russian areas.

In June 1994, Yeltsin signed a decree which gave FSK and MVD officers the right to enter premises, without a warrant, to examine documents and private papers. Cars could be stopped and the occupants questioned and searched. The reason for the new draconian powers was that existing laws were quite inadequate in the fight against crime. The Duma reacted as if stung by a wasp. In order to defend the dilution of democratic rights, the MVD claimed there were 5700 criminal gangs in Russia, totalling 100,000 members. In the first quarter of 1994, there had been 84 murders a day and many of these were contract killings. On 21 June, the Moscow MVD demonstrated what it could do. Backed up by 20,000 troops from the Dzerzhinsky division it combed Moscow and detained over 2200 persons, charging almost 800. Businessmen were not impressed and complained to Yeltsin that his decree had changed nothing. They were afraid to give evidence to the authorities for fear of reprisals. Criminal proceedings were begun against Barannikov and Dunaev, in April 1994, for corruption and abuse of authority. Their wives were accused of smuggling. They never appeared in court as they knew too much about high level corruption in the Kremlin.

General Erin lasted until June 1995, still battling unsuccessfully against crime and corruption. The President, however, did not dump him. In July 1995, he was transferred to the foreign intelligence service (SVR) as deputy director responsible for combating crime and terrorism with foreign links. As he had no expertise in foreign countries he was like a fish out of water. It was a typical Yeltsin appointment. Loyalty replaced expertise. Erin was succeeded by General Anatoly Kulikov who was also made a deputy Prime Minister. Kulikov was a much stronger character than Erin and was politically very ambitious. He was dismissed along with Chernomyrdin and Chubais, in March 1998.

Sergei Stepashin took over and when he became Prime Minister was succeeded by General Vladimir Rushailo. Between 1976 and 1988, Rushailo had worked in the criminal investigation branch of the main directorate of internal affairs of the city of Moscow. In 1988, he was appointed head of the department responsible for combating organised crime and between 1993 and 1996 did the same job for Moscow oblast. In 1996, Rushailo became a legal consultant to the Duma speaker. He returned to the ministry of internal affairs, in May 1998, as a deputy minister and, in May 1999, became the minister of internal affairs.

SECURITY

By the end of January 1992, there were five agencies which had taken over the functions of the KGB (Knight 1996: 34–7) (Table 6.2). The largest was the ministry of security which counted about 137,000 employees. It inherited the Lubyanka and its archive. Its main concern was counter-intelligence and it took over the functions of the second, third, fourth, sixth and seventh directorates and the directorate for the protection of the constitution from the former KGB. Yeltsin appointed Viktor Barannikov head of the new ministry in January 1992. A mark of Barannikov's closeness to Yeltsin was that he accompanied the President into the banya, bath house or sauna. One can call him one of Boris's banya buddies.

The KGB's eighth chief directorate, which was responsible for government communications and ciphers, became the federal agency for government communications and information (FAPSI). General Aleksandr Starovoitov, formerly deputy head of the KGB's eighth chief directorate, was appointed its chief. It supervised government communication lines and engaged in intelligence by intercepting and decoding information. One of its functions is to check the contents of e-mail messages. The ninth directorate, responsible for protecting government leaders, buildings and installations, became the main guard directorate (GUO) and this was entrusted to General Mikhail Barsukov. It had over 8000 men.

The President created the presidential security service (SBP) for General Aleksandr Korzhakov and it enjoyed autonomy within the GUO. Korzhakov managed to go independent in November 1993. The Alpha and Vympel (transferred from the ministry of security in September 1993) elite anti-terrorist troops were part of the GUO.

The fourth successor agency was the committee for the protection of the Russian border which inherited 180,000 troops. The former head of the KGB border guards, Ilya Kalinichenko, became the new head. In June 1992, when Yeltsin subordinated the border guards to the ministry of security, he appointed Vladimir Shlyatin the new head.

The KGB's first chief directorate was renamed the foreign intelligence service (SVR) and Evgeny Primakov became its first head. He had been chief of the central intelligence service which had been set up after the attempted coup. He had been associated with the KGB but had considerable foreign policy expertise and was an Arabist. The SVR took over the first chief directorate's large premises at Yasenevo, on the southern outskirts of Moscow. Primakov reported directly to Yeltsin as did all the other new chiefs. The President had toyed with the idea of ending the functions of the former KGB which were concerned with surveillance of the domestic population. He soon abandoned this as he needed to know what his political enemies were plotting. The more insecure the President became the more rapidly the intelligence services expanded.

THE SECURITY MARKET

In the Soviet Union the KGB had enjoyed a monopoly but in the new Russia the various agencies would have to compete for market dominance (Knight 1996: chapter 2). The agencies of greatest value to the President were those which could contribute to the defeat of his political opponents. First and foremost this involved the personal security of Yeltsin and his associates. Then there was intelligence gathering which included bugging telephones and conversations, intercepting mail and spreading disinformation. There was also the battle against ethnic unrest, corruption, organised crime and drugs. The borders of the country had to be secure so border troops could become important. Then there was the need to collect information on foreign countries, especially on economic and military affairs. There was also the task of dealing with the large number of spies in Russia.

Yeltsin and parliament differed fundamentally on the security services. The President wished to subordinate them to himself without any accountability to parliament or the legal agencies. Parliamentary conservatives, on the other hand, wanted the services to be accountable to parliament. This would permit the parliamentary majority to use them against the President in their political infighting. The parliamentary democrats wanted to ensure that the services were subordinate to the law as well as parliament. The Supreme Soviet's committee on defence and security defended Yeltsin's position since it was full of security officials. Its chair was Sergei Stepashin until mid-1993. He then returned to his post as deputy minister of security. In February 1994, he became head of the foreign counterintelligence service (FSK) and, in April 1995, of the federal intelligence service (FSB). Yeltsin strengthened his position through various decrees. These were normally drafted in Stepashin's committee. The decree on secrecy reimposed the old system. The ministry of security was to have representatives in all state agencies to ensure that secrets were not leaked to the public. The person appointed was often the previous KGB officer.

Yeltsin's first attempt to use force against his political opponents failed. The national salvation front, a far right grouping of communists and nationalists, began calling for the resignation of the President and the re-establishment of the Soviet state. The President issued a decree, in October 1992, banning the organisation for contravening the Russian constitution. He ordered the ministries of security and internal affairs to implement it. They hesitated as many officers shared the right wing views of the front. The constitutional court refused to confirm the decree. Barannikov and Erin would not act extra-legally and it was only a year later, after the bloody events of October 1993, that the salvation front was banned.

Public concern about corruption forced Yeltsin to engage in high-profile initiatives. In October 1992, he set up a commission to fight crime and corruption, headed by Vice-President Rutskoi. It brought together the ministry of security, the MVD, the SVR, economic ministries and the customs service. Its task was to prevent officials selling state property, economic secrets, raw materials and engaging in currency deals. One of the unintended consequences of this commission was to provide Rutskoi with ammunition against Yeltsin and his associates. The ministry of security announced sensational arrests of criminals and military officers from time to time but this was only the tip of the iceberg. Barannikov claimed that the main reason for corruption were the activities of foreign intelligence agencies. No one believed him. Yeltsin raged, in February 1993, that whole ammunition dumps were disappearing and the security services were doing nothing. Few cases ever got to court. The reason was that if an official were indicted for corruption a higher placed official, his patron, stepped in and stopped the case.

From March 1993 politics degenerated into accusation and counter-accusation. Rutskoi, in April, claimed that shock therapy had criminalised the country and pointed the finger at top officials. Gaidar, allegedly, had sold off Russia's gold reserves, Vladimir Shumeiko had granted sole import rights to foreign firms and Mikhail Poltoranin was involved in the illegal sale of Russian property in Berlin. Even more potentially damaging was the claim that Yeltsin and Gennady Burbulis were involved with a company in Ekaterinburg which manufactured and exported a strategic raw material, called red mercury. However this was a cover for exporting gold, uranium and other things. The director of the company stated that it worked closely with the ministry of security and the presidential administration and was absolutely above board. It was perfectly clear that the ministry of security, whose task was to protect state assets, was in business itself, just like the KGB. The ministry supervised the export of raw materials and high technology. It could provide Russian companies with information on their competitors, for a consideration, of course. Ministry officials also participated in joint ventures with foreign companies. Under Gorbachev, KGB officers were involved in setting up many of the new commercial banks and cooperatives. In 1990, this author negotiated a business deal, involving tourism, with a high-ranking KGB officer in a luxurious dacha just outside Moscow. He then asked for a $2 million loan to be arranged. Working with the KGB was good business because it could overcome any obstacle. One of the main concerns of ministry officials in 1992 was how to set up an offshore account. Money laundering then became feasible. What is money laundering? It is a legal phrase which refers to the criminal practice of moving ill-gotten gains through a succession of bank accounts so that ultimately they appear to be legitimate profits from legal businesses. The money is then withdrawn and used for further criminal activity.

Another agency which was quick off the mark was FAPSI. It had the right to lease government communication lines to commercial banks and enterprises for confidential operations such as the transfer of funds. Some of the profits of this lucrative business were used to upgrade technical equipment which made it more formidable.

Many ministry officials left to head private security companies, of which there were over 1000 in 1994. This had risen to about 10,000 in 1997. Banks and companies had their own in-house security and intelligence services. In mid-1998, about 2500 banks and 72,000 commercial organisations had their own security services. Some were very large. Gazprom, for instance, employed about 20,000 in its security organisation. Private organisations were usually staffed by former security, MVD and military personnel. After all they had the connections. They were also well armed. Altogether, in 1997, there were about a million employed in the private security industry. This compared to the 400,000 in the MVD.

BARANNIKOV DEPARTS

Even though Yeltsin had extended many privileges to the ministry of security, including many money-making activities, it was not wholly loyal to him. The President wanted to use it against his political opponents but Barannikov could not guarantee that it would act on his orders. Disturbingly for Yeltsin, there were hints that Barannikov was going over to the other side. He had piles of kompromat (compromising material) on military and MVD officers and pro-Yeltsin politicians. The procurator general sided with Barannikov and began proceedings over the red mercury scam. Yeltsin sacked Rutskoi as head of the commission on crime and corruption but this was bolting the door after the horse had gone. Who had given Rutskoi the eleven suitcases of incriminating evidence? The ministry of security and MVD. In July 1993, the procuracy, assisted by the ministry of security, searched Mikhail Poltoranin's residence and cross-examined him for three hours. Plans were afoot to arrest Vladimir Shumeiko. Yeltsin sacked Barannikov (and many of his top men) over an incident on the Tajik–Afghan border, in July 1993, when many Russians had been killed and wounded (Knight 1996: 67–9). Who had collected the incriminating evidence on Barannikov? A Russian businessman operating in Switzerland called Dmitry Yakubovsky. He had material revealing that Barannikov and his wife had been bribed by another Russian businessman in Switzerland, Boris Birshtein. It turned out that Yakubovsky was also collecting kompromat on Rutskoi, Ruslan Khasbulatov and procurator general Valentin Stepankov. Russia was experiencing its kompromat wars; Nikolai Golushko took over from Barannikov.

THE KOMPROMAT WARS

Yeltsin's new anti-crime commission reported that it had found no evidence of wrongdoing by Poltoranin and Shumeiko but had discovered that Rutskoi had stolen millions of rubles from the state. They also accused Stepankov of planning the assassination of Dmitry Yakubovsky. On 1 September, Yeltsin sacked Vice-President Rutskoi and first deputy Prime Minister Shumeiko pending investigations into the charges of corruption.

Yeltsin dissolved parliament on 21 September and expected the ministry of security to help implement the decree. However Golushko was circumspect in his comments, revealing that the ministry had no stom-

COLONELS AND SPIES 227

ach for violence. Barannikov claimed that about 7000 officers sided with parliament against Yeltsin. Clearly the ministry could not be relied upon when it came to the shedding of blood.

ENTER THE FSK

Yeltsin's solution was to disband the ministry of security on 21 December 1993. It was unreformable. The new organisation was the federal counter-intelligence service (FSK) and Golushko was to head it (Knight 1996: chapter 4). In a major departure, Yeltsin promised that political surveillance of the population was to cease. Was this promise credible given that the President's enemies were legion? The new agency was only to engage in counterintelligence, hence its name. Another reason for disbanding the ministry was that there were CIA agents within its ranks. In the previous year twenty officers had been sentenced. Their cover was presumably blown by Aldrich Ames, the best agent the KGB and ministry of security ever had inside the CIA. He was unmasked shortly afterwards.

Sergei Stepashin, Golushko's deputy, revealed that the operational strength of the FSK would be 75,000 officers, about half of that of the ministry of security. In typical Russian fashion the surplus officers were not sacked, they were transferred to other agencies such as the MVD. After all, the FSK was no longer to be responsible for countering economic crime; that duty now passed to the MVD.

It soon turned out that the MVD and the procuracy could not cope with the rising tide of crime and corruption. The FSK had to help and the number of officers far exceeded the envisaged 75,000. By the end of 1994, the FSK had more powers than the ministry of security. It also acquired a new head, in February 1994, when Sergei Stepashin replaced Golushko. The latter may have been fired for his lack of commitment to Yeltsin in October 1993.

The FSK committed many blunders in Chechnya. Its first major mistake was its failure to topple Dudaev. It was to have a bad war in Chechnya. Despite this it went from strength to strength domestically and, in March 1995, the President issued a decree on combating fascism and neo-fascism. These blanket terms could cover anti-Semitism, the promotion of ethnic and religious hatred, video nasties and nationalism. Who defined fascism and neo-fascism? The FSK and this gave it unprecedented power in Russia. Stepashin was not squeamish about using force against the President's enemies.

ENTER THE FSB

It was now time to change its name in line with its new powers. In April 1995, the FSK became the federal security service (FSB). Its increased standing was signalled by its head automatically acquiring the rank of army general. This meant that the FSB was now on a par with the KGB whose last head, Vladimir Kryuchkov, had also been an army general. Indeed one can say that the FSB was potentially more powerful than the KGB as it was not subject to juridical supervision. It only answered to the President. Democracy and the rule of law had to take a back seat in the fight against the President's enemies. The FSB believed in overkill when it came to informing the top people. In the first 11 eleven months of 1996, it forwarded 4157 analyses to the President, Prime Minister and secretary of the Security Council. This works out at over ten a day.

Stepashin was a hawk on Chechnya. What brought him down was his unskilful involvement in the Budennovsk crisis in June 1995. However MVD head Erin and deputy Prime Minister Nikolai Egorov were even more to blame. Yeltsin sacrificed all three in a successful attempt to entice the Duma to withdraw a motion of no confidence in the Chernomyrdin government. The man who took over the FSB was Mikhail Barsukov. According to one newspaper, Barsukov could consume great quantities of vodka. His other skill, closely related to this, was to get foreign guests drunk at his bacchanalian parties. As a boost to the FSB, the elite Alpha troops were subordinated to it. Barsukov fell victim to Chubais's superior cunning in June 1996 when he was sacked along with Korzhakov and Soskovets. Nikolai Kovalev succeeded him. This was the signal to reduce the size of the FSB and its numbers were cut to 40,000 in 1998 and 30,000 in 1999. The presidential guard counted 4000 in 1995 but this was down to 900 in 1999.

The financial collapse of August 1998 hit the FSB hard. Beforehand salaries had been low and afterwards officers only received about half their salaries. Salaries in the SVR were about 50 per cent higher. Berezovsky maintained, in March 1998, that members of the security services were trying to assassinate him. Kovalev came to the conclusion that the accusation was false and was just part of Berezovsky's ongoing war against the FSB. In his memoirs, Yeltsin (2000: 327) writes that Kovalev had an ingrained antipathy to anyone with money. He burrowed into the affairs of rich businessmen since he presumed they were 'enemies of the people'. Kovalev was sacked, on 25 July 1998, and succeeded by Vladimir Putin. Kovalev had been looking into corruption in FAPSI and someone had convinced Yeltsin that Kovalev was trying to take over FAPSI and become more powerful. After his appointment, Yeltsin proposed to Putin that he return to active service in the military with the rank of general. Putin turned this down, saying he had quit the KGB in August 1991 and wished to remain a civilian. He was content with the rank of colonel in the reserves.

In November 1998, Berezovsky repeated his accusation to Putin. Berezovsky went further and called the FSB a criminal organisation. At this time Berezovsky was executive secretary of the CIS. This stung Putin and he categorically denied Berezovsky's claims.

Putin was concerned about morale in the FSB and told the Duma, in November 1998, that even the best of his officers were leaving the force because of low pay. He was promised that FSB salaries would increase by 25 per cent in 1999. In 1997, about 600 graduated from the FSB academy and there were about ten applicants for each place at the academy. Putin was appointed Prime Minister, on 9 August 1999, and was succeeded by General Nikolai Patrushev. The latter is a close confidant of Putin.

THE SVR

The foreign intelligence service (SVR) was formed from the first chief directorate of the KGB, with about 12,000 personnel, on 18 December 1991, and has retained the same name ever since (in September 1992 there was a move to change the name but this was quashed the following month) (Knight 1996: chapter 5). It has a legitimacy which domestic security lacks. Even the most passionate democrat would not quibble about having an organisation to spy on foreigners and protect Russia's interests abroad. KGB officers who had served abroad were more acceptable to Russian democrats than those who had clamped down on dissent at home. A case in point was General Oleg Kalugin who leapt to fame in 1990 when he castigated the KGB. Democrats were willing to overlook the fact that he had been involved in nasty active measures. These included the murder of Georgi Markov, a Bulgarian dissident, with the poisoned tip of an umbrella. According to the SVR, uncivilised methods of recruiting agents would be a thing of the past; the days of blackmailing people to become agents were supposedly gone.

The first head of the SVR was Evgeny Primakov who had not been a professional KGB officer but had had much contact with the security organ, especially in the Middle East. Yeltsin appointed him after visiting Yasenevo and consulting high-ranking officers. Primakov even promised not to spy on CIS countries (the information could be collected by other means) or to send officers abroad pretending to be journalists (not kept) and he welcomed parliamentary supervision. He was a smooth talker indeed. He discussed cooperation with the CIA on combating nuclear proliferation, terrorism, drug trafficking and money laundering. Instead of their numbers declining, the stated aim, they almost certainly increased. Officers could go abroad as entrepreneurs and businessmen. The more money they made the more officers the SVR could afford. The SVR and MI6 agreed on an official SVR representative in London in 1992. The law on foreign intelligence stated that the main task was collecting economic and technological information in the west. High-tech spying could be very lucrative. It could benefit Russian industry but it could also be sold on to other countries. The SVR does not have a monopoly of foreign intelligence. The GRU, military intelligence, continued as before, and FAPSI has its own intelligence service.

An agreement on the basic principles of cooperation between the intelligence services of the CIS was signed in Almaty, in April 1992, by nine states. Azerbaijan, Georgia and Uzbekistan did not sign. Members were not to spy on one another. In 1995, twelve states signed an agreement in Tbilisi on cooperation on combating organised crime, international terrorism and drug trafficking. The first part of a CIS special services database was completed in July 1998.

Yeltsin visited the SVR's headquarters at Yasenevo, in April 1994. What he had to say boosted the morale of the officers. At a time of declining military expenditure, the SVR was the guarantor of Russia's security. Secret diplomacy was extensively used in international relations: 'We should be able to look under the cover of these secrets so as not to be caught unawares.' Its budget would be augmented. Intelligence would collect the most important information for decision making on domestic and foreign policy, the economy and scientific and technical progress. In early 1995, Yeltsin instructed the SVR to make a significant contribution to the Russian economy. Increased economic espionage was to help reduce the technological gap between Russia and the developed countries. The SVR was to counter western attempts to influence CIS states and Russian domestic policy. In other words, the SVR was to be a major player in foreign affairs. Primakov had long been transferring his officers to the ministry of foreign affairs, with the consent of Yeltsin. Primakov fitted this role perfectly as he often travelled abroad on special missions for the President. Primakov, in public, was quite frank about the need to spy. Cooperation with the west 'does not mean that we stop spying', he remarked in December 1995.

Primakov was appointed minister of foreign affairs, on 10 January 1996, and was succeeded by General Vyacheslav Trubnikov, his first deputy, responsible for south east Asia, since 1992. His expertise was in India and Pakistan. In 1994, he had claimed that the SVR was one of the four best secret services in the world. The other three were the CIA, MI6 and the Israeli Mossad. In July 1996, he was made a member of the Security Council and an army general in January 1998. Clearly he was a success. In May 2000, General Sergei Lebedev took over from him. He served with Vladimir Putin in the GDR and from 1988–2000 was head of the SVR's official office in Washington, DC. In June 2000, Trubnikov was transferred to the ministry of foreign affairs.

THE NEW MEN

The SVR seeks young men between the ages of 22 and 35 with higher education and who are physically fit; they should possess language and analytical skills. Women are not recruited as officers. The SVR no longer has the pick of the bunch as many private institutions offer better career prospects. It is up to its academy to bring the new recruits up to the mark. Operational strength is believed to be about 15,000. There is more work than ever to do. In December 1997, Trubnikov commented that, contrary to public perception, the confrontation between intelligence services since the Cold War had actually intensified. NATO enlargement and the desire of other countries to join increase the need to be active in those states. The perceived threat of Islamic fundamentalism requires increasing attention. Millions of Russians now live outside the country and this provides fertile ground for recruitment: for instance, there are over 200,000 Russians in London alone. Rich Russians are of special interest especially if they are businessmen. A trade-off can be arranged for services rendered.

7

MOSCOW DOES NOT RULE, OK? FEDERALISM AND THE REGIONS

A defining element of our society was and is the belief in myths. At various times in the past there was the myth of the good Tsar, peaceful revolution, communism, proletarian revolution and developed socialism. Nowadays for many there is the myth of federalism. (Valentei 1997: 3)

THE DEVELOPMENT OF THE RUSSIAN STATE

THE DEVELOPMENT OF THE RUSSIAN STATE, or statehood, has gone through four phases since August 1991 (Luchterhandt 1996; Solnick 1996):

1 The attempted coup of August 1991 to the beginning of the economic reforms of January 1992;

2 Early 1992 to the violent dissolution of the Supreme Soviet in October 1993;

3 The transition phase from the autumn of 1993 to the summer of 1994 during which the new Russian constitution was adopted and federal and local elections took place;

4 The rapid development of a constitutional system since mid-1994.

PLATE 5 Boris Berezovsky, left, a controversial business tycoon, and Roman Abramovich, Russian oil tycoon, with reported political connections, both parliament members, walk after the session of the State Duma, parliament's lower house, in Moscow, Russia in this January 26, 2000 photo. Two prominent moguls, Berezovsky and Abramovich, took the unusual steps of winning parliament seats in elections last December that secured them the immunity from criminal prosecution that all lawmakers enjoy. (AP Photo/Ivan Sekretarev, Staff).

PLATE 6 Balkan's special envoy Viktor Chernomyrdin gestures during a news conference June 17, 1999. President Boris Yeltsin told Defence Minister Igor Sergeyev on Thursday that Russia must insist on having its own zone in Kosovo during talks in Helsinki with U.S. Officials. (mf/Photo by Alexander Natruskin, Popperfoto/Reuter).

PLATE 7 Acting Prime Minister Sergei Kiriyenko applauded as he listened to lawmakers during the parliament session in Moscow, 24 April. Facing the threat of dissolution, the parliament held one final debate ahead of its crucial vote on President Boris Yeltsin's youthful candidate for Prime Minister, Sergei Kiriyenko. (Pool AP/ - /VG/nie/ao).

PLATE 8 Yevgeni Primakov during his first press conference after his appointment to the post of Foreign Minister (1996). (Novosti [London]).

AUGUST 1991 TO THE END OF THE SOVIET UNION

The declared goals of this phase were the destruction of the power of the communist party of the Soviet Union (CPSU). A functional executive, or rather presidential executive, came into being – a hierarchical pyramid in which the head of the executive at every level was not elected by representative institutions but was nominated by his or her immediate superior and was responsible for the implementation of orders which emanated from above. The only difference between this new, democratic pyramid and the former CPSU pyramid was that officials in the latter were formally elected. Immediately after the failure of the attempted coup, Yeltsin suspended some regional leaders who had supported it. They were replaced by those who were closely linked to Yeltsin or were known to him personally. The office of presidential representative was also introduced in these regions in order to serve as the eyes and ears of the President there. He (there were no women) was also to supervise the implementation of central directives at the regional level.

Yeltsin's goal of reducing the power of the centre was warmly welcomed by the regions. His slogan of 'take as much sovereignty as you can cope with' resulted in all 16 autonomous republics, four of the five autonomous oblasts and five of the ten autonomous okrugs declaring themselves sovereign republics. This was only a tactical move to win support in the non-Russian regions but it antagonised Russians living in the oblasts and krais who sought the same status within the federation. As one analyst put it, there were 23 million subjects, most of them non-Russian, living in a federal state and 124 million Russians living in a unitary state.

The local self-government law of 6 July 1991, passed by the RSFSR Supreme Soviet, took precedence over existing Soviet legislation. Later Russian legislation retained most of its provisions. Local self-government was to consist of various forms of direct local democracy, including local representative bodies, local ballots, meetings of local residents and other forms of public territorial administration. It guaranteed citizens full participation in local self-government. Local representative and administrative organs were recognised as juridical persons with their own powers of jurisdiction and were to be elected directly by the citizens. Natural resources, together with communal and other property, were to form the economic basis of local self-government. Local administrations were to be responsible for their own budgets.

ECONOMIC REFORM AND CONFLICT BETWEEN THE EXECUTIVE AND LEGISLATURE: JANUARY 1992–OCTOBER 1993

The President's goals during this period included:

■ the development of constitutional institutions, based on the principles of democracy, the rule of law and federalism;

■ the principal goal to be the adoption of a new constitution;

■ radical market reform (shock therapy) through price liberalisation, stabilisation and privatisation to ensure that the communists could not regain power and capitalism to be rendered irreversible;

■ draft proposals for a federal state to be elaborated so as to define the power of the centre and the regions in such a way as to ensure the unity of the Russian Federation.

The most significant achievements of this period were:

■ the rapid formation and expansion of executive organisations such as the presidential administration, the Security Council, the presidential guard and the main administration for the protection of persons and property;

■ as conflict increased, the heads of these institutions, especially those who were close to Yeltsin, began to play a more important role than many constitutional institutions. The restructuring of the security institutions was based on personal loyalty to the President;

■ the expansion of the vertical relationship between the centre and the regions aimed at making it easier for Moscow to direct events in the regions;

■ the signing of the federal treaty, in March 1992, by 87 of the 89 republics, autonomous oblasts and okrugs, krais, oblasts and two cities of federal significance (Moscow and St Petersburg). All these were classified as subjects of the federation but this did not resolve the conflicts between the various territorial entities in the federation. The 21 republics were recognised as sovereign states and promised expanded rights over their natural resources, external trade and domestic budgets; the oblasts and krais received few enhanced rights beyond the designation as subjects of the federation.

The President consistently attempted to increase his own powers (especially his extraordinary powers) and areas of competence.

One of the most significant developments of the reforms was the decreasing number of officials responsible for market reform. This conferred on those who remained greater and greater power. The increasing powers of the executive led at the centre and in the regions to the undermining of the legal system since policy was implemented mainly through decrees and regulations. These took precedence over existing legislation and the constitution.

A significant outcome of the 25 April 1993 referendum was that the President's support mainly came from the oblasts and krais with less than half of the republics (excluding Chechnya which did not participate in the poll) returning majorities in his favour. The Constitutional Assembly, in July 1993, attempted to resolve the problem of equal rights for all subjects of the federation. A draft was agreed which retained the essence of the federation treaty, including republican sovereignty. However this draft was only supported by eight of the 21 republics and received only a lukewarm response in other regions. Yeltsin's final attempt to win the support of regional and republican leaders for his draft of the new constitution, now critical in the light of the bitter struggle with parliament, occurred in Petrozavodsk, in Karelia, in August 1993. He proposed the creation of a Council of the Federation that would consist of representatives of the 89 subjects of the federation and would be the upper house of a new Russian federal assembly. The republican leaders took umbrage at the offer of equal status for all subjects of the federation. This would have resulted in their being comprehensively outvoted by the Russian regions. The Council of the Federation was finally rejected by republican and Russian regional leaders in mid-September 1993. The stage was set for the President to act unilaterally.

The conflict between the executive and legislature came to a head with unconstitutional decree no. 1400, dissolving the legislature on 21 September 1993 and ended with the brutal use of force in storming the White House, the dissolution of soviets at all levels and the dismissal of the constitutional court. The use of force transformed relations between the President and the regions. It was now dangerous to oppose Yeltsin. Regions which supported parliament against the President had attempted through convocation of the Council of the Subjects of the Federation to scale down the conflict, to call new elections to parliament and the presidency and to take power until these were completed. However at the meeting in St Petersburg, on 26 September 1993, only 41 representatives from subjects of the federation turned up. This gave the green light to Yeltsin to use force against the Supreme Soviet. It also underlined the age-old Russian tradition: in a conflict between Moscow and the regions, Moscow rules.

POWER TO THE EXECUTIVE: OCTOBER 1993– SUMMER 1994

This very significant phase was in two parts: the first until the adoption of the new constitution of 12 December 1993 and elections to the new parliament, the Federal Assembly, consisting of a lower house, the Duma, and an upper house, the Council of the Federation. The second part lasted until the summer of 1994 when elections to the legislative bodies in the subjects of the federation had been completed. During this period the President increased his own power substantially.

The new constitution treated republics, krais, oblasts, autonomous oblasts, autonomous okrugs, Moscow and St Petersburg, in essence, as equals and omitted previous references to republican sovereignty. Predictably the constitution did not go down well in the republics. Voters in nine of the 21 republics rejected it and in six others either boycotted it or the required 50 per cent of the registered voters failed to turn out to make the ballot valid. The republics were overruled as a majority in the federation had approved the draft constitution. Nevertheless Chechnya, since it had declared independence in November 1991 and therefore did not regard itself as part of the Russian Federation, and Tatarstan refused to recognise the new constitution. On 15 February 1994, President Yeltsin signed a bilateral treaty with Tatarstan which, in reality, granted the republic few significant rights over those granted the other republics in the constitution. This was not the real point of the exercise, which was to accord Tatarstan recognition as a special republic.

The day before parliament convened for the first time, on 11 January 1994, Yeltsin issued a presidential decree removing all those responsible for the security of the state at home and abroad – the ministry of defence, the ministry of internal affairs, the Border Troops, the secret services, the ministry of foreign affairs as well as radio, TV and archives – from subordination to the government and made them directly subordinate to himself. They were to come together in the Security Council, chaired by the President. Yeltsin had secured control over all the instruments of coercion in the state – all those carrying guns were subordinate to him personally. The government was left with the economy, social affairs, the environment, culture, education and science.

During this period the regional administrations concentrated as much power as they could in their own hands, all on the basis of presidential decrees: on the organisation of power in the subjects of the federation of 22 October 1993; on the reform of self-government of 26 October 1993; on elections in the subjects of the federation of 26 October

1993; and on the main principles of the organisation of self-governing authorities of 29 October 1993. The administrations were able to act without supervision after the soviets had been dissolved. Even more significantly they decided the structure, functions and the electoral rules of the representative bodies at their level. The results were predictable. The oblast dumas and those of the cities and villages were mainly decorative as most of the deputies elected were representatives of the executive.

The Russian constitution of 12 December 1993 recognises and guarantees local self-government as an independent entity subject to its own jurisdiction and whose agencies do not form part of the agencies of state power. Chapter 8 of the constitution states that the population shall decide 'questions of local significance' and owns, uses and disposes over municipal property. Local self-government is to be exercised by citizens through 'referenda, elections and other forms of the direct expression of [their] will' (article 130.2) as well as through elected agencies of local self-government. The population has the right to decide autonomously the structure of the agencies of local self-government (article 131.1). Agencies of local self-government shall 'autonomously administer municipal property, form, confirm and execute the local budget, set local taxes and charges, protect public order and resolve other questions of local significance' (article 132.1).

THE NEW FEDERAL STATE: 1994–98

This stage divides again into two periods: up to the brutal intervention in Chechnya on 11 December 1994, and afterwards. The first period was marked by a search for solutions by peaceful means but the second began with the violent use of force against mainly civilians. For the first time there was not only open, sharp conflict between and among state institutions and within the instruments of coercion but also within institutions. Examples of this were the military and the presidential administration and the army and the ministry of internal affairs. Even more significantly an open struggle developed between interest groups – clans, cliques, groups, financial groups – within various institutions.

During 1994 and early 1995 the President formulated his goals in general terms: the formation of a strong Russian state and the more effective use of state power; the development of federalism and self-government within a united Russia; a more resolute struggle against criminality, especially against organised crime (in 1993, the MVD identified about 3000 organised crime groups in Russia. A year later it was 5700 with three million members. Viktor Ilyukhin, communist chair of the Duma's security committee, in October 1994, claimed that 35,000 businesses in Russia were obliged to pay protection money to 135 Russian criminal organisations which employed 100,000 criminals. In December 1998, Yury Skuratov, the procurator general, estimated that about 50 per cent of all commercial banks and about 40 per cent of state owned companies were criminally controlled. This came to about 40–50 per cent of Russian GDP. The natural gas, oil and coal sectors were particularly prone to organised crime); increasing the authority of law; continuation of the economic reforms.

Several significant trends emerged during this period:

- The state began to use force more freely in resolving political and economic conflicts.

- Institutions not mentioned in the constitution expanded rapidly, especially the presidential administration which grew to shadow all government departments.

- Changing the personnel of the power ministries proceeded apace in the light of the failures during the Chechen war. Politically, in view of the 1996 presidential elections, many generals were becoming liabilities. The net result was that the Security Council, the ministry of internal affairs and the General Staff grew in stature and began playing a role as political actors.

- Moscow concentrated on preventing the regions freeing themselves from central direction and ensuring that regional power groupings did not emerge to challenge the centre. On 3 October 1994, a presidential decree banned the election of governors and mayors in the regions. In so doing the President clearly violated the principles of federalism in the constitution. Preventing the regions electing their own governors violated article 77 which affords subjects the right to determine themselves the 'system of agencies of state power'. The goal was to maintain the tradition of nominating from above the heads of the local administrations (even some mayors were appointed by Moscow) and to prevent a change of leading personnel in the regions. Elected officials would acquire greater legitimacy and become more powerful voices for local interests. The special concessions made to republics such as Tatarstan and Bashkortostan were to be whittled away. Appeals by the President to respect human rights, democracy and federalism fell on deaf ears, especially since the President acted outside the law almost at will. A glaring example was the suspension of the Russian constitution in Chechnya just after war broke out. This should have been accompanied by the declaration of a state of emergency. Indeed no formal declaration of war was ever made. Violations of the human rights laid down in the Russian constitution were documented by the human rights commissioner, Sergei Kovalev, but to no avail.

- Support for the President ebbed away as the brutalities of the Chechen war alienated the population.

- Against all the odds Boris Yeltsin was re-elected President in July 1996 (electoral fraud played its part). Relations with the regions were not given priority as the federal government sought ways of increasing tax revenue. Moscow's lack of revenue meant that it increasingly failed to meet its financial obligations to the regions. A tax revolt erupted, in February 1997, in the regions when Sakhalin oblast voted to withhold taxes in protest at the failure of the centre to provide the promised budgetary transfers. Moscow's response was swift. It paid part of its debt the following month in return for Sakhalin countermanding the decision. Irkutsk oblast ceased paying tax to the federal government, on 1 March 1997, claiming that Moscow owed it trillions of rubles. Moscow forced Irkutsk to reverse this decision a few days later. Tula oblast and Krasnodar krai announced publicly that they were toying with the idea of withholding federal taxes but after Moscow intervened thought better of it. However it proved a useful tactic to force Moscow to provide more revenue. Yeltsin came up with an astute solution to his problems in Kemerovo oblast, the centre of the Kuzbass. Aman Tuleev, a thorn in the President's side, was the odds-on favourite to win the gubernatorial election in the summer of 1997. Mounting labour protests were threatening to spread. Just before the election, Yeltsin summarily sacked his man, Mikhail Kislyuk, and appointed Tuleev as governor. Tuleev then began a crackdown on labour protests. He was elected with a large majority. The democratic press railed against the cynical deal which the President had done: power for Tuleev if he kept the workers in order.

THE FEDERAL STATE IN CRISIS: 1998–99

In August 1998, the federal government defaulted on its short-term debt, devalued the ruble and many citizens lost most of their savings. The economic collapse precipitated a revolt by the regions as they were obliged to act economically to limit the damage. The Republic of Buryatia and Kaliningrad oblast declared states of emergency, something which, according to the constitution, only the Russian President may introduce. Over 60 regions drafted austerity programmes, froze consumer prices, ceased to pay federal taxes and contemplated introducing local currencies and food vouchers. The Republic of Sakha banned the sale of gold to the federal government and together with Kemerovo oblast began to build up gold and foreign currency reserves. This, of course, contravened federal law. In October 1998, the Republic of Tatarstan thought of establishing its own citizenship. Sverdlovsk oblast examined the possibility of a separate currency, nationalising local banks and enterprises and issuing its own Eurobond. Khabarovsk krai declared it would no longer pay federal taxes because the centre owed it billions. Leaving Russia and becoming independent were, however, not possibilities. The regions desperately needed federal transfers but Moscow often could not oblige. During the winter of 1998–99 the situation in the Far North and the Far East was desperate. The greatest need was fuel. In December 1998, half of Vladivostok's buildings had no heating. The Russian Red Cross appealed for international aid to buy food and medicine for Kamchatka oblast and other northern regions.

The winter of 1998–99 was a turning point. Prime Minister Evgeny Primakov intervened energetically and relief aid was dispatched to the regions. He recognised the danger of the federation breaking up. 'We lost the Soviet Union but we will not allow Russia to be lost', he graphically declared. He was aware of how powerful the regions' governors had become. He warned them against acting like 'feudal princes'. Primakov favoured strengthening the centre in its relations with the regions and many governors agreed with him. For instance, the governor of Saratov oblast thought that Russia could become a confederation if Moscow did not vigorously combat economic separatism. Eduard Rossel, governor of Sverdlovsk oblast, advocated strong central management of Russia. Mikhail Prusak, governor of Novgorod oblast, thought that governors should be appointed by the centre and not elected by popular vote. The disadvantage of having elected governors was that they, as part of the executive, pursued local interests at the expense of the centre. The German model of large Länder was again considered. Yury Luzhkov, mayor of Moscow, and Evgeny Primakov, suggested 10–12 large regions. Aman Tuleev, governor of Kemerovo oblast, thought that 25–35 were more advisable with the new regions having the powers of republics, such as Tatarstan and Sakha. Primakov favoured the consolidation of regions, subordinating governors to the centre and greater centralisation of power. His dismissal as Prime Minister, in May 1999, however, put a hold on such plans.

The incursion of about 2000 Islamic rebels from Chechnya into Dagestan, in August 1999, caused a crisis in Moscow. Soon the second Chechen war was under way. The war underlined the split between Dagestan and Chechnya. The former did not aspire to separate from Russia and did not wish to be embroiled in Chechnya's conflict with Moscow. The same applied to Ingushetia which had to absorb over 200,000 refugees from Chechnya.

The Duma elections of December 1999 obliged the politicians to seek support in the regions. The new coalitions, Edinstvo, OVR and SPS had no regional organisations and, thus, had to rely on governors to organise support. Tatarstan and Bashkortostan, for example, backed Primakov and Luzhkov (OVR). OVR attracted governors from the more successful regions, revealing how Yeltsin's authority had slipped in the richer areas. Edinstvo targeted the poorer regions and promised them a greater say in drafting the federal budget. The major problem for the regions was to pick the winner in the 2000 presidential contest. Would it be Primakov or Putin or even Gennady Zyuganov, the communist leader? In 1999, only 13 regions paid more in taxes than they received from the centre. These were the cities of Moscow and St Petersburg, the Republics of Tatarstan and Bashkortostan, Krasnoyarsk krai, Lipetsk, Samara, Perm, Sverdlovsk, Moscow, and Irkutsk oblasts, and the Khanty-Mansy and Yamal-Nenets autonomous okrugs. The other 76 regions were recipient regions. Edinstvo had a large constituency.

The good showing of the Edinstvo coalition in the December 1999 Duma elections and the astonishing personal popularity of Vladimir Putin, based almost entirely on his campaign in Chechnya, caused some of the governors to reconsider their position. For instance, President Shaimiev of Tatarstan quickly moved into the Putin camp. Putin's intention to increase military expenditure was welcomed by the governors, many of whom had had to subsidise the troops in their region. When Putin was head of the FSB he strengthened the centre's control over FSB agencies in the regions.

A CONSTITUTIONAL OR A CONTRACTUAL FEDERATION?

Another way of looking at the Russian Federation is to say that a federation can be created on the basis of either the constitutional or the contractual principle (Zergunin 2000). In the former, the constitution defines the prerogatives of the federal centre and the members of the federation. In the latter, bilateral or multilateral treaties between the centre and the regions are signed (as in the former Soviet Union). The problem is that these two principles have been fused in the building of the present Russian Federation.

Initially President Yeltsin favoured the contractual principle. The Federal Treaty was concluded between Moscow and members of the federation, in 1992, with Chechnya and Tatarstan declining to sign. However the 1993 constitution applied the constitutional principle. Nevertheless, in 1994, under pressure from local elites, President Yeltsin began anew to sign agreements with regions by signing bilateral treaties with seven republics, Tatarstan being the first. By 2000, fifty treaties had been signed. Each treaty is different and is accompanied by a series of agreements which can be signed at any time after the conclusion of the treaty. The agreements are much more detailed than the treaties and reflect the differing conditions of the regions.

Besides these bilateral treaties, the republics adopted their own constitutions and krais and oblasts adopted charters. Many contravene article 71 of the federal constitution which defines the spheres which are exclusively under federal jurisdiction. Sverdlovsk, Tatarstan and Udmurtia claimed control over the operation of the defence industry and arms exports. The constitutions of Tatarstan and Bashkortostan permit these republics to establish relations and sign agreements with foreign states. Article 72 of the federal constitution lists areas of joint authority but many republics claim exclusive jurisdiction in finance, investment, environmental protection, culture and so on. It does not help that articles 71 and 72 are rather vaguely worded.

Moscow's attitude was not to define relations with the regions but to adopt a wait-and-see attitude. For instance, there is no federal law on private land ownership so various regions, for example, Saratov and Novgorod went ahead and adopted their own legislation, even granting foreigners limited land rights. The 1994 treaty with Tatarstan just described what was in place in areas such as foreign relations and trade. The Sverdlovsk treaty of 1996 granted the oblast the right to its own civil service and domestic legal regulation of the spheres of joint regional and federal jurisdiction. The oblast can even suspend the normative acts of federal ministries and agencies. Since regions have different foreign policy powers the Russian Federation can be called an asymmetric federation. Over time this leads to conflict between regions as the weaker try to gain the rights of the stronger. It can also destabilise the country.

In order to address these problems, Moscow passed various federal laws to regulate the international relations of the regions. The law of July 1995 gives regions the right to participate in drafting international treaties which impinge on their interests. This law, however, does not resolve the problem of existing regional international agreements. The law on the state regulation of foreign trade, of October 1995, envisages joint authority over the regions' foreign trade, foreign loans, free economic zones and so on. The regions may trade with foreign partners on their own territory, sign agreements with foreign partners and establish trade missions abroad. The regions viewed this law as providing a legal framework for their activities and extending their rights.

A presidential decree of March 1996 stated that treaties between Moscow and the regions and the accompanying agreements were not to contravene the federal constitution and were to respect its supremacy. The President also signed a decree instructing regions to inform the ministry of foreign affairs about their international activities. A federal law, of December 1998, limits the international activities of regions. They are permitted to deal directly with the regional and local governments of foreign states but when dealing with central authorities must go through Moscow. Missions abroad cannot be afforded diplomatic status. Agreements between Russian regions and foreign partners do not have the status of international treaties. A federal law, of June 1999, stated that regions should amend their legislation in order to conform with federal law. They were given one year to effect the necessary changes. Despite this, Tatarstan passed a law on international treaties, in July 1999, which contravenes federal legislation.

During the 1990s the regions signed over 300 international agreements, some of them in collaboration with the ministry of foreign affairs. However there were cases where Moscow was ignored and expressed concern. An example was the agreement between Kabardino-Balkaria and the breakaway Republic of Abkhazia in 1995. Moscow annulled the trade treaty between Kaliningrad oblast and Lithuania in 1995 because it contravened federal legislation.

Tatarstan has representative offices in 16 countries and it arranged for a Turkish general consulate to be set up in Kazan. Since 1995 regions have to fund their foreign missions from their own budget and this has put the brakes on. For instance, Nizhny Novgorod has only one representative abroad, in the German Land of North Rhine Westphalia. Novgorod has been particularly successful in attracting foreign direct investment worth an estimated $900 million in 1999. Only Moscow attracts more.

LOCAL GOVERNMENT

A comprehensive law on local self-government was passed on 28 August 1995 (Schneider 1998: 11–12). It confirmed the constitutional provision that local self-government was to cover the whole of the federation. Local representative agencies were afforded the right to enact laws and decide whether the head of a local administration should be elected directly by the citizens or by a representative body and whether he or she should be a member of that body. The legislation can also determine how many deputies shall be elected to the local representative body and how long it shall sit, although a minimum term of two years must be observed. Local self-government legislation has to be registered by the state and this can be denied if it contravenes the constitution or the laws of the Russian Federation or those of a subject of the federation. Local self-government agencies are expressly permitted to engage in foreign trade activities.

In practice local self-government has not developed as outlined in the legislation. There are two major reasons for this. Generally the heads of local administrations are appointed from above rather than being elected and are subject to vertical subordination. The other major reason is that local budgets are heavily dependent on higher authorities and subsidies. Appointed heads of local administrations are not keen to have competitive elections to local dumas (councils) and the heads prefer to arrogate to themselves the right to appoint local officials. Where elections are held it is normal for independent candidates to dominate. This is because the central political parties are unpopular and hence, for instance, a communist may prefer to stand as an independent candidate to attract more votes. Political parties, therefore, are only in their infancy at the local level. Voters judge according to the candidate and not according to party affiliation.

The law of 25 September 1997 on the financial basis of local self-government strengthened local self-government bodies and afforded regional government greater financial independence. Local self-government now had its own sources of finance. Only time will tell if this will amount to much, given the economic crisis Russia finds itself in. It may also have been intended to signal to the regions that the centre lacks the resources to finance local self-government.

The regions have been reasonably successful in gaining control over tax revenues (Table 7.1). In 1998, the regions' share of revenues had risen to almost 60 per cent. The process of negotiation is non-transparent and varies from year to year. However the obverse of the rise in revenues is that the regions are becoming responsible for more and more public services.

The same pattern evident in relations between the centre and the regions is developing in relations between the subjects of the federation and their local self-governing bodies. The centre is not willing to dilute its powers and share them with the regions if possible. A similar pattern is evident within the subjects. By mid-1997 the subjects of the federation had passed some 76 laws on local self-government. The Russian ministry of justice examined 68 of them and concluded that only four conformed to the articles laid down in the Russian constitution.

By 1996, it had become clear that the constitution did not reflect the real distribution of power within the state. According to the constitution the Security Council has no decision-making powers but during the Chechen war was clearly the key decision-making forum in the state. The presidential administration, not mentioned in the constitution, waxed in size and influence and became superior to the government.

A major reason for these phenomena is that the state no longer performs the role of legal guardian of each and every citizen. A flood of decrees emanated from the President, some unpublished, and this led to a confused legal environment. The Duma, with its anti-market ethos, declined to provide the required legal infrastructure for a market-oriented economy. Russian law, in contrast to English law, does not observe the principle of precedence. New English legislation takes precedence over all existing legislation. This is not the case in Russia. This leads to a situation where it is extremely difficult to discover exactly what the law is.

THE LEGISLATION OF THE SUBJECTS OF THE FEDERATION

Legislation passed at the federal and regional level has led to confusion and uncertainty since some of it contravenes the Russian constitution. Then there are the presidential decrees which have also sown uncertainty, hence the constitutional relationship between the federation and the regions is unclear. Article 5.4 of the Russian constitution states that 'all subjects of the Russian Federation shall be equal between themselves in mutual relations with federal agencies of state power'. Despite this the federal authorities have accorded many republics rights which others do not enjoy, not to speak of the oblasts and krais. The constitution affords the centre the right to clarify its relations with subjects through treaties. This can also be done through federal legislation but, in practice, this opportunity has been little availed of; there is at present no comprehensive legislation on defining the competence of state agencies, the rights of national minorities, a federal tax code, a federal land code, the right to natural resources and so on. Inevitably the subjects of the federation have attempted to compensate for the absence of federal legislation by passing their own laws. These sometimes contravene constitutional and federal law.

Article 61 of the constitution of the Republic of Tatarstan states that the republic is an associate member of the Russian Federation and can decide its own constitutional legal status. Article 60 of the Republic of Buryatia constitution permits the republic to alter its status if in a referendum half the ethnic Buryat citizens participate. Article 78 of the constitution of the Republic of Tyva states that the Supreme Kural, the parliament, may take decisions on peace and war. Another article permits Tyva to leave the Russian Federation. Tatarstan, Bashkortostan, Tyva and Sakha (Yakutia) have included in their constitutions articles which prevent Russian federal legislation 'harming' them. In essence, this means that these subjects can pick and choose which federal legislation they wish to implement. Indeed Buryatia, in November 1996, stated it would not continue to implement some Buryat and federal legislation. Bashkortostan has recognised Abkhazia as an independent state. Ingushetia has legalised polygamy and, a most interesting development, Sakha-Yakutia has adopted English as its official language.

The Russian constitution foresees treaties as the instrument for regulating relations between the subjects and the centre. The first treaty was signed on 15 February 1994 with Tatarstan, then with Kabardino-Balkaria on 1 July 1994, Bashkortostan on 3 August 1994, North Ossetia-Alenia on 23 March 1995, Sakha (Yakutia) on 29 June 1995, Buryatia on 29 August 1995 and Komi on 20 March 1996. All these agreements were with republics. Then came treaties with oblasts and krais: with Kaliningrad and Sverdlovsk oblasts on 12 January 1996, Orenburg oblast, Krasnodar krai and Stavropol krai on 30 January 1996 and Rostov oblast on 11 June 1996. All these treaties were to resolve ongoing conflicts between the regions and the centre (Chinarikhina 1996). The next rash of agreements appeared during the 1996 presidential electoral campaign when no less than 15 were signed during his peregrinations around the country. They were very hastily put together and were designed to respond to local needs. In short, they were electoral bribes, designed to ensure that regional elites and voters stayed loyal to the President. This fed suspicions among governors that their neighbours might have cut secret deals with the centre, deals which granted them special benefits.

Some of these treaties contain articles which contravene the federal constitution: e.g. article 2 of the agreement with Sakha (Yakutia) states that the federal and republican governments shall together assimilate and utilise the natural resources of the continental shelf of the Russian Federation. Article 72 of the federal constitution does not envisage such activities as being under joint control. There is also the federal law of 25 October 1995 which states that the exploitation of the continental shelf of the Russian Federation shall exclusively be the responsibility of the federal authorities.

According to Vladimir Lysenko, leader of the Republican Party, there are four types of treaty (Lysenko 1995). The first are those which were signed for purely political reasons as a result of pressure by subjects of the federation. These include the agreements with Tatarstan, Bashkortostan and Sakha (Yakutia). These treaties include articles which contravene federal and constitutional law. These subjects are accorded special rights as regards taxation and the use of natural resources. Several of the treaties signed during the presidential electoral campaign fall within this category. The second group provide support to the leadership of the subject during times of conflict, such as the republics of Kabardino-Balkaria and North Ossetia-Alenia. Thirdly, treaties with subjects to regulate relations with the centre, demarcating responsibilities. The first such treaty was with Sverdlovsk oblast which had been instrumental in proclaiming the Urals Republic. The centre declared it unconstitutional and proceeded to make concessions to the various constituent parts of the illegal republic. Besides the treaty there were many agreements signed which clarified joint areas of responsibility. Fourthly, there are treaties which regulate specific objects in the subject, such as a nature reserve in Kaliningrad oblast or Lake Baikal in Buryatia.

The strategic significance of the north Caucasus has led to many agreements being signed by the centre in addition to those mentioned above. For instance, Moscow had concluded six agreements with the Republic of North Ossetia-Alenia on property, the defence industry, on sanatoria and health, leisure and tourism, foreign economic relations, the use of natural resources and the protection of the environment, and on the use of land. Two agreements were signed with Chechnya on 12 May 1997 (in addition to the peace treaty between Chechnya and Russia) on monetary circulation and clearing transactions. There have been nine agreements with Krasnodar krai on topics ranging from education, law and order, the introduction of customs controls and various economic matters. The largest number in the region are with Rostov oblast. Eighteen agreements have been signed by Moscow and the administration of Rostov oblast, many of these being on economic matters. Others are on law and order, the ownership of land and minerals, education and the development of the fuel and energy industry.

In addition to the above there are several presidential and Russian government decrees the goal of which is to reduce the gulf between living standards in the north Caucasus and the Russian average. There are federal programmes to promote the oil and gas industry in Dagestan, the tungsten and molybdenum complex in Kabardino-Balkaria and the coal industry in Rostov oblast, among others. Given the location of the region, free economic zones have been established in Ingushetia, North Ossetia-Alenia and Kabardino-Balkaria.

A striking fact about treaties between the centre and the regions is that in almost all cases local citizens are excluded. Moscow's agreements are with the local executives, not with the regions' inhabitants. Treaties are signed by the Presidents (of republics) or the heads of the subjects (governors). Supplementary agreements are signed by the Russian Prime Minister and the regional head of the executive – according to the region this can be the Prime Minister or the governor. Few of these regional treaties have been published, indeed there is no legal requirement that they be so. They contravene, as a rule, existing federal and constitutional norms. Infringements of the constitution can be divided into three main groups:

1   The transfer of the responsibilities of the Russian Federation into joint responsibility of the federation and the subject. Nineteen subjects have established agencies concerned with defending state and territorial unity and security: the republics of Adygea, Bashkortostan, Dagestan, Ingushetia, Kabardino-Balkaria, Mordovia, North Ossetia-Alenia, Tyva, Udmurtia, Volgograd, Kemerovo, Omsk, Saratov, Sverdlovsk, Tver, Tomsk, Ulyanovsk oblasts, Nenets autonomous okrug, St Petersburg. The following have set up their own security councils: the republics of Adygea, Ingushetia, Kabardino-Balkaria, North Ossetia-Alenia, Mordovia, Tyva, Dagestan, Perm and Sverdlovsk oblasts. Ministries and authorities for security have been established in the republics of Bashkortostan, Dagestan, Ingushetia, Kabardino-Balkaria, Karelia, Khakasia, Mary El and Tatarstan. Defence and security, according to article 71.1 of the Russian constitution, are exclusively the responsibility of the federal authorities. Other examples are conversion from military to civilian use of enterprises in Sverdlovsk and Orenburg oblasts and elsewhere and the sale of weapons and military technology in the treaty with Tatarstan.

2   The transfer of the powers of the Russian Republic to the subjects of the federation. These include the right to engage in international economic relations, the establishment of national banks, republican citizenship in Tatarstan and the right of Kabardino-Balkaria to declare

a state of emergency. In many subjects the rights, freedoms and duties of the person and the citizen are linked to the citizenship of a given republic. This contravenes articles 15, 17, 18, 62 and 71 of the Russian constitution. For instance, the constitution of Dagestan permits dual citizenship (this does not contravene the Russian constitution) but Dagestanis, living outside the republic, may be granted citizenship without being citizens of the Russian Federation. In Irkutsk oblast the head of the executive branch may not have dual citizenship. This implies that the head has to come from Irkutsk oblast.

3 The transfer of joint powers to the subjects of the federation. These include the guarantee of human and civil rights, rights to own and use land and resources, the nature of republican agencies and their activities in Tatarstan and Bashkortostan.

The treaties mentioned above have produced a federation where subjects are not legally equal. Some regions have many agreements with the centre; for example, in 1997, Sverdlovsk oblast had 13, Orenburg oblast five, Bashkortostan 11, but some others had none. Some regions, through treaties with the centre, are able to render inoperable certain aspects of federal legislation. Presidential decrees have the same effect. It is extremely difficult to challenge these concessions on the basis of constitutional law.

The State Duma is the main source of federal legislation. The first Duma, 1993–95, passed over 400 laws but failed to agree on important legislation affecting the structure of the state. Glaring gaps were filled with presidential decrees. The Duma does not have the resources to employ enough legal advisers to help with the drafting of bills. The result is that much legislation is woolly, imprecise, declarative and of little practical use. Sometimes new laws contradict existing legislation or repeat it. Some legislation fails to state what the penalty is for contravening the law or failing to implement it. Lawyers have two main criticisms of Duma legislation: it is either too general, declarative or unnecessarily detailed or it is a moral statement which contains little law. An added difficulty is that article 114.2 of the Russian constitution states that the 'procedure for the activity of the government of the Russian Federation shall be determined by a federal constitutional law'. As yet this has not occurred and so the activities of the federal government remain undefined in law. According to article 115.1 of the constitution the government 'shall issue decrees and regulations and ensure their implementation' on a federal basis. Another law which has still not been promulgated is the law on the organisation of state power in the subjects of the federation which would coordinate the activities of the regional institutions.

Saratov oblast has found an original solution to the endless confusion over the ownership of land – it has enacted its own land law. The oblast duma passed legislation, on 12 November 1997, which confirms the right to private ownership of land and permits the free sale of land held as private property. The Saratov law is a breakthrough in that it permits the sale of privately owned land to any other person or organisation. However foreigners may not own or purchase land but are permitted to lease it. Only privately owned land may be sold, not state or municipal land. Following tradition, the Saratov law does not permit the change of use of agricultural land; farmland must still be farmed. The Saratov initiative spurred other regions into action and many began drafting their own land law modelled on the Saratov legislation. Samara's law, for example, permits ownership of land by foreigners. During the winter of 1997–98 Kemerovo passed its own land law and began distributing land to residents of the oblast. By late 1997, over 50 regions had passed legislation permitting the buying and selling of land in conformity with the Russian constitution. The impasse at the centre has resulted in regions acting unilaterally to resolve the problem. This testifies to the increasing confidence of local legislatures and, by extension, local elites. Land is an extremely important issue and it would appear that the regions are achieving their goal, control over their own land.

Regional legislation is heavily influenced by the head of the executive, the President or governor. Between 40 per cent and 70 per cent of this legislation contravenes federal and constitutional law. If there is a dispute at the regional level between the executive and the legislature over legislation it is the executive which has the authority to resolve it. The aggrieved party can take the matter to the constitutional court. However the court cannot cope with the number of submissions made to it and only provides judgments in a minority of cases.

A major headache for the centre is that it is extremely difficult legally to force the regions to amend their own legislation to conform to federal or constitutional law. Extra-judicial means have to be found to oblige regions to conform to federal norms. The lack of clarity in constitutional law has led to disputes between subjects of the federation. For example, the authorities in Yamalo-Nenets and Khanty-Mansy autonomous okrugs, part of Tyumen oblast, attempted to upgrade their status to that of oblast, and thereby become independent of Tyumen oblast, but were rebuffed by the constitutional court. In practice, the regional legislatures have very little influence on the federal legislature, the Duma.

This state of affairs can be called legal nihilism where central institutions have recourse to the law if it enhances their power and disregard it when it suits them. The lack of interest of the Duma in fashioning an efficient market-oriented system means that federal legislation is incapable of coping with the demands of a burgeoning market economy. Officials from various ministries and agencies at the centre form interest groups (or clans or mafia groups) and link up with regional groups to promote their own agendas. Legally they can hardly be combated. The usual method of dealing with them is for the President to sack the top officials. The new men then begin to fashion their own interest groups. This corruption also benefits the centre. It permits the federal authorities to cut deals with regional executives so as to keep them loyal. The concessions made to Bashkortostan were to ensure that it did not pursue its aim of merging with Tatarstan. The same applies to Sverdlovsk oblast which received many benefits from the centre to ensure that it did not return to its plan to form a Urals Republic.

REGIONAL ECONOMIC PERFORMANCE

Regions can be divided into winners and losers from the point of view of economic structure. Differences in economic structure among regions are immense and the structure of output can be explained by differences in the endowments of natural resources, labour and capital. Another major factor was the tendency of Soviet planners to concentrate the output of some products in a few large factories. Differences in economic structure are relevant since, over the years 1992–95, those regions which were dominated by the fuel and energy industry fared better than those in textiles and light industry. The economic structure turned out, over the years 1992–95, to be more important as an explanation for relative economic performance than economic policy (Van Selm 1998: 605). Policy differences have not had a significant impact on economic performance, at least so far.

The success story of the years under review was the city of Moscow. It experienced a decline in industrial production of over one third while the average for the Russian Federation was about a quarter. Nevertheless, in 1995, Moscow had the lowest official unemployment, the highest nominal income in the Russian Federation and its electricity production was 99 per cent of that of 1990. New sectors, especially financial services, have sprung up and transformed the capital.

Van Selm computed an index of overall economic performance which included industrial output, unemployment, exports, nominal income and electricity generation (Van Selm 1998: 611). Six of the ten regions with the most favourable industrial structure in 1993 were among the top economic performers in 1995: Lipetsk, Kemerovo, Tyumen, Irkutsk and Magadan oblasts, and Sakha (Yakutia). The ten regions with the least favourable industrial structure in 1993 were: the Chuvash Republic,

Moscow oblast, Bryansk, Vladimir, Pskov oblasts, Altai Republic, Jewish autonomous oblast, Kaluga, Ulyanovsk and Ivanovo oblasts, in that order. Not one of these was among the top ten performers in 1995 while two, Chuvash Republic and Ivanovo oblast, were in the bottom ten performers. The latter was dominated by the Muslim republics in the north Caucasus, such as Dagestan, Kabardino-Balkaria and Karachaevo-Cherkesia. One of the interesting findings was that there was no obvious correlation between economic policy and economic performance in 1995. This may mean that economic reform takes time and that 1995 was too early to expect tangible results. Agriculturally the most fertile parts of the country, the black earth belt or chernozem, have not fared well. Indeed the non-chernozem regions have been more successful. Most progress has been made in a band 50 km wide around major cities. This reveals the influence of the urban market and the ability to deliver food products to it. The areas which require the largest subsistence income are, not surprisingly, all in the north.

As mentioned above, the north Caucasus (defined as the Muslim republics, plus Krasnodar krai, Stavropol krai and Rostov oblast) had fared poorly by 1995. There is a sharp distinction, however, between the Muslim republics and the other regions of the north Caucasus. In 1996, the gross per capita regional product of Stavropol krai was 72 per cent of the Russian average. In Krasnodar krai it was 65 per cent and in Rostov oblast 63 per cent. The highest ranking Muslim republic was Adygea with 43 per cent, followed by Karachaevo-Cherkesia with 41 per cent, North Ossetia-Alenia with 37 per cent and Kabardino-Balkaria with 35 per cent. Right at the bottom were Dagestan with 21 per cent and Ingushetia with 20 per cent. Chechnya is not included. These figures reveal the great gap in living standards even within the north Caucasus.

The economic debacle of August 1998 hit the regions hard and led to many banks collapsing. In order to ensure access to revenue streams the authorities in St Petersburg and Ekaterinburg took over regional banks. The Nizhny Tagil metallurgy combine gave the Sverdlovsk oblast administration a 25 per cent stake in the company in return for a restructuring of its tax arrears and the cancellation of its overdue wages bill. These are only a few of the examples of how regional authorities have strengthened their positions in the wake of the August collapse.

REGIONAL SUBVENTIONS

Which regions are most successful in obtaining fiscal aid from the centre? Are those regions which vote for the President and for pro-presidential parties at Duma elections more likely to be winners in the lottery of state aid? Are regions which support the opposition punished by seeing their financial subventions from the federal budget shrink? Are regions which are economically backward more likely to obtain a higher per capita quota than the economic success stories? Treisman, in analysing federal finances in 1995 and 1996, comes to some surprising conclusions (Treisman 1998). The subject is complex and, given the state of Russia's finances, a hazardous undertaking. Nevertheless he finds that a clearer connection can be divined between net central transfers and indicators of social need than was true in previous years. In 1992, 1994, 1995 and 1996 larger transfers went to those regions which had voted clearly against central, pro-reform candidates. He finds evidence that those regions which had threatened the economy by striking or the President's political role by siding with parliament in October 1993, for example, were later rewarded with greater subsidies. The reason for this appears to be that the centre, aware of its weakness, will always attempt to mollify opposition. A particular goal is to prevent two or more regions coming together to form an opposition which could be joined later by other disgruntled regions. Attempts to alter the constitutional order are met with fiscal and jurisdictional concessions. The only exception is Chechnya where, it would appear, President Dudaev could not be bought off.

In 1997, differences between regions had widened further. For example, the gulf between average life expectancy in some regions had grown to 17 years for males and 12 years for females; the proportion of pensioners was up to five times higher in some regions; the average income of the population was 14 times higher in the richest region compared to the poorest region and the gulf in wages was 11.5 times. The purchasing power of the population in the richest regions was eight times higher than in the poorest regions.

A case in point is Dagestan. Its economic decline began in the 1980s but this was accompanied by a sharp rise in the population. In 1996, compared to 1983, the population had risen by 30 per cent. Global agricultural output continued to decline at the same time. This has widened the economic gulf between Dagestan and the Russian Federation as a whole. In 1996, per capita production was only 17 per cent of the Russian average, industrial production was 8 per cent and agricultural output was 36 per cent. The rise in the population and the drop in agricultural output have led to greater and greater imports of food, up to 65 per cent of consumption. This problem needs to be addressed quickly since Dagestan has the potential to produce all the food it needs.

One of the obstacles facing Dagestan is that those not of working age (per 1000 of those of working age) are double the Russian average. Children and pensioners now constitute 55 per cent of the Dagestani population. This enormous social security bill imposes a heavy burden on the budget. Unemployment is a scourge and is particularly high among young people. In the capital Makhachkala it is about half but in Khasavyurt raion it was 94 per cent in 1996. The poor economic prospects led, over the years 1991–97, to 11,500 Russians and 5100 Mountain Jews and Tats leaving the republic. Most of the Russians and Mountain Jews were employed in social institutions and in industry. One of the reasons for the exit was the collapse of military production in the republic.

Dagestan's weak economic position makes it dependent on the federal centre, Moscow. In 1994, federal transfers accounted for 87 per cent of the republican budget but this had dropped to 72 per cent in 1997. One of the reasons for the decline was that the Russian ministry of finance changed the way the transfer fund for the regions was calculated in 1996. The result was that the fund declined by about 50 per cent. The centre distributes funds to the regions according to certain criteria, one of which is the loyalty of the local elites to Moscow. The money is disbursed to the region but the centre pays little attention to the way it is spent. This fosters the influence of local oligarchies. The lack of supervision from Moscow has led to the black economy expanding quite quickly. One estimate puts it at 79 per cent of the global economy in 1997. It is expanding annually at the expense of the legal economy. The black economy pays little or no tax and so Dagestani budget revenue is likely to decline continually. This suits the oligarchs since it will strengthen their claims for increased transfer payments from Moscow.

Dagestan, as regards the average per capita income of the population, is below the average of Russia but also that of most north Caucasian regions. In 1997, in the Russian Federation only Dagestan, Ingushetia, Chita oblast and the Republic of Tyva had per capita incomes below subsistence level ($39 a month in 2000). In per capita income, in 1997, Ingushetia was last and Dagestan last but one of all the regions in Russia (excluding Chechnya). The lack of resources in Moscow has led to the centre transferring responsibility for financing an increasing range of services, such as education, culture and research institutes of the Academy of Sciences to the regions. Under present circumstances this is a slow sentence of death for these services.

Ingushetia is even more dependent on federal transfers than Dagestan. In 1996, the share of federal transfers accounted for 79.3 per cent of the net income of the republic. On this calculation they accounted for 55.5 per cent of net income of Dagestan. In Adygea they were 51.5 per cent but in Krasnodar krai only 19 per cent. The Russian average was 14.3 per cent.

The economic crisis of August 1998 and the penetration of the Chechen insurgents in August 1999 were body blows to Dagestan. The second Chechen war has ruined not only Chechnya but also resulted in a desperate economic situation in Ingushetia, indeed in the whole of the North Caucasus. Perhaps as many as 50 per cent of the population of the North Caucasus now live in poverty.

The Caucasus has remained a high poverty region but the same can be said of the Far North, the Far East and parts of Siberia. In 2000, the government stated that 10 per cent of Russian regions contributed 48 per cent of GDP. The Chuvash Republic now has a native majority and Tatarstan and Bashkortostan soon will. They are all in the Volga region. Would they be better off coming together to form a new republic? President Putin would not like that.

GUBERNATORIAL ELECTIONS

Fifty-five regions of the Russian Federation held elections for the post of head of the administration, governor, between June 1995 and March 1997 (*Vybory* 1997; Solnick 1998). In many regions there were also elections to the regional legislatures, mayors of the regional capital city, and for local councils. Forty-eight of these elections for governor were held in regions where the incumbent head of the administration had been appointed by President Yeltsin and had never faced the voters. The timing of the elections was significant. Yeltsin did not want elections to take place before the presidential elections of June and July 1996. Indeed the first election to be held, in St Petersburg, took place on 2 June and resulted in the defeat of the incumbent mayor (now governor), Anatoly Sobchak, by Vladimir Yakovlev.

The results of the gubernatorial elections surprised and disappointed many. The Yeltsin camp had expected another win over the communists. On paper the result was more or less a draw. About half of the incumbents were defeated revealing that either regional politics was different from pan-Russian politics or the presidential team had been incompetent. However this turned out to be only a formal defeat. Many of the communist and anti-Yeltsin governors immediately offered to work with the President. Regional voting did not follow the pattern of the presidential elections and a correlation between the economic standing of the region and voting was difficult to establish. The key reason for success in regional elections was the personality of the candidate and his or her (there is one new female governor, Valentina Tadeevna Bronevich of the Koryak autonomous okrug; she is of Itelmen nationality and a lawyer) links with the local political structures. This implies that pan-Russian parties have not succeeded in establishing significant regional branches. The trend of governors negotiating with the centre to secure concessions and investment seems set to continue. The willingness of communist governors, such as Aleksandr Rutskoi (Kursk), to work with the President appears to preclude factions in the Council of the Federation mirroring those in the Duma. This further fragments the political opposition and permitted President Yeltsin to play one group off against the other. There is little to indicate, at present, that there is a centrifugal flow of power in Russia and that the federation is under threat.

ISLAM

The Concept of National Security which was confirmed by the President's decree of 17 December 1997 stressed that Islamic sects, especially in the north Caucasus, were perceived as a threat to Russian national security. It was recognised that the poor socio-economic conditions of the region fostered such movements but the struggle for power was also a significant factor. This was a change of perspective. In the early 1990s, Moscow viewed local nationalists as the greatest threat to national security. Is the threat to the unity of the federation real or imagined? Is the centre merely using the spectre of Islamic fundamentalism to promote its own agenda in the region?

Islam is, according to the law on the freedom of conscience and religious associations signed by the President on 26 September 1997, one of the four 'traditional' religions of Russia. The others are Orthodoxy, Judaism and Buddhism. The main centre of Islam in Russia is Dagestan but there are several Muslim republics, such as Tatarstan and Bashkortostan, which are not geographically in the north Caucasus. It is now the tradition, in Muslim republics, for the President to be sworn in with one hand on the Koran and the other on the constitution of the republic. There has been a renaissance of Islam in Russia since the law on the freedom of religion, passed by the Russian Supreme Soviet in 1990. Nowhere has the growth been as spectacular as in Dagestan. Whereas in 1985 there were 27 mosques in Dagestan, in December 1996 there were 1600, 600 Mosque schools, 25 medreses and 11 Islamic institutions of higher education. About 2200 imams, mullahs and alims are employed in the mosques and educational establishments (*Dagestanskaya Pravda*, 18 December 1996). The Spiritual Board of the Muslims of the North Caucasus, established under Soviet rule, split in 1989 along national lines (there was a Kumyk Spiritual Board, then a Lak Spiritual Board and so on). However in September 1994 all the Spiritual Boards came together and formed the Spiritual Board of the Muslims of Dagestan. Among the duties of the Board were theology, services, Islamic learning, the running of the mosques and Islamic educational establishments, the organisation of the hadj (to Mecca; only 350 from Dagestan went on the hadj in 1990 but in 1998 this had risen to 13,500), the promotion of knowledge about Islam and the raising of the moral and spiritual level of the population. The Board works closely with the government of Dagestan. The constitution of 26 July 1994 declared Dagestan to be a secular republic and separated the religious institutions from the state.

Political movements and parties sprang up quickly from 1989 onwards. Almost all had come into being by 1994. The most significant are the Islamic Democratic Party of Dagestan, formed in 1994, the Islamic Party of Dagestan and the Islamic Renaissance Party. There is also the Wahhabi party, the Jamaatul Muslimin (see below).

In September 1995, the first Congress of the Muslims of Russia took place and elected Nadir Khachilaev chair. Soon afterwards the Congress of the Muslims of Dagestan set up the Dagestan branch of the Union of Muslims of Russia. In April 1995, the Nur [Light] Pan-Russian Muslim Social movement was founded. In June 1996 a Dagestani branch of Nur was set up. The movement spread throughout the whole of the north Caucasus. In early 1998, Nur was transformed into the Party of Muslims of Russia. There is also a growing Islamic press.

The above may be regarded as moderate, traditional and willing to function within the law of Dagestan. None of the above demands an Islamic republic or the replacement of the law by the Sharia (Islamic law). The more radical face of Islam is the Wahhabi movement. It appeared in Dagestan about 15 years ago and emanates from Saudi Arabia. It rejects much of the traditional teaching of the Sunnis, such as the pilgrimage to Mecca. It is not a single movement but consists of many groups. They have clashed with the Sufi tariquats and this has led to disorders in mosques in many raions. The police and government agencies have kept their distance. The Spiritual Board has acted vigorously against them but has called on the government to take action to eliminate extremism. This has led to the muftis working with the Federal Security Service. However the influence of the radicals has been felt in some raions where concerts, plays and films have been banned.

The Wahhabim in Dagestan and Chechnya have acted in concert and a political movement, the Nation of Islam, which includes political parties from both republics, headed by Movladi Udugov, the former foreign minister of Chechnya, promotes the unification of the two republics. They also advocate that the new state become an Islamic republic. They have instituted violence to radicalise the political situation such as the attack on the Russian military at Buinaksk, in December 1997, and the occupation of government buildings in Makhachkala. President Aslan Maskhadov has banned their activities in Chechnya. Chechen insurgents in Dagestan, in August 1999, were described as Wahhabim and proclaimed an Islamic republic. Such was Moscow's perception of the Islamic threat to its rule that a major war was launched to suppress it.

Little progress has been made in the dispute between North Ossetia-Alenia and Ingushetia over Prigorody raion. This is a potential flashpoint and trouble here could spread throughout the region.

Overall there is a depressing increase in the number of kidnappings in the north Caucasus and this points to a loss of authority of the governments there. According to the Russian ministry of the interior, 1094 persons were kidnapped in Chechnya, or neighbouring areas, between January 1997 and August 1999. Over 950 were still unaccounted for in late 2000 and many have been killed during the savage bombing of Chechnya by Russian forces. These official numbers do not include the thousands of Chechens abducted within the republic. Some families of victims pay the ransom and do not report the crime.

After the Russian withdrawal from Chechnya in 1996, Moscow was not in a position to halt the kidnappings or free the victims. The local Chechen government's security services rarely intervened for fear of fuelling clan conflicts. Indeed the Chechen police often cooperated with kidnappers or became kidnappers themselves. Customs officials could kidnap people while inspecting trains and busses. The abducted are often billeted with local villagers by the kidnap gangs and warned that if they allow the prisoner to escape they and their family will pay with their heads. A favourite method of execution is decapitation. Heads are then kicked around by the executioners. Some are put on poles for display. Sometimes a heart is cut out and nailed to a tree. A slave market developed as kidnappers bought and sold their captives. Russian soldiers have been known to sell their comrades into slavery. Russian soldiers, especially officers, are prize targets. This has led to a situation where Russian troops take no prisoners during engagements with Chechen rebels. It is either kill or be killed.

The market took off in September 1996 when Russia ran out of captured Chechen rebels to exchange for Russian POWs. The Russian Duma passed legislation permitting the amnestying of convicted Chechens in prison if they were exchanged for captive Russian soldiers and civilians. A similar amnesty law was passed in late 1999. The norm was three Russians to be exchanged for each Chechen. An unfortunate side effect of this is to step up the search for Russians to kidnap. After all the more Russians who are kidnapped the more Chechens will be released from Russian jails.

A kidnapped Russian can bring in between $2000 and $145,000. French citizens can be released for as much as a million dollars each. British aid workers Camilla Carr and Jon James were freed in September 1998 after a year in captivity. Their release was negotiated by Boris Berezovsky who denied paying a ransom but there were persistent rumours that several million dollars changed hands. Valentin Vlasov, President Yeltsin's envoy to Chechnya, was released in November 1998 after six months in captivity. Insiders said $3 million was paid. In December 1998, the heads of three British citizens and a New Zealander were found by the roadside. They had been working for a company setting up a mobile phone relay station. An American missionary was let go in June 1998 after a video showing his captors cutting off the tip of his right index finger was sent with a ransom demand. He stated that if the money did not arrive a finger would be cut off; others would be cut off until the money was paid.

8

BANDIT CAPITALISM

Spread the truth – the laws of economics are like the laws of engineering. One set of laws works everywhere. (Lawrence Summers, 1991)

There are no special countries. From an economist's point of view, if economics exists at all, then it is a science with its own laws and . . . all countries are one and the same. (Petr Aven, February 1992)

DURING THE 1990S RUSSIA PURSUED TWO economic policies. One was inspired by western neoliberal economic theory, shock therapy and its successors, and the other by Russian experience. Neoliberal economics was based on developments in Latin America in the 1980s. These were then applied to Russia and eastern Europe in the 1990s. They proved quite inappropriate in Russia and the CIS. Neoliberal economics was based on several assumptions:

- Men and women are natural, instinctive capitalists.
- Their natural entrepreneurial ability was held back by the planned economy until 1991.
- Since the institutions of a communist state are inimical to the spirit of enterprise, the best course to adopt is to destroy the communist state and its institutions.
- The institutions of a new capitalist society will emerge spontaneously.
- The role of the state is to establish the rules of the capitalist game and then watch it unfold.

- The instruments used by the state to permit the free expression of the entrepreneurial spirit are financial – regulation of the money supply, a balanced budget (the government spends as much as it collects in revenues from the population), etc.

- The first step is to liberalise prices in order to move from state-regulated prices to market clearing prices. During the transition some prices may, for a time, remain state-regulated.

- Privatisation of the state's assets is fundamental to the success of the new economy.

- Privatisation should be pushed through as quickly as possible.

- Privatisation should replace existing enterprise managers with new managers who are capable of working successfully in a market environment; in other words, insiders should be replaced by outsiders.

- Poorly executed privatisation is preferable to no privatisation at all.

- In Russia's case, it is acceptable that businessmen from the communist black, illegal economy become legal owners in the new economy. Their criminal backgrounds are of no consequence; their ability to succeed against all the odds under communism proves they have the talent for legal business in the new economy.

- Inflation will be high in the beginning but will decline and become manageable after about a year.

- Bringing down inflation is effected by stabilisation; simply put, this means balancing the budget. In order to reduce expenditure, the social security burden borne by the state should be reduced drastically; citizens should gradually move to paying for health and education according to their needs; this is done by taking out personal insurance policies; pensions will gradually be met from personal pension policies. In the short term there will be no safety net for the less successful. As the economy develops, the state can assume some responsibility for the less well off.

- Structural reform becomes very important; simply put, this means the survival of the fittest enterprises with the others going to the wall or bankrupt.

- Russia's economy was in urgent need of structural change as it was dominated by the military industrial complex. The industrial economy needed to become oriented to civilian products which were competitive on the world market.

- Agriculture occupied too many workers, about 25 per cent of the labour force, and needed to slim down.

■ The unemployed should move into the service sector which was grossly underdeveloped in Russia.

■ In the short term Russia could compete successfully in the world commodity markets because of its ability to export oil, gas, metals, timber, gold, etc.

■ The central economic ministries should be phased out and the management of the economy left to the market.

■ The ministries which represented monopolies in various sectors of the economy should be devolved into holding companies and these could then be privatised but the state would retain a holding in these privatised companies.

■ The exporting and importing of goods should be privatised.

■ Parliament should promulgate the legislation needed to establish a functioning market economy as quickly as possible.

■ The government does not concern itself with investment; the market will decide which sectors need investment and the more successful the sector the more investment will flow there.

Alan Greenspan, chair of the Federal Reserve, admitted, in 1997, that he thought the collapse of communism would automatically establish a free market entrepreneurial system. 'Much of what we took for granted in our free market system and assumed to be human nature was not nature at all, but culture . . . There is a vast amount of capitalist culture and infrastructure underpinning market economies that has evolved over generations: laws, conventions, [modes of] behaviour, and a wide variety of business professions and practices that has no important functions in a centrally planned economy.' Douglass North, who was awarded a Nobel Prize for his pioneering work on institutions (in other words, rules, laws and incentives), was even more direct, in 1993. 'We simply do not know how to create efficient political markets . . . The interface between politics and economics is still in a primitive state in our theories.' He added: 'Neoclassical [economic] theory is simply an inappropriate tool to analyze and prescribe policies that will induce development. It is concerned with the operation of markets, not with how markets develop.'

Side by side with the new economic philosophy, which was quite alien to Russia, was the old economic philosophy. The state manages the economy. This resulted in:

■ The state providing subsidies to enterprises and regions.

■ These subsidies could not come directly from the budget, which had to be almost in balance to satisfy the IMF and other western lenders, but had to be off-budget.

- The government ran the neoliberal economy and satisfied the criteria laid down by the IMF, etc. In this way more western aid flowed into Russia.

- The presidential administration played an important role in running the off-budget subsidies; these were needed because the economy was in sharp decline and enterprises did not have the resources to pay for their inputs and labour; the state had to decide which to subsidise.

- Since the government could not provide the subsidies directly, a sophisticated system had to be developed to provide them; this involved primarily the commercial banks, of which the big foreign trade banks were the most important; they received loans from the Russian Central Bank and then distributed them, taking their cut. As a reward, these banks, headed by the oligarchs, received government accounts and paid no interest to the government; they made substantial profits from exporting oil, gas, etc. but some of this money had to be passed on to loss-making enterprises in order to keep them afloat; the banks left a part of their export revenues in foreign banks abroad and they also paid little tax to the government. The banks did not decide which enterprises should receive loans, this was the responsibility of bureaucrats. Banks, as a result, had little interest in soliciting savings from private citizens; they also extended few loans using normal business criteria. As a result, a huge part of the banks' loan portfolio consisted of non-performing loans or bad debts; to compensate, the government wrote off some the banks' debt to it from time to time; the leading foreign trade banks were instructed by the presidential administration, from time to time, to acquire part of loss-making firms and media companies; they then subsidised them; the banks owned oil companies, for instance, and could deflect some of their profits to these newly acquired companies. They also had to continue delivering oil, natural gas, etc. to customers who could not pay.

- The government used the IMF and other currency inflows to provide off-budget subsidies and to pay for the import of consumer goods; this meant that the government was always short of money and needed more and more loans. Russia's foreign debt increased alarmingly and its servicing began to take up more and more of the budget.

- In order to increase revenue the government began to sell GKOs or short-term government bonds. These were acquired by the commercial banks; at first foreigners could not purchase them but gradually this was eased and foreign investors flooded in. The whole system broke down in August 1998 when Russia defaulted and devalued. Foreigners had their wealth confiscated by the Russian state.

■ Since the government was always short of revenue it did not pay wages on time. It also did not pay producers and farmers for their produce on time. Before elections it always cut these arrears substantially.

■ Privatisation was rigged in favour of outsiders; these were the clans around Yeltsin with Anatoly Chubais being the main actor. Since insiders, the existing managers, took over about 60 per cent of industry, the government began trying to bankrupt them. This was not to put them out of business but to allow them to be taken over by outsiders. Tactics used included imposing punitive taxes, denying them subsidies, sending in the tax police to go through their books, etc. Taxation was so onerous that it amounted to more than 100 per cent of profits! Manufacturing industry was thus not profitable but promised to be so in the long term. In the short term the outsiders concentrated on gaining control of the energy sector; why did the government continue with large-scale privatisation when so many insiders (the red nomenklatura) benefited so greatly? (The Academy of Sciences estimated, at the end of 1995, that 61 per cent of the business elite were from the red nomenklatura; as were about 75 per cent of Yeltsin's government and entourage and 82 per cent of the regional elites.) The reason appears to have been Gaidar's fear of a popular upsurge which could have forced the Yeltsin administration into revising its privatisation programme. The ordinary Russian and the middle class (scientists, lecturers, professors, teachers, engineers, doctors and those in the research and educational sectors) did not favour privatisation since it enriched existing and new elites. In order to head off popular protest Gaidar, Chubais and the team entered into an informal alliance with the old nomenklatura. This also meant allying with the mafia entrepreneurs. Hence the new ruling elites felt so insecure that they came together with the old ruling elites. Yeltsin consciously chose to avoid another 1917 revolution, which would have seen property transferred widely to the people and to continue the Soviet-era distribution of power. The only difference now was that the ruling elites owned the property instead of disposing of it. All those who could be co-opted were co-opted.

■ Privatisation resulted in huge benefits to insiders and outsiders. Over the period 1992–99 Russia scored a world record in the number of enterprises and facilities privatised when over 133,200 were sold for a grand total of $9.25 billion or about $69,500 per asset or less than the price of a new Mercedes. Revenues from 22,402 industrial enterprises came to $347.2 million or about $15,500 a time; the privatisation of 8100 construction companies raised $56.8 million or $7000 each; the sale of 3184 transport and communications enterprises realised $49.4 million or about $15,500 each. Compare this to Brazil's $66.7 billion between 1990 and 1998.

AN OVERVIEW

The process of transferring wealth from the state to private persons began in 1986 when Gorbachev began dismantling the state's foreign trade monopoly. Until then the ministry of foreign trade had a monopoly on foreign trade and hard currency deals. All funds flowed into Vneshtorgbank, the bank for foreign trade. Ministries competed for their share of this treasure trove. Gorbachev afforded other ministries the right to trade directly with the outside world and to handle their own hard currency. Then certain enterprises were permitted to do this and finally individuals. World market prices might be a hundred times that of Soviet controlled prices. Those who could get an export licence, knew how to get the goods abroad and deposit the money in a western bank account could become fabulously rich almost overnight. How was one to get a licence and get the goods abroad? Bribe the necessary officials, of course. The most valuable products were oil, gas, diamonds, gold and minerals. Manufactured goods were way down the list as almost all were uncompetitive on world markets.

The sale of gold, for instance, remained a state monopoly; however, gold mines were to receive a percentage of the dollar earnings, usually 25 per cent, and the rest in rubles. State officials could sell the gold, inform the mines of the price they had secured (much lower than the actual price) and promise them payment partly in dollars. This usually arrived very late and due to inflation the rubles had already devalued. The gold mines then tried to transfer the dollars abroad into a hard currency account. This author acted as a consultant to a foreign company and was always asked the same question by the Russians: 'how do we set up an offshore account?' As far as gold was concerned there was another question. 'How could the gold be exported without the permission of the Soviet authorities?' The author decided the Russians were much more cunning than he was when it came to finding a solution to this problem.

Another gold mine was financial speculation. New commercial banks could be set up in 1988 and hundreds came quickly into existence. Private banks could also be established. Often those involved had worked in the Central Bank and thus had the right contacts. The game was to borrow as much as possible from the Central Bank. Interest rates were always below inflation so, if one borrowed money for two months, one paid back less. However it was much more lucrative to buy dollars and transfer the money abroad. Some hit on a simpler wheeze. Set up a bank, borrow huge amounts from the Central Bank, exchange the rubles into dollars, transfer the money abroad, then liquidate the bank and disappear (the loot had to be shared with the Central Bank officials who had authorised the loan).

This was the basis of the greatest bank rip-off in Russian history, known as the great Chechen bank fraud, in 1992–93. It was so simple it was breathtaking. Two banks were set up. One would send a forged money transfer to the other, using Russian Central Bank codes. The bank would then present the order to one of the 1400 Central Bank payment centres and receive the money in cash. This gigantic scam netted, according to the Russian government, $500 million, but according to other observers, billions, before it was stopped (Klebnikov 2000: 27). The two banks disappeared. It was only possible because the Chechens were able to bribe high-level Central Bank officials and launder their money through a network of corrupt banks.

SHOCK THERAPY OR THE WASHINGTON CONSENSUS

On 5 November 1991, Egor Gaidar received a telephone call from the President, not Mikhail Gorbachev but Boris Yeltsin. He and his team or clan were to take over the transformation of the Russian economy. He would be acting Prime Minister and minister of finance. Gaidar, one of the cleverest economists of his generation, was frightened but as it turned out not frightened enough. He did not hesitate. After all he and his friends had been dreaming of this day for five years. He was the heir to a famous name. His grandfather had been a Red Army hero and writer of best-selling children's books. Yeltsin was partly under the spell of his name when he selected him. As he belonged to the nomenklatura Gaidar enjoyed a privileged education. He was aided by a photographic memory and was the finest speaker of Russian when in office. Even at secondary school he was reading about the capitalist alternative to communism. His brother gave him Adam Smith and he loved the Scottish economist's rational approach. Another delight was Paul Samuelson's classic textbook on economics. Unfortunately Gaidar believed the world described by Smith (history has revealed that Marx was a more perceptive analyst of capitalism than Smith) and Samuelson actually could exist whereas it still remains a mystery how the market economy actually functions. Samuelson's experience was based on the mature American economy and how it could be improved. It needed improvement. Labour productivity growth between 1973 and 1990 was sluggish and behind other economies, such as Japan. Real earnings of US production workers declined by 14 per cent between 1973 and 1995. Median weekly earnings of all men fell, while those of women stagnated. Gaidar's faith in the US economy, however, was justified. It took off spectacularly in 1995.

At Moscow State University, Gaidar read economics and the western texts from Ricardo to Milton Friedman (Keynes would have been more relevant). He did postgraduate research on econometrics under Academician Stanislav Shatalin. From 1983–85 Gaidar was a member of a government commission, established by Yury Andropov, to examine the reform of a socialist economy. This forum brought him into contact with several who would later join him. Gaidar convened a seminar near Leningrad, in 1986, and the 'dream team' was born; other participants included Petr Aven, Anatoly Chubais, Aleksei Ulyukaev and Sergei Vasilev. They playfully set about forming a post-planning government. Gaidar was a natural as Prime Minister because of intellectual pre-eminence and knowledge of western economic theory and Chubais's outstanding organisational talents were already evident. Gaidar and Chubais were members of the communist party.

In 1987, at the invitation of Aleksandr Yakovlev, Gaidar became editor of articles on economics in *Kommunist,* the party's theoretical journal, and a member of the board. In 1990 he became editor of the section on economic policy of *Pravda* and a member of the board. This was an extraordinary situation akin to having an atheist as the Pope's spiritual adviser in the Vatican. Gaidar and his friends were also in touch with reform economists in Hungary, Czechoslovakia and Poland through the Academy of Sciences. As it turned out it was Leszek Balcerowicz, in Poland, who was the first to attempt to put theory into practice when he launched shock therapy in 1990. Gaidar was a risk taker. On shock therapy he commented: 'We must simply shut our eyes tightly and take a leap into the unknown'.

TAKE-OFF: 2 JANUARY 1992

Gaidar's programme only existed in outline and was based on a few concepts: liberalise prices (this was not the first time he had advocated this policy – he had called for the full liberalisation of prices as the first move towards a socialist market economy in *Pravda* on 16 April 1990), stabilise the currency, set up a new tax system, privatise and restructure companies, and protect property rights and enforce contracts. In the beginning was price liberalisation which he hoped would kick start the economy. However the primary motive was political, not economic. 'Price liberalisation fosters depoliticisation because it deprives politicians of the opportunity to allocate goods' (Götz 2000: 1099). It was akin to giving a patient an electric shock in order to revive him. Gaidar expected that within a year Russia would have a balanced budget (revenues and expenditure equal). Inflation at the end of 1992 would be a few per cent and the decline of production 10–12 per cent.

Not all prices were freed. Prices of basic foodstuffs, energy, fuel, transport and communications were still controlled by the government. As regards oil this meant that the price of a packet of Marlboro cigarettes on Moscow streets (about $1) was equivalent to the state-controlled price of three tonnes of crude oil (the world price was about $100 a tonne). It was easy to become rich overnight. Buy at low domestic prices and sell on the world market. Maintaining low prices of oil, gas and metals favoured those who exported part of their output. All they needed were the requisite licences, rights and privileges. They obtained these from the young reformers in the government and sometimes from the President himself.

Gaidar was later to lament the fact that he had not been radical enough and freed everything. In reality, Yeltsin had prevented this. In May 1992, the President sacked Vladimir Lopukhin, a Gaidar appointee as minister of the oil industry. Yeltsin would continue to decide the price of oil, not the market. In fact, all critically important prices were controlled.

No attempt had been made to prepare the population for this experiment and Gaidar thought that he would only be in government until the summer when he would pack his bags and return to the Academy of Sciences. He opted for rapid privatisation of small-scale enterprises in services, trade and industry, a tight monetary policy and a large reduction in government spending. Inflation would be about 100 per cent in January and February, 10–12 per cent in March and April and a few per cent by the end of 1992.

The role of the state was to be cut back to permit the market room to develop. Reducing the role of the state would come through cutting public expenditure. This was the essence of stabilisation. The goal was to reduce the budget deficit to zero. Hence the state abdicated its responsibility to promote economic growth by regulating the economy and providing the necessary incentives. The responsibility for the social welfare of the population was also abdicated. What about a social safety net for those who could not cope? This was dismissed as a Marxist concept. In essence, the policy amounted to deindustrialisation. Heavy industry and the defence sector employed too many workers. There were also too many in agriculture. They should move into jobs in the services sector.

Ellman (2000: 1423) calculates that industrial production in 1999 was 54 per cent of that of 1991. Sharper declines were recorded by engineering and metal working, 48 per cent, and light industry, 17 per cent. The latter reflected Russia's inability to procure raw materials (Uzbek cotton, for example) and competition from foreign clothes and shoes which dominate the domestic market.

Economic development is shown in Tables 8.1 and 8.2.

Gaidar expected prices to rise threefold but was taken aback by the massive jump in prices. One of the consequences of this was the elimination of the monetary overhang, the huge amount of money held by the population. Of course, this meant that savings vanished as well. It also meant that state debts to the population had been wiped out. In January 1992, 10,000 rubles would have bought a car but by the end of the year it just might have bought a good pair of shoes. Yeltsin would promise, right up to 1996, to restore these savings. The state was never in any position to do so.

The red managers lobbied effectively in 1992 and began to win credits from the Central Bank (they totalled over 15 per cent of GDP in 1992 and 5 per cent in 1993) (Nagy 2000: 72). Viktor Gerashchenko, the head, did not believe that the most effective way to achieve stabilisation was to restrict the money supply. In September 1992, the government ordered the Central Bank to extend additional credits to enterprises. The purpose was to enable them to pay their VAT arrears. Hence the government was printing money, passing it onto enterprises and taking it back as tax. This was an Alice in Wonderland world and the only result was that inflation was soon out of control. The government manipulated profits tax in such a way as to grab more than the statutory 32 per cent. It did this by limiting the amount companies could deduct from their gross income. The result was that profits tax collection rose sharply and resembled the confiscation of profits reminiscent of the central planning regime. Collection remained high until the middle of 1993 but this led to enterprises demanding larger and larger credits. Companies siphoned off profits into other accounts and expanded barter deals in order to evade the punitive tax.

The government gave the impression that Gerashchenko was acting against it. In reality, he was carrying out government policy. The impression had to be given to the IMF that its instructions about cutting the budget deficit were being carried out. The branch commercial banks did not extend credit automatically to their enterprises. They acted on instructions from the ministry of finance and ministry of the economy (the old Gosplan) – the latter had over a thousand officials – and from the holding companies (Hough 2001: 40). Increasingly the foreign trade banks were permitted to keep more of their earnings in order to extend subsidies themselves. In return they were given government accounts and did not pay interest. They used the funds to earn profit. The leading banks were usually headed by oligarchs and this is another instance of how the government and the oligarchs worked together.

In 1993, inflation was over 2600 per cent. If the lobby for shock therapy was small in 1992 it was now wafer thin. Another tactic adopted by the government to increase revenue was to engage in foreign trade as a major player. It bought oil and gas at low domestic rates and sold them on world markets at high prices. One of the unintended consequences of this was that the state had an interest in keeping the gulf between domestic and foreign energy prices wide. It also promoted increasing corruption within the governmental apparatus. Since the government was collecting less revenue it could not meet its budgetary obligations. Privately, the government drew up a list of preferential beneficiaries and simply ignored the rest. Non-payment of bills became a governmental tradition. Inevitably enterprises claimed that the government's non-payment of its bills to them excused them from paying their taxes to government.

A sharp rise in tax evasion was observable from the second half of 1993. The government's answer to this, from 1994 on, was to cancel tax arrears by issuing credits to the enterprises for the same amount. Hence by 1994 enterprise managers had become a powerful lobby (they owned about 60 per cent of Russia's industrial assets) and were influential enough to prevent a strong state emerging. They wanted to take full advantage of the unique set of circumstances which existed in order to rob the state and enrich themselves. Enterprises were privatised at the local level and this permitted local authorities to exclude outsiders. Collusion between local authorities and managers led to mutual enrichment. After privatisation managers pressed for less taxation and more state subsidies.

One mourner to another: 'He paid his debts. RIP.' The tax burden is so high that it killed this poor taxpayer. Created by Igor Revyakin.

Those who managed their privatised enterprises badly could always lobby for credits.

The Russian Academy of Sciences, in summing up two years of shock therapy, was not very complimentary. The income of the top 10 per cent of the population was 10 times that of the lowest 10 per cent. A third of the population was below the poverty line of which 15 million had incomes insufficient for physical survival. The 'cavalry charge' to the market was not based on economic but on political criteria. As such it can be called 'neo-Bolshevik'. Too much emphasis was placed on foreign aid and the stimulation of business and investment in Russia ignored. All criticisms of the adopted policies were dismissed as coming from the 'enemies of reform'. The government refused to enter into a debate with its critics. It believed in its own infallibility (Medvedev 2000: 43–5). Needless to say this report was totally ignored and not even reported in the media.

PRIVATISATION

Chubais was in charge of privatisation from the very beginning. On 8 November 1991, Anatoly's wife contacted Sergei Vasilev in St Petersburg and asked him to draft a privatisation plan and present it to her husband the next day in Moscow. A few others joined the team to run the state privatisation committee, the GKI. They had to set up offices in all 89 regions and in all major towns. They started off with no staff but that was a decided advantage. Whereas Gaidar and the others had to rely on the existing bureaucracy to implement their polices and thereby suffer frustration after frustration, the GKI was staffed by hand-picked officials all loyal to Chubais. They were members of his clan.

The privatisation programme, from the very beginning, suffered from a fatal flaw (Freeland 2000: chapter 3; Gustafson 1999: chapter 2). The object of privatisation was to create a new generation of enterprise managers whose main objective would be profit maximisation. To this end it was proposed that management and labour would be able to acquire up to 40 per cent of the shares of the company. Outsiders, which could include the government, would have the other 60 per cent. There was only one snag; the red directors would not wear this. The other problem was that privatisation legislation had to pass the Supreme Soviet and the red directors were well represented there. In order to get the legislation through, in June 1992, Chubais took the fatal step of giving in to the directors. Another option was offered which gave management and workers 51 per cent of the voting shares in their company at a purely nominal price. Another 29 per cent of the company was to go to the rest of the population and the remaining 20 per cent remained with the state. Management could pay cash or in vouchers and labour could offset wage arrears against payment. State organisations were not permitted to acquire companies but bureaucrats quickly found a way round this obstacle. They founded private companies and transferred money to them by means of fictitious contracts. Often the resources came from state budget organisations. Thus red directors and their former bosses in the planning bureaucracy colluded and rapidly acquired control over enterprises.

The Supreme Soviet enacted the voucher legislation in the summer of 1992. Each citizen born by 2 September 1992 was to be issued with a voucher with a nominal value of 10,000 rubles or $25 (arrived at by dividing the value of the industrial assets of Russia by its population – the actual figure was 8467 but this was rounded off to 10,000 – in this way the national wealth was shared equally; Chubais called this people's privatisation), bearing his or her name and would not be able to transfer or sell it for three years. However, on 14 August 1992, when parliament was in recess, Yeltsin signed a decree enabling vouchers to be issued without names. This meant they could be bought and sold immediately. This permitted outsiders, including Yeltsin's team, to acquire valuable assets. About 144 million Russians paid the 25 rubles to obtain their vouchers and became a lobby group for privatisation. Vouchers were traded on the securities market and smart entrepreneurs quickly realised their potential. So did enterprise managers. They set about buying vouchers from workers who were ignorant of their real value. Vouchers accounted for about 20 per cent of the (deliberately undervalued) assets of the state enterprises. This meant that the assets to be privatised were valued at about $20 billion. By the time privatisation had been completed, inflation had cut this to about $5 billion, a mere fraction of their real value.

Another rich source which was mined were the 9500 enterprises which had been leased by the state to management. Annually they paid a fixed rent to the government and eventually they would become the property of the management and employees. However the high inflation of the early 1990s was never envisaged. This permitted the companies to pass into private ownership for a fraction of their real value. Another tactic was to value a state enterprise in 1991 prices and then transform the leased enterprise into another company using highly inflated 1992 prices. The latter could then buy the state enterprise for virtually nothing.

Management used many subterfuges to acquire shares held by their employees. They founded closed companies in which shares could only be traded with the consent of other shareholders. Management then offered to buy shares held by employees. If they declined, their wages were not paid. They soon sold their shares.

As a result of all these tactics new entrepreneurs acquired about 60 per cent of the country's industrial assets and the confidence to attempt to escape from state regulation. In 1999, of the 2.9 million registered enterprises, 2.1 million were wholly or partly privately owned and the remaining 800,000 enterprises and entities were state or communally owned. Most privately owned concerns, 1.7 million, are involved in trade and services, as are a further 600,000 state companies. There are about 200,000 industrial enterprises which are wholly or partly privately owned. Outside trade and services, the state owns 14,000 enterprises and a further 23,000 institutions (Götz 2000: 1110–11).

Yury Luzhkov, the mayor of Moscow, pointed out another anomaly of privatisation. There was no obligation, once the purchase had been completed, to continue in business. Luzhkov and the city government of Moscow bought ZIL, the automobile company, for $4 million. It occupied a prime site of 240 hectares. It was more profitable to rent the space out for warehouses. Another instance was an institute of chemistry which went for $200,000. The highly qualified chemists were sacked and the valuable land rented out to bring in over double that in one year (Klebanov 2000: 128).

Why did Chubais give in so easily to the red directors? Simply because the prime motive behind privatisation was political not economic. He believed that privatisation had to happen quickly lest the window of opportunity be slammed shut. No one could tell how long the Gaidar team would retain the President's confidence. Had every company been evaluated and restructured ready for privatisation, probably 200 a year at most, the process would have taken over one hundred years. Thus mass privatisation was the only option.

Chubais began to panic, in October 1992, as inflation roared ahead and output declined. He badly needed a voucher privatisation to provide a precedent. It looked as if Gaidar would be dismissed by parliament in December and the risk was that his whole team, including Chubais, would go as well. In order for an enterprise to be privatised it had to be a joint stock company. There were only eight of these in Moscow in November. Chubais's eye fell on the Bolshevik biscuit factory as the pilot project. The name was splendidly appropriate. Even more appropriate was that Lenin was lying in state in his mausoleum not far away. On 9 December, the company was sold and the Bolshevik management and workers were now shareholders. Someone else who was quick off the mark was Mikhail Fridman who had bought enough vouchers to acquire a nice slice of shares. On 14 December, Gaidar was sacked.

The whole process could have been compromised, on 3 October 1993, during the fighting between Yeltsin's forces and parliament. The opposition looted the Moscow mayor's building but failed to discover the 11 million used privatisation vouchers (worth about $55 million), some of them tied with condoms because the GKI could not afford elastic bands, which were stored there. Had they put them back into circulation there would have been considerable confusion.

Originally the vouchers were due to expire on 1 January 1994, but this was extended to 1 July 1994 when it became clear that the project was behind schedule. Nevertheless it was quite a feat to push through the most radical change in ownership since 1917. By 1996, the number of state-owned companies had fallen from 205,000 to about 91,000. Most of the latter were in the defence sector and hence outside privatisation. Universities, schools, hospitals and prisons were also not privatised. About 14 million Russians acquired shares in privatised companies and another 44 million became indirect owners through investment funds. About one third of all urban apartments became the property of the tenants. Many public buildings were passing into private hands. Dachas were sprouting up around towns like mushrooms after rain. Chubais was delighted. He never dreamed that privatisation could be pushed through so fast. He once remarked that his attitude was that he had only a short time in office. 'What can I do in the next two weeks to ensure the communists do not return to power?'

He knew that many of the emerging entrepreneurs would have criminal backgrounds. Leonid Abalkin reported him as saying privately that the task was to create a small number of real owners and it was inevitable that most would be ex-criminals. There were no others and without real owners and entrepreneurs Russia would never get out of the hole it was in (Hough 2001: 69–70). Outsiders had to be brought in, irrespective of the dangers.

Chubais had envisaged that privatisation would win lasting support among the population but his hopes were dashed. People rapidly perceived privatisation as benefiting the nomenklatura and the crooks, the mafia. The average person felt cheated in the face of insider dealing. This quickly led to an intense hatred of Chubais and his team.

Some of the auctions were badly flawed. In an auction if a small number of vouchers were bid for a company's shares, more shares were distributed per voucher. Inevitably this meant that insiders had a powerful incentive to discourage others from bidding. This could be done by siting the auction in an out-of-the-way place or changing the venue at the last minute. On the day of the auction the telephone lines were cut and access by road and air interrupted. If unwanted bidders still turned up heavies could dissuade them from entering the auction room. The more valuable the company the greater the incentive management had to use illegal tactics. Over a thousand companies were privatised by management cutting special deals with the government (needless to say both sides benefited financially from this move). Another wheeze permitted managers to acquire 30 per cent of their companies' shares cheaply if they came to an agreement with the workforce which would prevent the company going bankrupt for a year. Who decided whether the company would go bankrupt in a year or would not go bankrupt? The managers, of course. In other words, the managers were being handed a large stake in their companies virtually free of charge.

An intriguing question was the interrelationship between enterprises which was deliberately hidden from view (Hough 2001: 31–6). The new Russian government only inherited two industrial ministries, the ministry of industry and the ministry of the fuel and energy industry. Other industrial ministries had been hived off under Gorbachev into associations or holding companies. They all, effectively, became subordinate to the ministry of industry. Specialised ministries were gradually formed and the relevant associations passed under their supervision. Each association or holding company set up its own commercial bank whose main task was to provide loans for its enterprises. The associations organised the procurement and delivery of inputs to their own enterprises. This remained the dominant pattern until the autumn of 1993 when Yeltsin decided to dismiss parliament and introduce a new constitution. One of the consequences of this was a greater role for governors in the distribution of state subsidies. Privatisation led to many of the top officials in the holding companies becoming heads of joint-stock companies. That was where the money now was. The holding companies carried on and turned into trade associations, although many of the holding companies continued to exist. Roslesprom remained a state company and managed the timber industry. Rosugol did the same for the coal industry. Rostekstil looked after textiles. A key task was to win subsidies for their companies. In the oil industry, the government set up Lukoil, Sidanko, Sibneft, Rosneft, Tyumen oil, Yukos and VNK. United Energy Systems of Russia was formed as the monopoly holding company in electricity. Svyazinvest took over telecommunications. The government then sold majority stakes in these companies to outsiders.

Russia was a paradise for asset strippers. A simple tactic for managers was to set up companies and then sell their output to them at very low prices. In return, the main enterprise bought inputs from these new companies at highly inflated prices. The main enterprise could be billed for services it had never received from the other companies. Another approach was for managers to set up, say, 10 daughter companies to which 10 per cent of the enterprise's shares were transferred to each. In return, the mother company received shares from the daughter companies. The daughter companies then issued huge numbers of new shares, say 100 new shares for every existing share, thereby rendering the shares held by the mother company of very little value. The management could then buy the parent company shares for a pittance. Managers would not even have to use their own money as they could invoice the parent company for services it had not received from the daughter company. Hence they did not need to spend a kopek of their own money to take over their own company. And this was all perfectly legal at the time!

Managers quickly grasped the advantages of inflation in 1992 and 1993. They issued large numbers of new shares and distributed them among insiders, including themselves. Payment only became due when inflation had rendered the original price risible. Another démarche was to recalculate the value of the enterprise in line with inflation. Each time this was done shareholders should have received new shares reflecting the new value of the enterprise. Instead, these new shares were only issued to nominees of the managers who thereby enriched themselves.

Voucher privatisation unmasked the government's strategy. The question was who should gain control of the nation's industrial and other assets? Should it be the existing managers and workers or the young reformers and their clans and other members of the new Yeltsin elite? Parliamentary legislation, identifying the owner of each voucher, meant that outsiders would find it very hard to take over state assets. By turning vouchers into currency, the reformers could acquire enough to buy into and take over companies. As it turned out the insiders gained the upper hand. The government's tactic was then to try to bankrupt them by increasing taxation, denying them credits and delaying payment for their output so that they could be taken over by outsiders. A more rational economic policy would have been to provide incentives to the insiders to enhance the value of the enterprises by restructuring, shedding labour and providing credits. The insiders would then be permitted to sell their enterprises and keep the profits.

RUSSIANS ABROAD

It was not only in Russia that scams were highly successful. In early 2001, London police arrested two Russians involved in the most sophisticated credit card fraud encountered until then in Europe. A factory had been set up to produce imitations of credit cards which were capable of overriding every security measure then in place. Using state of the art machines, including a hologram stamp imported from Russia, the gang were able to produce near-perfect replicas of Visa, Amex and Master Card. These cards were then sold for £300, anticipating a month's spending spree before the cardholder noticed that something was amiss. The gang would also go on extensive Saturday spending jaunts in the West End. They bought designer clothes and electrical goods and sold these on the black market. In order to access holders' information, the gang employed waiters and bar staff from eastern Europe who placed illegal swipe machines in restaurants, hotels and wine bars across the capital. The waiters carried a tiny swipe machine, often on their belts, which they would use to reswipe credit cards after they had been used to pay the original bill. When the swipe box was full, they would be met as they finished their shift and given another. In return the staff would receive forged EU passports allowing them to work in Britain. The data on the black boxes were then downloaded through a computer at the factory in south London. Only the gang know how much they have netted with this scam. If it was so sophisticated, it had presumably been operating elsewhere in Europe undetected for some time.

This raises an intriguing question. Why do highly talented, highly qualified Russians choose a life of crime rather than engage in legitimate business? Is it because they believe they can make more money through crime? They are quintessential roving bandits. Their time horizon is always short.

WHO GOT THE LOOT?

In the public perception the richer the businessman was the more corrupt he was. He was a mafioso and hence a criminal. Not everything about the New Russians (nouveaux riches) was bad. Their legendary lack of finesse was the butt of many a story. A New Russian goes into a restaurant and pours the two most expensive French red wines on the menu into a single glass. His argument is that they must be twice as good if mixed together.

The red directors did very well but it was a Pyrrhic victory. They dominated manufacturing but the real money could be made in commodities, oil, gas, gold, timber, and raw materials. Here the New Russians dominated. Entrepreneurial skill was needed to succeed but the key factors were money, influence and connections. The struggle for property was and is a no-holds-barred conflict and is more brutal than many thrillers.

Russians consider there to be four natural monopolies: gas, telephones, railways and oil pipelines. Gas and telephones have been privatised but railways and oil pipelines have not. All four are managed by insiders who were in senior positions under Gorbachev and had the flair to become successful entrepreneurs. The luckiest one was railways. Transrail was established as a joint venture between the USSR ministry of railways and a Swiss-based group of European shipping companies. The Russian ministry of railways inherited the half share owned by its predecessor. In return for supplying the ministry with hard currency, Interrail was the ministry's favoured carrier. Naturally it was accused of sharp practice and other crimes by the new transport companies and, in 1997, it had to cede market share. However it still has about a half of the ministry's transit business. It is by far the biggest player in the market.

GAZPROM

Gazprom is Russia's largest and richest company. It supplies about 27 per cent of the world's gas production and owns about 40 per cent of the world's gas reserves. A conservative valuation would be about $600 billion but as the price of gas goes up so does Gazprom. It will one day become Russia's first trillion dollar company. Its previous name was the USSR ministry of the gas industry. Its top managers all learnt the business under communism. Gazprom is a company with two markets, the domestic and the foreign. In the former it makes losses and in the latter profits. In 1989, Viktor Chernomyrdin consolidated the whole of the gas industry in one company, Gazprom. It was privatised in 1993–94 for about $250 million. Management and workers acquired 15 per cent of the company by buying up vouchers cheaply. A further 10 per cent was retained by Gazprom, 35 per cent went to Russian investors and the state retained its golden share, 40 per cent. This was later handed back to Gazprom in trust by the government (after all Chernomyrdin was Prime Minister). In early 2000, the government still owned 38 per cent while the managers' official stake was about 35 per cent, most of which is owned by small groups of people who reportedly received stakes of one per cent to five per cent each. Each per cent stake is worth many billions of dollars. That left about 25 per cent in other hands, presumably Gazprom insiders. Viktor Chernomyrdin, for instance, is rumoured to be one of them.

When Chernomyrdin went into government he was succeeded by his deputy, Rem Vyakhirev, an Azeri. (Chernomyrdin returned to Gazprom in 1999.) Gazprom was a closed joint stock company which meant that shares could only be bought and sold with the board's permission. Gazprom took a risk in the late 1980s when it linked up with a German company, Ruhrgas, to attempt to penetrate the European market. Against all expectations, it succeeded. It was a learning exercise and Vyakhirev learnt very fast. Later these lessons could be applied to the Russian domestic market. Gazprom set up its own banks and kept a lot of its earnings abroad. Domestic prices were kept low by the government since

Russian industry and consumers could not pay world prices. Naturally Gazprom was compensated by the government, headed by Chernomyrdin. It did not pay export tax and was exempted from many import dues. During the 1990s these concessions were worth billions of dollars. This underlined the fact that Gazprom was more than just a joint stock company. It is also an arm of the federal government (if Moscow wants to bring Georgia to heel it gets Gazprom to cut off gas supplies), it extends loans to customers and it collects its own taxes. It contributes about one quarter of Russian taxes and, in 1998, was reported to be collecting only 10–15 per cent of its revenues in cash. In 1996, it owed $2.8 billion in back taxes and its customers owed it $8.9 billion (Hough 2001: 50).

It supplied gas to many CIS countries and Ukraine, especially, ran up huge debts. Some Gazprom critics saw it as the extended arm of the ministry of foreign affairs. It has built up a huge business empire, including the media, and may control up to 10 per cent of the Russian Gross Domestic Product. It owns about 150,000 km of pipeline and has about 350,000 employees. Then there are 20 farms, 67 meat processing plants, 31 dairies, a shipping company, numerous industrial enterprises, over 20 newspapers and at least 14 TV and radio stations. It also invests abroad and has a growing portfolio. If what was good for General Motors was good for America, the same can be said about Gazprom and Russia. Gazprom's reported revenues are over $30 billion annually but its true revenues are impossible to determine from the outside. It can transfer money to daughter companies. For instance, over $30 billion was transferred to an unknown company, presumably run by Gazprom managers (Black *et al.* 2000: 49). In August 1999, a deputy Russian Prime Minister complained that Gazprom was selling gas cheaply to middlemen who then sold it on at enormous profit.

It is a sobering thought that had Gazprom been privatised properly by the Russian state it would have raised enough money to have put the whole privatisation process on a sound footing. It goes without saying that had this been done there would have been no loans for shares scam. The roving bandits were just too strong and this was because some of them were in the government.

ALFA GROUP

Mikhail Fridman gained a valuable bonus when he moved part of his business to Prague in 1991. He witnessed voucher privatisation at first hand. This gave him a head start in Russia. He was smart enough to identify and recruit a young economist working for a foreign investment bank. The bank had a list of foreign companies eager to invest in Russia. The young man simply brought the list to Alfa. It then bought shares in the companies in which the foreigners were interested. Alfa made money but not a fortune from this démarche but it made the same mistake as many overseas investors. Investing in manufacturing was not worth the effort. Real money could only be made in commodities. Fridman's next step was to use his persuasive skills on Petr Aven, one of the Chubais clan and a minister of foreign economic relations. He left government and joined the Alfa group as a partner. Now Alfa had the connections to make real money through government contracts, export licences, handling government accounts and borrowing from the Central Bank. Aven was very frank about how to become a millionaire in Russia. 'One does not need business flair only good contacts in government, parliament, local authorities and law enforcement agencies. One fine day an obscure bank is authorised to handle state budgetary funds. Or very generous quotas are allocated for the export of oil, timber and gas. Put simply, one is appointed a millionaire.'

MENATEP

Menatep waxed rich through banking, first of all to enterprises, then to regions and finally to the government itself (Freeland 2000: chapter 6; Gustafson 1999: chapter 4). In 1992, the Russian state was teetering on the edge of collapse. Enterprises were not getting the money owed them by the government. Menatep stepped in, paid the companies and then collected the money from the ministry of finance. It then performed the same service for regions. This was reminiscent of the role played by Russian tax collectors in the Tsarist period. They had collected as much as possible and paid the Tsar as little as possible. Now it was the other way round. The next step and the step to riches was to handle the government's own finances. Ministry accounts and the movement of money from one part of the government to another provided Menatep with liquid capital which it could use to provide credits for lucrative imports and exports. With its inside knowledge it could speculate on the currency markets. It benefited from high inflation as the rubles it paid out were already devalued. The longer it could delay payment the more money it made. Khodorkovsky and the other lucky bankers received government deposits but did not pay any interest on them (inflation in 1992 was 2506.1 per cent and in 1993 was 839.9 per cent) and charged interest on lending out this money. Their rates of interest were as high as 800 per cent. This practice was still widespread in 1999. Khodorkovsky's connections were so good that he was appointed a deputy minister of fuel and energy in early 1992 and also headed the supervisory council of the ministry of fuel and energy. Khodorkovsky later commented that politics was the most profitable business in Russia. As an expert in chemistry, Khodorkovsky identified many important companies in the chemical industry and acquired them for next to nothing. Government officials soon caught on that they could also share in the new riches and so a government–business partnership developed, the object of which was mutual enrichment. Privatisation permitted Menatep to build up an impressive list of companies over a wide range of industries. The banks and the enterprises were welded together into a financial-industrial group and the goal was to monopolise a sector of the economy. These groups had a good friend at the centre of government, Oleg Soskovets.

Menatep also handled the finances Russia expended on its 1994–96 war with Chechnya and also the cash for the rebuilding of Chechnya. A Russian government audit later concluded that $4.4 billion of these funds never reached their intended destinations.

The management of Yukos, the Siberian oil holding company acquired by Menatep in the loans for shares scheme, is instructive (Black *et al.* 2000: 42–5). In 1996, Yukos reported oil revenues calculated at $8.60 a barrel whereas the real price was about $4 more. This money was presumably moved to an offshore account. Yukos acquired several oil companies and purchased oil from them at about $7.50 a barrel. These companies, before they became part of Yukos, were reporting pretax profits of about $1 billion. However they were soon reporting losses and not paying their taxes. All this was against Russian company law. Even the Russian securities commission intervened but had no power to do anything. In 1997 and 1998, Khodorkovsky borrowed heavily from western banks using Yukos shares and those of its subsidiaries as collateral. The August 1998 financial collapse hit Menatep very hard and Khodorkovsky did not use any offshore money to keep Yukos and Menatep going. He let them sink. Soon 30 per cent of Yukos shares would be seized by the western banks. However before this could happen he came up with a bright scheme for shareholders of Tomskneft, Yuganskneftegaz and Samaraneftegaz. On paper these companies were worth billions of dollars because of their oil reserves. They were the jewels in Yukos's crown. A huge new share issue would transfer these companies to offshore companies at prices below one per cent of their actual value. Enough shares would be issued to transfer ownership of Yukos to these new offshore companies. A long-term agreement would be concluded with the subsidiaries to sell their oil at 250 rubles a tonne (about $1.30 a barrel at the August 2000 exchange rate). Those share-holders who opposed these stratagems were invited to sell their shares back to Yukos at prices which valued the three subsidiaries (with proven oil and gas reserves of 13 billion barrels of oil equivalent) collectively at $33 million. This is not a misprint. Khodorkovsky needed share-holder approval to push through this breathtaking scheme. The day before the subsidiaries' shareholder meeting (they held 49 per cent of the shares) a malleable judge ruled that they were conspiring together, in contravention of the antimonopoly law. Thus they could not vote and Khodorkovsky got his way. He then transferred Yukos's remaining shares in two of the three subsidiaries to two offshore companies. The western banks were left without anything to seize. It may be coincidence or it may not be coincidence that the mayor of Nefteyugansk was mur-dered in 1998, shortly after demanding that Yukos pay its taxes and back wages. In early 1999, Evgeny Rubin, head of a company which had won a court case against Yukos, had his Mercedes blown up by a bomb, killing his bodyguards. He was elsewhere at the time. The whole episode did not hurt Khodorkovsky. He was accompanying Prime Minister Evgeny Primakov to the US to visit President Clinton when the visit was cancelled in mid-air after NATO began bombing Serbia. The head of the securities commission, Sergei Vasilev, resigned in frustration after fail-ing to gain government support for a court challenge. The other mem-bers then approved the share issues. Things continued to go well for Khodorkovsky and Yukos. In 2000, Yukos reported a net profit of about $2.5 billion, up from $1.15 billion in 1999.

After the financial collapse of August 1998 Khodorkovsky transferred what was left of Menatep to a new bank, Menatep-St Petersburg. Depositors and creditors were left with the shell Menatep. To ensure that the transactions could not be traced later, he arranged for a lorry load of Menatep documents to be driven off a bridge into the river Dybna, where they still lie (Black *et al.* 2000: 26).

ONEKSIMBANK

Potanin reluctantly concluded that Oneksimbank did not have the clout to participate in voucher privatisation. He had to stand on the sidelines and watch others enrich themselves. However his opportunity was not long in coming. Vneshtorgbank, the state bank for foreign trade, was on the point of collapse in late 1992. Its accounts, worth an estimated $300 million, were simply transferred to Oneksimbank. Potanin lobbied the companies to keep their accounts with his group and offered many of them loans. The next step was to take some of them over. Soon Potanin used his contacts to acquire two more valuable accounts, the state customs service and Rosvoruzhenie, the agency which sold arms. The beauty of this arrangement was that Oneksimbank's customers included some of Russia's largest importers and exporters. They had to pay customs dues. The money could be deducted from their Oneksimbank accounts but it remained in Oneksimbank until the government required its transfer elsewhere. Delaying payment to the government permitted the bank to use the money to make more money. It was the nearest thing to a licence to print money that existed in Russia. Oneksimbank also managed money for the ministries of finance and foreign trade. Then in 1994 along came the greatest money-making opportunity ever, the loans for shares schemes masterminded by Potanin (see below). Before the crash of August 1998 the Oneksimbank group may have owned about 10 per cent of the Russian GNP.

Potanin was not always concerned about his reputation among western investors (Black *et al.* 2000: 46–7). Sidanko is a Russian oil holding company in which Oneksimbank and its affiliates, particularly MFK, held 96 per cent of the shares in early 1998. Then Potanin decided to streamline the share ownership structure within the Oneksimbank financial-industrial group and dilute the 4 per cent minority shareholding in Sidanko. The chosen method was for Sidanko to issue convertible bonds to Oneksimbank affiliates in exchange for their shares in other group companies. The conversion price was about 0.1 per cent of Sidanko's current market price. Once the bonds were converted the number of Sidanko shares tripled and this neatly reduced the minority shareholder stake from 4 per cent to 1.3 per cent. After the securities commission began to investigate, Sidanko agreed to issue enough shares to minority shareholders to restore their holdings to 4 per cent. This was a Pyrrhic victory, however. When the August 1998 crash arrived Potanin removed most of Oneksimbank's remaining assets and stripped Sidanko and its subsidiaries. The money went into offshore accounts. Sidanko's minority shareholders, which included BP Amoco, which had paid $571 million for a 10 per cent stake in Sidanko, found that their holdings were practically worthless.

Oneksimbank was badly dented by the August 1998 crash. However, skilful restructuring transferred many of the assets to Rosbank. In December 2000, Rosbank reported total assets of $1.9 billion. It plans to repackage Oneksimbank and market it in due course. Rosbank has also been working on restructuring Inkombank but may not take over the bank. Inkombank owes money to companies in the Interros group, to which Rosbank also belongs.

LOGOVAZ

The automobile industry was one of the few to thrive during the 1990s. The elimination of the monetary overhang in 1992 meant that there was no longer a ten-year waiting list for new cars. Avtovaz's Ladas were in great demand. Hundreds of daughter companies were set up to deal in Ladas and spare parts. They were financed by Avtovaz Bank and were all linked to the management of Avtovaz. The company sold its cars at a loss and dealers could make a profit of 100 per cent on a sale. Management regarded these rip-offs as normal business practice. As one businessman observed: 'Collective property is property which belongs to everyone' (Klebanov 2000: 92). It was government policy which had promoted the development of an independent Logovaz dealer network. In 1992, the government insisted that cars be sold at low, controlled prices. Logovaz, aided by Berezovsky, set up companies which bought the cars at the low prices and sold them on at double or three times the amount. In no time they had the capital to establish a large dealership chain. Many of the Ladas were exported. Dealers had to pay only a proportion of the price in cash to Avtovaz. They then sold the cars for cash up front and delayed paying Avtovaz. With high inflation, every passing month increased their net profit. Dealers could also borrow money from Avtovaz Bank. When the ruble stabilised in 1995 dealers could invest in government short-term bonds with an annual return of around 100 per cent. The leading dealer was Boris Berezovsky. No wonder Avtovaz was regarded as the most criminally infested company in Russia.

Another lucrative venture was Avva, or the Russian automobile alliance. The company was launched in October 1993 amid great publicity and valuable tax breaks and import duty exemptions. A Russian people's car was to roll off new production lines in Avtovaz, in Togliatti. It was to be a joint venture with General Motors. People were invited to buy shares at 10,000 rubles each. Privatisation vouchers also just happened to have a face value of 10,000 rubles. A voucher would do instead of cash. Investors participated in a lottery for thousands of new Avtovaz cars. When Avva was completed investors could opt for cash or shares in the company. About $50 million was put in by the public. General Motors pulled out and in so doing pulled the plug on the venture. Berezovsky, Kadannikov and other Avtovaz managers had acquired a $50 million interest-free loan. In late 1996, Avtovaz announced that it was going to build a new car after all, in Finland. A joint venture with a Finnish company did produce some cars and one was given to Viktor Chernomyrdin. Then it folded (Klebanov 2000: 140–42). In essence, Avva was a pyramid scheme. It was also legal because, at that time, the Duma had not passed legislation banning such schemes.

By 1994 Berezovsky had made it to the top but he had collected enemies en route. In June 1994, outside his Logovaz office, in Moscow, a car packed with explosives was detonated as he sped past in his Mercedes. It decapitated his driver, severely wounded his bodyguard and almost set him alight. He suffered multiple burns and had to have months of treatment in a Swiss clinic. A mafia group was attempting to intimidate him but his own private security organisation was not cowed. As a mark of solidarity, Gusinsky lent him an armoured Mercedes until another arrived from Germany. Berezovsky's Obedinenny Bank was bombed soon afterwards. The mafia war continued into the winter of 1994–95 when Berezovsky and other leading businessmen agreed among themselves to end contract killings. The oligarchs had been using the mafia to take out business opponents. The ongoing battle between Chechen and Russian gangs for control of Moscow ended in a draw. The street-wise mayor of Moscow, Yury Luzhkov, knew he could not subdue the mafiosi. Instead, he taxed them. Some of the money was spent on public works. One of these was the rebuilding of the cathedral of Christ the Saviour in Moscow for which Luzhkov drummed up a billion dollars.

Another skill Berezovsky possessed was to place his men in top positions. One of these was Aleksandr Voloshin. When he graduated in 1986 he went into the ministry of foreign trade. On the side he became a consultant. This is when he came to Berezovsky's notice. Voloshin had an eye for turning his access to state commercial information into private gain. Berezovsky and he worked the voucher privatisation market to lucrative effect. In 1996, Voloshin was appointed head of the Financial Funding Corporation, part of the GKI, and responsible for supervising GKI auctions. Voloshin's critics claim that he helped Berezovsky and his associate Roman Abramovich to acquire 85 per cent of Sibneft, the Siberian oil company, at a knockdown price. Sibneft is reputed to have reserves of 4.1 billion barrels and is the largest producer of petrol in Russia with its own chain of petrol stations. Abramovich controls 40 per cent of the shares. Voloshin became head of the presidential administration in 1999 and retained the position under Putin.

Berezovsky was a wizard when it came to share dealing (Black *et al.* 2000: 45–6). Sibneft is controlled by Berezovsky and his partner Roman

Abramovich. Its main subsidiary is Noyabrskneftegaz which is 61 per cent owned by Sibneft. In 1996, it recorded profits of about $600 million but in 1997 there were no profits. The money turned up in the Sibneft account. At the Noyabrskneftegaz annual meeting in 1998 shareholders were asked to approve a new issue of shares. These were to be almost 2000 times as many new as existing shares. It went through as very few minority shareholders were present. Sibneft then issued Noyabrshneftegaz shares at about half the market price to four companies with which it enjoyed close relations. This had the effect of enhancing Sibneft's share price and depressing Noyabrskneftegaz's share price. As a magnanimous gesture Sibneft then proposed that each Noyabrskneftegaz share could be exchanged for four Sibneft shares. This was not as good as it sounded as shareholders ended up accepting about 4 per cent of the original value of the shares. The wise ones took the money and ran. Those who sued had their case rejected on the grounds that the lawyer's signature on the appeal papers differed from the signature on the original complaint. Of course, it did not and even if it had it would have made no difference in Russian law. In early 2000, one of Sibneft's subsidiary companies avoided repaying a $58 million loan to the European Bank for Reconstruction and Development by simply getting a malleable judge to confirm that it had repaid the loan. Those who wanted a quiet life and to stay alive did not cross Boris Berezovsky's path. A remarkable number of those who did not take this advice ended up dead, beaten up or jailed.

BEREZOVSKY PENETRATES THE KREMLIN

One of Berezovsky's strengths was that he did not know when to stop. His relationship with Kadannikov had made him a fortune but it only whetted his appetite. He was inspired by the success of a man like Aleksandr Korzhakov. One reviewer of his memoirs unkindly thought that Korzhakov had the intellect of a three-year-old. If Korzhakov could do it, so could Boris. After all he was intellectually a high flyer. But how could he ingratiate himself with Yeltsin? In expanding his media world he had come across Valentin Yumashev, a journalist who just happened to be ghosting Yeltsin's second volume of memoirs in late 1993.

Berezovsky saw his opportunity. He would become the man who financed the publication of the President's memoirs, *Zapiski Prezidenta*. Actually several publishing houses would have fallen over one another to publish the book without a subsidy, but Berezovsky got Yumashev to suggest to Korzhakov and Yeltsin that without a subsidy the book would not be published. Logovaz would finance the publication. So Yumashev brought Berezovsky to the Kremlin and introduced him to Korzhakov and then Yeltsin and the rest is history. Yumashev also introduced Berezovsky to Tatyana Dyachenko, Yeltsin's daughter. At the time her husband, Leonid, was working with the Omsk refinery and hence in close contact with Roman Abramovich, Berezovsky's partner. The book was published in Finland and it was translated into several languages. Yeltsin had visions of earning over a million dollars from the book; after all, if Gorbachev could do it, so could he. Yumashev brought the President his royalties each week and put the money in his safe. However, according to Korzhakov, the $16,000 which Yumashev delivered weekly was the interest on a $3 million deposit in Barclays Bank in London. So pleased was Yeltsin that Berezovsky was made a member of the Presidential Club.

This was a priceless gift to a man of Berezovsky's skills. He was unsurpassed in his ability to identify someone who could be of use in building up his empire. Once he had found his man he would massage him until he succeeded. Korzhakov complains in his memoirs that Berezovsky once followed him into the shower to promote a deal. Berezovsky was the only oligarch who became a member of the Presidential Club, reserved for members of the ruling elite. Other oligarchs might be invited on the rare occasion. The Club was where the Yeltsin family relaxed, playing tennis, swimming and so on. There was also a beauty salon for the women. Berezovsky now had regular contact with Tatyana Dyachenko, who was becoming increasingly important as her father faltered. Yeltsin had royalties to invest and eventually Berezovsky ended up as the family's banker. Tatyana was showered with gifts and went off on holiday with Berezovsky and his business partners. Berezovsky had a yacht and villas in the south of France and the south of Spain, to mention only two locations. She visited the Logovaz club, modelled on the President's Club.

Gusinsky's NTV irritated Yeltsin and Berezovsky. So Berezovsky proposed that the state television company, ORT, be built up to provide vigorous pro-Yeltsin information. Eventually he and his friends obtained 49 per cent and the state retained the rest (this was to ensure that the state continued subsidising it) but Berezovsky placed his men in key positions and it became his channel. Newspapers shaped public opinion as well so he acquired some, for instance, *Nezavisimaya gazeta*. In 1999, he took over the widely read *Kommersant*. Another battleground with Gusinsky were the Aeroflot accounts. The national airline was poorly managed but as Russia prospered it would prosper. Berezovsky arranged for two

Swiss companies to handle the revenues and ensure that everything was opaque. Tatyana's brother-in-law, Valery Okulov, was given a top position. Aeroflot became the family airline. Later the Swiss authorities would claim that the revenues had been systematically misappropriated. One of the Swiss companies was called Forus, which in English spells 'for us'. It had been set up in 1992 by Berezovsky as a financial company which organised credit and other financial services for Russian companies abroad. It also owned shares in many of Berezovsky's companies. It helped establish Obedinenny Bank, in 1992. This bank would become the main bank for Avtovaz and Aeroflot (Klebanov 2000: 89).

MEDIA-MOST

Gusinsky built up the first media empire in Russia. A major breakthrough was the launch of *Segodnya,* in February 1993, and it rapidly established itself as a leading liberal newspaper. Later in 1993 some ambitious journalists at ORT, led by Evgeny Kiselev, Russia's Jeremy Paxman, approached Gusinsky with the idea of setting up an independent TV production company. Gusinsky had been toying with the idea of setting up his own TV station and NTV (independent TV) was soon born. Igor Malashenko, recently sacked from ORT, was recruited as manager. Igor was a Dante scholar and became quite an expert in Catholic heresy. In 1983, he published an article on Dante in an East German literary journal and it drew general applause. This was quite a feat as the GDR was culturally under the heel of real, existing socialism. In 1985, he was recruited to counter the Italian young communist delegation, led by Massimo D'Alema, in Moscow, who were hot on euro-communism. Malashenko quoted from Dante's *De Monarchia* to demolish D'Alema's Marxist arguments. He knew that D'Alema had not read Dante as young Italian communists were expected to read Gramsci instead. Igor was quickly snapped up by the Yeltsin regime and made the transition from defending the conservatism of the Soviet communist party to defending the rapacious capitalism of the Yeltsin era effortlessly. Clearly Dante and Catholic heresy had provided him with all the necessary propagandistic tools.

Most applied for a licence but always ran into a brick wall. Luckily it discovered that the man blocking their application was Shamil Tarpishchev, Yeltsin's tennis coach, and a formidable money-maker himself. He had been appointed minister of sport and athletics in 1993. His National Sports Fund (NSF) was then managed by Boris Fedorov (not the man who was at one time minister of finance). The NSF was ostensibly concerned with helping sport and down-on-their-luck athletes but, in reality, was a highly lucrative organisation which imported alcohol and cigarettes duty free. Tarpishchev's charm was such that Yeltsin gave him what he wanted.

Tarpishchev was against the bid since he wanted to set up his own TV sports channel. Gusinsky promised Tarpishchev time on his channel for sport and the deal was done. Most paid practically nothing for the licence. Very quickly Kiselev was the top TV newsman and NTV the station which everyone watched. However Gusinsky became careless and the result was the Korzhakov raid in December 1994; Gusinsky moved to London and his banking and newspaper empire slowly declined as it was assumed that he had overstepped the mark.

THE MEDIA EMPIRES

The oligarchs grasped very early the importance of the media. They moulded public opinion. They set out to control the central and local press, radio and television in order to promote themselves, get their nominees elected to parliament and local councils, push the careers of friendly politicians and demolish their political and economic opponents. Table 8.3 gives a list of media barons and their holdings (Black *et al.* 2000: 19–21).

Given that the media were normally lossmaking, did the oligarchs need to become so deeply involved? The list in Table 8.3 may be only the tip of the iceberg. Hough (2001: 87) suggests that they were instructed to do so as part of their deal with the Yeltsin administration. They would then have to provide subsidies to the companies they had shares in. This may have been true of the low profile outlets but one should remember Berezovsky's comments about the media. He said he was not involved in the media to make money, because there was no money to be made there, but rather to shape public opinion.

THE LOANS FOR SHARES SCHEME

The idea, which originated with Boris Jordan, an American investment banker, was stunningly simple. Potanin and other bankers would provide the state with a $2 billion credit in return for managing the state's share in leading companies. Potanin invited other bankers to join him and they worked out the companies they wanted to take over. These bankers included Mikhail Khodorkovsky, Aleksandr Smolensky of Stolichny Bank, Vladimir Vinogradov, of Inkombank, Petr Rodionov of Bank Imperial, established by oil and gas interests, Vitaly Malkin of Rossiisky Kredit bank and Mikhail Fridman. Fridman got cold feet immediately. A group emerged and they divided up the spoils among themselves. Potanin was to get Norilsk Nickel, the producer of nickel, cobalt and the controller of the world palladium market, in the far north, and one of the most lucrative companies in Russia. After all, this was fair as he had advanced the scheme. Khodorkovsky was to get Yukos (Freeland 2000: chapter 8; Nagy 2000: 89–91).

Potanin presented the proposal to the Russian government in March 1995. He had already won over Oleg Soskovets, the friend of large business groups and responsible for industrial policy. Chubais, after initial hesitancy, had also come on board. The key reason was that the government desperately needed money as the economy floundered, inflation rose and the disastrous war with Chechnya had just got underway. Psychologically the timing was perfect and Potanin used his considerable presentational skills and knowledge of the establishment's mentality to excellent effect. The communists wanted to cancel privatisation, claiming that the state was not making money from it. The government had to come up with a scheme which looked good on paper.

Potanin and the bankers met government officials on many occasions to hammer out a deal. Gradually an inside group of bankers emerged. This did not include Vladimir Gusinsky (Most), Vladimir Vinogradov (Inkombank), Petr Aven (Alfa Bank) and Vitaly Malkin (Rossiisky Kredit Bank). The bankers would extend the government credit and in return would manage the state's stake in various companies including Norilsk Nickel, Lukoil (but only 5 per cent was up for grabs), Yukos, United Energy Systems of Russia, the electricity generator and distributor, and Rostelekom, the state telecommunications company. The last was eventually withdrawn from the auction. The conditions for the auctions were laid down in a presidential decree on 31 August 1995. To be valid, each auction needed two bidders and foreign investors were permitted to participate. The winners would extend the government credit for three years but gain control over the management and profits of the companies for five years. The state had the right to repay the credits but if this were not done by 1 September 1996 the winners would acquire the right to sell the shares and retain 30 per cent of the proceeds over and above the credits granted. In reality this meant that the winners could arrange the sale of the shares to themselves at a price just above that of the credits. It was also agreed that, in certain cases, if companies paid off their tax arrears the government would reward them with stakes in some companies.

In the end only 12 auctions took place (originally there were 29 but 17 red directors had the clout to ensure that their companies were removed from the list) and they were all fixed. In five of the 12 there was only one bidder. In November 1995, the pension fund of the valuable Surgutneftegaz oil company won simply by disqualifying all competitors. Bank Imperial put up the money. Just to make sure the local airport, Surgut, mysteriously closed down for the day. Needless to say Surgut could only be reached by air. Lukoil acquired the 5 per cent of its shares which were up for auction itself, backed by Bank Imperial. (In late 1999, Reforma Investment, a Cyprus-based company, presumably controlled by Lukoil managers, bought 9 per cent of the shares of the company from the government for $200 million. This was less than half the share price at the time. On yet another occasion Lukoil managers bought a block of shares from the government at less than market price.) Oneksimbank acquired 51 per cent of the voting shares (but 38 per cent of the shares) of Norilsk Nickel. It disqualified all other bids including one from Rossiisky Kredit for $355 million on the grounds that the bid exceeded Rossiisky Kredit's capital. A blind eye was turned to the fact that the same applied to Oneksimbank. It also acquired 51 per cent of the lucrative Sidanko oil company using the same technique.

In December 1995, Menatep acquired 45 per cent of Yukos. A consortium of Inkombank, Alfa Bank and Rossiisky Kredit Bank had offered $350 million, by far the largest bid. However the institution responsible for registering the bids was none other than Menatep. It disqualified the bid on the grounds that it was not entirely in cash. Menatep won an additional 33 per cent by promising to invest $150,125,000 million in Yukos. 'A nice little earner', as the immortal Arthur Daley, the lead character in the ITV series *Minder* would have commented. However in this case it was a nice big earner. Yukos, in reality, was worth at least $10 billion. Another nice little earner was the privatisation of Zarubezhtsvetmet. It was formed by Russia to hold a 49 per cent stake in a joint venture with the Mongolian government which managed Mongolia's Erdenet copper mine. Zarubezhtsvetmet's market value was perhaps $250 million but it was sold to insiders in the Russian ministry for metallurgy for $150,000 (Black *et al.* 2000: 16).

Berezovsky was determined to become an oil baron. He set up Sibneft (Siberian oil) by merging Noyabrskneftegaz, an oil company, and Omsk refinery with his partner, Roman Abramovich. Neither company initially wanted to merge but opposition to the deal just melted away after the managing director of the refinery was found floating, face down, in the river Irtysh. In late November, Berezovsky asked Alfred Kokh, head of the GKI, what he had to do to get Sibneft included in the loans for shares scheme. The paperwork had to be completed by the last day in November to ensure the sale went ahead in December before the deadline for the whole scheme expired. Kokh and Berezovsky agreed that the reserve price would be $100 million. Berezovsky got it for $100.3 million. There was another bid, $175 million by Sameko, a subsidiary of Inkombank. Just after the auction began, the Sameko managing director withdrew his bid. He had been made an offer he could not refuse. Withdraw or cease breathing.

Tables 8.4 and 8.5 show the values involved, and the winners, in the loans for shares scheme. It got even better for the oligarchs. The banks involved in the scheme had various government accounts. They simply advanced the government's money as loans back to the government. The result was that the government made a net loss on the whole transaction. However the crown jewels were a political bribe. The oligarchs would only acquire them after the re-election of Yeltsin in the summer of 1996. This ensured that they would all work together to ensure he won. Chubais and the government had manipulated the oligarchs for their own political ends. They thought that they could continue to manipulate them. However when the oligarchs acquired the wealth they began to manipulate the government.

The loans for shares episode is an important turning point in Russian politics. It marked a return to the policy of 1991 when Yeltsin offered economic benefits for political favours. It also marked the entry of the oligarchs into high government positions. After the re-election of Yeltsin two of the oligarchs entered the government. Vladimir Potanin became deputy Prime Minister responsible for economic policy while retaining his banking and business interests. Boris Berezovsky was appointed deputy secretary of the Security Council, in October 1996. Berezovsky made no bones about where his loyalties lay. He told *Newsweek*, in January 1997, that he was in government to protect his own interests.

Russia's privatisation has been dramatic and as regards the number of enterprises privatised the greatest the world has ever seen. A Russian company is regarded as private if the state's share holding in it is less than 50 per cent. The Czech Republic has privatised the largest proportion of its economy among formerly centrally planned economies (Table 8.6). Belarus is at the other end of the scale.

What about small private companies? One might expect them to flourish in an economy which had previously had few services. In 1995, the number of small Russian businesses was 877,000 but this fell to 829,000 in 1997. Small businesses are targeted by the tax inspectors since one of the persistent IMF conditions for its loans to Russia is for the state to collect more tax. Many large enterprises are subsidised by the state; one estimate in 2000 put subsidies at 15–20 per cent of GDP. Large companies just increase bribes if more pressure is put on them to pay tax. Small businesses do not advertise as a rule and business cards rarely have telephone numbers and addresses. Many businesses operate behind unmarked doors.

GOVERNMENT BONDS

On 1 July 1997, Thailand's financial system collapsed under a mountain of bad debt. Soon Indonesia, Malaysia and South Korea followed. The ripple effect of these events reached the Moscow stock market on 28 October when it dropped 20 per cent. Foreign investors were getting nervous and some had to sell to cover their losses in south east Asia. Another consequence was a sharp drop in oil prices. Oil accounted for about 20 per cent of Russia's exports.

On 23 March 1998, Yeltsin fired Chernomyrdin and Chubais. Berezovsky, a roving bandit, who opposed the plan to seize company assets in lieu of tax arrears, had conducted a whispering campaign against Chernomyrdin. Boris's nominee to take over was Ivan Rybkin but the opposition rallied and eventually Sergei Kirienko was chosen. He was installed in May but more than a month of valuable time had been frittered away. One of the casualties was Rosneft which the government wished to privatise, hoping to net at least $2 billion. On 26 May, defeat had to be admitted: no one wanted to buy the oil giant. This caused panic in the stock markets. The next day Moscow fell 10 per cent which meant that it had dropped about 40 per cent since the beginning of May.

One of the demands which the IMF reiterated ceaselessly as a condition of its loans was that Russia should gradually eliminate its budget deficit. This was impossible in the existing conditions but the government had come up with a solution in 1994. It began to sell short-term (GKO) and long-term (OFZ) ruble-denominated government bonds to the population and then to foreigners. Interest rates were sky high. In May 1998, government debt had risen to $140 billion in hard currency and $60 billion in rubles. Redeeming this debt was costing over $1 billion a week at a time when state revenues were declining to $3 billion a month. When this shortfall had happened in the past the state simply issued new bonds. This no longer worked as investors had lost confidence in the government. There was another solution, print money. However inflation was low and the ruble was strong, the two main achievements of the painful years of reform. There was another solution, albeit a short-term one: ask the IMF. Chubais was dispatched to Washington to work his usual magic. When it was mission impossible Anatoly was the man.

However Kirienko and the Russian government were out of their depth and could not see the gathering storm. The oligarchs acted and, on 16 June, they and Chubais debated the situation at Berezovsky's Logovaz club. The sum needed to save Russia had now risen to $35 billion. Chubais was again chosen for mission impossible. After agreeing they went to see Valentin Yumashev, head of the presidential administration, and then Sergei Kirienko. They of course agreed. A proposal, drafted by Potanin, was to be presented to the IMF. On 13 July, Chubais came up trumps and the IMF agreed to a $22.6 billion loan over two years. The first tranche of $4.8 billion arrived at the end of July. Some GKO debt was rescheduled to ease the pressure on Moscow. The government thought it had escaped by the skin of its teeth and that confidence would flow back into the financial markets. The opposite happened and those who could get out got out. They cashed in their GKOs and shares, bought dollars and transferred the money abroad. On 11 August, SBS-Agro (formerly Stolichny), run by Aleksandr Smolensky, and Inkombank, headed by Vladimir Vinogradov, defaulted. Two of the oligarchs had bitten the dust. They had followed the pattern of south east Asian banks, they had borrowed heavily and could not service their loans as their shares and investments plummeted in value. Bank Imperial was near the brink and banks began to default on loans to one another.

Surely this was another job for mission impossible man? However Chubais was touring the lush, green Irish countryside on the lookout for a castle. Sergei Dubinin, the chair of the Central Bank, was sunning himself in Italy. Mikhail Zadornov, the minister of finance, was at his desk but quite oblivious to what was coming. Even Egor Gaidar thought Russia would ride out the storm. What they did not grasp was that economics is as much about confidence as money. And confidence in the ruble was evaporating by the minute. Then came the blow which hastened the end. On 13 August, the *Financial Times* published an angry letter from George Soros. He wrote that the Russian financial meltdown was in its terminal phase. Russia had to devalue, perhaps by 25 per cent. Russia needed another $15 billion from the west, otherwise the country could collapse with incalculable consequences. As the stock market nose-dived, Kirienko assured everyone on television that things would work out. Some perceptive Muscovites began withdrawing their rubles and changing them into dollars. On 14 August, Bank Imperial defaulted. Yeltsin put his shoulder to the wheel. 'There will be no devaluation', he thundered.

As the Central Bank ran out of dollars, the inevitable had to be faced. Russia would have to default on its $40 billion ruble-denominated bond debt (about one third of this was held by foreigners). It would cheat those who had placed their faith in Russia with their money. The ruble would be devalued by about 50 per cent to 9.5 to the dollar. The oligarchs, some of whom had been advocating devaluation for weeks, were appalled by the decision to default on government bonds. How were they to service their loans since they were heavily into bonds? Eventually it was agreed that there was to be a moratorium on payments of foreign debt by all Russian companies and citizens. Kirienko announced the package, on 17 August, looking how he felt, utterly devastated. The moratorium was vital for the banks as it offered them the possibility of revenue during the 90 days in order to meet some of their obligations.

The ruble soon fell below 9.5 to the dollar and kept on falling. The collapse decimated the new middle class, the hope of the young reformers. Many lost their jobs and headed back to the provinces. Once again Russians had lost their savings. The clever ones had changed their rubles into dollars and kept them under the mattress. Those with dollar accounts in banks found they could not withdraw the money. Eventually the government agreed to pay up to five cents on the dollar on state bonds. Kirienko and his government fell as well, on 23 August.

The hardest hit in the August crash were the banks and two oligarchs, Aleksandr Smolensky (SBS-Agro) and Vladimir Vinogradov (Inkombank) became insolvent and left the ranks of the oligarchs. In July 1998, Inkombank had been the largest private bank and the fifth largest Russian bank with assets of 35.2 billion rubles ($5.9 billion). However, in September 1998, Inkombank had a stroke of luck when it obtained a $100 million loan from the Central Bank and the official who granted it also left hurriedly. He was Sergei Dubinin, the governor, and he made several such parting gifts to troubled commercial banks. Government policy was to save 'socially important' banks. Inkombank serviced about 10 per cent of Russia's foreign trade and about 5 per cent of the country's bank accounts. Unfortunately for Vinogradov he was on bad terms with the new Central Bank governor, Viktor Gerashchenko. Inkombank had its licence revoked on 29 October 1998 and Vinogradov stepped down as head of the bank. Among the reasons given was the excessive risk taking of the bank which had run up forward currency contracts of between $12 billion and $14 billion by mid-August. The bank's assets included 26 per cent of the giant Magnitogorsk steelworks but only 3 per cent was owned directly by the bank while the rest was held by affiliated companies. This permitted rapid asset stripping. It also owned many valuable oil paintings, including Red Square, the master-piece of the Russian modernist painter, Kasimir Malevich, and a con-trolling interest in the Rot Front sweet factory in Moscow.

In March 1999, an attempt was made to restructure Inkombank. This failed and a Moscow court declared it bankrupt with debts of at least $1.6 billion, including $200 million owed to private investors and $800 million to foreign creditors, and large off-balance sheet obligations.

SBS-Agro was designated a 'socially important' bank and survived. It was the third largest bank before the crash. Previously Smolensky had wisely donated 50 kg of gold ingots for the roof of the Cathedral of Christ the Saviour in Moscow. Another reason why SBS-Agro survived was that after Yeltsin's re-election, 1996, it had taken over the huge state-owned Agroprombank which channelled massive government subsidies to farms. This was Smolensky's reward for his financial help during the election campaign. The bank retained this business after the crash, along with Alfa Bank. Alfa Bank did rather well because it had little exposure to the short-term bond market. It also acquired the St Petersburg city budget account.

Contacts are everything, especially if one was a foreign investor in GKOs. Goldman Sachs, the US investment bank, arranged a $6.4 billion bond swap which it promoted to clients by buying ruble-denominated secu-rities. It closed a month before the August crash. Goldman Sachs itself did not lose anything because it disposed of its GKOs, worth hundreds of millions of dollars, just before the crash. George Soros and his funds may have lost close on two billion dollars in the debacle. American com-mercial and investment banking losses were over $1 billion. Barclays Bank, the British bank, lost over £250 million.

Chernomyrdin came back but the Duma would not have him. Evgeny Primakov took over. However Mikhail Zadornov stayed on as minister of finance. Primakov was a consensus-seeker and gradually looked like a presidential candidate. This was his undoing and he was sacked in May 1999. In came 'baby-faced' Sergei Stepashin, a man who had proved his loyalty before. In August, Vladimir Putin replaced him and began at once to deal with the Chechen problem. He also started putting his war machine in place. In November 1999, General Sergei Ivanov, deputy head of the FSB since August 1998, was made secretary of the Security Council. He is one of Putin's closest confidants. Then came the greatest surprise of all. On 31 December 1999, Yeltsin announced he was stepping down and appointed Putin as acting President. He was duly elected President, in March 2000. He had some economic luck. Oil and commodity prices rose sharply and Russia began to run up a large foreign trade surplus. Industry began to grow again as foreign goods became very expensive.

Table 8.7 shows foreign direct investment (FDI) in 1989–98. If one adds IMF, World Bank, German and all other state and private inflows, the situation changes dramatically. The grand total comes to about $150 billion. The main reason why foreign companies invested so little in Russia was the absence of a tariff policy which would protect their investment. IBM did set up a plant to assemble computers but the Yeltsin administrations gave insiders the right to import computers free of import duties and taxes. IBM could not compete and closed down. Pharmaceutical companies decided not to invest because they feared cheap imports from Turkey and India. Even joint ventures often did not work. Western oil companies did 50–50 deals with Russian companies but found they were responsible for all expenses. The Russian company had to deliver its oil virtually free to customers and hence had no money for investment. Foreign investment in Russian shares was also hazardous.

SHUTTLE TRADING

The rise and fall of shuttle trading is evidence of a maturing Russian economy. After the collapse of communism, thousands of Russians took off for Turkey, Italy, Poland, the United Arab Emirates, China and other exotic locations to buy up cheap consumer goods and sell them on Moscow's streets. The shuttle traders, predominantly women, lugged huge bags of merchandise through airports and railway stations on a regular basis. According to the Academy of Sciences, shuttle traders accounted for one in five of the 66 million Russian workers, in 1996. Shuttle trading, officially, imported $20 billion worth of goods, in 1996, but this fell to $8.7 billion in 1999. Profits were good, while it lasted. A shuttle trader could make $1000 to $2000 a month net profit. The goods most in demand were women's lingerie. The ruble devaluation of August 1998 was a body blow as it meant that Russians could not afford to buy existing stocks and traders found foreign goods increasingly uncompetitive on Russia's streets.

In 2000, shuttle traders were a dying breed. Importing has passed increasingly to air freight companies which deliver directly to the customer. They deliver on a regular basis and are parts of international networks. Russian industry has responded to the opportunities created by the August 1998 crash. It now produces many goods which are superior in quality to cheap foreign imports. Municipal authorities have been trying to push traders off the streets. Moscow has imposed a 5 per cent sales tax and many other cities have followed suit. Moscow also requires vendors to install cash registers. It is also closing down the city's bazaars. In 1999, 27 of Moscow's 224 bazaars ceased trading and another 43 are to close by the end of 2001. The objective is to move traders into indoor malls but this also means that profit margins will be squeezed as rent has to be paid and the tax inspector's work becomes simpler. The single trader will find it more and more difficult to survive as trading groups take over. Russia is becoming a normal trading country.

There are now two informal economies in Russia. The shadow economy or black market uses cash but, of course, pays no federal taxes. The virtual economy is the manufacturing sector which has not yet adjusted to the market and exists on state subsidies. The shadow economy, until the crash of August 1998, accounted for about 40 per cent of Russian GDP; the virtual economy for another 25 per cent. Hence the formal economy only produced about 35 per cent of GDP. This is one reason why the state found it so difficult to collect sufficient tax to maintain basic services. The fact that there are three economies in Russia does not mean that Russian producers act irrationally. Indeed, given the circumstances under which they operate, their behaviour is rational. They are responding to the incentives produced by economic reform. Russian savers also act rationally since the crash of August 1998. In November 1998, Evgeny Primakov, the Prime Minister, stated that there were 191.9 billion rubles in circulation or about $7 billion. However he estimated that there were a further $30 billion to $40 billion in US notes kept in apartments well away from commercial banks and the tax man. (In 2000, the number of US notes in Russia (official and private) was, according to one estimate, equal to the total circulating in the US.)

9

AGRICULTURE:
THE PEASANTS STAY POOR

IN THE WEST THERE WAS A widespread perception that agriculture was the Achilles heel of the Soviet system, hence there was always an agricultural crisis. This does not stand up to examination. Global agricultural output over the years 1961–90, by value, increased by 72 per cent while the population rose by 23 per cent. During these years grain output grew by 58 per cent, meat by 108 per cent, milk by 63 per cent and eggs by 190 per cent. Per capita food consumption kept pace with these advances. The farming economy was dominated by kolkhozes (collective farms) and sovkhozes (state farms). There were no private farms. On the face of it, socialist farming did well but this is not so. About one third of global agricultural output came from household private plots but they only worked about three per cent of the arable land. It gets even worse. An estimated one third of agricultural output was lost between the fields and the dining table. One can assume that waste on the private plots was minimal. Hence the problem of socialist agriculture was distribution, not production. This was due to an antiquated infrastructure of poor roads, communications, handling and storage facilities (tomatoes were sometimes delivered to the state in bulk, piled high in lorry loads, because there were no trays to place them in) and a lack of refrigerated wagons and lorries. Most crucial of all was that farms only produced and were not responsible for marketing. The quality of the produce was of no interest to them. Vast sums of money were invested in agriculture. Retail prices of food products were kept low resulting in state subsidies rising every year. The leadership was afraid of raising prices for fear of popular unrest. Under Brezhnev about one quarter of the budget was destined for agriculture and its inputs (machinery, chemicals, etc.). Even this was not enough. Billions of dollars (the US demanded cash which the Soviet Union obtained by selling gold and other commodities) were expended every year. For instance, in 1984, the USSR imported 46 million tonnes of grain, half a million tonnes of meat and meat products, over one million tonnes of animal and vegetable oil and other food products. All this would have been unnecessary had there been an efficient packaging, storage and distribution network.

Why was agriculture so inefficient and wasteful? The key reason was the lack of incentives to perform better. For instance, farms had to deliver almost all their output to the state. Had they been permitted to market their output, waste would have been reduced at a stroke. However this was ideologically unacceptable. It should be pointed out that Soviet farm managers and workers acted rationally within the limits of the system they worked in. They minimised the amount of work needed to achieve the plan. For instance, they delivered potatoes encased in clay because plan fulfilment was in tonnes. They were not being stupid, they were being sensible. This demonstrated the total lack of any feeling of social and moral responsibility towards society in general and the state in particular. This dreadful legacy was inherited by the Yeltsin era.

The author, in the early 1970s, visited an agricultural institute in Odessa, Ukraine. He was invited afterwards to an excellent lunch at a professor's home. The vegetables came from his garden as did the strawberries and other fruit for dessert. An Englishman would have been proud of the garden. He was told that the professor was a clever man because he kept his garden within the permissible limits. Any larger and he would be in trouble with the authorities. Here was the dichotomy of the Soviet system, efficient private agriculture and inefficient state agriculture. Needless to say farms around Odessa were as inefficient as elsewhere.

Ever since the Khrushchev years there had been out-migration from the countryside to the towns. There were no centres of higher learning in rural areas, one had to go to the town to study. The girls were first to leave, followed by the boys who wanted a woman. This brain drain increased the average age of farm workers and most were female. Gorbachev lamented the fact that farm workers were not made responsible for the use of land and other assets. Wages were almost the same for everyone which meant that the work-shy were paid the same as those

who worked. In 1987, he introduced the leasing of land for farm workers and, in 1991, over 63 per cent of collective and state farms had concluded leasing contracts. However, as with much under Gorbachev, this
was mere window-dressing. There was normally only one lease as this
was sufficient to meet the demands of the campaign. Under existing circumstances, farm personnel could not see any advantage in leasing land.

LAND PRIVATISATION

In December 1991, Yeltsin signed a decree to promote the privatisation
of collective and state farms (Wegren 1998: chapter 3). Farm members
were to receive a share of the farm on leaving. There were about 27,000
collective and state farms but about one in eight were on their last legs.
The best solution was for profitable farms to take them over but if there
were no takers the farm assets were to be sold to the workers. It was
not explained why a good farm should lumber itself with a bad one
and where the workers were to get the money from to buy the assets.
Who wants to buy a broken-down tractor? The basic rule in life is: if in
doubt blame someone else. The bankrupt farms blamed the state for their
condition. It had not met its financial and other obligations. The red
rural lobby secured its first victory. In March 1992, collective and state
farms were given the right to stay as they were if they so wished. An
opportunity was missed to oblige farms to restructure. They were
allowed to retain a collective form of labour organisation.

Under privatisation, if a member stayed on the farm his land share
remained with the farm and became general farm property. If he
changed his mind later he was compensated financially but received no
land. About 84 per cent of collective and state farms (90 per cent of
farmland) became joint stock companies and thus stayed exactly as they
were. Most farms chose to be closed joint stock companies (shares could
not change hands without the permission of the farm's general meeting and outsiders could not acquire them). If there was a profit at the
end of the year members received a dividend. This was the same as a
bonus under communism.

Farm reorganisation led to the first flare-up between President Yeltsin
and Vice-President Aleksandr Rutskoi. The latter thought private farming was too expensive and the state should not be devoting scarce
resources to it. In the interests of increasing food output existing farms
should be helped. Rutskoi was sacked in April 1993. Rutskoi received
some support from Viktor Khlystun, minister of agriculture from 1992
to October 1994 and again from May 1996. Khlystun and Aleksandr

Nazarchuk, minister of agriculture from October 1994 to May 1996, were both members of the Agrarian Party, the country sister of the KPRF. Hence there was always tension between the young reformers in Moscow who favoured private farmers and the minister who did not. Yeltsin's attacks on collective and state farms alienated the countryside at a time when Moscow needed allies to transform agriculture. Due to the government's inability to collect taxes it could not keep its financial pledges to transform the countryside. The rural voter lost faith in the Yeltsin regime. This was borne out in the elections in December 1993, December 1995, June–July 1996 and December 1999. The countryside belonged to the opposition. The only friend the government had in rural areas was the Association of Peasant Farms and Cooperatives of Russia (AKKOR) which represented private farming interests. In 1998, only about six per cent of land was held by private farmers. Private farms and private farmers were unpopular in the countryside.

In January 1994, farm reorganisation was almost complete. About 95 per cent of farms had reregistered. About 34 per cent of collective and state farms chose to retain their former status while the others became joint stock companies. Virtually all these farms adopted some form of collective labour organisation. Hence privatisation changed little and this made it very difficult for the private farmer. The economic environment was hostile, the urban market was unreliable, credit was very difficult to obtain and inputs expensive. Private farmers were poor and have remained poor. Even the government did not want them to become big farmers. It was politically unacceptable to recreate the large estates which had existed until 1917. The resistance to private farming is reminiscent of the period 1906–17 when Stolypin's 'wager on the strong' sought to break up the village communes and establish a new class of rural peasant landowners. He needed twenty years of peace for it to take root but he was only afforded eight. The main factor against private farming was the egalitarian culture of the Russian village. This remains the case today.

As a general rule the best opportunities exist for farms within a 100 km radius of a city. There are reduced opportunities within the next 100 km radius. Farms which are over 200 km from a city have few market openings and find themselves in the back of beyond. It is striking that in the most favoured area, within reach of the city, private farms did not immediately appear in considerable numbers. There are various explanations for this. The best age for a private farmer is between 30 and 40 but this age group is under-represented and about one third of farm workers were too old to take on new responsibilities. Women easily outnumbered men as well. Overall the percentage of farmers capable of private farming was quite small. However many private farmers initially came from outside agriculture. In late 1991, in the non-black earth region as many as 80 per cent came from the cities with no technical preparation at all. Aleksandr Rutskoi estimated that, in July 1992, only 3000 of the 150,000 private farms in Russia were viable. In 1997, the average size of a private farm was 44 hectares but in the more fertile north Caucasus it was only 21 hectares. There was great initial enthusiasm to set up private farms and this peaked in 1993 when 87,094 appeared. However this declined rapidly to 9223 in 1994 and in 1996 the total number declined by 1387. The greatest decline was in the Urals but in the north Caucasus 4882 new farms were set up. In 1996, over 25,000 private farmers gave up the uneven struggle and quit. Of those who stayed in business an estimated 75 per cent were loss-making. In 1999, the area of privately owned land contracted by 400,000 hectares.

A private farmer usually received a parcel of good land and a parcel of average land. They were not contiguous. It was also normal to allocate land to private farmers in the least advantageous location. Where was he to get his inputs of machinery, energy, fertilisers, seed and so on when there was no wholesale market? He had to rely on the mother farm for them. This put him at the mercy of the management. On one occasion a farmer went to Moscow for the day and returned to find 26 piglets dead. The mother farm had switched off the electricity when he had departed. On another state farm potatoes were rotting because they could not be harvested. However the director would not allow a private farmer to pick them even though he desperately needed them as fodder for his animals. Credit was another problem as few banks would accept land as collateral.

The government was concerned in the spring of 1992 about the impact of price liberalisation on agriculture. In order to boost output it announced subsidies. However it made no attempt to promote farm efficiency but distributed subsidies on an egalitarian basis. It just continued the old Soviet practice. The weaker the farms and the weaker the region the greater the subsidies they received. Animal husbandry had never been profitable before 1991 and despite the new subsidies continued to be loss-making. The number of cattle on collective and state farms declined from 47.1 million head in 1991 to 31.1 million head in 1995. Pigs almost halved in the same period. This was in marked contrast to the number of animals owned by the population on private plots. Their numbers increased significantly so that in 1995 about one third of Russian pigs and 40 per cent of Russian cattle were on private plots.

RADICAL NEW MEASURES

Government policy became more radical after the Supreme Soviet was forcibly disbanded in October 1993. Ideology now played a more important role. Collective agriculture was deemed bad and private agriculture bad. Foreign advisers and funding played a major role in this transformation. Subsidies should be cut back and farms should be allowed to sink or swim. Western specialists giving this advice conveniently forgot that European Union, Canadian and US agriculture is heavily subsidised. The general rule is the more developed the state the greater the subsidy. The only exception to this is New Zealand but there agriculture dominates the economy.

A document leaked in March 1994 revealed the advice that Yeltsin was being given to reform agriculture. It described a countryside dominated by private farms. The state was to use financial levers to undermine farms working on the basis of collective labour organisation. These farms were to vote for dissolution and the land handed to associations of up to thirty private farmers. The minister of agriculture called the document absurd and this was a polite word for it. Yeltsin backed off and stated that there was no intention of forcibly breaking up farms. The reformers' dream that private farms could feed the country more economically than collective and state farms remained a dream. In 1997, private farms contributed about three per cent of the nation's food supply. The way ahead was to make collective and state farms more efficient. Indeed one could coin the maxim: what Stalin had bound together let no man tear asunder.

THE NIZHNY NOVGOROD EXPERIMENT

Grigory Yavlinsky had worked with Boris Nemtsov, the governor, to promote market reform but the impetus for private farming in the region came from the World Bank, the British Know-How fund and the Canadians. In November 1993, a joint stock farm was sold to its members and 12 new private farms emerged ranging in size from 915 hectares to 5 hectares (Wegren 1998: 94–107). Other farms were sold off and Viktor Chernomyrdin actually smiled after attending one of the auctions. A decree, in April 1994, stated that the Nizhny model was to be adopted throughout Russia. It was but to little effect. Returns on private farms were not significantly better than on collective and state farms. Setting up small private farms also flew in the face of western experience. There small farms were disappearing with large farms gradually taking over the countryside. The economies of scale are significant in developed agriculture.

RURAL POLITICS

The young reformers were urbanites and they took it for granted that the way to reform agriculture was from the top down. This had been the Soviet tradition. None of them had any particular interest in the rural economy and hence failed to realise that in order to reform successfully they had to build up support in the countryside. Reform was not economically but politically driven. The goals were to decollectivise the countryside and to create a new class of private farmers who would provide a political base in rural areas. Those who advocated privatisation failed to understand the dominant social role collective and state farms played in the countryside. They provided housing, schools, health facilities, pensions and other social services. A private farmer cut himself off from these. The government later admitted that it had only implemented the first stage of agrarian reform. The second stage was to set up agricultural banks to provide credit including the acceptance of land as collateral. Then a new social security net had to be established. The reason for this was the government's inability to collect taxes and keep its promises to fund agriculture. Among those hardest hit were the private farmers when the state delayed paying them for their produce. By 1994 the government's rural reform policies had alienated almost everyone in the countryside. Price inflation led to reduced demand for food and the hardest hit were the food processing plants. The nouveaux riches preferred foreign imports and the average Russian could not afford domestic produce. In 1995, about 40 per cent of Russian food was being imported and it was estimated that up to 80 per cent of Moscow's food was imported. In 1996, Russia was spending about $1 billion a month on food imports or, on an annual basis, four times as much as the government invested in Russian agriculture. In 1996, agriculture was allocated only 3.2 per cent of the budget, about an eighth of the halcyon Brezhnev days. In reality it received less as state revenues dwindled. Capital investment in agricultural infrastructure was gradually switched from the central to the local budget.

The terms of trade turned against agriculture. During the first year of price liberalisation agricultural prices rose by a factor of ten but industrial prices rose by a factor of 26. In 1993, and afterwards, agricultural prices always limped behind industrial prices. One of the sharpest increases was the price of fuel over the period 1991–95 which rose by a factor of 44. A reason for this huge disparity was that essential food prices were not freed in January 1992 but remained state controlled. Farms could simply not cover their production costs. They could also not feed their animals and their numbers declined rapidly. To compound the problem taxes rose as farm revenue fell. By 1995, agricultural employees had the lowest income of any group, about one third of that of urban employees.

GLOBAL PRODUCTION AND CONSUMPTION

Global production fell during the 1990s as the arable (crop) area dropped. Yields per hectare also declined. Over the period 1990–95, global production fell by an estimated 33 per cent. It fell another 8 per cent in 1996 and 7 per cent in 1997. There are various explanations for this. The drop in capital equipment has led to a drop in labour productivity. Animals are not as well fed as in 1990 and hence they yield less meat when slaughtered. Cows give less milk. The north Caucasus, the largest grain producing region in Russia, saw grain yields decline by 27 per cent between 1991 and 1994. The same story is repeated in other regions. Another reason were the high interest rates which very few farms could afford to pay. When they borrowed it was for basic production. Farms cut back on the sown area and food production. This resulted in lower farm income. This, in turn, meant they could not reduce losses and wastage.

Table 9.1 outlines global grain production and state purchases from 1986 to 2000. The statistics do not accurately reflect actual grain (wheat, rye, buckwheat, barley, oats and millet) production as farms hold back up to 25 per cent of their harvest to cover employee wages, sales to private traders and until prices rise, usually the following spring. This also ensures they evade paying tax on this part of their output. A common trick is to write off part of the sown area claiming that the crop has been destroyed by hail, storms, locusts or fire. For instance, in 1999, the area sown to crops was 42.6 million hectares but of this 7.7 million hectares were written off. Since 1990 the area sown to crops has declined by about 20 million hectares. Russia needs 74 million tonnes annually to be self-sufficient in grain. The real 2000 output was put at 70.5 million tonnes by the head of the Russian Grain Union.

After 1993 state control of grain trade declined very rapidly and this pattern was followed in other foodstuffs. However it was one thing for Roskhleboprodukt, the state procurement agency, to purchase (usually at above market rates) but another thing for it to pay. Its arrears to farmers by the mid-1990s had climbed to several billion dollars. This made producers reluctant to sell to Roskhleboprodukt.

Livestock numbers dwindled rapidly during the 1990s. In 1990, there were 47.2 million cattle but this had dropped to 17.5 million in 1999.

The corresponding numbers for pigs were 31.2 million and 10 million and for sheep and goats, 42.1 million and 4.8 million.

Food consumption improved steadily in the Soviet Union and by the late 1980s was adequate. However, consumers complained about quality which did decline. Cheese was of fine quality until the late 1970s but afterwards was less inviting. This led to some young people giving up cheese.

Table 9.2 outlines patterns in food consumption from 1990 to 1997; those most affected by the decline in consumption were women and pensioners. The latter ate much less than the national average with males of working age consuming much more. There was hunger in certain cities, even Moscow, and food was rationed in certain areas. Regions adopted the policy of restricting the export of food to other areas. As subsidies were removed from food the structure of the Russian diet changed. Meat and milk products increased in price faster than bread. Russians now eat more bread and potatoes and less meat and milk products. The Agrarian Party claimed in 1995 (an election year) that Russians consumed 40 per cent less protein than the healthy norm and the vitamin deficiency was 60 per cent.

AGRARIAN POLITICAL MOVEMENTS

Rural political organisation began with the Association of Peasant Farms and Agricultural Cooperatives of Russia (AKKOR) which convened its founding Congress in January 1990 (Wegren 1998: 138–47). Its primary aim was to represent the interests of newly private farmers and leaseholders. The USSR Union of Leaseholders and Entrepreneurs appeared in June 1990. Workers in the agro-industrial complex split from the All-Union Central Confederation of Trade Unions and set up their own trade union, the trade union of workers in the agro-industrial complex, in March 1990. It claimed about 15 million members. At the third Congress of People's Deputies, in March–April 1990, agrarian deputies decided to form their own parliamentary faction. It became the Russian Agrarian Union but it never became a political party. It represented the interests of collective, state and private farms, leaseholders and those in the food processing industry. AKKOR soon withdrew claiming that the Union really represented collectivised agriculture. The Union wanted to restrict government interference in collective and state agriculture and lobbied for more investment and subsidies. The main theme at its second congress, in June 1993, was the declining fortunes of the rural economy. Predictably they argued in favour of increasing subsidies for rural producers.

The party which emerged from the Agrarian Union was the Agrarian Party of Russia (APR). It held its founding convention in Nizhny Novgorod in December 1992 and its founding Congress in February 1993 in Moscow (Wegren 1998: 141–7). The decision to set up the APR was taken at the All-Russian Congress of Kolkhozniks (collective farmers) in early 1992. Mikhail Lapshin was elected chair of the central council. The Congress convened two weeks after the founding of the communist party of the Russian Federation (KPRF). Lapshin had been head of the agrarian faction, the largest faction, in the Russian Supreme Soviet. He was also a member of the founding committee of the KPRF and was elected one of the six vice-chairs of the party. The APR has its own weekly newspaper, *Zemlya i Trud.* In the December 1993 Duma elections the APR secured 33 seats with 8 per cent of the votes. The agrarian faction in the Duma had 55 members. In the December 1995 Duma elections it only obtained 20 seats because its share of the vote fell to 3.8 per cent or below the 5 per cent threshold required to secure party lists seats. In December 1999 only one agrarian deputy was elected to the Duma. Most of its former support switched to the communists.

The APR was the main voice in the countryside opposing agricultural reform and it increased its influence after December 1993 in the wake of declining rural living standards. Viktor Khlystun, Aleksandr Nazarchuk and Aleksandr Zaveryukha, ministers of agriculture from 1992–97, were members of the APR. Ivan Rybkin, speaker of the first Duma, was also a member. Its poor showing in the December 1995 Duma elections (lost votes went mainly to the KPRF) resulted in the head of the party losing his seat as did the head of the Agrarian Union. Rybkin was replaced as speaker by Gennady Seleznev (KPRF).

Given the widening of wage inequality to a level not experienced for over 50 years one might have expected much more social protest. The APR did organise demonstrations but they had little impact. It is hard to attract attention unless everyone comes to Moscow to demonstrate. Russia is simply too large for this to become a repeated occurrence. There was a social contract between town and countryside before 1991. Cynics would say that everyone was equal in poverty but everyone was looked after. In 1993 the government dropped this policy and attempted to force farms to reorganise or sink. Farms responded by cutting production and not restructuring. The government got the worst of both worlds.

THE PRESENT SITUATION

The main reason why agriculture today is in a difficult situation is the determination of the government to ensure cheap food for the cities. This is the chief reason for not approving the buying and selling of land. Shortly before the presidential election in March 2000, Vladimir Putin told the APR central committee that if there were a real *khozyain* (boss) in the countryside there would be order and wealth in Russia. However he ducked the key question: is a *khozyain* the owner of the land and able to buy and sell it or a lessee or simply a good manager? After ten years of post-communism the subject remains that sensitive.

About 80 per cent of Russian farms are loss-making and in 1999 total debts were 180 billion rubles ($6.3 billion) or 28.9 per cent of global agricultural production. Russia requested food aid from the United States for the second year running. Those who advocate the buying and selling of land are met with furious opposition in the countryside. Given that country people are poor, the land would be snapped up by the new Russians and foreigners, rendering them landless. It would be a new form of serfdom. The APR and KPRF sing the same song in order to win the rural vote. After all there are 40 million rural residents involved in agriculture.

A land market does exist but it is very small. In 1998, about 126 million hectares of agricultural land out of a total of 455 million hectares, or 28 per cent, had been privatised. However almost all of this land belongs to 11.9 million individuals who are members of former collective and state farms which have converted to joint stock companies. They own the land collectively and their labour is organised collectively. Collective and state farms account for 328.5 million hectares with 28.2 million hectares being owned by individuals (6.2 per cent) and 98.2 million hectares by organisations. An estimated 30 million hectares of agricultural land has, in effect, been abandoned. One of the reasons for this is that the terms of trade have turned strongly against farmers. If the rise in the price of agricultural products during the 1990s is taken as equivalent to a hundred, the prices for inputs such as spare parts, fuel and machinery were between 450 and 700.

The second stage of privatisation, the establishment of land banks to provide financial support for those who wish to become private farmers, still only exists on paper. A federal law on agricultural mortgages has been talked about for ages. Probably only about 20 per cent of present private farms are viable. Those who advocate a market in land argue that the land shares of collective and state farm employees should be separated out. Then the owner can decide what to do with his or her land: rent it out, work it or sell it.

Even if a land code did permit buying of land there is no guarantee there were be a great rush of buyers. Rent and land taxes at present are very low. In some regions these taxes are a few rubles a year. In Novgorod, rent and land taxes are only about 2800 rubles ($100) for a 200 hectare farm. However, in 1999, in Saratov, which is one of the few regions to have passed legislation permitting the buying and selling of land, buyers paid about 60,000 rubles ($2200) for a 200 hectare farm. Saratov began selling land in 1998 but sold only 43 plots in 1998 and 25 in 1999. The price was 780 rubles per hectare in 1998 but this came down to 300 rubles in 1999. Contrary to the nightmares of the APR and KPRF no New Russians or foreigners have bought any land.

A shadow market in land has developed but it concerns private plot and dacha land. The New Russians have no interest in agriculture but they are extremely keen to acquire land on which to build a dacha. A New Russian without a dacha is like a dog without a bone. Practically every Muscovite aspires to a private plot and dacha. The rush began in 1991 and those who were slow off the market had to go further and further out of Moscow. The urban dwellers were a curiosity to the locals. When they suggested the rural dwellers should also buy a plot and build a dacha they were met with disdain. The urban dwellers had a thirst to own land but the locals regarded this as foolish. The average plot was 100 square metres and near Moscow could cost up to $1000. It had to be registered with the local soviet or council and in order to reduce taxes the land was listed at a fraction of its real price. In 1998, the Russian government estimated there were 450,000 land transactions and an equal number which went unrecorded. The average land transaction, involving private plots, averaged 0.23 ha. Altogether about 40 million hectares passed into private ownership.

The private plot keeps Russians alive and, in 1999, produced 91.2 per cent of the potatoes, 79.6 per cent of the fresh vegetables, 88.1 per cent of the honey, 56.9 per cent of the meat, 48.3 per cent of the milk, 30.1 per cent of the eggs and 55 per cent of the wool of the national output. On the other hand they only produced 0.9 per cent of the grain. These baby farms can be up to 1000 square metres. In 1999, one institute estimated these private plots produced 64 per cent of Russian global agricultural output. In 1991 it was 31.2 per cent.

Dedushka (granddad) and *babushka* (grandma) play an important role as they usually live on the plot during the summer. Part of their job is to ensure that no one makes off with the produce. When a pensioner found two men stealing his potato crop near Moscow he shouted at them to clear off. One produced a knife and the pensioner shot him dead with his gun. Even the local police chief said he was a hero. Another thief found stealing vegetables was locked in a metal cage; another was required to walk on all fours as he was attached to a dog kennel with a heavy metal chain. A rumour circulated that a woman had captured a local thief; she allowed him to go free after he agreed to service her for a year. Collective and state farms also confront the same problem of theft of new machinery. The director usually keeps machinery in his private plot to ensure that no one steals or cannibalises it.

The extraordinary productivity of private plots has a reverse side. It reduces the demand for farm produce. Farms, as a result, cannot sell their produce and therefore run up debts. By 2000 barter had almost totally replaced monetarised exchange in agriculture. The plots pay no income tax and use traditional tools. They have very little interest in new technology. This remarkable phenomenon points to technical regression in Russian agriculture. One can also call it the growing primitivisation of the sector. An indication of this is that the number of horses in Russia more than doubled in 1991–97.

A LAND CODE

The Duma and Council of the Federation have debated a new land code on many occasions since 1996 (Wegren 1998: chapter 5). Two were passed but vetoed by President Yeltsin because they did not provide for the sale of land. The present draft, being promoted by the APR and the KPRF, is framed in such a way as to make it extremely difficult to qualify for private land. One has to lease it for 10 years but in order to get a lease one has to pass an agricultural examination. However a key provision is that the land acquired is only for agricultural use. A real market will only develop when agricultural land can be used for commercial purposes. Even if a liberal land code were passed it would only be the first step towards a flourishing land market. According to the state land committee at least another twenty laws have to be passed. These laws would define what was federal, regional and municipal land, would legislate on land sales and the registering of these deals and on the mortgaging of land. Many of these laws exist in draft form but cannot be passed until the land code is law. Using land as collateral is essential if farms are to raise capital since at present commercial banks have little interest in agriculture. Those state banks which funnel credits to agriculture, such as SBS-Agro, have a remarkable propensity to lose some of the money en route.

Turning land into a marketable commodity will create social problems. What will become of those who are alcoholics, handicapped, too old or too young who may be turned off the land because the new private owner has no need of them? They will have to steal to survive. This is already happening in Orenburg oblast which borders on Kazakhstan. Kazakh workers turned off farms cross the border and steal from Orenburg farms. Facilities such as schools and hospitals are on collective and state farms. Private farmers require access to them so a partnership needs to develop. The state would like to opt out of providing social services in the countryside. No wonder people are leaving the countryside and the Russian population is declining.

The above situation has resulted in clan chiefs and oligarchs paying little attention to the countryside. There are no bandits roving the countryside. This is eloquent testimony to the fact that if someone is bent on making money the countryside should be avoided.

10

A SOCIETY IN CRISIS

A RUSSIAN WIT REMARKED THAT ONE should not think of death as the end. 'Just think of it as a very efficient method of reducing expenses.'

DEMOGRAPHY

Russia's population is declining by about 700,000 a year and there are fears that the number of Russians will halve by the middle of this century. In October 2000, the population was 145.0 million. There are now 1136 women per 1000 men. The shock of perestroika, the transition to a market economy and the loss of superpower status has had a catastrophic effect on the population. Alexander Zinoviev termed this phenomenon katastroika. But it is not merely a post-communist malaise. The decline in the growth rate of the population can be traced back to the 1960s when more resources were poured into defence and less into health, education and social security. In 1980, the natural increase in the Russian population was about a million a year but by 1989 this was down to half a million. In 1991, it was only 224,600 and by 1993 the number of deaths had exceeded births by 750,400. Russia thus became the first industrial state to experience such a decline for reasons other than war, famine or disease (Field and Twigg 2000: 13). A major reason is that the birth rate declined by about a half between 1985 and 1996. The economic situation led to women simply not wanting to give birth. Women are almost ten times more likely to die in childbirth in

Russia than in the west. Another reason is the rising tide of domestic violence. The police rarely react to claims of rape and assault by adult women.

Birth control has escalated. In 1994, 3.7 per cent of women used oral contraceptives and 19.8 per cent intrauterine devices. However abortion was and is the most common method of birth control. Since 1970 abortions have outnumbered births by at least two to one (1985 was an exception). In 1994, the number was 217.0 but these were only the registered abortions. There may be as many as four abortions to each birth at present. The number of illegitimate births doubled between 1970 and in 1995 when it was 21.1 per cent (urban and rural areas were almost the same). This rose to 25 per cent in 1997. Most of these children are born to single mothers, often teenagers, who find it emotionally and economically difficult to look after the child. Many of them are abandoned and become street urchins where they fall into the hands of street gangs. The Orthodox Church estimated, in December 2000, that there are now between two and five million vagabond children in Russia and up to 30 per cent of children kept in children's homes have only one parent. The divorce rate and separations, which may be around 70 per cent, is contributing to these numbers.

The birth rate in Russia is one of the lowest in Europe. It is well short of the level necessary for the reproduction of the population (about 210 births per 100 women or a fertility rate of 2.1). In 1996, the fertility rate was 1.28, in 1997 1.23, in 1998 1.24 and in 1999 1.17. Such a low level of reproduction is unprecedented in Russia and is one of the lowest in the world. This has serious consequences for the Russian economy as the workforce declines. In the United States the fertility rate is 2.0 but the average for wealthy countries is only 1.7 which is 81 per cent of the level needed. Britain and France record 1.7 which is typical of the developed group but in Italy it is only 1.2 and in Spain 1.1. Russia is now competing with Spain for the lowest rate of reproduction in the world.

The decline in the fertility rate in Russia is the most rapid in the industrialised world. It halved between 1988 and 1998. Ireland comes second with a fertility rate of 3.2 in 1980 dropping to 1.9 in 1997. In the United Kingdom, between 1991 and 1999, the number of those between the ages of 16 to 29 fell by 13 per cent. This is one of the most profound demographic changes ever seen in Britain. Russia's ministry of health estimates that at present between 10 per cent and 25 per cent of couples are infertile. Infertility is now growing at three per cent annually.

About one in ten newborns dies of infection. Girls are having sex earlier and earlier and the usual method of birth control is abortion. When she comes to have a child the chances of a healthy baby have declined to about one in ten. Abortion still takes precedence over contraceptives as the former is free and the latter expensive.

The city of Ryazan, east of Moscow, illustrates the trend, in late 2000. The news is not good for males. 'There are no normal men left', complained a 37-year-old woman. 'They have all got inferiority complexes because they cannot earn enough money to support a family. All of them live with their mothers and earn between 1000 rubles and 1500 rubles a month ($35–$55). Who would want to have a child with a man like that?' Apparently, hardly anyone. In Ryazan over the last decade, the marriage rate has plummeted by 30 per cent, the divorce rate has jumped 60 per cent and the birth rate is down 40 per cent. One of the city's four maternity hospitals closed in 1999 as only seven women in every thousand produced a baby. Despite this most couples would like two children. The main reasons at present why this is not happening is lack of money and tiny apartments shared with parents. Then there is fertility. A doctor at a fertility clinic commented: 'No one knows how many Russians couples are infertile.' Perhaps one in ten as Russia's obstetrician general says, or one in five, as the ministry of health retorted, or one in six as doctors in Ryazan estimate. It is one in twelve in the United States. Half of the infertility cases involve men, compared to 20 per cent a decade ago. Doctors blame alcohol, an inadequate diet and venereal diseases, from herpes to chlamydia to hepatitis. There is more bad news for the boys. Young women can wait no longer and are going abroad for a man.

About 45 per cent of the parents of Moscow's 1.4 million children were single in mid-2000. Almost all were women. This is an estimate since many couples live together without getting married. These mothers are social outcasts and receive a monthly allowance of 300 rubles ($10) from the state per child. Almost all single parents are poor. The law provides for mothers to take three years' maternity leave after giving birth but this is seldom observed in practice. Most employers decline to take on young women with children as they are likely to stay at home when the children are ill. A law on alimony does exist but is rarely enforced. Single fathers who raise their children do not qualify for the child allowance which mothers receive. The number of single mothers is on the rise. In 1998, of 1.3 million children born, almost 346,000 were to single mothers. Some single mothers do not marry in order to qualify for state child support.

The mortality rate is the highest in Europe. In 1993, in St Petersburg there were three deaths for every birth. The last time this was recorded was during the siege of the city between 1941 and 1944. One of the most affected groups are the younger males. However the highest rate of population decline is in central Russia. The total excess of deaths over births, between 1992 and 1997, in Russia was 3.89 million. At least a third of these died prematurely. Left-wing politicians call this the genocide of the Russian nation and, of course, see it as a deliberate policy. Half of Russian males now die before they reach the retirement age of 60. The rate of the annual population loss in the mid-1990s was higher than during the period of Stalinist oppression and mass famine during the first half of the 1930s. It is worth adding that between 1975 and 1985 there was an excess of 1.6 million deaths among males aged between 20 and 50. Death rates among girls in their teens and young women have been rising sharply since 1997. Specialists ascribe this to the fact that prostitution has become the main source of income for a part of this population cohort.

Infant mortality, a good expression of a nation's health, rose from 24.7 per 1000 live births in 1972 to 27.4 in 1974. This was deemed so embarrassing that Soviet authorities ceased publishing data until the Gorbachev era. Hence the malaise of Russian society can be traced back to the 1970s. Infant mortality actually declined between 1980 (22) and 1995 (18). However the Russian rate in 1995 was over twice that of the Czech Republic but the only country in which it was higher was Romania with 23. The maternal mortality rate over the years 1989–95 was 52 per 100,000 live births. This was over five times the rate of Poland and Hungary and even higher than Romania (48) and Ukraine (33). In the European Union in 1995 it was 6.

May one blame only the breakdown of the health service, the poor diet and poverty for the high death rate since 1991? If male death rates accelerated one would also expect infant and elderly mortality, the most vulnerable social groups, to have risen as well. This is not the case. Infant mortality, for instance, declined from 18.6 in 1994 to 16.6 in 1998 (Field and Twigg 2000: 25). The shock of the transition appears to have played a role and it is working age males who find it most difficult to cope. Refuge from social stress is sought in alcoholism and drug abuse. It is particularly difficult for Russian males to cope with cataclysmic events as the communist society suppressed private initiative. All key decisions were taken for a person and if one worked harder, for instance, there was no added reward. Social responsibility and discipline were not nurtured. As a consequence psychological disorders are on the increase. In

1999, about 3.5 million Russians were treated for psychological disorders, over one third higher than in 1989. However the ministry of health estimates that up to a third of the Russian population may be suffering from psychological disorders of various degrees.

During the transition the individual is required to act responsibly in his or her own interest. This is of key importance as far as health is concerned. The individual has to resist smoking (Russia produced over 280 billion cigarettes in the first ten months of 2000, 10.2 billion more than the whole of 1999; Russian cigarette exports in 2001 are expected to reach $1.5 billion), resist alcohol and drug abuse, take exercise, reduce the intake of fats and engage in safe sex. The average Russian often demonstrates a wanton disregard for his or her health. They are high risk takers in private life but low risk takers in their working life.

Russia has an unusually high rate of deaths among the economically active population. In 1998, 202,000 of the 520,800 who expired in their economically active years died because of external reasons, such as murder, suicide, accidents, poisoning and injuries. This was 60,000 more than in 1990. The probability of accidental death in Russia, in 2000, was 4.5 times higher than in Europe on the whole and the number of accidents in the country was expected to reach 150,000 by the end of 2000.

Life expectancy in 1999 at 59.8 years for males was extremely low by European standards and 72.8 years for females was also modest. The gulf between male and female life expectancy is the highest of any industrialised nation. In 1900, life expectancy for males was 31 years and for females 33 years. This rose to 40 and 46 years by 1941. After 1945 life expectancy continued to grow until 1987 when it was approaching world levels (70 years). Afterwards a decline set in and reached a low point in 1995 (see Table 10.1).

In some republics and oblasts in the Urals, west and east Siberia the situation is worse. Life expectancy is between 49 and 57 years for males and 62 and 71 years for females with an average of 55 to 64 years for the population as a whole (Glazyev 1999: 15). Russia is now on a par with Mongolia and Morocco. Why is the gender difference so great in Russia? After all men and women live in the same environment. The average for the developed world is about six years. Indeed in America in 1920 the life spans were almost the same. The difference in Russia is the highest ever recorded anywhere in the world. Women are able to cope with disasters and difficulties better than men but this would not account for all of the difference. The situation is even worse in the Russian countryside. In 1993, the mortality of males was five times greater than that of females and in urban areas it was four times higher. If this trend continues, the virile country male is a dying species.

It is interesting to note that the gender difference in many former Soviet republics parallels that of Russia. In Estonia, Latvia, Lithuania and Belarus it is between 12.3 and 12.5 years. In Kazakhstan it is 11.2 and in Ukraine 11.8. This would suggest that a communist-type society is a major factor. Males were expected to sacrifice themselves for the motherland and to increase labour productivity. An instance of this was the clean-up operation at Chernobyl in 1986 when troops worked unprotected. One may commend their courage but they were in effect committing suicide. In the two years 1991–93 over 100,000 Russians actually committed suicide. Suicides have risen 60 per cent since 1991; the peak was reached in 1994 when Russians descended into deep despair at the economic collapse. The suicide rate is about 40 per 100,000 persons or about four times that of the US. Fathers who cannot provide for their families take their own lives (this also happens in the west). Scientists commit suicide to draw attention to the plight of science.

Infectious diseases are spreading like a plague in Russia, especially tuberculosis. Indeed being sent to prison today is almost a death sentence because of the prevalence of tuberculosis and hepatitis. More and more strains are proving resistant to existing drugs. In 1997, the mortality rate from cardiovascular diseases was up to six times greater in Russia than in the west.

There are an estimated 20 million alcoholics and another six million engage in drug abuse. The latter are almost all between 13 and 25 years of age. Between 1994–97, the number of drug addicts among children and university students increased almost eight times. There were only 5.3 cases of syphilis per 100,000 recorded in 1990 but this rose to 265 in 1996 or by 50 times. In 1999, it had risen to 77 times the 1990 level. Gonorrhea peaked at 230.1 cases in 1993 but declined to 139.2 cases in 1996. Real national monetary incomes between 1992 and 1996 declined by 43 per cent and pensions by 45 per cent. Over 30 million Russians or 20 per cent of the population had incomes below subsistence level. After the August 1998 crash this grew to 40 per cent. The chances of a family of more than two children living below subsistence level is now 50 per cent.

Another way of looking at the problem is to ask how many of today's 16-year-old males in Russia will survive until they are 60. In the United States it is 83 per cent but in Russia it is 54 per cent. A hundred years ago in European Russia the figure was about 56 per cent. Many of those who survive will be quite ill.

Another factor contributing to the decline of the Russian population and fertility is the growing prostitution industry. In 1998, over half a million women and girls from the former Soviet Union were working abroad as prostitutes. The overwhelming majority were from the Russian Federation. In most cases they had been lured abroad by offers of employment by legitimate companies. When they arrived their passports were seized and they were sold as sex slaves. The traffickers in human flesh cannot be prosecuted under Russian law as there is no legislation prohibiting this activity. Areas from which large numbers of women have been lured are Yaroslav, Novgorod, Moscow and Leningrad oblasts, the Urals region, Buryatia and Karelia.

Women are attracted to jobs abroad since they appear glamorous and promise a way out of unemployment and poverty. According to the Russian ministry of labour, in 1993, 63 per cent of the unemployed were women and, in 1997, this figure had risen to 80 per cent. About 70 per cent of the female unemployed are over the age of 29. About 80 per cent of single-parent, single-income households are female and of these 80 per cent are unemployed. Even some of the worldly wise among these women find prostitution abroad attractive. Those who escape and return to their home village cannot prosecute those who are trafficking in their village. They normally live in hiding for fear of retribution. The Duma is reluctant to legislate on trafficking because the sexual exploitation does not occur on the territory of the Russian Federation. The companies which recruit them and send them abroad are legal and papers are in order. Russian consulates abroad usually refuse to help them since they have violated the terms of their visas by working as prostitutes. Since their passports have been taken by the pimps they are abroad illegally and therefore have no legal standing. The flesh business is a multi-billion dollar concern and highly organised. Those involved will use extreme violence to protect their investments. In the terminology of this book they are all roving bandits, taking from but putting nothing back into society.

An interesting fact about the former Soviet republics is that the population is declining in only the Slavic group, Ukraine since 1991, Russia since 1992 and Belarus since 1993. In all other ex-republics the population is growing.

Within the Russian Federation, the ethnic Russian part of the population is declining fastest. In 1989, the population declined in seven of the subjects of the Russian Federation but in the first quarter of 2000 this was occurring in 77 (out of 89) subjects. The only regions in which the population is growing are Dagestan, Ingushetia, Tyumen oblast, the republics of Tyva and Sakha-Yakutia, and the Taimyr, Evenk, Aginsk-Buryat and Chukotka autonomous okrugs. There are 130 ethnic groups in Russia and the only one which is slowly dying is the Russian. The density of the population in the Russian Federation is very low. There are 8.6 persons per square kilometre. Beyond the Urals (Asiatic Russia), there are only 2.5. In comparison, China has 122 persons per square kilometre. According to international norms about 30–50 persons per square kilometre are needed to provide a modern social environment.

EDUCATION AND HEALTH

By 1997, Russia had become a small state as regards expenditures and revenues (see Table 10.2). There were no states which were still large states (50 per cent or over). Kyrgyzstan and Kazakhstan recorded the greatest decline and this was reflected in the diminished provision of social services and the rise of poverty. China is an exception. The economy almost quadrupled between 1978 and 1997 which resulted in the state provision of social services actually increasing.

Spending on education (see Table 10.3) has not dropped so precipitously as in other public sectors. Over the years 1992–96 budgetary educational spending dropped by about 19 per cent in real terms. In the Soviet Union about 40 per cent of the educational budget was financed locally but this rose to 87 per cent in 1996. Under socialism enterprises were responsible for pre-school and primary education and the whole community availed themselves of these facilities. This was also the case with certain types of health care. These outlays were equivalent to about 3 per cent of GDP in 1994 and should be added to educational and health care expenditure. Bankrupt enterprises could no longer perform these functions and joint stock companies became reluctant to devote resources to them. Russian secondary school enrolment at 96 per cent of the age group (12 to 17 years) was higher than in the European Union in 1980 but by 1993 it was down to 88 per cent whereas it had jumped to 117 per cent in the EU. Higher education enrolment was 46 per cent in 1980, the highest of any Soviet republic and much higher than in eastern Europe. It only dropped to 45 per cent in 1993 (the highest that year was recorded by the United States with 81 per cent). Enrolments in secondary schools and higher education have dropped since and hence have come down to the levels of many other countries.

Universal access to free medical care was one of the major achievements of the Soviet Union. The proportion of the budget devoted to health and health related issues peaked at 20.8 per cent in 1955 but by the early 1960s was down to about 6 per cent (Field and Twigg 2000: 43). It declined further under Gorbachev. Health care was in crisis in the 1980s as basic medicines disappeared from chemists' shelves and waiting lists lengthened. Russia responded in 1991 by introducing compulsory medical insurance and all the laws were in place in 1993. Employers have to pay a health tax of 3.6 per cent per worker and regions pay a per capita amount to cover non-earners. The monies are paid into regional funds, one for each of the 89 subjects of the Federation. Patients claim their costs from private insurance companies who in turn are reimbursed by a regional fund. The aim is that private insurance companies compete with one another for patients and thereby improve standards. This has not happened. There are six insurance companies in Moscow but they cover separate parts of the city and do not overlap. This implies that they are part of the same economic clan. Doctors' salaries are low and thus they have little incentive to increase their patient load. Hospitals and polyclinics have never competed with one another for patients.

Over 82 per cent of the Russian population is now covered by medical insurance. Until 1995, health care spending was reasonable (but the federal budget contributed under 10 per cent) but afterwards more and more regions defaulted on their payments (Table 10.4). One source calculated that, in 1997, only 37.5 per cent of the amount needed to fund the care promised by the insurance companies was available. Health staff and patients suffered. Doctors and nurses now go on strike and patients resort to the old Soviet practice of paying the doctor in kind. Some have even been offered coffins for treatment. Moscow is best served with per capita spending up to six times that in the north Caucasus and central black earth region.

The general practitioner did not exist in Soviet medicine. Students chose a narrow specialty from a list of over one hundred (many of these do not exist in western medicine). This leads to endless referrals of the patient. Some doctors may only work in a certain environment such as a neighbourhood clinic or at the workplace. Several medical schools have recently introduced courses to train general practitioners and there are now about 400 GPs working in Russia (Field and Twigg 2000: 58).

About 80 per cent of doctors today in Russia are female. Little has changed since 1950 when they comprised 76 per cent of doctors. A major reason for the poor state of medicine today is that it is a female profession; as such it has little political clout and doctors have few entrepreneurial skills. Their medical training is not up to western standards (Russian doctors in Israel have found it difficult to compete) and they lack access to western literature. Medicine is one aspect of the problem facing women in Russia today. About 70 per cent of the unemployed are female and most of these are over 30 years of age. Women form the majority of workers who go unpaid. There is also a reluctance, a carryover from Soviet days, to discuss specifically female health problems such as sexually transmitted diseases and teenage pregnancies. Russian society has become more male-dominated with women reverting to traditional gender roles. Pornography and prostitution have mushroomed and downgraded the status of women. These are hugely profitable businesses and pimps can flout the law with impunity. About 80 per cent of violent crimes in Russia occur in the home, overwhelmingly committed by males. This has led to the view that Russia is not a democracy (people power) but a virocracy (man power). This is reflected in the prison population. In 1999, of the 1.7 million who committed crimes, 1.5 million were male. Only 11 per cent of the prison population in the same year were female.

The feminist movement has had little impact in Russia despite the increasing difficulties of women. A major problem for women doctors is that their patients are poor and cannot afford to pay very much for care. Doctors have remained loyal to their patients instead of going off into private medicine. Many doctors spend most of their time on house calls. This is a tradition which grew up in the Soviet Union when patients regarded the doctor as being at their beck and call. The Soviet state deliberately cut itself off from contact with western medicine and thereby did not participate in the medical technology revolution. The clinics for the Soviet nomenklatura were the exceptions to this.

Foreigners who fall ill in Moscow are now almost always taken to the huge Botkin hospital, north west of the Kremlin. Those who have had heart attacks, if conscious, will be able to admire the standard of intensive care offered free of charge. There are millions of dollars' worth of American heart-monitoring and resuscitation equipment ready for the 2000 patients treated there every year. Moscow city government installed the equipment five years ago. The equipment is fine but the food is poor. Also one is not guaranteed hot water because of unpaid power bills. If one asks if one should pay something, the doctors reply that gifts are welcome. Western embassies' advice to their nationals who fall ill in Russia is very simple. Take the first flight home.

Doctor to patient: 'Allow me to introduce you to our anaesthetist!'
Russian medicine is short of resources! Created by Igor Revyakin.

Before August 1998, about 60 per cent of medicines in Russia were imported or made from imported raw materials. Russian-produced medicines are cheaper and are bought more frequently by Russian consumers. About 90 per cent of raw materials are imported and this is not exceptional. About 80 per cent of the bulk pharmaceutical chemicals used by US manufacturers to produce prescription drugs are imported. Drugs such as insulin are provided free by Moscow city authorities. However the patient needs ingenuity to obtain them free of charge. In Russia, 45 million persons have the right to free or subsidised medicines at a discount of 50 per cent. Federal and local authorities are quite incapable financially of meeting this commitment. Prior to the August crash, 40 per cent of the cash assets of compulsory medical insurance, by law, had to be invested in short-term government bonds (GKOs). The bonds are now virtually valueless, thus exacerbating the problem of drug supply.

VODKA

Before 1914 the state had the vodka monopoly and about one third of the budget came from the clear spirit. The communists drank like everyone else and alcoholism was a blight on society. Various attempts, all futile, were made to reduce alcohol consumption. The approach was either to increase the price, in which case more of the family budget went on booze, or to restrict its supply. This inevitably increased the output of samogon, hooch. One was always offered the latter in the countryside in Russia. The best advice was to avoid imbibing it at all costs. Foreigners who declined to take this advice were normally paralytic for three days. The well-meaning Gorbachev continued Andropov's war on vodka but only inflated the profits of the bootleggers. They ploughed the money into the newly legalised cooperatives and thereby accelerated graft and corruption.

The roving bandits came into their own in 1992 when the state abandoned its alcohol monopoly. In 2000, the vodka market was worth an estimated $12 billion, half legal and the other half sold on the black market. Big money has brought big bandits, making it a high-risk business. Competition is ferocious and it is quite usual for a vodka tsar to be discovered full of holes. Many of the vodka tsars have sought legality and are now Duma deputies. In 1999, vodka production in Russia was officially 1.34 billion litres, up 60 per cent on the previous year. However Russia's chief health inspector, in January 2001, put alcohol production, official and clandestine, at 4 billion bottles a year and average adult male consumption at 40 litres annually. This must surely be a world record, the type no country is proud of. The World Health Organisation regards eight litres of alcohol per capita as the upper limit for consumption before serious health problems occur.

In April 2000, police uncovered a secret still run by two Chechens and employing 120, all Chechens. It was producing 10,000 bottles of vodka daily. Profits were counted in millions after a few months. (This meant that the Chechen owners opted to liquidate the business rather than pay the bribes the police were demanding for continued operation. They would then look for another location.) According to the ministry of internal affairs, 25 million litres of vodka were seized in 1999 and 4700 clandestine stills shut down. They were found in the most extraordinary places, inside strategic military bases, retirement homes and luxurious country dachas. One bandit had a cellar full of 26,000-litre vats. When one bandit is put out of business another fills the hole in the market. If all the illicit stills were closed down it would not solve the problem.

Others would start up elsewhere. The craving for alcohol is so great that supplies will always be forthcoming. Where there is demand there will always be supply, irrespective of any government's legislation. In the first half of 2000, almost 25,000 Russians died from alcohol poisoning, almost as many as during the whole of 1999. The ministry of health estimates that over 250,000 died during the 1990s. One report claims that half of Russian males when they die are drunk. A bottle of vodka cost 60 rubles ($2) in 2000 and a bottle of samogon, half as much. Unfortunately samogon is remarkably easy to distil, another reason why anyone can make easy money quickly. The situation is now exacerbated by the fact that the state has woken up to the fact that if it increases the duty on a bottle of vodka it can collect more revenue. In order to do this it is attempting to take over vodka distribution. The predictable result has been clan wars and an upsurge in samogon production. Inevitably the death rate from poisoning has also climbed.

Russians are also heavy smokers. Two thirds of men and one third of women smoke. Smoking accounts for up to 30 per cent of deaths from heart diseases and cancer. This is about twice the death rates in the US.

DRUGS

Drug abuse is the greatest threat to the survival of the Russian nation. It is even more lethal than vodka. All statistics are estimates because drugs are illegal and as in the United States, for instance, there is huge disagreement on the size of the problem. The Russian ministry of health's published material reveals that the number of registered addicts jumped fourfold between 1991 and 1997 and reached 120,606 in early 1998 (Field and Twigg 2000: 104). The four regions with the highest level of addicts were all in west Siberia. Drug abusers, but not addicts, rose 3.7 times over the same period. The ministry of health surmises that the actual number in 1997 was possibly 700,000. Those who have experimented with drugs may be double this number. There are even higher figures, over ten million. Illicit drug abuse among youths in Russia may now be higher than in the United States. One factor which contributes to this is that about 1.5 million children and teenagers do not go to school or work. In 1999, the Russian authorities estimated that some two per cent of the population, between 1.5 million and 2.5 million, are injecting drug abusers.

The drug market is divided between the New Russians who can afford imported drugs such as cocaine and heroin and the great majority who get by on hashish, synthetic drugs and volatile substances. The MVD identifies Afghans, Pakistanis and Central Asians as controlling the luxury end of the market in heroin, ethnic Russians and Nigerians run the cocaine market, Ukrainians are in control of cannabis and central Asians the market in raw opium. The MVD estimated the drugs market to be worth $1.2 billion in the first half of 1998. Officially, drug trafficking is now a threat to Russian national security. About one third of drugs on the Russian market are imported. Russia is a major transit route for drugs from Asia to Europe. The excess capacity of the chemical industry has been put to use in producing synthetic drugs. In 1997 alone the police closed down 848 laboratories. However it is doubtful if this held back the expansion of production. Russian-made amphetamines have now penetrated the American market. Russians who cannot afford to buy drugs make their own. This is a potentially lethal underground activity.

AIDS

According to Academician Vadim Pokrovsky, Russia's leading specialist on Aids, in July 2000 there were about 300,000 in Russia who were HIV-positive. Aids is now a 'national threat' and he predicts that it will spread as rapidly in Russia as in South Africa (where about 10 per cent of the population are infected) over the next ten years. In January 2000, he came up with the prediction that 10 per cent of the Russian population will be HIV-positive in 2005. This would mean about 14 million sufferers in 2005. Others calculate that there will be 10 million with the disease in 2005. All estimates of the prevalence of HIV infection are guesses but local testing has come up with disturbing results. In Krasnogorsk, in Moscow oblast, 3 per cent of those between the ages of 15 and 25 were found to be infected. This is comparable to the rate in Angola or Ghana. Most of those infected now in Russia will be dead by 2010. They are the conscripts, family founders and workers, in other words, the future of the nation. The main route to infection is the use of drugs followed by sexual intercourse (especially with prostitutes) and the commercialisation of the blood donor market. The main centres of infection in Russia are the city of Moscow, Moscow, Kaliningrad, Krasnodar, Tver, Nizhny Novgorod, Irkutsk and Saratov oblasts.

The major problem facing Russia is that officials pretend that Russia has a first-world Aids problem whereas it has a third-world Aids problem. Many Aids centres were set up in the Aids hysteria of the 1980s but today their main purpose is to count the number of cases of HIV infection. The directors of Aids centres now claim that they have the epidemic under control. What they mean is that they carry out over 20 million tests annually to track the disease. Most tests are administered without consent and as it is a criminal offence to put anyone at risk of HIV infection those who sense they may have it will do practically anything to avoid being tested in clinics. Those who are found to be HIV-positive must sign a form which can be used in court against them. Over 80 per cent of the infected are intravenous drug users. The Aids centres know where these unfortunates are to be found – in prisons, detention centres and detoxification centres – but have no idea how to locate the other infected people who may now be in the majority. Despite its drawbacks the present testing system has indicated that Russia has the fastest-growing HIV epidemic in Europe.

Aids was first identified in the west in 1981 although there had been deaths from it in west Africa in the 1930s. The Russian press began writing about it in 1985 and the first fatality was in 1987. In that year, Gennady Gerasimov, the silver-tongued official spokesman of the USSR ministry of foreign affairs ruminated that perhaps Aids was God's punishment for the doubtful morals of the world. This is a strange sentiment for the representative of an atheistic state to express! A group of medical students, in mid-1987, wrote to Pokrovsky saying they hoped that a cure would never be found because Aids would wipe out all drug addicts, homosexuals and prostitutes.

In 1989, 49 children and nine mothers were infected while in a children's hospital in Elista, near the Caspian Sea. A nurse had injected the children with different needles but had used the same syringe because others were not available. Other cases were reported in the press. Initially doctors would not treat patients for fear of becoming infected themselves. The main reason for the spread of the disease today is the sharing of syringes among intravenous drug users. Another is the multitude of prostitutes who work Moscow, St Petersburg and other cities. Perhaps one in ten of the 70,000 ladies of the night in central Moscow are HIV-positive. They have no use for condoms. The average prostitute may have up to 1000 partners a year and the impact that this may have is sobering. Before 1993, male homosexuality was a crime (there was no legislation on female homosexuality) but not always applied. Researchers have found a fatalism among Russian homosexuals about their chances of contracting Aids. Russia's large prison population is another source of infection. Homosexual acts are common and the incidence of contagious diseases high. Special camps are being set aside for prisoners with Aids. HIV tests are not always reliable as they may be falsely negative for an average of six weeks. The range is between two weeks and six months. Budgets to combat Aids are small (an Aids test in the US costs $160) and Pokrovsky suspects that there is a group around the leadership who deny that the disease is a problem. The Russian ministry of health regards HIV and Aids sufferers as a warning to healthy people not to engage in bad behaviour. It also plays down the appalling health and demographic situation because it does not want to accept responsibility for it.

A World Bank study, in late 2000, stated that the Aids problem had 'literally exploded in Russia'. Russian authorities recorded an estimated 50,000 new HIV infections in 1999. This number is 'more than the total number of infections registered between 1987 and 1999'. The main reason, according to the World Bank, is the sharing of contaminated needles and syringes by those using illegal drugs. By the end of 1999, the number of infections throughout the former Soviet Union and eastern Europe had reached 360,000. Most infections have occurred since 1995 with the greatest number of cases occurring in Ukraine, Belarus, Russia, Moldova and Kazakhstan. The situation in Ukraine is worse than in Russia. The number of diagnosed HIV infections jumped from practically zero before 1995 to about 20,000 annually between 1996 and 1999. New infections from drug abuse are declining but those from unprotected sex are rising.

Russia offers practically no treatment to those who are HIV-positive. It has not adopted the common short-term therapy proved most effective in preventing in-utero HIV transmission from mother to child, even though the drug required, AZT, is manufactured locally. Many local doctors are opposed to HIV-positive women becoming mothers with the result that the drug is kept from the needy. Other antiretroviral drugs could be manufactured locally but they will not be. Licences have just been granted to some western pharmaceutical firms to manufacture 12 compounds, the high price of which will ensure that Russian patients cannot afford them. Pokrovsky estimates that treating an HIV patient costs between $9000 and $22,000. The 1999 Russian Aids prevention budget was only $800,000.

It is debatable whether Russians are aware of the risks they are running when injecting drugs intravenously. Intercourse, whether it be anal, oral or vaginal, carries with it a 2 per cent risk of infection if the partner is HIV-positive. Infection from female to male via vaginal intercourse without a condom or other diseases in either partner occurs approximately in 3–4 per cent of cases, male to female is approximately 10 per cent. Anal intercourse increases the risk to around 40 per cent without other diseases, and oral is unknown. However there is speculation that oral sex is becoming the most common route of increase among heterosexual couples in the US. In the case of female to male transmission via vaginal intercourse, if one partner has another sexually transmitted disease the risk goes up from 2 to 40 per cent. If the partner has two diseases it rises to 80 per cent.

Given the limited information which the authorities disseminate about sexually transmitted diseases it is likely that there is widespread ignorance of the risks being undertaken. There is still a school of thought which would like to see all birth control and other sexual information, including Aids, banned. Some Duma deputies articulate this view. This appears to be based on the perception that sex information stimulates sexual activity. There is some truth in this as the incidence of sexual activity among Russian youth is now on a par with the United States. What is different is that it has happened very suddenly in Russia and the young are finding it difficult to cope. However western countries with their information programmes are also finding that the young are resistant to advice. For instance, in England, in 1999, gonorrhea increased by 25 per cent and chlamydia by 16 per cent. The Orthodox Church advises young people to remain celibate until marriage and then stay faithful to one's partner. This assumes partners stay together but the evidence now is that up to seven marriages in ten fail. There are villages where celibacy before marriage is still the norm but not in Moscow. There, bonking is a major urban pastime.

According to the Moscow city police there are now at least 30,000 underage homeless persons living in the capital. One in three of these children has syphilis or gonorrhea and one in ten is infected with Aids. More than half of them engage in prostitution. Pimps can be as young as 16 and can earn $200 a day on Red Square from noon until 8 pm. They live on Pepsi Cola and pizzas. They take a cut of 20 per cent but the fatality rate is quite high. The next senior boy takes over as pimp. When the pimps want to relax they rent young girls for the night. Prices of child prostitutes range from 500 rubles ($17) to $200. It all depends on the age of the child and the nature of the services: the rule is the younger the child the higher the price. Most of the customers are businessmen. The children are not on display, only the pimps. Many of the boys arrive in Moscow after hearing tales that it is easy to make money there; then their bosses have raped them. Social workers say that many of the boys suffer from various mental illnesses but are not aware of this. They blame Duma deputies for talking about but not passing legislation to protect children. Even when the police arrest a customer it is very rare to get a conviction. The customer has a high-level protector and the boys are afraid to give evidence. Police in early 2000 raided a brothel and found the names, addresses and telephone numbers of 180 customers, many of them from the top drawer. Only vague hints about one customer were ever published.

SEX

During glasnost, Vladimir Posner became a star on Soviet television by staging live discussions between American and Soviet citizens. On one occasion a young American asked about sex. A Komsomol girl stood up and stated that in the Soviet Union there was no sex. Taken literally this would have meant that the population would die out. However what the young maiden meant was that there was no sexual intercourse before marriage. Sex was a taboo subject. In Ireland, in the 1930s, the same applied. Doctors refused to discuss human sexuality for fear of trouble with the local Catholic priest, who would maintain that sex was only for procreation and not for pleasure. A psychologist might say that since the priest was denied sex himself he was bent on ensuring other males enjoyed as little of it as possible. One young couple tried hard for a child for several years but without success. They had been practising anal sex. Once they discovered that vaginal sex was the route to motherhood the children came.

On the surface the communist state was just as puritanical and found any discussion of sex very embarrassing. The young maiden may have believed that there was no sex but others got on with the job. As a postgraduate in Moscow in the late 1960s the author heard complaints, especially from Africans, that Russian girls would not climb on top when having sex. Sergei Mikhalkov's film *Burnt by the Sun*, was an overnight sensation: one scene showed a woman on top of her lover. This became known as Mikhalkov-sex and apparently was a revelation to many Russians. Readers wrote to newspapers asking for information on Gaidar-sex and Zhirinovsky-sex. Gaidar has a happy home life (three children) so presumably there are no revelations to report. Zhirinovsky is quite a different matter as he cannot keep his mouth shut when the subject of sex comes up. One of his presidential electoral promises was that he would provide every woman with a man. Since there were more women than men in the population this presumably meant there would have to be some asset sharing.

The personal columns reveal the abysmal ignorance about sex among the population but at least answers are given. As in the west, sex

Created by Igor Revyakin.

quickly became a commodity in Russia. Young healthy males were in great demand. Russian wives found that their husbands, well before middle age, could not make love any more. Parents advertised for a male to service their daughter. They were quite specific: his organ had to be in good working order. Presumably the previous applicant had not been up to the job. The New Russians do not have a good reputation; they devote almost all their energies to making money. However one of the oligarchs has a penchant for young, nubile girls. When he picks one he buys her an apartment and car, pampers her and when he tires of her, usually after six months, he pays for her university education. When a western journalist related this story to a Russian friend she was shocked by the response. 'Would it be possible for my Katya to meet this oligarch? After all she is very mature [big-breasted] for her age'. As far as the mother was concerned the reward for six months' labour was very attractive.

Russians love to have sex but refuse to talk about it. The leading sex-ologist, 72-year-old Igor Kon, teamed up with the ministry of education in the mid-1990s to help develop sex education courses in the nation's schools. The project never got off the ground as the media savaged a

The average Russian man's dream woman. Created by Igor Revyakin.

pilot sex-education programme. According to them, children's morals would be destroyed. In 1997, the project was dead in the water. Kon wants sex education to help stem the frightening rise in HIV, Aids and other diseases. He is concerned about the intolerance shown towards homosexuals. Only in 1993 did homosexuality cease to be a criminal offence, and it was only in 1999 that it ceased to be classified as a mental illness. Not surprisingly, in 2000, 31 per cent of Russians still regarded it as a disease or mental illness.

THE DISABLED

In 1998, over 9 million persons were in receipt of disability pensions. There are over a million disabled in Moscow and the city government provides about one third of the population with some sort of aid. War has left its mark on many in Russia with perhaps half a million disabled veterans from the Great Fatherland War. Another 2.66 million are veterans who have not suffered any wounds. The conflict in Afghanistan also left its mark. About 3 per cent of the 168,000 Russian veterans are disabled. The Afghantsy are well organised even though they enjoy little sympathy among average Russians. In 1991, President Yeltsin signed a decree establishing a fund for Afghan veterans which may have received over a billion rubles.

There may have been about five million homeless in Russia in 1998, with up to 350,000 in Moscow. Many of these are disabled and ill. The incidence of tuberculosis is about 70 per 100,000 but in prisons it is 3395 per 100,000 (Field and Twigg 2000: 159). The number of disabled children has been growing rapidly and in 1996 was over 460,000. Overwhelmingly the disabled live in poverty. Disabled children have the right to an education but this depends on being able to walk to school. Many parents protest against their children being educated together with the disabled, hence a major problem for disabled children is social isolation. Disabled children especially those suffering from Down's syndrome, are often abandoned by their mothers. The author visited a clinic in Moscow, in 1993, which was full of these children. They were left on their own most of the day as there were no teachers to help them. They were absolutely delighted to see a stranger and smiled broadly. The superintendent explained that when they reached the age of 16 they would have to go to make way for younger children. When asked where they could go she shrugged her shoulders and pointed to the street.

In Soviet society 2 per cent of jobs were to be set aside for the disabled but this has gone by the board in present-day Russia. However sometimes the work they do adds to their sense of uselessness. One group knitted socks while another unwound them so that the others could start knitting again. They received some money for their efforts. It was considered uneconomic to sell the socks because that would involve finding buyers and also yarn to knit more socks. This neatly emphasises the dimensions of the problem of finding gainful employment for the disabled.

The disabled and pensioners have now lost most of the free benefits to which they were entitled. Free medicines are no longer free and many medicines are too expensive to purchase. One source in 1998 estimated that about 30 per cent of the population could not afford a minimum healthy basic diet.

WOMEN

Politically, women in Russia are where women were in Britain in the 1920s. There are women MPs but they are regarded with amused disdain by many of their male colleagues. In 2000, there is one woman among the 178 senators of the Council of the Federation and 34 out of 450 in the lower house, the Duma. Irina Khakamada, a liberal and an entrepreneur, left the 12 December faction in the 1995 Duma, which she had co-founded with Boris Fedorov, because of his refusal to take her views seriously. The minister for social protection in the Russian government is normally a woman. Her political clout is almost non-existent. The view is still prevalent that women and politics do not mix.

Unemployment has hit women harder than men because the industries which were traditionally female-dominated, such as textiles, have fallen on hard times. Social services have been cut back and many child-care centres closed. Under Yeltsin and now under Putin, there is a view that women belong in the home. This is reinforced by the declining fertility rate and rising child delinquency. Activists complain that overt sexism is permitted in job adverts. Sometimes females are required *bez kompleksov* which means that sex is part of the job. Valentin Rasputin, an influential writer, has argued that women have been over-emancipated. He belongs to the village prose school of writing which underlines traditional Russian rural values. Such values are patriarchal. The man is always on top. The more nationalist a writer or politician is the more likely he is to think traditionally about women. Television reinforces the image that females are playthings. There are now nude shows (only the women are naked) and the weather forecast is handled by a naked beauty. When she says it is going to rain she puts up her umbrella and it rains, when it is sunny she puts up her parasol. One does not have to be Freud to understand the symbolism.

However there are intrepid women who have become entrepreneurs. The association of women entrepreneurs estimates that between 30 per cent and 40 per cent of the 890,000 registered businesses in Russia, in 2000, were owned by women. Small businesses employ about 25 million people, including part-time workers and family members. They contribute between 10 per cent and 12 per cent of Russian GDP. Most women start up with a loan from their husbands since credit for women is hard to find. This has led to such groups as the Russian women's microfinance network which extends loans to female entrepreneurs. It says that women default less than men and pay their bills on time. Women tend to start small and gradually build up whereas men want initially to borrow big and start big. There is a consortium of women's non-governmental organisations which follows their progress closely. It says that women count in kopeks but men in thousands of rubles. Women have to deploy considerable skill to overcome male prejudice to get all the signatures required to be in business legally. Almost all women are in business to make money, not to prove they are as good as men.

It is worthy of note that only 27.9 per cent of civil servants are male. This is the norm in all levels of the administration but the very top – it is almost exclusively male-dominated. Men still dominate industry, agriculture, construction and transport. The proportion of men in management, trade and public catering is gradually growing. The ratio of men and women engaged in the health services and education has not changed of late, it remains one to five. The ratio in arts, culture, finance and insurance is about one to two. The only field in which both sexes are equally represented is science.

UNEMPLOYMENT AND POVERTY

The number of employed in Russia, in 1991, 73.8 million, was almost the same as in 1980. However numbers began to dip afterwards. In 1992, there were 72 million employed but this gradually dropped to 65.3 million in 1997. Over the years 1992–95, the structure of employment changed dramatically with industry declining 19.5 per cent. Transport and communications shed more labour, dropping 21.4 per cent. Trade and catering grew by 16.1 per cent while credit, finance and insurance showed the greatest increase, 40 per cent, but this was from a small base. The bureaucracy, significantly, expanded by 13.3 per cent.

The impact of privatisation is immediately evident. Labour left large enterprises and moved to small and medium-sized firms. In 1994–95, those employed in small firms, up to 20 employees, grew from 6.8 million to 8.8 million (Field and Twigg 2000: 194). As early as 1995 almost half the labour force was employed in the private sector. In 1996, almost 60 per cent were in the private sector and 10 per cent of the employed were self-employed. In 1998, 19.3 per cent of the labour force was self-employed or in new private concerns. This is much lower than in, for example, Poland. There was considerable levelling of wages under communism but after 1991 wage differentiation grew apace. Fuel and energy did best with wages 2.7 times the average, in 1995. The worst off were textiles where wages were only one eighth of those received by Gazprom employees.

The massive decline in industrial output in 1992 and 1993 did not result in millions of workers being sacked. Factories kept on labour but did not pay them or paid them very little, sometimes in kind. Enterprises ran up huge debts to one another. Far from abandoning labour, the government developed a sophisticated policy of social support, based on the enterprise. The goal was to maintain consumption in the cities even as output fell. Export earnings and foreign loans were used by the government to subsidise consumption. The reverse of this policy was that vitally needed investment was neglected. Since the IMF insisted that the budgetary deficit should not exceed 5 per cent of GDP, there were, in effect, two budgets. The official one for IMF eyes and the unofficial one which provided the necessary subsidies. In 1993, unofficial subsidies amounted to about 9 per cent of GDP. The government simply informed the IMF it was carrying out its instructions and the IMF was happy to accept this.

The decline in Russian GDP during the 1990s was unprecedented in an industrialised country in peacetime. Between 1989 and 1998 it fell by 44 per cent. It brought Vladimir Putin to the Kremlin. In Germany, between 1929 and 1932 it only declined by 15 per cent but this helped bring Adolf Hitler to power. During the Great Depression in the United States, from 1929–33, the decline was only 28 per cent and this brought Franklin D. Roosevelt to the White House. This stood as the world record until Russia acquired that dubious honour. Russia's performance was in stark contrast to that in Poland, the Czech Republic and Hungary. In Poland GDP grew by 23 per cent between 1993 and 1996 (the comparable figure for Russia was minus 25 per cent) and this meant that the country had recovered as GDP was 4 per cent higher than in 1989. In Hungary, GDP only fell 13 per cent over the years 1989–96.

Unemployment, according to Russian data, increased from 0.8 per cent of the labour force in 1992 to 3.5 per cent in 1996 and then declined to 2.6 per cent in 1998. These are only registered unemployed. However according to the International Labour Office's much wider definition of unemployment, 4.8 per cent were unemployed in 1992 and this rose steadily to 11.5 per cent in 1998. One has to add to these statistics those who were on enterprises' payrolls but not paid. A reason for retaining these workers is that they hold shares in the company and can prove useful if a battle develops over ownership. A large, lowly paid workforce also depresses the average wage and thus protects the company from excess-wage taxes. When workers are sacked they qualify for three months' severance pay. It is therefore cheaper to keep them on the payroll, send them on long unpaid holidays or pay them nothing. This phenomenon of large unpaid workforces is uniquely Russian and hence has no parallel in eastern Europe. Unemployment benefits are very low and retraining almost non-existent. Some who have been laid off receive their unemployment benefit in kind, in manure. It is not as crazy as it sounds because urban dwellers are happy to accept manure which they can apply to their private plots and thereby increase yields. The more ambitious might think of moving to Moscow to find work but a housing market hardly exists to provide accommodation. Also the capital still requires a *propiska* or residence permit in order to live and work there legally. The *propiska* is constitutionally illegal but that is ignored by the Moscow city government. About 80 per cent of Russian GDP goes through Moscow and this has meant that unemployment has been very low there, at least until the crash of August 1998. Moscow is a magnet and has retained the Soviet method of controlling immigration.

The Russian rate of unemployment (ILO definition), in 1997, was about the same as in Poland and Hungary but in Bulgaria it was higher. In the Czech Republic, it was 5.2 per cent and in the Baltic States it was 7.8 per cent. In the European Union, it was actually higher, 11.1 per cent, than in Russia and in the booming US economy it was 4.9 per cent.

Given the dramatic decline in wages, one would have expected Russian workers and their trade unions to have become militant but this has not been the case. Under communism workers slowed down the production process, made goods for private sale and stole from their enterprises. Striking was a high-risk activity and only began in the Gorbachev era with miners in the forefront. Strikes escalated in Russia and peaked in 1995, 1996 and 1997; in the latter year just over six million work days were lost. However the surprising thing is that those who went on strike were doctors, nurses and teachers. The educational sector, for instance, accounted for about 92 per cent of strikes in the first quarter of 1997. The key is that education and medicine are still state dominated whereas many workers in industry have switched to the private sector. Also what is the point of workers whom management cannot pay going on strike? What would they achieve? When workers go on strike it is usually with the support of management. They are striking against the government not their bosses. Doctors and teachers can hardly be compensated in kind nor can they earn money on the side outside the main cities. Given the above it is not surprising that trade unions have struggled to increase membership and organise protests. The average worker sees them as irrelevant. Membership of trade unions has dropped precipitously. The federation of independent trade unions claimed it represented 60 million of the 73 million workers in Russia. In 2000, it may have less than 40 million members. Multi-nationals are often anti-union. In June 1999, workers at the Coca-Cola plant in Ekaterinburg voted to join a union but withdrew after the management made it clear that if they stayed in the union they would lose their jobs. Union activists face threats and violence and some are murdered. The KPRF never attempted the mass mobilisation of labour against the Yeltsin administration but instead always sought to cut a deal with the government. Yeltsin was always ready to make concessions to the communists.

Unemployment and poverty are also high among Jews who have emigrated to the United States and Israel. Since the early 1970s, about half a million Jews have moved to the United States, 400,000 of whom reside in the New York area. Now one Jew in ten in New York is a Russian immigrant. In 1999, about a quarter of New York's Jews were near or below the poverty line (calculated at 50 per cent above the official poverty line of $17,000 a couple a year). This is the highest level since 1945. Sixty per cent of Russian immigrants are university graduates yet a large number of those needing welfare are graduates over 55. Russian immigrants are the new poor among New York Jews. This reveals how difficult it is for ex-Soviet citizens to adapt to a market economy. One might have surmised that it would have been easy to adjust in the vibrant US economy but this has not been the case.

The other side of the coin is the increasing consumption of coffee. In 2000, Russia imported three times as much coffee as in 1999. Russian consumption per head is still very low by developed world standards. It is now approaching 400 g compared to almost 5 kg a head in the US. This reveals the economic turnaround in Russia after the collapse of August 1998. One is tempted to say that the population is now divided into coffee and tea drinkers. The upwardly mobile drink coffee and the poor drink tea.

Table 10.5 outlines the percentage of the population existing in poverty in 1987–88 and 1993–95. Russian official statistics (Goskomstat) give the proportion of the population in poverty as lower but the trend is quite clear. Russia far exceeds eastern Europe, except Romania. Ukraine is worse off than Russia as is Central Asia. Only the Baltic States have managed to reduce levels of poverty.

A survey in late 1996 found that Russians had personal savings of $140 billion, of which 3.3 per cent belonged to the poorer 71 per cent of the population. The richest 5 per cent had 72.5 per cent of total savings. This meant that over half of Russian savings were in the possession of about 2 per cent of the population. Over half of personal savings were held in cash, usually in US dollars.

Russia has inherited an extremely complex system of benefits to alleviate poverty. There are 156 types of federal benefit which distinguishes

236 categories of recipient. About 45 million people in mid-2000 qualified. The only problem was that the federal budget does not provide the funds to meet its statutory obligations. The economic programme covering the years 2000 to 2010 aims to cut federal budgetary social expenditure even further.

MIGRATION

The collapse of the Soviet Union led about nine million people to leave their homes and seek protection elsewhere. In the post-war era, only the conflict between India and Pakistan after the departure of the British in 1947 resulted in greater internal migration.

The conflicts in Nagorno-Karabakh, Chechnya, Ingushetia, Abkhazia, south Ossetia and Tajikistan produced millions of refugees. Ethnic Russians in the Baltic States and Central Asia (apart from Tajikistan) have been returning to Russia for mainly economic reasons. In 1998, there were about 325,000 refugees and asylum seekers in Russia with almost another million granted forced migration status. The greatest single cause of forced migration has been the two Chechen wars which have displaced over 600,000. About 200,000 of these were ethnic Chechens and they have returned home. Thousands of Afghans, supporters of the ousted Najibullah regime, reside in Moscow. Stavropol and Krasnodar krais, in the north Caucasus, have experienced an influx of migrants from the Caucasian conflicts and Central Asia. Armenia houses over 200,000 ethnic Armenians who have fled Azerbaijan. About 800,000 Azeri refugees have moved to Azerbaijan from Armenia. Tens of thousands of ethnic Georgians fled Abkhazia and a settlement was reached in 1997 which permitted their return but little has happened since. The Tajik civil war displaced about a million with the educated elites moving to Uzbekistan and Russia.

The greatest tension between ethnic Russians and their host nation is experienced in Estonia, Latvia and Kazakhstan. Lithuania escaped this as ethnic Russians only made up about 10 per cent of the population in 1991. As a consequence Lithuania granted citizenship to all legal residents in 1991. Many Russians have left Estonia and Latvia.

Since 1989, about 3.2 million Russians in the non-Russian states have migrated to Russia, leaving about 22 million still there. The largest outflow of ethnic Russians has been from Kazakhstan where about 1.3 million migrated to Russia between 1991 and 1998. Russians now make up about one in four of the Kazakhstani population, a far cry from 1989 when they constituted 37.8 per cent of the population. Only Turkmenistan permits dual citizenship and this unsettles many Russians living in the former Soviet republics, the near abroad.

About half the Russians in the three Transcaucasian states and Tajikistan have left. Of the total net migration to Russia since 1989 about 88 per cent have been ethnic Russians. Those migrating to Russia in the largest numbers have been Armenians, Georgians, Azeris and Tajiks, following in the footsteps of the ethnic Russians. There has been a flow of non-Russians from Russia to the other former Soviet republics but, on balance, there has been a net inflow into Russia. Migration within Russia has been greatest in the Far North (Arctic) where about 11 per cent or just over 1 million have left. The greatest exodus has been from Magadan, over 40 per cent, and Chukotka, 58 per cent. Those leaving are predominantly the young and able-bodied.

Given present trends Russia's population will decline to 125 million in 2015 or the same as that of present-day Japan. If the Russian economy recovers it will need many more workers and an obvious source would be immigrant labour. There are still about 10 million ethnic Russians in Ukraine but they may decide they have a better future there. Russia will then have to contemplate non-ethnic Russian immigrants. President Putin, for instance, sees inward migration as the only solution to Siberia's demographic problems.

The ethnic German community who had been in Tajikistan for over a century have departed. Ethnic Germans have also left Uzbekistan in large numbers. Over 70 per cent of the one million ethnic Germans in Kazakhstan have left for Germany. (It is worth mentioning that these migrants have encountered considerable hostility in Germany. They remain in tightly knit communities, build their own homes, work hard and have prospered. The German government also provides them with generous resettlement grants. Local Germans disparagingly refer to them as Russkies. These Germans speak German to their neighbours but Russian among themselves. Ethnic German migrants from Romania do not encounter the same hostility.) Perhaps 300,000 Crimean Tatars returned to the Crimea from Uzbekistan and over 200,000 live elsewhere. The Ukrainian authorities welcome the Tatars as they reduce the dominance of ethnic Russians in the peninsula.

THE GOLDEN OLDIES

Given the traumatic history of Russia in the twentieth century, it is astonishing that, in 2000, about one Russian in eight is 65 years or older. In

1950, only about six per cent of the population were over 65 or older. The country with the largest proportion of golden oldies in the world today is Italy where just over one in six belongs to this category. The Russian golden oldies are overwhelmingly female. There are 45 males for every 100 females among those who are 65 and older and this declines to 24 males per 100 females at age 80 or over. No other country in the world has such sexual imbalance. The universal maxim that married men live longer also applies to Russia. In 1994, about 80 per cent of men aged 65 and over were married but only 28 per cent of the women. If you want to live longer get a woman. Widowers remarry much more often than widows. Remarkably, only 1.6 per cent of males 65 and over have never married. Women are more likely to live on their own. In 1994, about one third of women of 70 and over were on their own compared with 12 per cent of the men. This is very low by European standards. In the Czech Republic and Scandinavia about half of elderly females live alone. The ageing of the Russian population imposes greater strains on an already inadequate health service. Long-term care is a problem that is not being addressed. Not surprisingly, life for the elderly is more difficult in the countryside where one in three of the population live. In 1996, only 23 per cent had running water and only three per cent had indoor toilets. Table 10.6 reveals that there are more golden oldies as a proportion of the population in Ukraine and Belarus than in Russia. Turkmenistan, at the other extreme, has a remarkably young population.

Table 10.7 shows the proportion of GDP going into public pension funds in Russia and elsewhere. There was a sharp decline in revenue flowing into the pension fund after 1994 because of non-payment of contributions which were due. The average pension declined as a percentage of the average wage. In 1990 it was 38 per cent but in 1996 it was only 28 per cent.

THE ORTHODOX CHURCH

Emile Durkheim, the founder of sociology, was fascinated by the role religion played in society. He concluded that God is an expression of the human sense of community. The individual needs a sense of belonging to a community. It dominates him but also protects and uplifts him. Believers personalise this and regard God as the creator and ruler of the universe. Prayer is regarded as the best therapy for one's problems. If one has no problems one prays for others with problems. One has a moral responsibility to live a good life and to help one's neighbour. Society would be perfect if everyone shared these beliefs. Non-believers think of society and want to promote social justice and equality. Society could become perfect if everyone acted rationally and practised altruism (unfortunately there is no evidence this is happening at present).

Everyone in Europe was a Catholic (except Jews and Muslims) until the Reformation and the church saw itself as the church of the whole community. There was no salvation (one's sins have been forgiven by God) outside the church. Protestantism challenged this and promoted the concept of individual salvation: every person was responsible for his or her own salvation. The Orthodox Church belongs to the pre-Reformation Catholic tradition. To be Russian is to be Orthodox. If one joins another religion one has lost part of one's Russian identity. Before 1917 the Orthodox Church symbolised the togetherness of Russian society; it attempted to heal the wounds of social conflict. Orthodoxy requires the believer to stand during mass. The congregation wants to be uplifted and feel nearer to God. It places little significance on a catechism of beliefs, and Bible reading is not as much promoted as in western Christianity. Rationalism has not much penetrated Orthodoxy and westerners find that a discussion (or dispute) on Orthodox theology does not result in a meeting of minds. East and west belong to different universes. Many Russians attend church but this appears to have little impact on their secular lives, especially their moral lives. This is something that baffles westerners.

The communists had to find a substitute for the church and ended up substituting the party for the church. The party leader was the father of the nation. Gorbachev realised that there was a moral void in society and brought the Orthodox Church increasingly back into Soviet life. This was because Gorbachev was the only Soviet leader with a moral sense. He did not use force to stay in power. Yeltsin had the same problem. He also had to define what Russia was and what a Russian was. There was a ready-made answer, the Orthodox Church. It was restored to its pre-1917 role and had an important part to play in helping Russia during the transition from communism to something better. However it was not as simple as that. Yeltsin took the American route to riches and shaped policy according to American advice. The church was appalled by this as it regarded the idolatry of everything American as the march of Satan. Tension was often acute but, in 1997, the Orthodox Church got its way. Legislation was passed which may eventually mean the expulsion of all foreign Christian missionaries from Russia.

About half of the Russian population (excluding Jews, Muslims and Buddhists) regard themselves as Orthodox but less than 10 per cent go to church regularly. Many young urban educated are to be found among regular churchgoers but congregations consist mainly of the old and the quite young. Many parishes have been created and new churches built. The number of priests has increased dramatically. The church is aided financially by the state which grants it concessions such as importing alcohol, cigarettes and other goods duty free. There are many other Christian denominations with Catholics, Baptists and Pentecostalists well established. All denominations have seen their numbers rise and this has alarmed the Orthodox Church. The Catholic Church has expanded quite rapidly and the resulting tension has postponed Pope John Paul II's visit to Russia. About 5 per cent of the population may attend non-Orthodox services on a regular basis, hence non-Orthodox regular attendance may now be approaching that of the Orthodox Church. It is rare for a Jew, Muslim or Buddhist to convert to Christianity. There are those who find that Orthodoxy is too impersonal to deal with their problems. They seek help to achieve a personal relationship to God and they find this in the Catholic and Protestant churches.

Some western commentators claim that a significant proportion of those who turn to religion in Russia do not do so out of conviction but as a form of self-identification, a sign that they belong to a certain group and are different from others. In 2000, about 85 per cent of Russians stated that they would celebrate Easter but the number attending services in Moscow on 30 April (125,000) was lower than a year previously.

No political party is directly linked to the Orthodox Church and its leadership. There are Christian democratic movements and groups but they are dominated by lay members. (Some Orthodox priests such as Father Gleb Yakunin, a staunch supporter of the democrats, have served as Duma deputies. However the church made it clear it did not favour this overt participation in politics. The real reason may have been that the hierarchy did not like Yakunin's progressive views.) It is worth noting that politically they made little impact. The Church does not advise believers whom to vote for in elections but the symbolism is quite clear. President Yeltsin was photographed many times in the company of Patriarch Aleksi II. During the 1996 presidential campaign both Yeltsin and Zyuganov regularly attend services. President Putin has continued this tradition. Members of Yeltsin's government were also to be observed at services, especially the Prime Minister. The Orthodox Church's role in the military has been increasing.

The 1993 Russian constitution states that Russia is a secular state and guarantees the freedom of religion and its propagation. It also states that there is to be no national ideology. However, in September 1997, a law on the freedom of conscience and religious associations was passed which declared that there were four main religions in Russia, Orthodoxy (technically Orthodoxy is not a religion but a branch of Christianity), Islam, Judaism and Buddhism. Others were either religious associations or groups. The latter are cults or sects which the authorities would like to see disbanded. Many local authorities had been passing restrictive legislation before 1997 and some of this found its way into the federal legislation. The first draft was rejected by President Yeltsin, the US government having protested strongly, and returned to the Duma. The final draft, in the view of many observers, was less liberal. Before it was passed Baptists and other denominations met Orthodox clergy and others to discuss the new draft. However they were not permitted to see the final draft. Instead of demanding to see the draft legislation they merely made their position clear and departed. Religious organisations are officially registered associations. In order to qualify they have to present documentary evidence that they have operated on the territory in question for at least 15 years. However in 1982 the Soviet state persecuted believers and normally refused to register their churches. Groups are not permitted to own property, erect buildings, employ anyone, conduct services in hospitals and elsewhere, distribute literature, engage in charity work or have international links such as inviting foreign guests.

Orthodoxy is the main faith in Belarus and Ukraine and again one encounters the view that to be Belarusian or Ukrainian is to be Orthodox. President Alyaksandr Lukashenka of Belarus often proclaims his Orthodoxy but has also stated that he is an Orthodox atheist! Some Orthodox have come up with a snappy slogan: Orthodox of the world unite!

In August 2000, the Orthodox Church broke with tradition and published a document running to over a hundred pages on the Church's views on subjects ranging from cloning to homosexuality, from contraception to divorce and from nationalism to globalisation. The document was drafted over a period of six years by the twelve-man Holy Synod which administers the Church from day to day. The Council of Bishops, which is formally superior to the Synod, passed the document in less than a day without debate. Previously bishops and priests have only had private views on pressing matters of the moment. The Church itself always avoided commenting on contentious issues. It has now followed the Catholic Church which speaks out on moral and social issues on a regular basis.

The document roundly condemns homosexuality and abortion. The latter is viewed as murder and similarly euthanasia is viewed as murder or suicide. Cloning is an 'undoubted challenge to the very nature of man'. Reproductive technologies are not permitted except for the artificial insemination with a husband's semen which is viewed as not violating the sanctity of marriage. On contraception Catholic and Orthodox views diverge. Whereas Catholic doctrine condemns contraception, Orthodox doctrine states that while contraception should be discouraged in Christian families, it does not destroy an embryo and 'should not be equated with abortion'. Bearing children is one of the main goals of the 'divinely established matrimonial union' and therefore deciding not to have children for 'egotistical reasons' is a sin. 'Leniency' is counselled for women who have aborted a pregnancy which threatened their lives. Priests are advised to give such women penance but not to deny them holy communion. The only truly responsible Orthodox attitude to child-bearing is voluntary abstinence from sex. The document points out that sex is not to be disparaged and that non-church marriages should not be considered adulterous. This is a reminder to some radical priests who have adopted sexophobic attitudes (all Orthodox priests are required to marry. All those in senior positions are celibate).

The list of legitimate reasons for a Church divorce is extended to include cases where one's spouse has contracted Aids, is a medically attested alcoholic or drug addict, or when a wife has an abortion without her husband's consent. The reasons which previously permitted the dissolution of the marriage included adultery by one's spouse, impotence, syphilis or sexual abuse. Homosexuality is a 'sinful damage of human nature' and can be overcome by penance, fasting and prayer. While the Church has pastoral responsibility for homosexuals it resolutely opposes attempts to present this sinful tendency as a norm or a subject of pride to be emulated. The Church recognises freedom of conscience but refuses to endorse it as truth. The Church recognises any form of government but a true spiritual revival is necessary in society to produce the conditions which could lead to the restoration of the monarchy. This would be spiritually 'higher' than democracy. The Church is all for 'active patriotism' but implacably opposed to 'aggressive nationalism' which turns one's nation into a god. Globalisation is bad because it unifies the world on the basis of consumerism and godless values. Sport is fine if its goal is physical fitness but sport which gives rise to pride and is record-oriented is to discouraged. In God's eyes the physically weak and the ill are just as valuable to Him as the fit and the strong. The Church has traditionally been hostile to the media but the document recognises that this attitude has played into the hands of its enemies. Priests are not to sue journalists but should attempt to resolve disputes by mediation. If this fails the priest may publicly break with the journalist or media. An immediate task for the Church is to stop building new cathedrals but to fill the existing ones with Christian life. This codification of the Church's teaching is to serve for the next few decades.

In 1998, the Orthodox Church had 151 bishops in 127 dioceses. About 19,700 clergy served in over 19,000 parishes. There were 478 monasteries and convents and of these 299 were on the territory of the Russian Federation. In Moscow, the Church had 428 churches and 39 chapels with 539 priests and 206 deacons. The Church also owns property in Europe, North America and Israel.

The Orthodox Church, through affiliated companies, has developed many lucrative businesses across Russia. One of the Church's largest known earners is the international economic partnership, a large oil exporter. The Moscow patriarchy was a cofounder and owns 40 per cent of the shares. The company had a turnover of about $2 billion in 1999. In 1996, the Church imported 10 per cent of the cigarettes sold in Russia and also imported alcohol. Yeltsin had granted the Church a concession which meant it imported these wares duty free.

11

FOREIGN POLICY: WILL THE EMPIRE STRIKE BACK?

THE NEAR ABROAD

PERHAPS THE KEY REASON FOR THE dissolution of the Soviet Union was the struggle between Presidents Mikhail Gorbachev and Boris Yeltsin. It was a conflict at a personal level but also a national one, between Russia and the Soviet Union. A new Union under Gorbachev was unacceptable so when the Commonwealth of Independent States (CIS) (there is no territorial entity in this title – this followed the tradition of the Soviet Union) appeared it was stated explicitly that it was not a successor state. Eventually 12 of the 15 republics joined with only Estonia, Latvia and Lithuania remaining outside. But what is the CIS? It is still unclear. What is clear is that it is not an equal commonwealth since Russia dominates it by its size, economic resources and the fact that it is a nuclear power.

An active foreign policy towards the near abroad (Moscow regards the former Soviet republics, including the Baltic States, as the near abroad, and the rest of the world as the far abroad; wits poke fun at this by pointing out that, for instance, Poland, the far abroad, is physically nearer Russia than Tajikistan, the near abroad) first emerged in the latter part of 1993. This was due to the desire of Russia to forge a partnership with the 'civilised world', mainly the United States. That was where the money was. Another reason was the fraught domestic scene which consumed much energy and also there was the belief that the successor states would gradually gravitate towards Russia because of common ties, especially security and economic ties. Also most Russians did not regard Belarus (the Russians decline to adopt the new names of the successor states: hence they continue to call Belarus Belorussia and Kyrgyzstan Kirgiziya) and Ukraine as sovereign, independent states. Ukraine, for one, took umbrage at this. Another problem for Moscow was how to define Russian national interests. Russia, due to the fact that it was multi-national, did not develop as a nation-state alongside other European powers in the nineteenth century. The dilemma of what is Russia still persists today. Sergei Witte, the architect of Russia's industrial growth between 1907 and 1914, expressed the view that Russia did not exist: only the Russian empire existed. Those who shared this approach after 1991, who can be called empire-savers, nationalists or great Russian chau-vinists, were constantly critical of Kozyrev's concept of foreign policy. He was forced to take on board these criticisms in 1993.

In the aftermath of the collapse of the Soviet Union, Russia's policy can be characterised as withdrawal, a desire to end all expensive economic and military commitments outside its new state borders. Domestic economic reform took absolute priority. Military interests had low priority. Russia became responsible for all Soviet troops who were not inside new states. Hence it withdrew troops from Nagorno-Karabakh, Azerbaijan and began withdrawing from the Baltic states. In 1992, Russia concerned itself with state-building and paid no attention to state-building within the CIS. Well before the December 1993 Duma elec-tions, a general consensus was building that Russia was a great power and should be treated as such. The near abroad was defined as an 'his-toric sphere of interest' and Russia's leading role in this region was a precondition of its great power status. In 1993, Russia became more active in helping to prevent the fragmentation of states in the near abroad by intervening in civil conflicts and forming a web of bilateral agreements. Russia also revealed a willingness to take on the responsibility of peace-keeping and conflict resolution in the CIS. The Russian military pres-ence was to be regulated by agreements on military bases.

Moscow also intervened in civil conflicts to promote its own inter-ests. A case in point is Georgia where it sided with the separatists in Abkhazia in 1993. Georgia, which had tried to stay outside the CIS, was obliged, in order to gain Russian military help, to become a member, sign the treaty on collective security and a treaty of friendship and cooperation which included an agreement on Russian military bases in Georgia. Azerbaijan, due to setbacks in Nagorno-Karabakh, had to join the CIS and also signed the treaty on collective security in 1993. By 1993

Russia had achieved its two main objectives in the near abroad: establish a leading position and exclude foreign powers from the region. In the draft military doctrine of May 1992 defending ethnic Russians abroad became the task of the Russian military (Hansen and Heurlin 1998: 115).

Only in September 1995 was a coherent policy document on the near abroad published. The near abroad was afforded top priority in Russia's national security and strategic interests. The goal was to strengthen Russia's position and integrate the region economically, militarily and culturally. The CIS was clearly Russia's backyard and a Russian Monroe doctrine was applied. CIS states were to be persuaded not to join alliances directed against any member state. Political, economic and military pressure could be applied by Russia on CIS states in order to redress the human rights violations of Russian minorities. When Evgeny Primakov succeeded Andrei Kozyrev as foreign minister, in January 1996, he immediately stressed the importance of the CIS to Russia's security and proposed closer integration of member states.

President Yeltsin presented the new national security doctrine in June 1996. The world was not becoming more cooperative but geopolitical, geoeconomic and geomilitary competition were increasing. Central to this was the competitive US-Russian relationship. There was a discernible trend among Muslim countries and the west to hinder CIS integration in order to prevent the emergence of a serious political and economic rival. Russia was losing its geopolitical dominance in the near abroad. There was a fierce struggle for influence in Central Asia by China, Turkey, Iran, Pakistan, Saudi Arabia, the USA and NATO countries. An arch of instability was forming, embracing Central Asia and the Caucasus, which could lead to a buffer zone of states that would not be friendly towards Russia. Primakov, in December 1996, saw the world as a series of centres. The US was the leading economic and military power but would soon be overtaken economically by the European Union (here he was completely wrong) and during the 21st century China, Japan and south east Asia would become strong centres. Russia's task was not to ally itself with any one centre but to cooperate with all.

Russia could not make up its mind about how to promote integration in the CIS. It could become a donor state and enter into expensive economic and military agreements but this ran counter to Russia's interests. The race was on to find a policy which promoted Russian influence but which cost almost nothing. In the spring of 1996, Russia, Kazakhstan and Kyrgyzstan announced deeper economic cooperation.

All this really came down to was promoting more trade. In a policy document, published in April 1996, cold realism was evident. Russia should not take on any expensive commitments and integration should proceed from below – at enterprise level – and not at state level. It was recognised that some states favoured a closer relationship to Russia while others did not. Hence a differentiated approach was advisable (Hansen and Heurlin 1998: 121).

CIS states are opposed to the organisation taking on any supra-state characteristics (favoured by Moscow) and it has developed solely on the basis of bilateral agreements. If a state abstains from a decision it need not implement it. States can decide their own speed of integration and closeness to one another. National parliaments, when ratifying documents, often add restrictions. In general, CIS decisions are not implemented. States are wary of closer military cooperation and this only occurs when the military are needed as firefighters in local conflicts and to engage in peacekeeping. Russia has warned that the CIS treaty on collective security would be transformed into a military alliance if NATO expanded up to its borders. NATO expanded into Poland (Kaliningrad oblast borders on Poland), the Czech Republic and Hungary in 1999 but no CIS military alliance appeared.

The west is an important factor in Russian policy towards the CIS. All CIS states are members of the Organisation for Security and Cooperation in Europe (OSCE), the North Atlantic Cooperative Council (NACC) and the NATO Partnership for Peace (except Tajikistan). Russia and Ukraine are members of the Council of Europe. The UN and OSCE are involved in conflict resolution and peacekeeping.

Table 11.1 outlines CIS agreements and their signatories between 1992 and 1996. An economic union agreement was signed in September 1993 (Ukraine signed as an associate member) and also a payments union in October 1994. These are the only agreements which all members have signed. The customs union of March 1996 was only signed by Russia, Kazakhstan, Kyrgyzstan, Tajikistan and Belarus. The treaty on collective security of May 1992 was signed by these countries plus Armenia. Indeed the only countries which have signed all agreements are Russia, Kyrgyzstan, Tajikistan and Belarus. Kazakhstan has signed all except the statute on peace-keeping forces of January 1996. Armenia has signed everything except the customs union agreement of March 1996. Hence there is a core of states which agree almost always with Russia. The main reason is that they are desperate for Russian credits (Bowker and Ross 2000: chapter 13).

In March 1996, Belarus, Kazakhstan, Kyrgyzstan and Russia formed the community of integrated states and extended an invitation to other CIS states and indeed any other state to join. In 1998, Tajikistan took up the offer but no one else has expressed interest. However this quadrille has had no more success in harmonising trade regulations, import duties and restrictions than any other CIS agreement. The situation became even more complicated in October 1998 when Kyrgyzstan was admitted to membership of the World Trade Organisation. On the other hand, Azerbaijan and Moldova have only signed two of the eight CIS agreements, Ukraine two agreements and an associate membership and Turkmenistan only three. Russia repeatedly complains that member states sign agreements, assume obligations and then do not honour them. This applies especially to paying their bills. In January 1994, Kazakhstan, Kyrgyzstan and Uzbekistan formed the Central Asian economic union and in March 1998 Tajikistan joined. However this union is more formal than real.

An indicator of how important the CIS was to Russia is to count the number of meetings of CIS presidents. In 1992, they met six times, in 1993, five times, but only once in 1998 and once in 1999. This spurred states to look for sponsors other than Russia. Azerbaijan turned to Turkey, Moldova thought of union with Romania, Ukraine and Georgia cast envious eyes at the west and Uzbekistan and Turkmenistan closed themselves off from the outside world.

The IMF advised the successor states not to establish their own currencies but to retain the ruble. Russia was too distracted at home to devote attention to its interests in the CIS. CIS countries received rubles from the Russian Central Bank because the only printing presses were in Russia. All states discovered that if they issued credits to their own enterprises the Russian Central Bank paid. If CIS companies bought goods in Russia and were issued with credit the Central Bank met the bills. Besides goods and services there were also oil and gas. Russia was exporting energy at about 5 per cent of the world price. One estimate is that Russia exported 11.7 per cent of its GDP to CIS countries in 1992. This was an enormous aid budget (developed countries provide less than one per cent to the third world) which Russia could not afford. The aid added 52 per cent to the GDP in Georgia, 49 per cent in Armenia and 26 per cent in Azerbaijan. Egor Gaidar and Boris Fedorov, the finance minister, decided to put a stop to this and in April 1993 CIS countries could no longer issue credits. In July 1993, the Central Bank announced a currency reform and only Russians could exchange existing rubles for the new ones. The republics were then advised by the IMF to establish their own currencies (Azerbaijan had already issued its manat in August 1992 as a parallel currency). Given their weak economic base it was inevitable that their currencies would be very weak. The ruble zone ended in 1994 (in 1995 in Tajikistan). This caused considerable problems for many Russian enterprises which received their inputs from CIS countries. One of the republics hardest hit was Kazakhstan whose industry was closely integrated with Russian enterprises which bordered on the republic. These republics received short shrift from Fedorov. A man of strong opinions, he treated as almost a personal affront the claims of Belarus, Kazakhstan and, especially, Ukraine to be sovereign, independent states.

Russia regards the borders of the CIS as its security borders. Hence it patrols the Armenian border with Turkey and Iran and Tajikistan's border with Afghanistan. All countries belong to the joint air defence system except Azerbaijan and Moldova. Russia promotes the resolution of local conflicts as this is in its own interests. It also provides peacekeeping forces in, for instance, Tajikistan, along with other states. This is the only case where troops other than the locals and the Russians are involved. A major concern is to prevent the rise of Islamic fundamentalism in Central Asia. Of great concern to Russia is the possible spread of NATO into the CIS and the Baltic States. The latter have expressed a desire to become members as has Georgia. Ukraine is of key importance and Kiev has been developing closer ties with the US and Germany.

In the heady days of 1992 Russia accepted the concept of deep involvement by the international community in its security affairs. In December 1992, Kozyrev suggested joint action with the UN and the OSCE in heading off regional conflicts, including the use of military force. Moscow debated involving the UN or NATO in peacekeeping in areas of ethnic conflict in the CIS. All that changed when Russia claimed special responsibility for keeping the peace in the former Soviet Union. It requested UN endorsement of this mission. When the UN refused, Russia then proposed that the CIS be recognised as the legitimate entity to perform this mission. Russia has an ambivalent attitude towards the involvement of the UN and the OSCE; it has requested their presence on CIS territory but is wary of foreign influence in what it regards as its own backyard. It is particularly interested in burden sharing and has repeatedly requested aid from the UN to defray its operational costs in the CIS. In 1996, Russia declared that it welcomed UN and OSCE cooperation in the CIS but insisted that it had the right to take the key decisions.

The OSCE deployed long-term missions in Georgia (Abkhazia and South Ossetia) in November 1992, in Moldova in April 1993 and in Tajikistan in February 1994. UN missions in Abkhazia and Tajikistan are more active than the OSCE. The UN Security Council, in 1994, recognised Russian intervention in Abkhazia as a collective CIS undertaking. This was the first time that this had occurred. Russia accepts UN and OSCE peacekeeping forces but strenuously opposes the involvement of national military forces. In December 1994, the OSCE set up an international peacekeeping force in accordance with the wishes of the signatories to an agreement on Nagorno-Karabakh. No Russian peace-keeping troops have been deployed in Nagorno-Karabakh due to objections by Azerbaijan. The conflict has received more attention from international organisations (chiefly the OSCE) than any other conflict in the CIS. This conflict follows a pattern whereby military means are no longer capable of advancing the interests of any one side. The other separatist conflicts, in Abkhazia, South Ossetia and Transdniestria, are effectively in limbo at present. In Tajikistan, the Tajik government and the United Tajik Opposition signed an agreement in June 1997.

There has been a trend to form regional groupings, for instance, the Central Asian Union and GUAM (Georgia, Ukraine, Azerbaijan and Moldova). It was established by the first three states in 1996 and then Moldova joined a year later. Then Uzbekistan came on board in 1998 and it became GUUAM. Its primary economic motive is to ensure the supply of Azeri oil by pipeline through Georgia and then by tanker along Black Sea ports to provide oil for Moldova and Ukraine. They also combined to resist attempts by Moscow to revise the conventional forces in Europe treaty in such a way as to permit higher levels of Russian forces in or near GUUAM countries. In 1999, they appointed coordinators to promote economic cooperation both within the group and with western partners. Little flesh has been put on these bones so far. It is striking that key meetings of GUUAM take place abroad: in 1997 in Strasbourg, in 1999 in Washington and in 2000 in New York. The goal is a free trade area as this has failed to materialise in the CIS. Russian protectionism is blamed. The GUUAM are also in favour of westbound oil and gas pipelines. In 2000, Russia pulled out of the CIS agreement on visa-free travel but the GUUAM retain it. GUUAM is looking to add western members and countries such as Romania are considering joining. The attraction is the transit of Caspian oil via the Black Sea to the Balkans. Hence there are two groupings in the CIS: GUUAM is increasingly pro-western and the others can be described as pro-Russian (Belarus, Kazakhstan, Kyrgyzstan and Tajikistan).

National peacekeeping forces have been created in several CIS states and can only be deployed under a UN mandate. This applies to the peacekeeping forces set up since 1996 in Ukraine, Georgia, Kazakhstan, Kyrgyzstan and Uzbekistan.

When Evgeny Primakov replaced Andrei Kozyrev as foreign minister, in January 1996, pragmatism became the guiding principle of Russian foreign policy. He favoured the withdrawal of Russian forces (peacekeeping forces would stay) from the CIS. There were about 8500 Russian troops in Georgia, 6400 in Moldova and 16,500 in Tajikistan in 1996. He thought it more productive to use political and economic levers rather than military might to increase Russia's influence in the CIS. The exception to this trend is Armenia which cleaves close to Russia as it feels internationally isolated. There were about 5000 Russian troops stationed in Armenia in 1994. In November 1999, Russia agreed to evacuate its four remaining military bases in Georgia: Vaziani, near Tbilisi; Gudauta, in Abkhazia; Akhalkalaki, in Javakheti; and Batumi, in Ajaria. However the airfield in Viziani will pass under Georgian control but Russia will be allowed to use it to a certain extent, that is, as long as there are Russian bases in Georgia. The withdrawal is complicated by the fact that the Abkhaz are insisting on full independence before they will negotiate with Tbilisi on the closure of the Russian base at Gudauta.

The situation in Afghanistan continues to cause great concern and President Islam Karimov of Uzbekistan is very exercised by opposition, especially when it has an Islamic tinge to it. In early 1998, Russia, Uzbekistan and Tajikistan set up a coalition to resist 'Islamic extremism'. Fighting continued in 1999 and involved Kyrgyzstan, where insurgents took hostages, and Uzbekistan. Marshal Igor Sergeev estimated there were, in mid-2000, about 5000 Islamic Movement of Uzbekistan fighters and their numbers are growing all the time. They now have the ability to go over to the offensive against Uzbek and Kyrgyz forces who are ill-equipped to fight against rebels in mountainous terrain. Resentment has been caused by arrests of many Uzbeks accused of distributing religious literature. Kyrgyzstan has moved families away from the Kyrgyz-Tajik border for their 'protection'. Some observers see their removal linked to their sympathies for the rebels. Fighters are trained in Afghanistan by the Taliban and then infiltrate through Tajikistan. The Islamic Movement of Uzbekistan's goal is the removal of President Karimov and the establishment of an Islamic state. A major reason feeding sympathy for the fighters is that many in rural areas in Tajikistan, Kyrgyzstan and Uzbekistan are living in dire poverty.

On nuclear weapons Russia has got its way. It consistently demanded that Belarus, Ukraine and Kazakhstan transfer their nuclear weapons to Russian territory. The United States has played an important role by providing financial compensation and non-specific security guarantees. In 1994, Ukraine signed the nuclear non-proliferation treaty as a non-nuclear state and thereby laid to rest any ambitions it might have had of remaining in the nuclear league. In 1996, all remaining warheads were transferred to Russia.

Anticipating his election as Russian President on 26 March 2000, Vladimir Putin convened a CIS summit in Moscow on 25 January 2000, which proved to be a watershed in relations between Russia and the other members of the CIS. Energy debts to Russia were put at $4 billion but probably much higher. Only Azerbaijan and Turkmenistan had no energy debts. Putin cut bilateral deals with members in return for their support. Kazakhstan traded its $240 million energy debt for shares in its state energy company; Ukraine's debts were restructured once again as were those of other states. Putin expressed a personal desire to help forge solutions to problems in the Caucasus; all signed an agreement to combat international terrorism. This was tacit support for Russia's anti-terrorist campaign in Chechnya.

Russia is pressing ahead with a union with Belarus and Putin appears to believe that Minsk's strategic position is worth the cost of shoring up its poorly performing economy. On 25 February 2001, the communists gained 71 of the 101 seats in the Moldovan parliament. Vladimir Voronin, the party leader, immediately declared that Moldova would seek to join the Russian-Belarusian union.

THE FAR ABROAD

Jack Matlock, the skilful US ambassador, once remarked that Gorbachev and the Soviets gave the Americans 120 per cent of what they asked for. Yeltsin and Kozyrev were determined to go further and give the Americans everything they wanted. If Grim Grom Andrei Gromyko was known as Mr Nyet, Mr No, smiling Andrei Kozyrev was called Mr Da, Mr Yes. In return, they expected to join the 'civilised world', become a member of the G7, receive limitless economic aid in order to become a rich country and to be afforded equal status with the greats of the world. This was the kindergarten approach to foreign policy – the grown-up world does not operate like this.

Yeltsin always devoted great attention and energy (while it lasted) to foreign policy. He was a natural actor and loved playing the Tsar of Russia abroad. Bill Clinton developed an insatiable curiosity and fascination with Russia and at times it appeared that US foreign policy only consisted of relations with Russia. His main adviser on things Russian was deputy secretary of state, Strobe Talbott, a Russophile, with an encyclopaedic knowledge of Russian literature and culture and who was always willing to look on the bright side of dark events in Russia. His inexhaustible optimism about Russia led some of his critics to wonder if he had read too many Russian fairy tales. Others saw him as Russocentric, always taking Russia's side in relations with the successor states. Clinton and Yeltsin hit it off straightaway. This was predictable as both were consummate political actors. The Bill and Boris show took the road and was much appreciated by the audience. It was often unscripted as no one was quite sure what Boris would do or say next, least of all Boris himself. Boris ate too much (at his first summit in Vancouver he surprised the Canadians, big eaters themselves, by his gargantuan appetite) and of course he drank too much. Clinton developed a brilliant response to offensive pronouncements: he simply laughed loudly and long enough until the atmosphere warmed up again. America always knew that Boris's heart was in the right place and when it came to the crunch he always sided with the west.

Relations got off to a good start with the Camp David declaration of February 1992, stating that the two countries were forging an 'alliance of partners' and cooperating against the common dangers which faced them (Bowker and Ross 2000: chapter 14). There was even a hint of a military alliance. Yeltsin talked of Japan as a potential partner (Japan was a member of the G7) but Russia was still technically at war with Japan as the issue of the Kurile islands had held up a peace treaty. The G7 got round the ticklish economic aid problem by handing the problem over to the IMF. It came up in mid-1992 with a package worth $24 billion. However when it was examined most of it turned out to be debt relief and bilateral loans linked to US exports; there was precious little cash available. The following year the IMF came up with a $43.4 billion offer but again it contained little hard cash. In return, the IMF wanted rapid economic reform which included more tax collection and a small budget deficit. Both sides were to be disappointed.

In 1992, opposition to the Atlanticist bias in foreign affairs was expressed by a wide spectrum of critics, from democrats to communists and nationalists. Some democrats regarded the near abroad as the natural place to start to resurrect Russia's great power status. They regarded relations with Europe, especially Germany, as of equal importance to those with America. Communists and nationalists wanted a policy of reintegrating the successor states. The spectre of Islam was never far from Russian minds. Then there were the Eurasianists who thought that Russia should be equidistant between Europe and Asia. Kozyrev was forced to take these criticisms on board and to assert Russia's leading role in the near abroad and to aim for great power status. The problem was that no one trusted Russia's intentions. The former satellites in eastern Europe were working hard at gaining entry to NATO as the solution to their security problems. The Baltic States had the same aspirations but membership of NATO's partnership for peace may be all they achieve. The west did not afford Russia much influence in resolving the consequences of the Yugoslav wars of succession. The Russians simply did not have the resources to compete with the Americans in Bosnia.

Clinton never missed an opportunity to praise Yeltsin's democratic credentials and turned a blind eye to his transgressions. In January 1994, in a Moscow summit, Clinton virtually gave Russia *carte blanche* to intervene in the near abroad if he deemed it necessary. He spoke of American intervention in Panama and Grenada in the same breath. This was too much for his critics such as Zbigniew Brzezinski and Henry Kissinger. The former was always suspicious that the new Russia was the old Soviet Union with a face lift. The arrest of Aldrich Ames, the highest ranking CIA officer who ever spied for the Soviet Union and Russia, in February 1994, was grist to his mill. The fact that Ames had continued spying after the break-up of the Soviet Union meant, in the eyes of Brzezinski and the Republicans, that Russia was not a partner but a rival. Brzezinski favoured the promotion of Ukraine and other states as a counterweight to Russian influence. Clinton did take note and began to mention that the interests of a renewed Russia and America would not always coincide. Ukraine received much attention from the US and Germany and attracted an IMF loan. Uzbekistan, which made no pretence of moving towards a liberal democracy and market economy, became the focus of US military concern. Britain had misjudged the situation in Central Asia and had concentrated its efforts on Kazakhstan. It then had to acknowledge that the most important capital in Central Asia was Tashkent, Uzbekistan. Oil was the magnet and the region had huge reserves. The problem was how to get the oil to world markets as all pipelines went through Russia. The oil companies convinced the US government that the region was of strategic importance and military and political ties were developed.

The more realistic approach to Russia led to a volte face in thinking about NATO expansion. In 1992, Strobe Talbott informed the Russians that

NATO would not expand eastwards. By late 1994, the die was cast and America had decided that Poland, the Czech Republic and Hungary should be invited to join NATO. One of Clinton's campaign promises had been to cut US defence spending and in a defence review in late 1993 he delivered. This was met by a Republican wave of protest that he was putting national security at risk. He might have ridden out the storm had it not been for the victory of the anti-Yeltsin camp in the December 1993 Duma elections. Vladimir Zhirinovsky's anti-western rhetoric had struck a cord with Russian voters. Clinton stopped talking about cutting defence spending.

In March 1994, the IMF agreed a $1.5 billion loan to Russia, not a spectacular amount but it signalled that Washington and Moscow were still working together. Had the IMF refused the loan it would have been read as the west abandoning Yeltsin and the reformers. The argument could be made that the west would gain some influence over the way the Russian economy was developing. However the problem was that the IMF had not woken up to the fact that roving bandits were running the Russian economy and that western advisers had limited influence. The European Union weighed in with a trade agreement. In July, Russia was invited to the G7 meeting in Naples. Kozyrev was most pleased but Russia did not become a full member. There were G8 discussions about politics in which Russia participated but when it came to hard economics Russia was outside.

In December 1994, Yeltsin came out against NATO expansion eastwards and Russia invaded Chechnya. Eventually America and its allies turned a blind eye to the human rights violations in Chechnya and conceded that Russia had the right to use force inside its own country. The IMF continued lending and other states extended loans.

The idealist Kozyrev, who had seen his dreams turn to dust, was replaced by the pragmatist Primakov. His hero was Aleksandr Gorchakov, the Russian foreign minister for a quarter of a century after the Crimean war defeat of 1856. Gorchakov had played a weak hand so skilfully that Russia had regained its great power status. Primakov would try to do the same. Primakov would balance Russia's interests in east and west. The problem was that no one thought of Russia as a big hitter in international affairs. The countries that wanted help were Libya, Iraq and Iran but they were outsiders. When Israeli-Palestinian peace negotiations came to a dead stop in September 1996, Yassir Arafat, the Palestinian leader, and Binyamin Netanyahu, the Israeli Prime Minister, boarded planes to Washington.

The west was very relieved when Yeltsin was re-elected in July 1996 but found the rhetoric during the campaign confusing. It was uniformly anti-American and there was precious little to distinguish between speeches by Yeltsin and those of Zyuganov. The west comforted itself with the thought that the rhetoric was for domestic consumption and that afterwards normal service would be resumed. One of the conclusions the west drew was that Yeltsin's victory represented the final victory of the reformers: a successful market economy was only a matter of time in Russia. As events were to demonstrate this was profoundly wrong.

Yeltsin shocked America and the west by sacking his whole government in March 1998. Al Gore, the Vice-President, had struck up a close relationship with Viktor Chernomyrdin and it was assumed that the former Gazprom man would be the next Russian President. The collapse of August 1998 was the end of an era. Critics of the IMF and President Clinton immediately posed the question: 'Who lost Russia?' As a wag said: 'Not me, the last time I looked it was still there.' The IMF was quick off the mark and, in November, called a conference to examine its Russian loan policy. Predictably it concluded that the reason why the IMF policy had failed was because Russia had not implemented it. There was some truth in this. On reflection, the $19 billion the IMF had poured into Russia had enriched the roving bandits. The White House, desperately searching for something positive to say, maintained that policy since 1992 had borne some fruit. Russia had moved away from isolation and was embracing the world community. Washington was not pleased when Evgeny Primakov took over as Prime Minister. Madeleine Albright, the secretary of state, was very stern and stated that America was very concerned about the direction Russia was taking. This was an admission that the US had limited influence over Russia's development. The partners had divorced. Primakov's successor as foreign minister was Igor Ivanov, a deputy minister of foreign affairs since 1993 and a specialist on Spain. The high-profile Primakov gave way to the professional diplomat Ivanov. Foreign policy decision making gradually moved from the ministry of foreign affairs to the Security Council.

Scholars and analysts wallowed in gloom and doom. They competed with one another to paint black scenarios. One stated that even though Russia only accounted for about one per cent of global GDP it could spark off a crisis which could engulf the world. This was not written by Zhirinovsky or Zyuganov but by the *Wall Street Journal*. Martin Malia, a respected American historian of Russia, was in deep despair and thought that all was lost. They were all wrong, profoundly wrong. Primakov stabilised Russia by building consensus and avoiding economic experiments.

Primakov was no friend of the west and one can call him a pragmatic anti-westerner. His dander was up in March 1999 when NATO began bombing Yugoslavia in an effort to solve the Kosovo crisis. Serbia was Russia's ally in the Balkans and both countries saw themselves faced with an Islamic threat. Why was NATO siding with the Muslims in Kosovo and Chechnya? The bombing produced an almost unanimous anti-American front in Russia, from the liberals to the communists and nationalists. General Lebed proposed the transfer of anti-aircraft weapons to Belgrade. Nothing came of this but had Russia acted NATO would have stopped the bombing post haste because the Americans were not willing to take casualties. Ninety per cent of the Russian population regarded NATO bombing as a mistake. A fault line developed in Russia. Very few Russians henceforth thought that Russia's best interests would be served by integrating with a US-dominated west. Russia could not afford a war so it became the champion of peace. Yeltsin moved to restrict Primakov's growing popularity in Russia by appointing Viktor Chernomyrdin as his special envoy to Yugoslavia. The latter was likely to search for a solution which benefited Russia and the west. Eventually President Milosevic backed down when Russia stated it would no longer support him.

Primakov was succeeded as Prime Minister by Sergei Stepashin and he by Vladimir Putin. They could not be accused of being starry eyed about America or the west. They liked Coca-Cola and American films but were pragmatists; Russia's way forward would be decided by Russians and not by advisers sent from Washington. Putin said that Russia did not need IMF loans. All this was disappointing for American businessmen who had made some money during the halcyon days of the Yeltsin presidency but nothing like what they thought they could make. Putin's task is to transform the roving bandits into stationary bandits. Roving bandits regard foreign direct investment as money to steal. Only stationary bandits think in the long term. American business, the IMF and the White House were deeply disappointed by the course of events in Russia during the 1990s. Russia now seeks to forge alliances which will challenge American hegemony throughout the world. Russia had moved from being an adversary to being a partner and back again to being an adversary.

12

SUCCESS NOT FAILURE: THE BALTIC STATES

THE BALTIC STATES ARE THE SUCCESS story of the post-Soviet era. They are on a par with the countries of central Europe. The major reason for this may be that they were independent states in the inter-war years with constitutions, political parties and market economies. Historically and culturally, they looked outwards to central and northern Europe and not southwards towards Russia and Ukraine. They are predominantly Lutheran and Catholic and not Orthodox.

Under communism they were the most developed republics (technically Belarus had a higher per capita income than the Baltic States). Gorbachev's perestroika and self-management allowed them to articulate the view that they could manage their own affairs more efficiently and effectively than the planners in Moscow. After independence, in September 1991, there were three main issues: democracy, a market economy and, internationally, escape from Moscow's hegemony. Eventually they chose divergent paths to achieve these goals. Lithuania moved towards a presidential system while Latvia and Estonia favoured a parliamentary path. Political parties proliferated, many resurrected from pre-1940 days. Economically, Estonia emerged as the star and has remained so (Table 12.1). Lithuania, more dependent on agriculture than the others, has found it more difficult to catch up. The economic policies chosen varied according to the country. Lithuania, with a strong presidential system, chose a gradual adjustment to the market while

Estonia, with its parliamentary system, opted for shock therapy. In foreign affairs, Lithuania adopted a relaxed attitude towards its small Russian minority while Estonia engaged in full-frontal confrontation with its large Slav population. Not unexpectedly, Tallinn's relations with Moscow become frosty and have remained uneasy ever since.

The collapse of communism engendered euphoria and united political and social groups. Their interests were secondary to producing a new state which would meet the aspirations of the people. This period did not last long as debate over new constitutions got under way. The core issues were the form of central government and the electoral system. There were two main arguments: a strong executive (President) which could forge stability and implement radical policies, and a strong parliament which could gain legitimacy through consensus-building and participatory democracy (Norgaard 1996: 5). There was also a lively debate on the type of elections to be adopted. Should they be based on the first past the post principle or on proportional representation? The political parties which formed seldom reflected economic or social interest groups in society. They were centred around various leaders who set out to gain support rather than providing a forum to search for solutions and compromises to the problems facing a new system. Issues which became important to leaders were often of little importance to the electorate.

The problem of moving from a planned economy to a market economy was that there were no agreed guidelines. Almost everyone wanted a market economy because it was synonymous with rich, western states. A problem was that capitalism is synonymous with inequality. Hence economic expectations had to be dampened in the early years as states fought with rising inflation and structural adjustment. As elsewhere there was a debate about the speed of economic reform. Should it be rapid, shock therapy, or more gradual?

ESTONIA

Estonia did not enjoy the option of reintroducing its pre-1940 constitution as it was not a democratic one. The constitutional issue was resolved by a compromise between the Supreme Council (the Soviet parliament) and the Estonian Congress. The Congress recognised the Supreme Council as the legitimate representative institution and that the new constitution should be based on existing institutions. The Congress thereby gave up its claim to be the sole legitimate representative institution in the country. The Supreme Council made concessions on the ethnic issue and as a result about 40 per cent of the population were denied citizenship. So the Russian minority were disenfranchised. A constituent assembly composed of equal numbers from the Supreme Council and the Estonian Congress was to agree on the new institutions of state. Those favouring a parliamentary system were in the majority but Arnold Rüütel, head of the Supreme Council and former leading communist, fought for a presidential system but garnered little support. Clearly there was a residual fear that a President could become dictatorial. On 28 June 1992, over 90 per cent of votes were for the draft constitution. The constitution states that parliament, the Riigikogu, with 101 deputies, is the central political institution and the President performs a ceremonial role. It is strikingly similar to the German system. The President proposes a candidate as Prime Minister to parliament. If, after 14 days, he or she has not been accepted a new candidate is proposed. If he or she fails to gain support parliament takes over and appoints its candidate. The electoral system also mirrors the German. Small parties can be represented if a member wins in a constituency but need 5 per cent of the national vote in order to obtain additional seats based on party lists.

President Lennart Meri, elected in 1992, has always tried to expand the role of the presidency. Although chosen by parliament he has sought to play a more direct role in foreign policy and on matters such as the status of immigrants. In January 1994, however, he had to concede defeat in his efforts to influence the appointment of a new Prime Minister. He has been more successful in immigrant policy as he claims to represent all inhabitants of Estonia. All Estonian governments are coalition governments. The administration of Mart Laar, who came to power after the 1992 elections, succeeded in passing much reform legislation until it foundered in 1994 as further reform became more contentious. Laar was also involved in a scandal over the selling of the rubles which had been withdrawn from circulation in 1992 when Estonia adopted the kroon. Meri wanted Siim Kallas, the governor of the Bank of Estonia, as Prime Minister but parliament chose Andres Tarand. He was only a caretaker Prime Minister and Tiit Vähi headed a new coalition government after the March 1995 elections. He resigned in February 1997, following allegations of corruption, and was replaced by Mart Siimann. Right of centre parties won the March 1999 parliamentary election and Mart Laar, of the Pro Patria Union, became Prime Minister again. The 1999 election was contested by 13 parties, many of them coalitions, compared to 30 in 1995. This indicates gradual consolidation of the political spectrum but politics is still strongly personality-based.

Estonia's population has declined by 8.1 per cent since 1989, the year of the last census. Although the crude death rate peaked in 1994, and it has since declined considerably, it still exceeds the birth rate. Improved contraception and a trend towards small families combine to keep the birth rate below the reproduction rate. In 1999, Estonians made up 65.2 per cent of the population, with Russians accounting for 28.1 per cent.

LATVIA

In October 1991, the Latvian Supreme Council resolved that only those who had been citizens in 1940 could vote in elections. This disenfranchised about 25 per cent of the population – immigrants who were predominantly Russian. It also neatly ensured that ethnic Latvians had a near monopoly of political power. However much economic power rested with the immigrants. After the 1993 elections a compromise was proposed but, to the surprise of many, parliament reintroduced the 1922 Latvian constitution. The situation is complicated by the fact that the 1922 constitution does not mention legal institutions and the 1977 constitution of Soviet Latvia is valid if it does not contradict the 1922 constitution. The 1922 constitution provides the President with a mainly ceremonial role but, as in Estonia, President Guntis Ulmanis tried to expand his role. He wanted a constitutional amendment passed which would permit the direct election of the President rather than being appointed by parliament.

Parliament, the Saeima, with 100 deputies, is the central political institution. The President proposes a candidate as Prime Minister and parliament decides. Weak coalition governments have been the norm exacerbated by a conflict between the largest party, Latvia's Way, and the national bloc in parliament. In June 1995, the national bloc obtained a majority on Riga city council and used it as a platform to attack the government. Two parties, Harmony for Latvia, and Equal Rights consistently criticise the government on immigrant issues. This issue polarises parliament and population (Norgaard 1996: 72). The Latvian threshold for representation in parliament is 4 per cent. The country is divided into five large constituencies. Candidates may run in more than one constituency but take up only one seat in parliament. This is a useful tactic to attract votes to less well known party candidates.

The general election of September-October 1995 changed the political landscape. The largest number of votes went to the left-of-centre Saimnieks Democratic Party, followed by Latvia's Way. The shock result was the strong showing of the nationalist People's Movement for Latvia. In order to ensure the nationalists did not enter the government, the President nominated Andris Skele, non-party, as Prime Minister. He brought together a coalition government and embarked on economic reform. Skele proved unable to keep the coalition together and he gave way to Guntars Krasts, of For Fatherland and Freedom party. However Krasts proved a weak leader. Skele's liberal People's Party emerged as the largest party (24 seats) in the October 1998 general election but was excluded from the centre-right coalition government, under Vilis Kristopans, of Latvia's Way. In July 1999, Andris Skele took over as Prime Minister, heading a three-party centre-right coalition. He resigned, in April 2000, and was succeeded by Andris Berzins, a leading member of Latvia's Way.

Vaira Vike-Freiberga, a Canadian academic, was elected President, after seven inconclusive ballots in the Saeima, on 17 June 1999. She had only returned to Latvia in 1998. In 2000, she was rated Latvia's most popular politician.

The last Russian troops left Latvia in August 1994, but tension between Latvians and the large ethnic Russian population persisted. In early 1998, it almost developed into an economic war but the collapse of August 1998 in Russia led to both sides seeking mutually beneficial ties. Relations were further improved by Latvians voting, in October 1998, for amendments to the citizenship law, which opened up the way for the naturalisation of all Russian residents. In December 1999, Latvia revised its strict minority language law, under international pressure. An added incentive for non-Latvians to seek naturalisation is that their Soviet-era passports expired in 2000, thus rendering them stateless.

Latvia's population has been declining since independence, due to emigration and the falling birth rate. It was 2.42 million at the beginning of 2000 or 8 per cent lower than in 1992. In 1999, ethnic Latvians made up 55.7 per cent of the population, with Russians at 30.3 per cent the largest minority. One fifth of the population are over 60 years of age.

LITHUANIA

The two dominant political forces, the Lithuanian Democratic Labour Party (LDLP) and the popular front Sajudis, agreed quickly that a new constitution was needed. This revealed that there was no political problem over enfranchising Russian immigrants as they did not constitute any threat to ethnic Lithuanian dominance. Sajudis wanted a strong presidential system (one is tempted to comment that this fitted the personality of Vytautas Landsbergis) which permitted the President to dismiss the government and form a new one without parliamentary approval. He would have the right to veto any law passed by parliament. The LDPR, on the other hand, favoured a more parliamentary system where the President would be influential in foreign policy. Sajudis was sure it could win a presidential election but was wary of the LDPR, the successor to the communist party, which might mobilise parliament against the President and block reforms.

In the spring of 1992, Sajudis split into two factions and lost its majority in parliament. There was no decision on the presidency but Sajudis was able to collect the signatures necessary to force a referendum on 23 May 1992. In the run up, the Sajudis faction boycotted the work of parliament and paralysed it since the other deputies could not form the necessary quorum. Sajudis was demonstrating to voters that parliament was a weak body and therefore the country needed a strong presidency. A majority voted yes in the referendum but the turnout was below the 50 per cent of all voters needed to amend the constitution. LDLP recommended that its supporters simply stay at home. Sajudis and LDPD tried to reach a compromise before the parliamentary elections of 25 October 1992. The draft constitution was agreed, but only two weeks before the elections, and therefore there was no time for an informed public debate. Since Sajudis and the LDPD did not trust one another, the constitution is a balance between parliament, the Seimas, and the presidency. The President is directly elected and appoints the Prime Minister who is endorsed by parliament. The government has to present a working programme to parliament but if this is not approved the government has to be replaced. This system was tested in June 1994 when the Lithuanian Social Democratic Party collected the necessary one fifth of deputies' signatures to call for a vote of no confidence in the government. Before the vote the Prime Minister, Adolfas Slezevicius, re-organised the government with the consent of President Brazauskas, elected in February 1993. He had replaced over half the members of his government and this led parliament to request a new political programme. He survived the vote. The threshold for parliamentary representation is also 4 per cent but this does not apply to parties representing national minorities. Unlike Latvia, the 141 seats in parliament are filled by a mixed system of first past the post (71 seats) and proportional representation (70 seats). Each voter has two votes, one for a candidate in his or her constituency and one for a party list.

The norm in Lithuania has been for governments to stay in office a short time. Between 1990, when Lithuania declared independence, and 1995 there were six governments. Before 1992, Vytautas Landsbergis, leader of Sajudis and speaker of parliament, acted as President and dismissed

Prime Ministers when a problem arose. LDPD governments have been much more successful mainly due to the enormous popularity of President Brazauskas. According to the constitution the President is actively involved in foreign policy and may take the legislative initiative in the Seimas. The President has built up a group of advisers who act, in reality, as a shadow government. The President has not taken the initiative in foreign policy and has concentrated on domestic policy, especially the reform of the economy. He may appoint members of the board of the Central Bank and the establishment of the currency board, in 1994, increased his direct influence on economic affairs. Not surprisingly, the President and the LDPD government have filled many administrative positions with members of the old communist nomenklatura. Sajudis was bitterly disappointed at losing the presidency to Brazauskas and also its majority in parliament. As a result, parliament was polarised and Sajudis expended much energy in accusing the President and government of acting unconstitutionally. By 1995, this conflict had abated.

In December 1995, Lithuania was in political crisis after the collapse of two of its largest banks. It transpired that the Prime Minister and others had received preferential interest rates from one of the banks and had withdrawn their deposits before the collapse. The President had to force Adolfas Slezevicius to resign. In the October–November 1996 general election the Homeland Union (Sajudis) regained power by winning 70 seats in the Saeima. Gediminas Vagnorius was appointed Prime Minister.

In January 1998, Vytautas Landsbergis, the Homeland Union leader, was defeated in a presidential election by Valdas Adamkus, born in Lithuania but a US national. Relations between the President and the Prime Minister deteriorated rapidly and Vagnorius resigned, in April 1999. He was succeeded by Rolandas Paksas, a former mayor of Vilnius and a Homeland Union member. His coalition government gradually fell apart and he resigned, in October 1999. Andrius Kubilius, of the Homeland Union, took over, facing severe economic problems.

Lithuania, with 3.7 million, is the most populous of the Baltic States but this represents a decline of 1.2 per cent since 1992. Average life expectancy reached its lowest ebb in 1994, 62.7 years for men and 74.9 for women. This rose to 66.5 and 76.9 years in 1998. The main reason for the wide discrepancy in the life expectancy of males and females is the high alcohol intake of males. Lithuania is the most ethnically homogeneous of the region: in 1997, Lithuanians made up 81.6 per cent of the population. There were 8.2 per cent Russians and 6.9 per cent Poles. About one in eight of the population are over 65 years of age.

A major problem throughout the Baltic States has been recruiting competent civil servants who are capable of adjusting to the new ethos. Pay is not as high as in the private economy and this led to many qualified personnel leaving. In Estonia, civil servants are ethnic Estonian and are young. This mirrors governments which are also full of young people. In Latvia, young ethnic Latvians are recruited. Corruption is a widespread problem throughout the region. Loyalty in Estonia and Latvia is to the system but in Lithuania it is to the government. Making bureaucrats accountable to the public is an uphill task as the previous culture was one in which the public was ignored. The language law only applies to public sector jobs in Lithuania but in Latvia and Estonia it also applies to the private sector. Immigrants see it as a way of keeping them out of many jobs but the language requirement is not always applied. Narva, north east Estonia, is predominantly Russian and continues to communicate in Russian. A more liberal language law was passed by the Latvian parliament in December 1999.

In Estonia and Latvia, Russian and other non-citizen economic elites have been almost disenfranchised politically. These elites are quite strong in Latvia and have sought to strengthen the presidency as a way round the problem. Since they cannot influence parliament from within they have attempted through bribery to influence the drafting of legislation and to gain other concessions. A stronger presidency in Latvia might mean that Russian businessmen, very influential in industry and finance, could circumvent parliament. Russian speakers are now represented in the Estonian parliament by deputies who are bilingual in Estonian and Russian.

The Baltic States are the only part of the former Soviet Union where political parties and movements play a significant role in national life. Political parties have passed through two phases: before and after independence. Before independence there were popular fronts, independence movements and the communist party (CPSU). After independence the popular fronts broke down into parties, the communist party almost disappeared and new parties emerged. In Estonia, the communists formed the Estonian Labour Party but failed to get into parliament. In Latvia, most communists joined other parties but the remainder split into Equal Rights and the Latvian Democratic Labour Party. Equal Rights is dominated by ethnic Russians and advocates citizenship for all residents at independence. Its leader was Alfreds Rubriks who was deprived of his seat as he had supported the attempted coup d'état in August 1991. The party process is different in Lithuania since the communists successfully transformed themselves into a democratic labour party. In December 1990, Algirdas Brazauskas renamed the communist party of Lithuania the Lithuanian Democratic Labour Party (LDLP) and took over the organisation and resources of the communist party. In the parliamentary elections of 1992 the LDPD won a majority of seats and, in January 1993, Algirdas Brazauskas was elected President. Hence there are no communists in the Estonian parliament, many in the Latvian parliament but the Lithuanian parliament is dominated by former communists.

The Baltic States have a plenitude of political parties but less than one per cent of the population belongs to a political party. This reflects the lack of public trust in parties, parliaments and governments. Parties find it difficult to represent interest groups as these groups are in the process of formation. The exception to this is the LDPD which has about 15,000 members. No other party in the Baltic States has even 1000 members. In Estonia, coalition governments have tended to move leftwards in response to the desire of voters for social protection against the rigours of an emerging market economy. Latvian coalition governments have been mainly centrist groupings.

Laws on citizenship have led to acrimonious disputes except in Lithuania where it was decided, in 1989, that citizenship be granted to all who had been citizens in 1940 and their descendants. All others who were permanent residents and had a fixed income also qualified. According to the citizenship law of December 1991 anyone who has been resident for ten years and has a fixed income may become a citizen. Almost all Lithuanian residents are now citizens. Vilnius was multi-national and only acquired a Lithuanian majority in 1997. In 2000, there were Russian and Polish minorities of about 17 per cent each and a Jewish minority of one per cent. The majority of these Jews had immigrated from Russia as almost all the native Lithuanian Jews, 220,000, were murdered during the German occupation of 1940–44. Over 17,000 Lithuanians helped the Nazis exterminate them despite Lithuania being a haven of tolerance before 1940. Several thousand Lithuanians risked their lives by not reporting hidden Jews.

In Latvia and Estonia it was quite different. In 1991, about 48 per cent of the population in Latvia were non-Latvian and in Estonia it was 38 per cent. Both states believed that these rates were far too high if their nation was to flourish. Many Latvian nationalists spoke of 20–25 per cent non-Latvians as the norm. President Ulmanis of Latvia refused to sign the citizenship law passed by parliament on 22 June 1994. He found it discriminated too much against non-Latvians. This was to replace the provisional law on citizenship of 15 October 1991 which had left about 700,000 residents without citizenship. This meant that few non-Latvians could participate in parliamentary and local elections. Nationalists won local elections in May 1993 in five of Latvia's seven largest cities, including Riga, where non-Latvians constituted the majority. An amended law was passed on 22 July 1994 which replaced the restrictive quota system with a multi-stage process for applications. In November 1998, 11,432 persons had been naturalised since independence. Ukrainian, Polish and Lithuanian minority schools have been set up. The Riga Jewish secondary school was the first non-Russian minority educational institution to be founded in Latvia and the first such school on the territory of the former Soviet Union.

In Estonia, parliament decided in November 1991 to reintroduce the former law on citizenship. Hence pre-war inhabitants and their descendants became citizens and the other third of the population was faced with a naturalisation process. This meant that immigrants could not become citizens before the spring of 1993. Hence Russians could not vote in the June 1992 referendum on the constitution or the subsequent parliamentary elections. Towns such as Narva in north east Estonia had non-citizen majorities of over 90 per cent and this presented problems for local elections. Estonia promised the Council of Europe that non-citizens could vote and hold office. After admission, in the summer of 1993, Estonia reneged on this promise. A law on naturalisation eventually became effective on 1 April 1995. It excludes those who served in the Soviet armed or security forces. About 50,000 non-Estonians had been naturalised by March 1995 and were able to vote in the elections. The Russian bloc succeeded in getting six members (out of 101) elected to the Riigikogu (Norgaard 1996: 202). Russians also have the right to vote in Russian presidential elections. In July 1996, they voted overwhelmingly, 77 per cent, for Gennady Zyuganov. By November 1998, 105,032 persons had been naturalised, the overwhelming majority being ethnic Russians. In 2000, of the half million non-Estonians, over 112,000 had been naturalised. A further 80,000 non-Estonians hold Estonian citizenship by birth. Half of the remaining 300,000 non-Estonians carrying aliens' passports live in Estonia with residence permits because they are citizens of the Russian Federation.

ECONOMIC SUCCESS AND FAILURE

The economic chaos which swept over the Soviet Union hit the Baltic States hard (see Tables 12.1 and 12.2). One of the conclusions they drew from it was to introduce their own currencies swiftly. This was not the conventional wisdom of the IMF and other international institutions. However as history has shown, the IMF has often been wrong. Estonia introduced the kroon in June 1992. It was tied to the German mark at 8 kroons = 1DM. It has maintained this rate ever since. This under-valued the kroon by about 600 per cent and was to enable the currency to resist the inevitable inflation which followed the liberalisation of prices. It was intended to make Estonian goods competitive in foreign markets; it also made foreign goods very expensive in Estonia and thereby pro-tected the fledgling domestic economy. Monetary policy comes under a currency board which is not subordinate to the Central Bank. The currency board has to exchange all the national currency it is offered into a reserve currency. Hence the national currency is fully backed by foreign reserves and the money supply only increases as the foreign reserves increase. Inflation was 1069 per cent in 1992 but this dropped to 28 per cent in 1994.

Lithuania also has a currency board, adopted in March 1994, but has found the transition more difficult to manage. This was partly due to polit-ical interference and stabilisation was not achieved until well into 1993. Inflation was 1021 per cent in 1992 but this fell to 45.1 per cent in 1994. The talonas was introduced in October 1992. Then the currency board introduced the litas at the fixed rate of 4 litas to the US dollar. Latvia, in contrast to Estonia and Lithuania, has adopted a standard central bank policy, based on the German Bundesbank. The Central Bank is only per-mitted to finance the budget deficit within tight limits. In July 1992 the Latvian ruble was introduced at the rate of one Latvian ruble to one Russian ruble. Rampant inflation in Russia caused the Latvian ruble to be revalued constantly. In October 1993 the lat became the only national legal tender. The exchange rate is 0.5 lat to the US dollar. Inflation was brought down from 958 per cent in 1992 to 35.9 per cent in 1994.

Estonia has been the most successful in curbing inflation and balanc-ing the budget. In Estonia and Latvia state subsidies to companies have been abolished while in Lithuania some large enterprises have gained concessions by postponing tax payments. Estonia adopted a standard rate of tax of 26 per cent in December 1993 and the following year Latvia set its rate at 25 per cent. In Lithuania, 1995 legislation put the ceiling of personal income tax at 35 per cent. Estonia liberalised its prices most quickly and by mid-1994 only a few public services were still controlled. From 1993, almost all goods could be imported and exported without tariffs. In Latvia price liberalisation began in July 1992 and all import controls were lifted in early 1992. Some export duties have to be paid.

Lobbying by farmers' groups resulted in import duties on some agricultural products being raised in June 1994. Lithuania also liberalised its prices in 1992 and the only subsidised good is heating. In foreign trade it is much more restrictive than the other two states, especially in agricultural goods. Given the weight of agriculture in the economy this is not surprising. Banking is strictly regulated in Estonia and almost to the same extent in Lithuania. However in Latvia regulation is light and, as a consequence, Riga is the leading financial centre in the Baltic states. The concomitant of this is that there are financial scandals from time to time. One of the biggest was in June 1995 when the Bank Baltija collapsed with debts of $300 million (Norgaard 1996: 132).

Estonia set up a central agency to privatise state assets. Small companies were sold at public auction (most were sold by late 1992) but medium and large companies were put out to international tender. A system of vouchers was used to privatise houses, flats, farms and companies expropriated during the communist era. From mid-1994, the vouchers could be used to purchase shares in companies, invest in investment funds or to acquire state bonds. Latvia has proceeded more slowly than Estonia but this is due to the fact that it was last to hold parliamentary elections and to pass a citizenship law. Initially ministries were responsible for privatising enterprises under their control but a privatisation agency was set up in 1994 to take over privatisation of large companies. Small companies are auctioned off. Vouchers were issued in 1992 to those whose families had been resident in Latvia in 1940 and according to the number of years the person had worked for the Latvian state. Immigrants after 1945, consequently, received fewer vouchers.

Lithuania has adopted a more egalitarian approach than the other states. In 1991, all Lithuanians received vouchers which could be redeemed to acquire a house or flat, land or shares. After the victory of the LDLP in 1992 management and employees were afforded certain privileges during the privatisation of their company. However this did not lead to many companies being privatised and in January 1995 privatisation was to be by cash sale. Few foreign investors were attracted. Restitution has proceeded differently in the three states. In Lithuania, only residents qualified and due to the small Russian minority it proceeded quite smoothly. Estonia has been beset with problems especially in agriculture. In Latvia, the process has been more rapid due mainly to the fact that in agriculture it was handed over to the farmers themselves. Another reason for the speed of rural restitution is that farmers are predominantly ethnic Latvians. The problem is much more complex in industry where ethnic Russians dominate.

GDP declined in the region in 1992 and 1993 by between 25 and 50 per cent with Lithuania coming off worst. Industry suffered badly. In Estonia, the drop was 39 per cent in 1992 and 26 per cent in 1993. In Latvia, it was 34.8 and 23 per cent and in Lithuania, 48.5 and 47 per cent. Estonian industry grew 2 per cent in 1994 and this contributed to GDP growth of 5 per cent. In Latvia, GDP growth in 1994 was zero and in Lithuania 0.6 per cent. This striking turnaround was due to the expansion of services, small private companies and foreign trade. Over the years 1995–99, Latvia and Lithuania managed a respectable 3 per cent GDP growth. In Latvia, inflation, over the same period, averaged 11.8 per cent and in Lithuania, 15.8 per cent. Estonia achieved more. Over the years 1995–99, average annual GDP growth was 4.4 per cent. Over the same period, inflation averaged 15.0 per cent annually. However, in 1999, inflation was down to 3.3 per cent.

Real wages in Estonia declined by 36 per cent in 1991 and 38 per cent in 1992 but rose by 6 per cent in 1993. In 1994, about 10 per cent of families were very poor. However the average wage has increased dramatically since 1995 when it was 2395 kroons ($140) a month. In June 2000, it was 5031 ($288). The best paid are securities brokers, at 2.2 times the national average, and the worst off are hunters and farmers, at 55.4 and 55.7 per cent respectively. The situation in Latvia and Lithuania was more serious than in Estonia. The average monthly wage in Latvia is the lowest of the Baltic countries and a large part of the population regards itself as living below the poverty line. One of the consequences of the downturn in Lithuania is that the suicide rate there is the highest in the former Soviet Union. In 2000, the minimum monthly wage in Lithuania was $130 while the average monthly wage was $274. It is a sore point among Lithuanians that whereas GPD per head in Poland is 30 per cent higher than in 1989, in Lithuania output is well below its 1989 level. Lithuania was only just recovering in 2000 from the August 1998 Russian financial collapse.

Market reforms were easier to implement in Estonia than in the other states. The industrial sector was small and dominated by Russians. However they were disenfranchised and could not vote in elections to register their opposition to privatisation. Likewise they had no redress against the tight monetary and fiscal policy. The economic decision makers could follow IMF advice but the impoverished Estonian workers and farmers, the main victims of the free market and liberal foreign trade, hit back in 1995 when they helped to vote the Mart Laar government out of office.

In Latvia, over half of the immigrant population had been disenfranchised and this meant that they had to adopt wildcat privatisation in order to cling on to their enterprises. Before the regularised privatisation of large companies commenced, about 50 per cent of industry was in private hands. This has promoted conflict between an ethnic Latvian administration and Russian-dominated industry. Baltic governments have long feared that Russian political dominance would be replaced by Russian economic dominance. Hence they have striven to attract western investment to prevent Russian investors acquiring assets. Native capital is in short supply. Sajudis pushed transition to the market very rapidly, especially in agriculture, and this was the main reason why they lost to the former communists. The social costs were perceived to be too high by Lithuanian voters. In 2000, about 70 per cent of industry was private with many companies sold to westerners. The main legacy of the Soviet period is a huge energy sector. In 1999 the Mazeikiu oil refinery was sold to a US company. Lithuania has agreed to close one of the two large nuclear reactors at Ignalinia as part of its drive to qualify for EU membership. Much agricultural land still lies idle because collective farms were dissolved before private owners were agreed. Estonia is the most western-oriented mainly due to its close ties with Finland. Latvia has been developing a closer relationship with Sweden.

Roving bandits, so prevalent in Russia, have not had the same success in the Baltic states. These countries do not possess the mineral and hydrocarbon wealth which has spawned so many roving bandit careers. There are a few Baltic roving bandits, mostly Russian. Bank scandals in Latvia and Lithuania reveal that they had penetrated banking. Tight state control in Estonia effectively excludes them. The collapse of Bank Baltija, in 1995, was due to the illegal sale of assets to a Moscow bank in return for Russian state bonds which were not worth their face value. This was a classic roving bandit scam. Roving bandits are to be found in the black economy, especially in the transit trade involving the illegal export of Russian output. The prime difference between Russia and the Baltic States is that whereas the roving bandits took over the Russian state they have had limited impact on government in the Baltic region. This is a major reason for the success story of these states.

SECURITY

The Baltic States fear the Russian bear. When it growls everyone shivers. Security and foreign policy since 1991 have been a search for protection against the Russian bear. Militarily they are dwarfs when confronting the might of Russia. They need a giant partner, NATO, which will provide them with an umbrella. The other solution is to become a member of the European Union because its philosophy is that an attack on one member is an attack on all.

What lessons can the Baltic States draw from Russian policy in the near abroad? Russia is too economically weak to achieve its policy objectives. Aspiration and reality are quite far apart. CIS countries have success-fully resisted closer integration and western presence in the region has influenced the agenda. Russian nationalists refer to the Baltic States as the near abroad but the Russian government seldom does. There have been notable exceptions. The otherwise mild-mannered Andrei Kozyrev was given to using abusive language about the Baltic States and spoke of 'apartheid' and 'ethnic cleansing' to express his opposition to poli-cies aimed at ejecting some Russian residents. On such occasions he placed the region in the near abroad. An unkind critic would say that Andrei only growled at those states which could not growl back.

Lithuania is concerned about the Russian enclave, Kaliningrad oblast, dominated by the Russian military (formerly the north east part of German East Prussia). There is an agreement which permits Russian troops to cross Lithuania entering and leaving the area. The oblast is controlled by roving bandits with Moscow exercising a light touch. It is a special economic zone but it has attracted little official business. The most profitable unofficial business is smuggling vodka and cigarettes (worth an estimated $200 million in 2000) to Poland. The next is to smuggle girls to the west to work as prostitutes. Average incomes, in 2000, were three times higher in neighbouring Lithuania and six times higher in Poland. Aids and TB infections are among the highest in Russia. The oblast cannot afford sewage plants and pumps untreated waste into the Baltic.

Lithuania established good working relations with Russia after 1992 and this led to the withdrawal of Russia troops in August 1993. Despite this, Lithuania spends more per capita on defence than the other two Baltic countries.

The Baltic States immediately after independence sought to join inter-national bodies in order to internationalise their security concerns. They joined the UN and the CSCE (now OSCE) in September 1991; the Council of the Baltic Sea states in March 1992; the North Atlantic Cooperation Council in December 1992; the Council of Europe in the summer of 1993; and became associate members of the EU in the summer of 1994. They also had access to the West European Union permanent council.

Lithuania was the first of the states to apply formally for NATO membership, on 4 January 1994. A week later a common statement supported partnership for peace membership as a route for developing cooperation between NATO and the Baltic states. The establishment of the Baltic Battalion (Baltbat), in September 1994, was the first tangible fruit of this relationship. It is coordinated by Denmark and trains in Latvia. The Balts were disappointed, in September 1996, when NATO declared that the Baltic States would not be among the first wave of new entrants. Some would like to see the states combining into a military alliance but all that is desired at present is cooperation. Support for a military alliance can be articulated in the Baltic Assembly but its resolutions have no binding power on the three governments. The Baltic Council of Ministers, set up in June 1994, also provides a forum. An argument against a military alliance is that NATO does not admit defence blocs, only individual countries.

EU membership is viewed as critical for the political and economic development of the states. The states signed free trade agreements with the EU which entered into force in January 1995, joined the European stability pact in the spring of 1995, had association agreements from the summer of 1995 and applied officially for EU membership at the end of 1995. The parliaments have been engaging in the harmonisation of legislation which is necessary to become members of the EU. The first stage involves 1300 EU directives. One of the fruits of this was the free trade agreement which formed a single market for agricultural and industrial goods. The EU is reluctant to provide a list of criteria which have to be met for membership. However it has stated that stable borders are essential. This presents a problem for Estonia because Russia and it cannot agree if the treaty of Tartu (1920) is still in force. It embraces more territory than present-day Estonia. The EU does not want to take on another unresolved problem, that of the Russian minority in Estonia which regards Russia as its motherland. Another bone of contention between Estonia and Russia is the support for Chechnya articulated by Estonian deputies.

A source of ongoing tension between the Baltic States and Moscow is the very different attitude to the Second World War. Russia, as the main successor state to the Soviet Union, has never recognised the illegality of its occupation of the three Baltic States in 1940. Russia has only grudgingly acknowledged the post-war deportations of Baltic nationals. Russians in the Baltic regard their victory over Germany in 1945 as one of their greatest national achievements. However, the Baltic peoples welcomed the Nazis as liberators in 1941 when they invaded the Soviet

Union. They also provided troops to aid the German war effort and this included the SS. From their point of view they were engaged in a grand war of liberation. Consequently these states are reluctant to prosecute SS veterans and others who served in punitive battalions. They murdered many Jews, Russians, and others. There have been parades of SS veterans in Latvia and, in Estonia, in the national history museum, in Parnu, there is an exhibit which records the feats of the SS and Adolf Hitler. At the same time trials are underway of Russians accused of collaborating with the Soviet Union. In Latvia, the leader of a Red Army partisan band is accused of killing Latvians during his engagements with the Wehrmacht. Not surprisingly, this deeply offends Moscow.

13

WILL THE IMAMS RETURN?
THE COMMONWEALTH OF
INDEPENDENT STATES

TABLES 13.1 TO 13.3 RECORD THE Presidents of the CIS, the GDP of CIS states 1992–96 and agricultural output for the same period.

Georgia has experienced the most rapid decline in GDP since 1991 (see Table 13.2). Ukraine is in an even more parlous situation than Russia. On these statistics Uzbekistan and Turkmenistan have performed best of all but they began at a modest level in 1991.

MIGRATION

Table 13.4 shows arrivals and departures in the CIS, 1991–96.

Western diplomats privately put the number of departures from Azerbaijan at 1.5 million, from Armenia at 2 million and from Georgia at 1 million. This suggests that Azerbaijan and Georgia have lost about a fifth of their population and Armenia over a half (*The Economist,* 19–25 August 2000). The ambitious and qualified are going. A local joke is that the DHL minority – decent, honest and law-abiding – is an endangered species in the Caucasus.

BELARUS

Belarus enjoyed the highest per capita income of any Soviet republic in 1990, followed by Latvia and Russia. In 1989, 77.9 per cent of the population were Belarusians and 13.2 per cent were Russians. This level of ethnic homogeneity protected it from the ethnic tension which exploded in other republics. The downside of this was that there was a low level of national consciousness compounded by the fact that most Belarusians spoke Russian as their first language. The Chernobyl disaster of 1986 hit Belarus hard with over 70 per cent of radioactivity falling on the republic. About a quarter of the most fertile agricultural land was lost.

Stanislau Shushkevich, of the Popular Front, replaced Mikalai Dzemyanti, chair of the Supreme Soviet, sacked because he had supported the attempted coup against Gorbachev. Shushkevich favoured a move towards a liberal economy and a parliamentary democracy. However the overwhelmingly communist legislature advocated a strong presidency along Russian lines. The new constitution, adopted in March 1993, provided Belarus with a strong presidency and a new bicameral legislature. Shushkevich wanted Belarus to be a neutral country but most deputies proposed that Belarus sign the CIS treaty on collective security. This occurred in January 1994 and resulted in the removal of Shushkevich. Myacheslau Gryb took over but only as caretaker until a presidential election was held. Alyaksandr Lukashenka, a former collective farm chair, was the winner. He was determined to downgrade parliament and had many confrontations with the legislature. Confrontation with the President continued after the parliamentary elections of December 1995 which saw many independent deputies elected. Lukashenka circumvented opposition in parliament by holding two referendums, in May 1995 and November 1996. They increased the powers of the President, supported closer integration with Russia and restricted the private ownership of land. Parliament attempted on numerous occasions to impeach the President but always failed. In May 1997, when pro-Lukashenka deputies achieved a majority for the first time, the President dissolved parliament and set up the National Assembly, full of his nominees. This brought the period of dual power, which began in 1991, to an end. The constitutional court, which in the past had often ruled that the President's actions were unconstitutional, was packed with presidential appointments. Opposition parties now operate outside parliament, opposition newspapers are printed abroad and the country has one of the highest ratios of police and military to the population which are used by the President to suppress demonstrations and dissent. Using the Russian analogy, the communist roving bandits were replaced by a democratic leader but the roving bandits united against him and removed him. Lukashenka was a roving bandit in 1994 but gradually became the leading roving bandit and as such became an autocrat. Belarus is the only state which has passed from the disintegrating authoritarianism of Gorbachev to the beginnings of democracy and then back to authoritarianism.

The Belarusian economy made quite a promising start to the 1990s but the advent of Lukashenka reversed the trend towards liberalisation and reintroduced a modified version of the command economy. The economy has been in decline ever since. The financial services industry and the national bank of Belarus, by 1998, were under state control. In 1996, the registration of new enterprises ceased and all existing firms were required to reapply for registration. This drove many thriving businesses into the black economy. In January 1998, the President acquired the power to intervene in the management of businesses. He can veto any fundamental change, including appointments. In 1997, over 65 per cent of prices were state controlled. Privatisation has been put in reverse and by the late 1990s only 12 per cent of property and 10 per cent of the labour force were private. Inflation rose from 247.5 per cent in 1991 to 2096.5 per cent in 1993, dropped to 2059.9 in 1994 and in 1997 was 163.1 per cent. The post-1994 figures are Lukashenka figures and as a result some economists believe they understate considerably the real situation. Belarus used to export food to other republics but by the late 1990s the state's agriculture was only producing about half the food needed to sustain the population. As in Russia vegetables are almost all grown privately. During the early 1990s many farms were privatised but Lukashenka reversed this and today only about one per cent of agricultural land is privately farmed. The decline in living standards of the population has been precipitous. Whereas 13.1 per cent of the population was calculated to be on or below the poverty line in 1991 this had risen to an alarming 80.4 per cent of the population in 1995. Almost all family incomes are spent on food.

Belarus produces about 15 per cent of its demand for oil and 3 per cent of its natural gas needs. The shortfalls are met by imports from Russia. The Druzhba oil pipeline en route to Ventspils, Latvia, runs through Belarus and the Northern Lights gas pipeline crosses Belarus to Poland. As a consequence there are oil and natural gas refineries whose capacity far exceeds Belarus's own needs.

According to some scientists, only about 3 per cent of Belarusian children are completely healthy. This is a legacy of Chernobyl but the state does not allocate sufficient resources to health. There are gloomy prognostications about the gene pool of Belarusians being irreparably damaged. The fertility rate declined from 1.8 in 1991 to 1.3 in 1996. The population has not declined so far and in 1997 was almost the same as in 1990.

Belarus is one of the most stable societies in the CIS with most citizens having a limited awareness of national identity. About 78 per cent of the population are Belarusian but they are almost indistinguishable from the Russians and Ukrainians. They all speak Russian.

Belarus under Lukashenka has aspired to union with Russia and in April 1996 Presidents Yeltsin and Lukashenka signed a treaty establishing the Community of Russia and Belarus. In April 1997, they signed another treaty which transformed this into the Union of Russia and Belarus. On 25 December 1998, they signed another agreement which envisages supranational bodies to oversee economic and defence policies. The union has not been consummated because of the economic cost to Russia. One of the reasons why Moscow has walked in tandem with Belarus is that Belarus borders on a NATO country, Poland. There are very good security reasons why the two countries should act in unison. There is a heavy Russian military presence in Belarus and they are expanding their facilities there. In May 1999, President Lukashenka declared that Belarus had kept its nuclear missile facilities even though it had given up its atomic warheads. He said he regretted giving up the nuclear weapons in 1996.

UKRAINE

Tables 13.5 and 13.6 give statistics for industrial and agricultural production in Ukraine and its regions, 1992–97.

Leonid Kravchuk, chair of the Supreme Soviet, made a seamless move from being a conservative communist to being a Ukrainian nationalist and won the presidential election in December 1991. The national democrats grouped in the popular movement for restructuring (Rukh) were bitterly disappointed but discovered that nationalism was only strong in west Ukraine. The main reason for this was its recent history. Part of the Austro-Hungarian empire until 1918, it became part of Poland and was then incorporated in the Soviet Union, in 1939. President Kravchuk's term of office (1991–94) was marked by instability as clans fought for influence. There were three Prime Ministers but no constitution to resolve conflicts. In such a climate there could be no successful economic reform. Indeed, Ukraine was appalled by Gaidar's shock therapy and was certain it would fail. The majority of the elites banked on Russia returning to a state-dominated economy. Russian privatisation found few imitators in Kyiv. Dual power, the President and the parliament, was the norm with regional elites acting in their own interests. Miners' strikes in June 1993 were only resolved by the promise of parliamentary and presidential elections. Elections to the new 450-member Supreme Council (renamed the Narodna Rada or People's Council under the new constitution) were held in March 1994 but the national democrats and pro-reform groups were again disappointed when the results were declared. Political parties were not very important and over half of those elected were independents. Parliament was split between the communists and their allies, the centre (representing many of the former nomenklaturists) and the national democratic groups. Voters had the opportunity to elect a President in the summer of 1994 and Leonid Kuchma just beat the incumbent President, polling 52 per cent of the votes. To an outsider, there was very little to choose between the candidates or their programmes. Kuchma has implemented some reform and has moved the country away from dependence on Russia. He also forced through the new constitution, in June 1996, which affords considerable power to the President, makes Ukrainian the only official language and declared Ukraine as a unitary state with Crimea as an autonomous republic within it. The unitary status of Ukraine has avoided the regional conflict which has occurred in Russia.

Kuchma has kept parliament in check and has sacked two Prime Ministers who presumably opposed his centralising tendencies. One of them, Pavlo Lazarenko, skilfully used energy export licences to enrich himself. He acquired property in the US and Switzerland – a highly successful roving bandit indeed. New parliamentary elections in March 1998 changed little. Half of the 450 seats went to the winners in the 225 electoral districts and the other half according to party lists (parties qualified if they scored more than 4 per cent of the total vote), almost a carbon copy of the Russian Duma. The centre again held the balance of power. In October 1999, Leonid Kuchma was re-elected President.

The regional factor is important in Ukraine. It is usual to divide the country in two, along the river Dniepr, between a western region, ethnically Ukrainian and leaning towards the west, and an eastern region, industrialised and Russified. A more precise approach would identify five regions. The eastern region consists of the heavily Russian oblasts of Donetsk and Luhansk which traditionally have had close links with Russia. Part of the coal-mining Donbass is in Russia. The eastern region declined rapidly during the 1990s and hence is wary of moves towards the market. The western region is the centre of Ukrainian nationalism and is dominated by agriculture and light industry. It favours closer relations with the west. The large central region speaks Ukrainian but Russian is the main language in Kyiv. It is moderate politically and has fared better economically than the east. In the south Ukrainian national consciousness is low and is more urbanised. Crimea only became part of Ukraine in 1954 and this has led to much tension with Russia. This was exacerbated by the fact that the Russian Navy's main base in the Black Sea is Sevastopol. The issue was resolved in March 1995 when Kyiv suspended the Crimean constitution, abolished the Crimean presidency and ended all talk about joining Russia. Crimea acquired a new constitution in late 1995. Russia acquiesced as it did not wish to fuel the aspirations of separatists within Russia.

Despite its declared aim of becoming a nuclear-free state in 1990 Ukraine held on to its nuclear weapons as a bargaining chip in its relations with Russia and the United States. It also wanted guarantees that if it returned its nuclear weapons to Russia they would not be used against it in the future. Ukraine also asked for financial assistance. In January 1994, it signed an agreement with Russia and the United States in which it undertook to give up its nuclear weapons and was rewarded with $1.2 billion to cover the costs of dismantling them. This was in marked contrast to Kazakhstan and Belarus which gave up their nuclear weapons without a whimper. President Kuchma has steered a middle course between Russia and the west. Ukraine was the first country to enter a partnership for peace with NATO. By 1997, the IMF had extended loans worth about $3.5 billion and only Israel and Egypt receive more US aid than Ukraine.

Ukraine has oil but about 80 per cent of its needs have to be met by imports. It has reserves of natural gas but at present it imports almost all its needs from Russia and Central Asia. Ukraine has five nuclear power plants but is planning to close down Chernobyl altogether.

MOLDOVA

When Moldova became independent in 1991 it was the first time in its history that it had enjoyed this status. Its elites were faced with formidable problems which pulled it in various directions. What should its relations be with Ukraine, Romania and Russia? A primary task was to foster a Moldovan national identity but how could this be done given the ethnic mix of the population? A referendum was held to adopt a new constitution in July 1994. It did not confirm a presidential system as Mircea Snegur, President since 1991, would have preferred. It avoided concentrating too much power in the hands of the President. The Russian experience was a major factor in this decision. Snegur did not win a second term in the presidential election of 1 December 1996, being defeated by Petru Lucinschi, like Snegur a member of the former communist nomenklatura. The President chooses the Prime Minister-designate and then elaborates a draft programme with him. The programme and ministers have to be confirmed by at least 52 of the 101 deputies in parliament. Deputies are elected by proportional representation according to party lists. In the elections of February 1994 the democratic agrarian party won 56 seats. However in the 1998 elections the communists gained the largest bloc, 40 seats. The centrist bloc, which supports President Lucinschi, acquired 24 seats. Lucinschi retained the Prime Minister, Ion Ciubuk, but the economic crisis led to his resignation on 1 February 1999. Ion Sturza formed a coalition administration from all the non-communist groups in parliament. President Lucinschi, like his predecessor, eventually concluded that a presidential republic was needed but a referendum in May 1999 was void because the minimum 60 per cent turnout to validate it was not achieved. This underlined the increasing political apathy which is exacerbated by the selection of deputies according to party lists. This means that no deputy identifies with a particular constituency or interest group.

In 1990, those who were opposed to union or close association with Romania, in Transdniestria, set up the Dniestr Moldavian republic in Tiraspol. About 48 per cent of the population were Russian and Ukrainian and 40 per cent Moldovan. When the Gagauz, also opposed to closer Romanian ties, became autonomous in March 1992, the same status was offered the Transdniestrians. They refused. The civil war in the summer of 1992 led to the intervention of General Aleksandr Lebed. The republic today imposes import duties on goods from the rest of Moldova, regarding them as foreign goods. About 40 per cent of the industry of the Soviet period is located in the republic. Compromise appears as far away as ever.

Moldova is energy-dependent on Russia and Ukraine and in no position to pay for oil and gas in hard currency as demanded by suppliers. Moldova has much good land but the market for agricultural products in Russia and Ukraine is depressed. The political uncertainty has reduced foreign direct investment to a trickle. The Russian financial crisis of August 1998 hit Moldova hard and increased the economic gloom which now envelops the republic.

THE CAUCASUS

Tables 13.7 and 13.8 show the real GNP and gross industrial output for the Caucasus, 1991–97.

There are over 3000 km of borders in the Caucasus but only the shortest, the 9 km stretch between Azerbaijan's Nakhichevan region and Turkey, is truly friendly. The two countries have a special relationship which embraces language, culture, economics, politics and defence. The Caucasus is a transit route from east to west and should bring Azerbaijan, Armenia and Georgia closer together. Russian is the lingua franca of the region and there are common economic problems to be resolved. The Caucasus is the route out for oil and gas around the Caspian Sea. Reserves are put at between 18 billion and 35 billion barrels or America and the North Sea combined. It could triple if the finds off the Kazakh coast are confirmed. Despite this most borders in the Caucasus divide rather than unite. When relations are good, as between Azerbaijan and Georgia, roads and communications are poor. It is easier to fly in from Istanbul or Moscow than from regional capitals.

Armenia and Georgia are Orthodox Christian and Azerbaijan is Muslim. Russian immigration in these states has been limited and this ensures that the titular nationality easily dominates. Only in Georgia have there been separatist tendencies and this led to much civil strife after 1992. The conflict over Nagorno-Karabakh between Azerbaijan and Armenia has ensured that the cooperation necessary to develop the region has not been forthcoming. The region has stunning natural beauty and therefore great tourist potential but the strife and political uncertainty have killed off interest.

Strongly nationalist candidates were elected Presidents of Georgia and Armenia, Zviad Gamsakhurdia, in May 1991, in Georgia and Levon Ter-Petrosyan, in October 1991, in Armenia. The more moderate Abulfaz Elchibey became President of Azerbaijan in June 1992. Gamsakhurdia'a autocratic style led to his having to flee Tbilisi in January 1992 and two war lords vied for power. Gamsakhurdia committed suicide in November 1993. In March 1992, Eduard Shevardnadze, Gorbachev's foreign minister, became chair of the State Council which ruled Georgia after Gamsakhurdia's departure. He displayed an iron hand and was elected President in October 1992 and re-elected in November 1995 and 1999. There have been several well-planned attempts on his life, the most recent one being in February 1998. Then the driver had the presence of mind to drive on after a rocket hit the engine of the car thus taking the President out of the firing line of the waiting assassins. Georgian sources blame the Russians but this does not mean that the Russian government was involved. After the attack Mercedes-Benz provided Shevardnadze with two armoured cars. He expects more attempts on his life.

Civil war has reduced the very beautiful Abkhazia to pauperism. Its President, Vladislav Ardzinba, even thinks this is a virtue. He sees poverty as the mother of invention. Its capital, Sukhumi, is unique in Europe in not having Internet access, no mobile phones and no hotels. In one day in 1992 the civil war cost it all its main cultural buildings and they still lie in ruins. There is no work, no hope, nothing but apathy and the airport is full of bits of crashed aircraft. It does not occur to anyone to clean up the mess. Energy is supplied by Russia but the ambitious have left for Georgia or Russia and the republic is full of the young and the old. The local UN and OSCE peacekeeping missions provide the only worthwhile work in town and the locals have renamed them piece-keepers, ensuring that this jewel remains in Russian hands. Abkhazia is not Georgia's most depressed region; that unwanted sobriquet goes to Armenian-populated Javakheti. The main employer is a Russian military base.

The failure of Azeri troops to prevent the Armenians taking over Nagorno-Karabakh undermined President Elchibey and he was forced to flee to his home region of Nakhichevan. Heydar Aliyev took over. He had been head of the Azerbaijani KGB and communist leader from 1969 to 1982 when he departed to Moscow to become a deputy Prime Minister of the Soviet Union. Gorbachev forced him out amid charges of corruption and he repaired to Nakhichevan. The rebellion against Elchibey coincided with the signing of a lucrative oil contract and Aliyev set about negotiating it. Again there were rumours of Russian involvement. Aliyev was elected President in October 1993 and re-elected in October 1998.

In Armenia, President Ter-Petrosyan came under heavy criticism for not dealing with abuses of human rights but was re-elected President in September 1996. He was forced to resign in February 1998 and was replaced by Robert Kocharyan. He was elected President in March 1999. He immediately met President Aliyev in an effort to resolve the Nagorno-Karabakh problem. The Armenian Prime Minister was murdered in October 1999 under mysterious circumstances and some have suggested he was killed because he was discussing a draft peace plan with Baku. These three states have presidential systems but the leaders are not as authoritarian as those in Central Asia.

Oil is the black gold of Azerbaijan and has attracted many foreign companies. The oil can be exported through pipelines running to the Georgian coast on the Black Sea or through the Russian port of

Novorossiisk. Armenia has gold and Georgia tropical products. Trade has gradually moved away from reliance on Russia and other countries of the CIS. Iran is Azerbaijan's main trading partner and number two in Armenia after Russia. The west promotes the cooperation of these states and also those in Central Asia because of the importance of oil and natural gas in the region. Reserves of oil in the Caspian basin may be equal to those in north America or the North Sea. Gas reserves are almost equal to those in north America.

Georgia suffered the most precipitous decline of any CIS country, dropping to 23.4 per cent of the 1989 level in 1994. Armenia bottomed off at 37 per cent in 1995 (Table 13.2). Inflation was worse than elsewhere, reaching 22,470 per cent in Georgia, 4964 per cent in Armenia and 1664 per cent in Azerbaijan, in 1994. This problem had been brought under control by 1998. Georgia again holds the record for the fastest decline of industrial production, in 1995 it was only 15.8 per cent of the level of 1989 (Table 13.8). The flow of new oil from Azerbaijan only began in late 1997 and this has improved the economic situation considerably. Armenia is kept going by US aid and the remittances of its wealthy diaspora. The American diaspora does influence US policy towards Armenia.

Most agricultural land has been privatised in the region as have small and medium-sized companies. By 1997, the private sector was producing about 55 per cent of GNP in Armenia and Georgia but only about 40 per cent in Azerbaijan.

Russia does not want to be forced out of the Caucasus as it was from the Baltic. It is twitchy about Azerbaijan and Georgia toying with NATO and EU membership and sees the hand of America as grasping and penetrating. The Georgians would like the large Russian military base near Tbilisi to be handed back to them. Russia has sharply criticised Azerbaijan and Georgia for aiding Chechnya but they consistently deny any links with Chechnya. Armenia has even floated the idea that it might join the Russian-Belarusian union. Russia has taken to issuing passports to practically any ex-Soviet citizen who requests one and there has been a considerable take up in Abkhazia, South Ossetia and Javakheti which may lead to a situation where Russian citizens form a majority there. Moscow could then require Georgian citizens to acquire visas for travel to Russia. The same could apply to Azerbaijan. This would undermine the thriving economic links between the Caucasus and Russia. Many Caucasians work in Russia.

MAP 3: Central Asia.

CENTRAL ASIA

Economic trends are illustrated in Tables 13.9 and 13.10. Central Asia is bounded on the west and south east by mountains which are inhospitable and by deserts in the centre and west. The settled population is to be found in the rest, with the fertile Fergana valley a focal point. The large reserves of oil and natural gas and deposits of many minerals have brought the region in from the cold internationally. China, Russia, Iran, Turkey and the United States now compete for influence.

Communist leaders became nationalist leaders overnight in the region, the only exception being Kyrgyzstan. In Kazakhstan, Nursultan Nazarbaev, communist leader from June 1989, was elected President in December 1991. He was the only candidate. He was re-elected in January 1999 amid criticism from international observers about the way the poll was conducted. In Turkmenistan, Saparmurat Niyazov, communist leader from 1984, was elected President, unopposed, in October 1990. He was re-elected, unopposed, in June 1992 and in January 1994 he had his term in office extended. In October 1993, he had himself declared Turkmenbashi, the leader of the Turkmen. As such only the scythe of time will remove him from office. An extraordinary cult of the leader has developed around him exceeding that of former Romanian President

Nicolae Ceausescu. A golden statue of him in the capital, Ashgabat, rotates all day to face the sun.

Islam Karimov dominates Uzbekistan although he only became communist leader in 1989. In December 1991, he was elected President and his term of office was extended to 2000 by a referendum in March 1995. In Tajikistan, Kakhar Makkhamov, communist leader from 1985, was elected President by the Supreme Soviet, in November 1990. He was not nimble enough during the attempted coup of August 1991 and came out for Gorbachev far too late. He was pushed aside and Rakhmon Nabiev took over. The civil war was then under way and was more about regional conflict than ideology or religion. Imamoli Rakhmonov was made head of state by a communist government, in November 1992. He was elected President, in November 1994, by voters in areas controlled by the government. These were around Dushanbe, the capital, and the region of Kulob. The civil war formally came to an end in June 1997 and the leader of the Islamic Renaissance Party, Sayed Abdullo Nuri, became chair of the new national reconciliation council, in July 1997. Rakhmonov remained President. The exception to the rule in Central Asia is Kyrgyzstan where the communist leader failed to become President. Instead Askar Akaev, chair of the Kyrgyz academy of sciences, was elected President in October 1991. In December 1995, he was re-elected. He is the only leader who has made any attempt to introduce an embryonic democratic system.

The strongest loyalties are along clan lines but also regional association is important. Kazakhstan is divided into three zhuz, literally part but also horde. The big horde is in the south and east, centred on the former capital of Almaty, the middle horde contains the new capital Astana (Akmolinsk, Tselinograd in Russian) and the small horde occupies the north west and west. Kyrgyzstan is in two parts, the north, centred on Bishkek, the capital, and the home of President Akaev, and the south which includes a part of the Fergana valley. President Islam Karimov has repeatedly attacked the idea that Uzbekistan is divided into four regions. He is particularly sensitive to criticism, especially from the large Tajik population and Islamists. Namangan in the Fergana valley is the main base of Islamic fundamentalism. Addressing the Uzbek parliament, in May 1998, President Karimov attacked 'Islamic fundamentalists' and remarked that if parliament were not prepared to adopt stricter legislation, he would shoot them himself.

Niyazov is strong enough to eliminate any regional divisions although there are over a thousand clans. However pressure on the religious has been increasing. In August 1999, Hare Krishna temples in Mary and Ashgabat were demolished. This is believed to be the first time since the end of the Soviet period that government authorities in any of the ex-Soviet republics have deliberately demolished places of worship in an attempt to halt religious activity. In November 1999, the Adventist church in Ashgabat was demolished. The persecution appears to be a legacy of the Soviet era rather than militant Muslim opposition. Religious observance in Turkmenistan among Muslims is low and only about 180 make the *hadj* to Mecca annually.

The mineral and hydrocarbon wealth of Kazakhstan makes it the potentially richest state in the region. Over a thousand types of valuable ores can be exploited and Kazakhstan is the world's leading producer of barite, lead and wolfram. It is second in the world in production of chromite ore, silver and zinc and is third in the world for manganese. Its mineral reserves may exceed $1 trillion. It has about 8 per cent of world reserves of iron ore. It is the sole producer of chromium in the northern hemisphere and has about 30 per cent of world deposits. About 25 per cent of world deposits of uranium are in Kazakhstan. In 1993, the US company Chevron and Kazakhstan formed the Tengizchevroil joint venture worth $20 billion. The Tengiz field has an estimated 6 to 9 billion barrels of reserves. The discovery of the huge Kashagan oil field on Kazakhstan's Caspian Sea shelf has increased optimism. President Nazarbaev has stated that the Kashagan find could yield six times as much oil as the Tengiz field. Western companies and Gazprom are involved in developing the large Karachagansk gas field. Kazakhstan is the third largest producer of energy in the CIS and has one nuclear power plant. It also has one of the largest goldfields in the world at Vasilkovskoe.

An important problem for Kazakhstan is how to get its hydrocarbons to outside markets. It supports the Baku-Ceyhan (Turkey) pipeline project but it has other options. In 1997, Kazakhstan signed a $9.5 billion deal with China on oil production and shipment. In 1998, the China national petroleum corporation purchased 60 per cent of the Aktobemunaigaz oil production company for $325 million and promised to invest $4 billion in it over the next 20 years. Kazakhstan and China have discussed building a 3000 km oil pipeline from western Kazakhstan to western China costing $3.5 billion.

Kyrgyzstan has many minerals but at present gold is the most valuable export. It now produces less than a million tonnes of oil but may have considerable reserves awaiting discovery. Electricity is a major export earner. Turkmenistan relies almost entirely on oil and gas exports. Tajikistan has many minerals, especially silver and gold, but the civil war has wreaked havoc with its economy. It has one of the world's largest deposits of uranium. It has reserves of oil and natural gas but both only provide 6 per cent of domestic demand. Almost all of its natural gas imports come from Uzbekistan and Turkmenistan. Turkmenistan has the world's third largest deposits of sulphur and huge reserves of sodium sulphate, sodium chloride and kaolin. Oil production is growing but export pipelines are a problem. It has the world's fourth largest reserves of natural gas. Uzbekistan has huge hydrocarbon wealth and it is estimated that 63 per cent of the country is sitting on hydrocarbons. Its gold deposits are the fourth largest in the world and about 70 tonnes are extracted each year. It is also a large copper and uranium producer.

EPILOGUE

THE SPY WHO TOOK OVER RUSSIA: VLADIMIR PUTIN

RUSSIAN WOMEN VOTED VLADIMIR PUTIN THE sexiest man in the country in 2000. One explained: 'He doesn't drink, he doesn't smoke, he is into sport, he loves his wife and children. What more do you want?' Another offered a different view: 'I am frightened of him – that means I want him'. Putin is on firm ground: there are nine million more women than men in Russia. At the end of 2000 his approval rating was over 70 per cent. Clearly many men liked him as well. What is his secret?

Sport dragged him off the streets of St Petersburg, his home town. First it was boxing but after breaking his nose he gave up. Then it was sambo, a Russian mixture of judo and wrestling and then, finally, judo. 'It is more than a sport, it is a philosophy', he comments in his biography (Gevorkyan 2000: 19). Putin had to channel his great physical energy into some positive activity. He learned to discipline himself in this way. However he did not do the same intellectually. At school, he was bright but disorganised. It was inevitable that a life of action would attract him and he was quickly bowled over by stories about the Cheka, especially the *Chekisty* who were spies abroad. He boldly approached the KGB and told them he wanted to join. They told him to go away and read law at university. Anyway, one did not approach them, they approached you. So law it was at St Petersburg university and then into spying. His parents did not understand and his judo coach thought he had taken leave of his senses. He did his best to deflect him from this goal but

Putin revealed his determined streak: he would brook no opposition to achieve his dream.

University life was not all study. He became a sambo black belt and a judo master two years later. He became the city judo champion. In his fourth year, he was approached by the KGB. He was in. Soon he was sent to the Andropov institute in Moscow for further training and he made it into foreign intelligence. He married his St Petersburg girlfriend, an airline stewardess, when he was thirty. His first foreign assignment was to the German Democratic Republic or East Germany. However he ended up in Dresden, where there were only ten other officers, instead of the much more glamorous East Berlin. His work consisted mainly of liasing with the Stasi, the KGB's east German sister. He took to life in the Saxon capital and put on weight and became fluent in German, including learning some of the local dialect. He made some trips to West Germany but always returned to the east.

The fall of the Berlin Wall, in November 1989, changed his life. The GDR was collapsing around his ears and there were important tasks: liquidate Soviet assets, set up dummy companies to extract as much money as possible from the West Germans and grasp a once in a life-time opportunity to make a lot of money. One of Putin's jobs was to help sell the property belonging to the Soviet ministry of culture in East Berlin. There were also the property of the various Soviet-GDR friend-ship societies.

Anatoly Sobchak, the mayor of St Petersburg, invited Putin to join his staff after he returned home in January 1990. Of course, he was still a KGB officer. He was made head of the committee on foreign relations and this included dealing with foreign businessmen who wanted to trade and invest. He resigned from the KGB in August 1991 but he did not leave the communist party. 'The CPSU just ceased to exist', he says.

One of the foreign businessmen attracted to St Petersburg was Harry Giesbrecht, a Canadian. His company was building a $22 million hotel in St Petersburg. However there was a problem. He could not find gravel to make concrete for the hotel. In stepped Putin and the problem was resolved. In 1994, when Putin was deputy mayor, Giesbrecht was involved in a project to build a hydrogen plant to supply hospitals and medical centres. He invited Putin to Canada to study similar facilities. He spent about ten days touring Ottawa, Toronto and Winnipeg, with a tourist trip to Niagara Falls. The deal, however, fell apart.

In 1996, Anatoly Sobchak lost his post as mayor to Vladimir Yakovlev, governor of Leningrad oblast. Putin campaigned for him but got carried away and called Yakovlev a Judas. Clearly he had no future in the new administration. (In 1998, as head of the FSB, Putin helped Sobchak to cross into Finland when the procurator general wanted to question him about alleged corruption.)

Pavel Borodin invited Putin to be his deputy in the presidential administration, in August 1996. He was responsible for the legal department and Russian property abroad. In 1998, he was deputy head of the presidential administration, then head of the FSB, then secretary of the Security Council. In 1999, he became Prime Minister and acting President. A star – no, a shooting star.

One of those who had nothing but good to say about Putin was Boris Berezovsky. He, Roman Abramovich and some other partners, set about taking control of some of Russia's largest aluminium smelters. In February 2000, Sibneft announced that certain shareholders had acquired controlling stakes in the Bratsk and Krasnoyarsk smelters, the two largest. Novokuznetsk, the fifth largest, revealed that Logovaz had acquired a controlling stake. With breathtaking speed Berezovsky, Abramovich and the others had acquired over two thirds of the Russian aluminium industry. Russia is the second largest aluminium producer in the world and aluminium is a major export.

A deal of this magnitude must have crossed the acting President's desk. He decided to remain passive and to leave the oligarchs to get on with business.

Putin told voters he was not going to campaign. Nevertheless he went on a whirlwind tour of the regions, flew to Chechnya in a jet fighter, spent a night in a submerged submarine and came across as a healthy, virile male. He revealed no policies, only that he favoured a strong state. This permitted nationalists, liberals, communists and everyone else to dream about his fulfilling their preferences.

The only doubt about Putin becoming President was whether he would win over 50 per cent of the popular vote on 26 March 2000 in the first round or whether it would go to a second round and see a head-on confrontation with Gennady Zyuganov. His campaign managers decided not to take any risks and the Central Electoral Commission declared that he had received 39.7 million votes or 52.9 per cent in the first round (Table E.1). He was declared duly elected. He was to be sworn in on 7 May. The ceremony was symbolic. The dominant colour was red. Mikhail Gorbachev and Vladimir Kryuchkov, the KGB mastermind of the failed coup of August 1991, were also there. Henceforth Boris Yeltsin was to be addressed as the first President.

There were mutterings about electoral fraud. Does water run off a duck's back? The communists pointed out that there were a million more registered voters than during the Duma elections in December 1999. Creative counting of ballots and bullying by local bosses helped ensure victory. Ambitious politicians wanted their region to record a yes vote; there was no point in being put on a blacklist by Putin from the word go. The accusations were not investigated. Putin would have defeated Zyuganov in the second round anyway. It was always a one horse race; declaring his candidacy, Grigory Yavlinsky lamented that no one could ever hope to beat Putin.

Putin had a mandate to reform. After inauguration, he began strengthening the power of the centre vis-à-vis the regions. He referred to this as the vertical line of power. He divided the country into seven federal districts and appointed a representative in each; five of the seven were either former KGB or military officers. The best-known civilian was Sergei Kirienko. The regions coincided with military districts and none had its centre in a (non-Russian) republic. Representatives were members of the Security Council and ranked somewhere between a deputy head of the presidential administration and a deputy Prime Minister. Legislation was pushed through the Duma permitting governors and city mayors who contravened federal laws to be removed. On the contrary, he has ensured that the Duma pass legislation which permits some powerful governors to run for a third term, strictly prohibited by current law. Mintimer Shaimiev, President of Tatarstan, is one who has benefited from this. Another law deprives governors of their automatic seats in the Council of the Federation and the loss of immunity from prosecution which goes with membership. However, each of them can nominate two representatives to sit in the Council of the Federation.

Putin is well aware of how the governors behave. During his time in the presidential administration, he is reported to have unearthed over 9000 cases in which federal funds, amounting to 3 trillion rubles ($104 billion at the exchange rate prevailing at the end of 2000), were spent by the regions on projects other than those designated by Moscow. The governors now sit in a State Council to advise the President on major policy problems; however, he nominates all the governors.

Putin and his advisers have said that they do not agree that the media should be privately owned. They took exception to Gusinsky's NTV's reporting on the war in Chechnya and excluded its journalists from the military press pool: the media should report the Russian side and not give space to the rebels. Andrei Babitsky, a Radio Liberty journalist, was

Gusinsky, the owner of NTV, the TV company, ends up in a soup kitchen. The dish is inscribed: NTV plus. Created by Igor Revyakin.

arrested in January 2000, traded to masked men whom Moscow stated were Chechen rebels, and then allowed free after five weeks of captivity. No wonder many were mystified as to why Russians authorities should trade a Russian journalist to the Chechens. The general conclusion was that it was a warning to independent journalists to stay out of Chechnya and not to report the war from the Chechen side. In May, Gusinsky's Media-Most was raided by the tax police. The following month, Gusinsky was arrested and spent three nights in jail. He promised to sell his majority stake in NTV to Gazprom in order to be allowed to leave the country for Spain. He claims that he only made the promise under duress. In December, he was arrested by Spanish police, acting on an Interpol warrant and extradition proceedings began. (Eventually the Spanish authorities refused to extradite Gusinsky.)

Boris Berezovsky, who claims that he contributed handsomely to Edinstvo's campaign fund during the December 1999 Duma elections, has fallen out with Putin. He resigned his Duma mandate to fashion an anti-presidential political party. This idea turned out to be rather fanciful and pressure was put on him to sell his stake in ORT; he found it advisable to move abroad. The Russian procurator general has reopened an investigation into alleged corruption at Aeroflot.

The worst misjudgement by Putin in his first year in office was during the attempts to rescue the 118 men trapped on the seabed, after explosions had sunk the submarine Kursk, in August 2000. He continued on holiday at Sochi, remarking that all that could be done was being done. This badly misread the public mood. He hastily returned to Moscow to supervise proceedings and his approval ratings recovered. There is another way of looking at the Kursk episode. Putin declined to play the strong leader because this would have involved him in condemning the old regime, the Yeltsin regime. This did not prevent Yeltsin, in his regular meetings with Putin, chiding him for his handling of the affair. Putin sees Yeltsin at Gorky-9, the government residence, which has an array of aides, servants and medical personnel. It was given to Yeltsin as part of the deal with Putin. The former President also has access to the presidential aircraft.

Gone are the days when the President feared the Duma. Putin has tamed the unruly legislature and the communists are willing to do his bidding. The nationalist rhetoric now comes from the President. He has sought to recover what was good from the past and merge it with the present. Yeltsin's national anthem, an extract from Glinka, has been replaced by the 1943 Soviet anthem. New words have been coined but communists can sing the old words. The Tsarist two-headed eagle has been added to the national flag and the military have the old Soviet standard back.

Putin's number two is Sergei Ivanov, minister of defence. Like the President, Ivanov is a career intelligence officer and is also from St Petersburg. He studied Swedish and Finnish and is an expert on Scandinavia. Before becoming defence minister Ivanov was secretary of the Security Council. Under him it increased its influence and helped draft the foreign policy and national security doctrines. It fashioned the information concept which imposes greater restrictions on the Russian press and also foreign journalists working in Russia. Ivanov merged the two agencies which export arms. One of these was the notoriously corrupt Rosvoruzhenie. In February 2001, Ivanov casually mentioned that Russia had abandoned plans to forge the CIS into a political and economic union. In future bilateral relations with the various members would be the norm. This reverses Yeltsin's declared policy.

Putin has travelled the world and has an insatiable thirst for more knowledge. He has repaired fences with North Korea, Cuba and Iraq and sought to fashion a grouping with China and India to stem American hegemony. He is a pragmatist and is still making up his mind about how to proceed on the world stage. He often wears the mask of a career spy but behind the glum exterior is a sharp mind and excellent memory. He attends Orthodox services with his wife. He is the first Russian leader since Brezhnev who is seeking to rebuild his country rather than engage in experiments to take it to new shores. He moves slowly and cautiously and is seeking Russian solutions to Russian problems. In 2000, the $60 billion trade surplus (capital flight was put officially at $24.6 billion) blunted the urgency to proceed rapidly with economic restructuring. Meanwhile the world outside is changing fast. Will it leave Putin's Russia behind?

The warning signals are there. Russia's production assets are wearing out and 2003 is seen as the critical year. Russian industry desperately needs substantial investment. On the bright side, Russia has more natural resources ($10.2 trillion) than Brazil, the Republic of South Africa, China and India combined. Russia's great weakness is its inability to attract foreign investment: in 1999, total accumulated foreign investment was $29.3 billion compared to $600 billion in China. Putin's task is awesome.

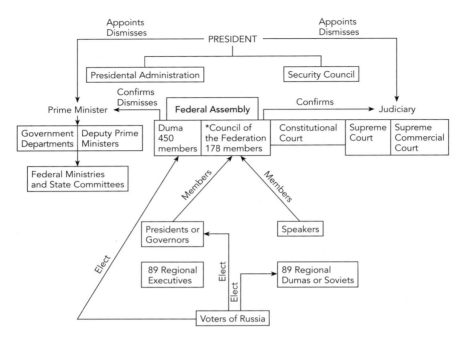

FIGURE 3.1 Key institutions of the Russian Federation (1993 Constitution)
Source: Based on Huskey 1999: 36.
* In 2000, membership of the Council of the Federation was amended. Each President or governor now nominates two representatives to sit in it. A State Council has been established. President Putin appoints Presidents and governors to it.

TABLE 3.1 Elections to the State Duma, 12 December 1993

Party/bloc	Party lists			Single-member constituencies		Total seats	
	% votes	Number of seats	% seats	Number of seats	% seats	Number	%
Russia's Choice	15.51	40	17.8	30	13.3	70	15.6
Liberal Democratic Party of Russia	22.92	59	26.2	5	2.2	64	14.2
Communist Party of the Russian Federation	12.40	32	14.2	16	7.1	48	10.7
Agrarian Party	7.99	21	9.3	12	5.3	33	7.3
Women of Russia	8.13	21	9.3	2	0.9	23	5.1
Yabloko	7.86	20	8.9	3	1.3	23	5.1
Party of Russian Unity and Concord	6.76	18	8.0	1	0.4	19	4.2
Democratic Party of Russia	5.52	14	6.2	1	0.4	15	3.3
[5 per cent threshold]							
Democratic Reform Movement	4.08	–		4	1.8	4	0.9
Dignity and Charity	0.70	–		2	0.9	2	0.4
Civic Union	1.93	–		1	0.4	1	0.2
Russia's Future-New Names	1.25	–		1	0.4	1	0.2
Cedar	0.76	–		–		–	
Against all	4.36	–		–		–	
Spoiled ballots	3.10	–		–		–	
Independents	–	–		141	62.7	141	31.3
Postponed	–			6		6	
Total		225		225		450	

Source: White 2000: 40.

TABLE 3.2 Elections to the State Duma, 17 December 1995

	Party lists			Single-member constituencies		Total seats	
	% vote	Number of seats	% seats	Number of seats	% seats	Number	%
Communist Party	22.3	99	44.0	58	25.8	157	34.9
Liberal Democrats	11.2	50	22.2	1	0.4	51	11.3
Our Home Is Russia	10.1	45	20.0	10	4.4	55	12.2
Yabloko	6.9	31	13.8	14	6.2	45	10.0
[5% threshold]							
Agrarian Party	3.8	–	–	20	8.9	20	4.4
Power to the People!	1.6	–	–	9	4.0	9	2.0
Russia's Democratic Choice	3.9	–	–	9	4.0	9	2.9
Congress of Russian Communities	4.3	–	–	5	2.2	5	1.1
Women of Russia	4.6	–	–	3	1.3	3	0.7
Forward, Russia!	1.9	–	–	3	1.3	3	0.7
Ivan Rybkin bloc	1.1	–	–	3	1.3	3	0.7
Pamfilova–Gurov– Lysenko bloc	1.6	–	–	2	0.9	2	0.4
Communists–Working Russia–For the Soviet Union	4.5	–	–	1	0.4	1	0.2
Party of Workers' Self-Management	4.0	–	–	1	0.4	1	0.2
Trade Unions and Industrialists	1.6	–	–	1	0.4	1	0.2
Govorukhin bloc	1.0	–	–	1	0.4	1	0.2
Fatherland	0.7	–	–	1	0.4	1	0.2
Common Cause	0.7	–	–	1	0.4	1	0.2
Transformation of the Fatherland	0.7	–	–	1	0.4	1	0.2
Party of Russian Unity and Concord	0.4	–	–	1	0.4	1	0.2
Party of Economic Freedom	0.1	–	–	1	0.4	1	0.2
89 Regions of Russia	0.1	–	–	1	0.4	1	0.2
Bloc of Independents	0.1	–	–	1	0.4	1	0.2
Other parties	8.9	–	–	0	–	0	–
Independents	–	–	–	77	34.2	77	17.1
Against all lists	2.8	–	–	–	–	–	–
Invalid vote	1.2	–	–	–	–	–	–

Source: White 2000: 52.

TABLE 3.3 First round of the presidential election, 16 June 1996

Candidate	Percentage vote	Number
Boris Yeltsin	35.3	26,665,495
Gennady Zyuganov	32.0	24,211,686
Aleksandr Lebed	14.5	10,974,736
Grigory Yavlinsky	7.3	5,550,752
Vladimir Zhirinovsky	5.7	4,311,479
Svyatoslav Fedorov	0.9	699,158
Mikhail Gorbachev	0.5	386,069
Martin Shakkum	0.4	277,068
Yury Vlasov	0.2	151,282
Vladimir Bryntsalov	0.2	123,065
Aman Tuleev*	0.0	308
Against all candidates	1.5	1,163,921
Invalid ballots	1.4	1,072,120
Turnout	69.7	75,587,139

* Withdrew from election at last moment in favour of Zyuganov
Source: White 2000: 98.

TABLE 3.4 Second round of the presidential election, 3 July 1996

Candidate	Percentage vote	Number
Boris Yeltsin	53.8	40,203,948
Gennady Zyuganov	40.3	30,102,288
Against both candidates	4.8	3,604,462
Invalid ballots	1.0	780,592
Turnout	68.8	74,691,290

Source: White 2000: 98. The registered electorate was 108,589,050.

TABLE 4.1 Elections to the State Duma, 19 December 1999

	Party lists		Single member constituencies	Total seats	
	% vote	No. of seats	No. of seats	No.	% seats
KPRF	24.3	67	46	113	26
Edinstvo	23.3	64	9	73	16
OVR	13.3	37	31	68	15
SPS	8.5	24	5	29	7
Zhirinovsky bloc	6.4	17	–	17	4
Yabloko	5.9	16	4	20	5
NDR	1.2	–	9	9	2
Nikolaev-Fedorov	0.6	–	2	2	–
Army	0.6	–	2	2	–
ROS	0.4	–	2	2	–
Pensioners	2.0	–	2	2	–
KRO-Boldyrev	0.6	–	1	1	–
Russian Socialist Party	0.2	–	1	1	–
Spiritual Heritage	0.1	–	1	1	–
Agrarian Party	–	–	1	1	–
Independents	–	–	100	100	23
Total		225	216	441	

KPRF   Communist Party of the Russian Federation
OVR   Fatherland-All Russia
SPS   Union of Right Forces
NDR   Our Home is Russia
ROS   Russian All-National Union
KRO-Boldyrev   Congress of Russian Communities and Yury Boldyrev Movement
The turnout was 62 per cent (a minimum of 25 per cent is required for the election to be valid). New elections will be held in nine constituencies in which more people voted against all candidates than for any candidate.
Source: Central Electoral Commission, 23 December 1999; 29 December 1999.

TABLE 5.1 The President's personal apparatus*

Chancellery
Counsellors' Service
Administration of Affairs (Property Department)

Presidential Administration
- Analytical Centre
- Awards
- Cadres
- Citizenship
- Citizens' Letters
- Civil Service
- Documents
- Finance and Budget
- Information
- Monitoring
- Organisation
- Pardon
- Parties and Public Associations
- Centre for Presidential Programmes
- Protocol
- Special Programmes
- State and Legal
- Territories

Presidential Commissions and Councils

Source: Based on Huskey 1999: 55. This was the situation in May 1994.
* Throughout this book the term presidential administration is used to describe the President's personal apparatus. Strictly speaking, the presidential administration is a part of the personal apparatus.

TABLE 5.2 Membership of the Security Council (15 December 1998)

President of the Russian Federation*	B. N. Yeltsin (Chair)
Head, Presidential Administration	N. N. Bordyuzha
Secretary, Security Council*	N. N. Bordyuzha
Director, Federal Agency for Government Communications (FAPSI)	V. P. Sherstyuk
Prime Minister*	E. M. Primakov
First Deputy Prime Minister	V. A. Gustov
First Deputy Prime Minister	Yu. D. Maslyukov
Minister of Foreign Affairs*	I. S. Ivanov
Minister of Internal Affairs (MVD)	S. V. Stepashin
Director, Federal Security Service (FSB)*	V. V. Putin
Minister of Defence*	I. D. Sergeev
Minister for Emergencies	S. K. Shoigu
Minister of Finance	M. M. Zadornov
Minister of Atomic Energy	E. O. Adamov
Minister of Justice	P. V. Krasheninnikov
Head, Federal Protection Service (FSO)	Yu. V. Krapivin
Director, Federal Border Guards	K. V. Totsky
Director, Foreign Intelligence Service (SVR)	V. I. Trubnikov
President, Russian Academy of Sciences	Yu. S. Osipov

*Ex-officio permanent member.
Source: Huskey 1999: 75.

TABLE 6.1 Russian defence expenditure (per cent of GDP)

	1989 (ex USSR)	1992	1993	1994	1995	1996	1997
Federal budget	8.0*	4.5	4.2	4.6	2.6	2.3	2.7

*Estimates vary and can be as high as 15 per cent. Russia had always contributed more per capita to defence than any other republic. In 1985, it was about two and a half times more. Gorbachev attempted, in 1985, to spread the burden more evenly among the republics but failed. Another attempt, in 1991, also failed. Yeltsin also discovered a great reluctance to contribute to defence spending within the Russian Federation. The city of Moscow contributes the most per capita and the regions as little as they can. Hence Yeltsin also failed to redistribute defence spending per capita evenly around the Russian Federation. This is now a major task for Putin.
Source: Nagy 2000: 27; and others.

TABLE 6.2 Soviet-Russian security services

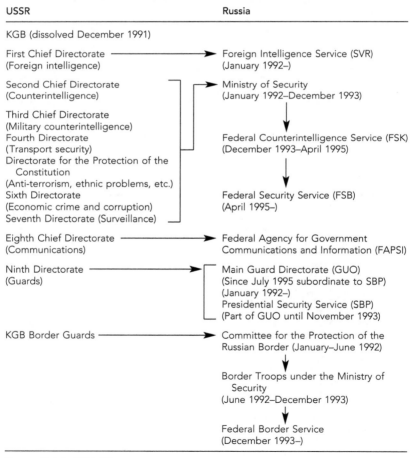

USSR	Russia
KGB (dissolved December 1991)	
First Chief Directorate (Foreign intelligence) ——→	Foreign Intelligence Service (SVR) (January 1992–)
Second Chief Directorate (Counterintelligence)	Ministry of Security (January 1992–December 1993)
Third Chief Directorate (Military counterintelligence) Fourth Directorate (Transport security) Directorate for the Protection of the Constitution (Anti-terrorism, ethnic problems, etc.) Sixth Directorate (Economic crime and corruption) Seventh Directorate (Surveillance)	Federal Counterintelligence Service (FSK) (December 1993–April 1995) ↓ Federal Security Service (FSB) (April 1995–)
Eighth Chief Directorate (Communications) ——→	Federal Agency for Government Communications and Information (FAPSI)
Ninth Directorate (Guards) ——→	Main Guard Directorate (GUO) (Since July 1995 subordinate to SBP) (January 1992–) Presidential Security Service (SBP) (Part of GUO until November 1993)
KGB Border Guards ——→	Committee for the Protection of the Russian Border (January–June 1992) ↓ Border Troops under the Ministry of Security (June 1992–December 1993) ↓ Federal Border Service (December 1993–)

Source: Knight 1996: 35.

TABLE 7.1 Federal-local revenue sharing

	1992 Federal	1992 Local	1993 Federal	1993 Local	1994 Federal	1994 Local	1995 Federal	1995 Local
VAT	75	25	64	36	73	27	74	26
Profit tax	41	59	33	67	35	65	35	65
Personal income tax	0	100	0	100	0	100	10	90
Alcohol tax	50	50	50	50	50	50	50	50
Energy tax	100	0	100	0	100	0	100	0
Natural resource tax	52	48	48	52	22	78	35	65
Foreign trade tax	98	2	98	2	100	0	100	0
Total tax revenue (excluding transfer payments)	57	43	48	52	46	54	49	51

Source: Nagy 2000: 117.

TABLE 8.1 Economic indicators, 1990–97 (1990 = 100)

	1991	1992	1993	1994	1995	1996	1997
Gross domestic product	95	81.2	77.1	67.3	64.5	61.3	61.9
Industrial production	92	75.4	64.8	51.1	46.9	48.1	48.8
Fixed capital investment	85	51	44.9	34.1	31.7	25.9	23.4
Agricultural production	95	86.4	82.9	72.9	67	62.3	59.2
Real wages	97	65	65.3	60.1	43.3	46	48
Increase or decrease of population (thousands)	103.9	−219.8	−750.3	−893.2	−840.2	−777.6	−756.5

Source: Glazyev 1999: 32.

TABLE 8.2 Economic trends, 1992–99

	1992	1993	1994	1995	1996	1997	1998	1999
GDP (per cent change)	−14.5	−8.7	−13.0	−4.0	−3.4	0.9	−4.9	3.5
Unemployment rate (per cent of labour force)	4.8	6.1	7.8	9.0	10.0	11.2	13.3	12.1
Prices (per cent change)	2506.1	839.9	215.1	131.3	21.8	11.0	84.4	36.5
Treasury interest rate (all maturities)	–	103.2	136.8	100.8	38.7	36.6	–	–
Exports (billion dollars)	–	44.3	67.5	81.1	88.6	88.2	74.2	75.8
Imports (billion dollars)	–	32.8	50.5	60.8	68.8	73.7	59.1	39.6
Exchange rate*	0.4	1.3	3.6	4.6	5.6	6.0	20.7	27.0
Reserves, inc. gold (billion dollars)	4.5	8.9	6.5	17.2	15.3	17.8	12.2	13.0
External debt (billion dollars)	107.7	111.7	121.5	120.4	125.1	125.7	145.0**	155.0

Source: IMF, EBRD, *Russian Economic Trends*, various years; *Russia Quarterly Forecast Report, Q3 2000* (London 2000).
* In new rubles to the dollar. One new ruble = 1000 old rubles at conversion on 1 January 1998.
** $103 billion of this was accumulated Soviet debt.

TABLE 8.3 The media barons (in mid-2000)

	Main companies	Media interests
Vagit Alekperov	Lukoil; Bank Imperial	Izvestiya newspaper (with Potanin) TV-6 (with Berezovsky)
Boris Berezovsky (linked to the Yeltsin family; Viktor Chernomyrdin; Aleksandr Voloshin)	Sibneft, Logovaz, Aeroflot and Transaero airlines, Avtovaz Bank, Obedinenny Bank	ORT TV (with Fridman), TV-6 (with Alekperov, and STS TV stations, Vremya TV programme, NSN radio, Nezavisimaya gazeta, Novaya Izvestiya and Kommersant, Ogonek magazine
Viktor Chernomyrdin	Gazprom	See Vyakhirev below
Mikhail Fridman (linked to Aleksandr Voloshin)	Alfa group holding company, Alfa Bank, Tyumen oil holding company, Alfa cement, various property, construction and export companies	Alfa TV, ORT TV (with Berezovsky) STS (network of TV stations)
Vladimir Gusinsky (linked to Yury Luzhkov, mayor of Moscow)	Media Most holding company, Most Bank	Segodnya, Novaya gazeta (with Smolensky), Obshchaya gazeta,7 dnei and Smena newspapers, Ekho Moskvy radio, NTV and NTV+ (with Vyakhirev), and TNT TV stations, Itogi and Lisa newspapers
Mikhail Khodorkovsky (linked to Evgeny Primakov)	Rosprom holding company, Bank Menatep, Yukos and VNK oil and gas holding companies, various manufacturing, copper, chemical, timber and retail companies	Moscow Times, St Petersburg Times and Literaturnaya gazeta newspapers
Yury Luzhkov (mayor of Moscow)	*Guta Bank, Bank Moskvy, Bank for Reconstruction and Development, believed to take a stake in every significant property deal in Moscow	Moskovsky komsomolets newspaper, TV-Centre (Moscow's TV station)
Vladimir Potanin	Interros holding company, Oneksimbank, RosBank, MFK Renaissance investment bank, various insurance companies, Norilsk Nickel (nickel and other non- ferrous metals), Sidanko (oil and gas holding company), Novolipetsk (steel), 25 per cent of Svyazinvest (telephone holding company), Perm Motors (aircraft), various metallurgical, shipping and industrial companies	Izvestiya (with Alekperov), Komsomolskaya pravda (with Vyakhirev) and Russky telegraf newspapers, Ekspert magazine
Aleksandr Smolensky	SBS-Agro Bank, may be co-owner of Sibneft with Berezovsky	Novaya gazeta (with Gusinsky) and National News Service newspapers, Dengi magazine
Rem Vyakhirev	Gazprom, managing director and shareowner, Bank Imperial (with Alekperov), Inkombank (minority stake), Gazprombank, National Reserve Bank, Promstroibank, Komitet oil company	Komsomolskaya pravda (with Potanin), NTV and NTV+ TV stations (with Gusinsky), Rabochaya tribuna, Trud, and Profil magazines, various regional newspapers and TV stations, minority stake in Media Most (see Gusinsky)

* These are owned by Moscow city government but Luzhkov has a stake in each.

TABLE 8.4 Loans for shares

	Packet in auction (per cent of shares)	Price of packet offered		Formal winner	Real winner
		Starting price ($ million)	Winning price		
Norilsk Nickel	38	170	170.1	Oneksimbank	Oneksimbank
Yukos	45	150	159	Laguna	Menatep
Sidanko	51	125	130	MFK	Oneksimbank
Sibneft	51	100	100.3	SBS-Agro Bank, Oil Finance Company (NFK)	Sibneft, through Oil Finance Company (NFK)
Surgutneftegaz	40	66.7	88.3	Surgutneftegaz Pension Fund	Surgutneftegaz, Oneksimbank
Lukoil	5	35	35.01	Lukoil, Bank Imperial	Lukoil, Bank Imperial
Novolipetsky Metallurgical Combine	15	30	31	MFK	Oneksimbank

Source: OECD 1997.

TABLE 8.5 Nominal and real values of companies involved in loans for shares scheme ($ millions)

Company	% auctioned	Auction price (Nov–Dec 1995)	Market capitalisation on basis of auction	Market cap. on stock market (1 August 1997)
Lukoil	5	35.01	700	15,839
Yukos	45	159	353	6,214
Surgutneftegaz	40	88.3	220	5,689
Sidanco	51	130	255	5,113
Sibneft	51	100.1	196	4,968
Norilsk Nickel	51	170.1	333	1,890

Source: Klebnikov 2000: 209.

TABLE 8.6 State ownership of companies (per cent of GDP produced by companies)

	1990	1998
Russia	95	30
Ukraine	90	45
Belarus	95	80
Kazakhstan	95	45
Kyrgyzstan	90	40
Uzbekistan	90	55
Turkmenistan	90	42
Moldova	90	55
Estonia	90	30
Latvia	90	40
Lithuania	85	30
Czech Republic	95	25
Poland	75	35
Bulgaria	90	40
Romania	85	40
China	95	75
United Kingdom	11	3
Italy	–	24

Source: Nagy 2000: 50.

TABLE 8.7 Foreign direct investment (FDI)

	Total FDI in 1989–98 ($ billions)	FDI inflow as per cent of GDP in 1997
Russia	9.2	0.8
Czech Republic	8.5	2.4
Hungary	16.9	4.6
Poland	12.4	2.2
Ukraine	2.7	1.2
Kazakhstan	5.7	5.9
All transition economies	74.5	1.8

Source: EBRD 1998.

TABLE 9.1 Global grain production and state purchases, 1986–2000 (million tonnes)

	Grain harvest	Federal and regional purchases as percentage of harvest
1986–90(average)	104.3	33.0
1991	89.1	25.0
1992	106.8	24.0
1993	99.0	28.2
1994	81.3 (71.4)	12.1
1995	65.4 (55.5)	9.5
1996	69.2 (59.8)	8.6
1997	89.0 (74.5)	–
1998	51.9 (41.9)	–
1999	54.7	–
2000	65.4	

Source: Wegren 1998: 136 and Goskomstat, various years; the figures in brackets are grain production, after processing.

TABLE 9.2 Food consumption, 1990–95 (kilograms per person)

	1990	1995	1997
Meat and meat products	75	55	48
Milk and dairy products	386	253	235
Eggs (number)	297	214	173
Bread and cereal products	119	121	–
Fish and fish products	15	–	9
Potatoes	106	124	108
Vegetables and melons	89	76	–

Source: For 1990 and 1995: Wegren 1998: 130; for 1997: Glazyev 1999: 22.

TABLE 10.1 Male and female life expectancy in Russia, 1980–99 (years)

Year	Males	Females	Difference
1980–81	61.5	73.1	11.6
1984–85	62.3	73.3	11.0
1986–87	64.9	74.6	9.7
1989	64.2	74.5	10.3
1990	63.8	74.3	10.5
1991	63.5	74.3	10.8
1992	62.0	73.8	11.8
1993	58.9	71.9	13.0
1995	58.3	71.7	13.4
1996	59.8	72.5	12.7
1997	60.8	72.9	12.1
1998	61.3	72.9	11.6
1999	59.8	72.8	13.0

Source: Field and Twigg 2000: 22; data for 1999 from Aleksandr Pochinok, minister of labour and social development, before the Duma, 17 November 2000.

TABLE 10.2 State expenditures and revenues (per cent of GDP)

	Expenditures		Revenues
	Last pre-transition year*	1997	1997
Russia	58.4	35.4	27.9
Ukraine	73.3	43.6	38.4
Belarus	46.0	46.8	46.1
Kyrgyzstan	34.2	23.5	17.3
Kazakhstan	31.9	27.1	19.8
Uzbekistan	49.7	32.8	30.5
Turkmenistan	28.9	29.2	29.2
Moldova	49.0	40.2	33.9
Estonia	33.6	37.0	38.9
Latvia	28.9	38.5	38.9
Lithuania	75.8	34.6	32.6
Czech Republic	61.1	43.4	41.3
Hungary	46.0	48.5	43.7
Poland	42.1	47.5	44.4
Bulgaria	65.6	34.1	31.6
Romania	38.7	34.3	30.7
China**	36.8	12.9	11.4

* Last pre-transition year for the former Soviet Union is 1992 because of lack of data for 1991. In eastern Europe it is 1990.
** Last pre-transition year is 1978.
Source: Nagy 2000: 57.

TABLE 10.3 Russian state expenditure on education (per cent of GDP)

	1989 (in USSR)	1992	1993	1994	1995	1996
Total expenditure of which:	4.7	3.5	4.1	4.5	3.1	3.0
Federal government	–	1.2	0.8	0.9	0.5	0.4
Local government	–	2.3	3.3	3.6	2.6	2.6

Source: Nagy 2000: 24.

TABLE 10.4 Russian state expenditure on health (per cent of GDP)

	1989 (in USSR)	1992	1993	1994	1995	1996
Total expenditure of which:	2.6	2.5	3.1	3.2	2.3	2.2
Federal government	–	0.3	0.3	0.4	0.3	0.3
Local government	–	2.2	2.8	2.8	2.0	1.9

Source: Nagy 2000: 20.

TABLE 10.5 Poverty

	1987–88	1993–95	1993–95
	(Per cent of total population)		(millions of people)
Russia	2	50	74.2
Czech Republic	0	<1	0.1
Hungary	1	4	0.4
Poland	6	20	7.6
Romania	6	59	13.5
Bulgaria	2	15	1.3
Ukraine	2	63	32.7
Baltic States	12	9	2.3
Central Asia*	15	66	30.7
All transition economies	4	45	168.0

* Not including Tajikistan.
Source: Nagy 2000: 33.

TABLE 10.6 Pensioners in Russia and the Commonwealth of Independent States, 1999

Country	Population	Pensioners*	Per cent of population
Ukraine	49,811,000	11,641,000	23.4
Belarus	10,402,000	2,231,000	21.4
Russia	146,394,000	30,270,000	20.7
Georgia	5,422,000	978,000	18.0
Moldova	4,461,000	735,000	16.5
Armenia	3,409,000	504,000	14.8
Kazakhstan	16,825,000	2,174,000	12.9
Azerbaijan	7,908,000	919,000	11.6
Kyrgyzstan	4,546,000	471,000	10.4
Tajikistan	6,103,000	475,000	7.8
Uzbekistan	24,102,000	1,936,000	8.0
Turkmenistan	4,366,000	321,000	7.4

Source: Field and Twigg 2000: 260.
* Pensionable age is 55 years for females and 60 for males.

TABLE 10.7 Public pension funds (per cent of GDP)

	1989 (in USSR)	1992	1993	1994	1995	1996
Russia						
Expenditure	6.2	6.9	6.1	6.1	4.6	4.5
Revenue	–	8.9	6.5	6.3	4.6	4.3
Balance	–	2.0	0.4	0.2	–	−0.2
Czech Republic			7.3			9.7
Hungary			10.6			9.7
Poland			13.4			14.4
Bulgaria			14.1			9.5
Romania			6.2			8.7
Ukraine			8.3			8.7
France			14.4			
Italy			17.1			
Germany			14.3			
United States						4.6

Source: Nagy 2000: 26.

TABLE 11.1 CIS agreements

	Treaty on Collective Security May 1992	Collective Security Concepts May 1995	Treaty on Joint Border Protection May 1995	Treaty on Joint Air Defence Feb. 1995	Statute on Collective Peacekeeping Forces Jan. 1996	Economic Union Sept. 1993	Payments Union October 1994	Customs Union March 1996
Armenia	*	*	*	*	*	*	*	
Azerbaijan						*	*	
Georgia		*	*	*	*	*	*	
Russia	*	*	*	*	*	*	*	*
Kazakhstan	*	*	*	*		*	*	*
Kyrgyzstan	*	*	*	*		*	*	*
Tajikistan	*	*	*	*	*	*	*	*
Turkmenistan				*		*	*	
Uzbekistan		*			*	**	*	
Ukraine				*		*	*	
Moldova						*	*	
Belarus	*	*	*	*	*	*	*	*

Source: Bowker and Ross 2000: 246.

* Signatory

** Associate member

Azerbaijan, Georgia and Uzbekistan signed the Treaty on Collective Security in May 1992 but withdrew in January–April 1999.

Tajikistan signed the Customs Union in February 1999.

The economic union of September 1993 never became a reality because it was not ratified by the Russian parliament.

TABLE 12.1 Change in real GDP, 1991–97 (1991 = 100)

	1992	1993	1994	1995	1996	1997
Estonia	85.9	78.6	72.5	75.5	78.6	83.3
Latvia	65.1	55.4	55.8	55.3	56.9	59.0
Lithuania	66.0	46.0	46.4	47.7	49.4	51.7

Source: Human Development Report 1999: 14.

TABLE 12.2 Gross domestic product, 1995–99

	1995	1996	1997	1998	1999
Estonia	4.3	3.9	10.6	4.7	−1.4
Latvia	6.1	3.3	8.6	3.9	0.1
Lithuania	3.3	4.7	7.3	5.1	−4.1

Source: EIU, various years.

TABLE 13.1 Presidents of the CIS

Armenia	Levon Ter-Petrosyan (1990–98); Robert Kocharyan (1998–)
Azerbaijan	Ayaz Mutalibov (1991–92); Albulfaz Elchibey (1992–93); Heydar Aliyev (1993–)
Belarus	Stanislau Shushkevich (1991–94); Myacheslau Gryb (1994); Alyaksandr Lukashenka (1994–)
Georgia	Zviad Gamsakhurdia (1990–92); Eduard Shevardnadze (1992–)
Kazakhstan	Nursultan Nazarbaev (1990–)
Kyrgyzstan	Askar Akaev (1990–)
Moldova	Mircea Snegur (1991–97); Petru Lucinschi (1997–)
Russia	Boris Yeltsin (1991–99); Vladimir Putin (acting December 1999–March 2000) (2000–)
Tajikistan	Kakhar Makkhamov (1990–91); Rakhmon Nabiev (1991–92); Imamali Rakhmonov (Chair of the Supreme Soviet 1992–94; President 1994–)
Turkmenistan	Turkmenbashi Saparmurat Niyazov (1991–)
Ukraine	Leonid Kravchuk (1991–94); Leonid Kuchma (1994–)
Uzbekistan	Islam Karimov (1990–)

TABLE 13.2 GDP of CIS states, 1992–96 (1991 = 100)

	1992	1993	1994	1995	1996
Armenia	58.2	53.1	55.9	59.8	63.3
Azerbaijan	77.4	59.5	47.0	42.2	42.7
Belarus	90.4	83.5	73.0	65.4	67.1
Georgia	55.1	39.0	34.9	35.8	39.8
Kazakhstan	94.7	86.0	75.2	69.0	69.3
Kyrgyzstan	86.1	72.8	58.1	55.0	58.9
Moldova	–	–	69.1	67.8	62.5
Russia	85.5	78.1	68.1	65.4	62.2
Tajikistan	–	83.7	65.9	57.7	48.1
Turkmenistan	–	101.5	84.5	78.0	78.1
Ukraine	90.1	77.3	59.6	52.3	47.1
Uzbekistan	88.9	86.9	82.3	81.6	83.0

Source: Goskomstat 1998, 1999.

TABLE 13.3 Global agricultural output of CIS states, 1992–96 (1991 = 100)

	1992	1994	1995	1996
Armenia	87	112	117	119
Azerbaijan	75	56	52	54
Belarus	91	81	77	79
Georgia	87	85	97	102
Kazakhstan	101	77	58	53
Kyrgyzstan	95	70	68	78
Moldova	84	69	71	62
Russia	91	76	70	67
Tajikistan	100	82	64	53
Turkmenistan	91	87	72	71
Ukraine	92	78	75	68
Uzbekistan	94	87	90	85

Source: Goskomstat 1998, 1999.

TABLE 13.4 Departures and arrivals in the CIS, 1991–96

	1991	1992	1993	1994	1995	1996
Arrivals						
Azerbaijan	112,320	76,971	50,449	31,782	27,901	–
Armenia	70,526	36,536	28,155	18,154	13,135	–
Belarus	345,581	331,815	287,724	232,660	205,229	214,094
Georgia	48,512	24,267	–	–	–	–
Kazakhstan	593,000	521,851	450,383	394,397	372,981	288,557
Kyrgyzstan	125,841	94,884	82,138	76,776	72,472	67,159
Moldova	117,472	102,486	84,667	67,426	60,149	43,679
Russia	4,382,838	4,192,511	3,825,721	4,163,302	3,971,787	3,518,037
Tajikistan	69,915	50,645	71,174	43,142	37,067	–
Turkmenistan	71,974	62,659	61,773	–	42,668	–
Uzbekistan	305,027	333,590	295,535	219,082	166,007	147,014
Ukraine	–	–	–	–	–	851,818
Departures						
Azerbaijan	126,162	107,575	65,259	49,932	47,325	–
Armenia	42,679	35,492	34,080	35,913	19,973	–
Belarus	306,080	263,149	246,341	230,363	198,075	198,070
Georgia	66,701	41,930	–	–	–	–
Kazakhstan	537,407	580,086	583,023	706,279	513,325	392,744
Kyrgyzstan	142,659	162,231	195,872	120,870	83,636	72,987
Moldova	120,463	122,221	88,321	77,910	72,529	59,571
Russia	4,113,358	3,703,292	3,336,364	3,216,905	3,275,890	2,990,335
Tajikistan	90,435	139,131	140,128	86,139	73,180	–
Turkmenistan	77,301	74,469	56,736	–	51,771	–
Uzbekistan	349,251	405,806	340,004	346,181	243,145	190,247
Ukraine	–	–	–	–	–	939,275

Source: *Naselenie* 1998: 25.

TABLE 13.5 Ukraine, 1992–97 (per cent)

	1992	1993	1994	1995	1996	1997
GDP	−12.5	−7.2	−24.3	−12.0	−10.0	−3.2
Industrial production	−9.0	−7.4	−28.0	−11.5	−5.1	−1.8
Agricultural production	−11.0	−16.5	−16.0	−4.0	−9.0	−7.2
Inflation	1,210	4,738	842	375	39	10
Foreign debt ($ million)	–	396	3,624	4,828	9,170	10,243

Source: Heenan and Lamontagne 1999: 82.

TABLE 13.6 Ukrainian regions, 1996 (per cent)

	Proportion of Ukrainian population	Urban population	Ethnic Russians	Proportion of total agricultural production	Proportion of total industrial production
West	22.1	49.8	5	22.0	16.5
Lviv	5.4	60.9	7	3.9	5.1
Ternopil	2.3	43.7	2	3.3	1.5
Ivano-Frankivsk	2.9	43.3	4	2.1	2.2
Centre	26.7	64.4	10	34.1	23.9
East	35.7	82.7	34	26.4	48.2
Donetsk	10.1	90.3	44	4.9	13.9
Luhansk	5.4	86.4	45	3.3	7.4
South	10.1	65.2	24	12.8	8.3
Crimea	5.1	70.5	67	4.7	3.1
All Ukraine	–	67.8	22	–	–

Source: Heenan and Lamontagne 1999: 84.

TABLE 13.7 Real GNP*, 1991–97 (1989 = 100)

	1991	1992	1993	1994	1995	1996	1997
Armenia	83.4	48.6	44.3	46.7	49.9	52.8	54.4
Azerbaijan	87.7	67.9	52.2	41.9	37.0	37.4	39.6
Georgia	67.0	36.9	26.1	23.4	24.0	26.6	29.6

Source: UN Economic Commission for Europe, 1998.
* Gross domestic product plus the income accruing to domestic residents arising from investment abroad less income earned in the domestic market accruing to foreigners abroad. Real GNP is adjusted for inflation.

TABLE 13.8 Real gross industrial output, 1991–97 (1989 = 100)

	1991	1992	1993	1994	1995	1996	1997
Armenia	85.4	44.2	39.7	41.8	42.4	43.0	43.4
Azerbaijan	98.2	74.9	69.7	53.9	44.6	41.6	41.7
Georgia	73.0	39.6	29.0	17.5	15.8	17.0	18.4

Source: UN Economic Commission for Europe, 1998.

TABLE 13.9 Real GNP in Central Asia, 1991–97 (1989 = 100)

	1991	1992	1993	1994	1995	1996	1997
Kazakhstan	88.1	83.4	75.8	66.2	60.8	61.1	62.3
Kyrgyzstan	96.5	83.1	70.3	56.2	53.1	56.9	62.5
Tajikistan	91.7	63.3	53.0	41.7	35.6	30.4	30.9
Turkmenistan	97.0	82.5	83.7	69.7	64.4	64.4	54.8
Uzbekistan	98.7	87.7	85.7	81.2	80.5	81.9	86.1

Source: UN Economic Commission for Europe, 1998.

TABLE 13.10 Real gross industrial output in Central Asia, 1991–97 (1989 = 100)

	1991	1992	1993	1994	1995	1996	1997
Kazakhstan	98.3	84.7	72.2	51.9	47.7	47.8	49.7
Kyrgyzstan	99.1	72.9	54.5	39.2	32.2	35.1	52.8
Tajikistan	97.6	73.9	68.1	50.8	43.9	33.4	32.6
Turkmenistan	108.2	92.0	95.7	72.1	67.5	79.5	55.7
Uzbekistan	103.3	96.4	99.9	101.5	101.6	107.7	114.7

Source: UN Economic Commission for Europe, 1998.

TABLE E.1 The presidential election, 26 March 2000

Candidate	Votes	Percentage of votes
Vladimir Putin	39,740,434	52.94
Gennady Zyuganov	21,928,471	29.21
Grigory Yavlinsky	4,351,452	5.80
Aman Tuleev	2,217,361	2.95
Vladimir Zhirinovsky	2,026,513	2.70
Konstantin Titov	1,107,269	1.47
Ella Pamfilova	758,966	1.01
Stanislav Govorukhin	328,263	0.44
Yury Skuratov	319,263	0.43
Aleksei Podberezkin	98,175	0.13
Umar Djabrailov	78,498	0.10
Against All Candidates	1,414,648	1.88

Source: *Rossiiskaya Gazeta*, 7 April 2000.

BIBLIOGRAPHY

Adomeit, Hannes (1998), *Imperial Overstretch: Germany in Soviet Policy from Stalin to Gorbachev*, Nomos Verlagsgesellschaft, Baden-Baden.

Anderson, John (1999), *Kyrgyzstan Central Asia's Island of Democracy*, Harwood, Amsterdam.

Aron, Leon (2000), *Boris Yeltsin: A Revolutionary Life*, HarperCollins, London.

Aslund, Anders (1995), *How Russia Became a Market Economy*, The Brookings Institution, Washington, DC.

Baranets, Viktor (1998), *Eltsin i Ego GeneralyZapiski Polkovnika Genshtaba*, Kollektsiya Sovershenno Sekretno, Moscow.

Barkhatov, Aleksandr (1998), *General Lebed ili Moya Lebedinaya Pesnya*, Politbyuro, Moscow.

Black, Bernard, Reinier Kraakman and Anna Tarassova (2000), 'Russian Privatization and Corporate Governance: What Went Wrong?', *Stanford Law Review*, 52.

Blandy, C. W. (1996), *The Significance of Pervomayskoye*, Conflict Studies Research Centre, Sandhurst, April (P19).

Blandy, C. W. (2000), *Dagestan: The Storm Part I – The 'Invasion' of Avaristan*, Conflict Studies Research Centre, Sandhurst, March (P30).

Blasi, Joseph R., Maya Kroumova and Douglas Kruse (1997), *Kremlin Capitalism: Privatizing the Russian Economy*, Cornell University Press, Ithaca, New York.

Bohr, Annette (1998), *Uzbekistan Politics and Foreign Policy*, Royal Institute of International Affairs, London.

Bowker, Mike and Cameron Ross (eds) (2000), *Russia After the Cold War*, Longman, Harlow.

Brudny, Yitzhak M. (1998), *Reinventing Russia: Russian Nationalism and the Soviet State, 1953–1991*, Harvard University Press, Cambridge, MA.

Campbell, Robert W. (1995), *Soviet and Post-Soviet Telecommunications*, Westview Press, Boulder, CO.

Chinarikhina, Galina (1996), 'Dogovor kak sposob razgranicheniya polnomochii i predmetov vedeniya mezhdu subetktami federativnykh otonoshenii', *Vlast*, no. 9.

Cohen, Stephen F. (2000), *Failed Crusade: America and the Tragedy of Post-Communist Russia*, W. W. Norton, New York.

Craumer, Peter (1995), *Rural and Agricultural Development in Uzbekistan*, Royal Institute of International Affairs, London.

Davisha, Karen and Bruce Parrott (1994), *Russia and the New States of Eurasia: The Politics of Upheaval*, Cambridge University Press, Cambridge.

De Soto, Hernando (2000), *The Mystery of Capital: Why Capitalism Triumphs in the West and Fails Everywhere Else*, Bantam Press, London.

Drobizheva, Leokadiya (ed.) (1996), *Govorit Elita Respublik Rossiiskoi Federatsii*, Rossiiskaya Akademiya Nauk, Moscow.

Drobizheva, L. M., A. R. Aklaev, V. V. Koroteeva and G. U. Soldatova (1996), *Demokratizatsiya i Obrazy Nationalizma v Rossiiskoi Federatsii 90-kh Godov*, Mysl, Moscow.

Earley, Pete (1997), *Confessions of a Spy: The Real Story of Aldrich Ames*, Hodder & Stoughton, London.

Elletson, Harold D. H. (1998), *The Changing Face of the Military in Soviet and Russian Politics 1968–1997: A Case Study of the Military Service and Political Career of Lieutenant General Alexander Ivanovich Lebed*, unpublished doctoral dissertation, University of Bradford.

Ellman, Michael (2000), 'The Russian Economy under El'tsin', *Europe-Asia Studies*, vol. 52, no. 8.

Field, Mark G. and Judyth L. Twigg (2000), *Russia's Torn Safety Nets: Health and Social Welfare During Transition*, St Martin's Press, New York.

Forschungsstelle Osteuropas an der Universität Bremen (ed.) (1997), *Das Neue Rußland in Politik und Kultur*, Edition Temmen, Bremen.

Forschungsstelle Osteuropas an der Universität Bremen (ed.) (1997), *Rußland Fragmente einer Postsowjetischen Kultur*, Edition Temmen, Bremen.

Freeland, Chrystia (2000), *Sale of the Century: The Inside Story of the Second Russian Revolution*, Little, Brown, London.

Friedman, Robert I. (2000), *Red Mafiya: How the Russian Mob Has Invaded America*, Little, Brown, Boston.

Gaidar, Egor (1997), *Dni Porazhenii i Pobed*, Bagrius, Moscow.

Galeotti, Mark (1995), *The Age of Anxiety: Security and Politics in Soviet and Post-Soviet Russia*, Longman, Harlow.

Galeotti, Mark (1995), 'The Kremlin's Agenda: The New Russia and its Armed Forces', *Jane's Intelligence Review*, London.

Gelbras, V. G. (ed.) (1994), *Kto est Chto Profsoyuznye Obedineniya i Tsentry*, Ministerstvo Ekonomiki Rossiiskoi Federatsii, Moscow.

Gevorkyan, Nataliya *et al.* (2000), *First Person: An Astonishingly Frank Self-Portrait by Russia's President Vladimir Putin*, Hutchinson, London.

Glazyev, Sergei (1999), *Genocide (October 1993–August 1998) Russia and the New World Order*, Executive Intelligence Review, Washington, DC.

Götz, Roland (2000), 'Die Privatisierung der russischen Industrie in Theorie und Praxis', *Osteuropa*, 10.

Gorbachev, Mikhail (1996), *Memoirs*, Doubleday, London.

Gustafson, Thane (1999), *Capitalism Russian-Style*, Cambridge University Press, Cambridge.

Hansen, Birthe and Bertel Heurlin (eds) (1998), *The Baltic States in World Politics*, Curzon, Richmond, Surrey.

Hedlund, Stefan (1999), *Russia's 'Market' Economy A Bad Case of Predatory Capitalism*, UCL Press, London.

Heenan, Patrick and Monique Lamontagne (eds) (1999), *The CIS Handbook*, Fitzroy Dearborn Publishers, London.

Henderson, Karen and Neil Robinson (1997), *Post-Communist Politics An Introduction*, Prentice Hall, London.

Hough, Jerry (2001), *The Logic of Economic Reform in Russia*, Brookings Institution Press Washington, DC.

Human Development Report for Central and Eastern Europe and the CIS 1999 (1999) UNDP, New York.

Huskey, Eugene (1999), *Presidential Power in Russia*, M. E. Sharpe, Armonk, New York.

Ioffe, Grigory and Tatyana Nefedova (1997), *Continuity and Change in Rural Russia*, Westview Press, Boulder, CO.

Kaiser, Robert J. (1994), *The Geography of Nationalism in Russia and the USSR*, Princeton University Press, Princeton, NJ.

Klebnikov, Paul (2000), *Godfather of the Kremlin: Boris Berezovsky and the Looting of Russia*, Harcourt, New York.

Knight, Amy (1996), *Spies Without Cloaks The KGB's Successors*, Princeton University Press, Princeton, NJ.

Knight, Amy (2000), 'The Enduring Legacy of the KGB in Russian Politics', *Problems of Post-Communism*, vol. 47, no. 4, July–August.

Kokh, Alfred (1998), *The Selling of the Soviet Empire: Politics and Economics of Russia's Privatization – Revelations of the Principal Insider*, Liberty, New York.

Komulainen, Tuomas and Iikka Korhonen (eds) (2000), *Russian Crisis and Its Effects*, Kikimora Publications, Helsinki.

Kornai, Janos (1992), *The Socialist System: The Political Economy of Communism*, Clarendon Press, Oxford.

Kosals, Leonid (1994), *Why Doesn't Russian Industry Work?* I. B. Tauris, London.

Kostikov, Vyacheslav (1997), *Roman s Presidentom Zapiski Press-Sekretarya*, Vagrius, Moscow.

Kto est Kto v Rossii i v Blizhnem Zarubezhe (1993), Novoe Vremya, Moscow.

Kurochkin, Viktor (1997), *Missiya v Chechne*, Pomatur, Moscow.

Lapidus, Gail W., Victor Zaslavsky, with Philip Goldman (1992), *From Union to Commonwealth: Nationalism and Separatism in the Soviet Republics*, Cambridge University Press, Cambridge.

Layard, Richard and John Parker (1996), *The Coming Russian Boom*, The Free Press, New York.

Lloyd, John (1998), *Rebirth of a Nation An Anatomy of Russia*, Michael Joseph, London.

Luchterhandt, Galina (1996), 'Der Aufbau der nationalen Staatlichkeit Russlands', in Forschungsstelle Osteuropas an der Universität Bremen (ed.), *Russland Fragmente einer postsowjetischen Kultur*, Edition Temmen, Bremen.

Luchterhandt, Galina (1998), *Parteien in der Russischen Provinz: Politische Entwicklung in den Gebieten des Ural und der Wolgaregion*, Edition Temmen, Bremen.

Luchterhandt, Galina, Sergej Ryshenkow and Alexej Kusmin (1999), *Politik und Kultur in der Russischen Provinz, Nowgorod, Woronesh, Saratow, Jekaterinburg*, Edition Temmen, Bremen.

Lysenko, Vladimir (1995), *Razvitie federativnykh otnoshenii v sovremennoi Rossii*, Moscow.

McCauley, Martin (1992), *Directory of Russian MPs People's Deputies of the Supreme Soviet of Russia-Russian Federation*, Longman, Harlow.

McCauley, Martin (1993), *Longman Biographical Directory of Decision-Makers in Russian and the Successor States*, Longman, Harlow.

McCauley, Martin (1993), *The Soviet Union 1917–1991*, 2nd edition, Longman, Harlow.

McCauley, Martin (1998), *The Longman Companion to Russia since 1914*, Longman, Harlow.

McCauley, Martin (1998), *Gorbachev*, Longman, Harlow.

Mau, Vladimir (1996), *The Political History of Economic Reform in Russia, 1985–1994*, The Centre for Research into Communist Economies, London.

Medvedev, Roy (2000), *Post-Soviet Russia: A Journey Through the Yeltsin Era*, Columbia University Press, New York.

Mickiewicz, Ellen (1999), *Changing Channels Television and the Struggle for Power in Russia*, Duke University Press, Durham, NC.

Nagy, Piroska Mohacsi (2000), *The Meltdown of the Russian State: The Deformation and Collapse of the State in Russia*, Edward Elgar, Cheltenham.

Naselenie i Usloviya Zhizn v Stranakh SNG (1998), Moscow.

Nelson, Lynn D. and Irina Y. Kuzes (1994), *Property to the People: The Struggle for Radical Economic Reform in Russia*, M. E. Sharpe, Armonk, New York.

Nolan, Peter (1995), *China's Rise, Russia's Fall: Politics, Economics and Planning in the Transition from Stalinism*, Macmillan, London.

Norgaard, Ole, with Dan Hindsgaul, Lars Johannsen and Helle Willumsen (1996), *The Baltic States Since Independence*, Edward Elgar, Cheltenham.

Olcott, Martha, Valery Tishkov Brill and Aleksei Malashenko (eds) (1997), *Identichnost i Konflikt v Postsovetskikh Gosudarstvakh*, Moskovsky Tsentr Karnegi, Moscow.

Olson, Mancur (1982), *The Rise and Decline of Nations*, Yale University Press, New Haven, CT.

Olson, Mancur (1993), 'Dictatorship, Democracy, and Development', *American Political Science Review*, vol. 87, no. 3, September.

Olson, Mancur (2000), *Power and Prosperity Outgrowing Communist and Capitalist Dictatorships*, Basic Books, New York.

O'Prey, Kevin, P. (1995), *A Farewell to Arms? Russia's Struggle With Defense Conversion*, The Twentieth Century Fund Press, New York.

Reddaway, Peter and Dmitri Glinski (2001), *The Tragedy of Russia's Reforms: Market Bolshevism Against Democracy*, United States Institute of Peace Press, Herndon, VA.

Remington, Thomas F. (1994), *Parliaments in Transition: The New Legislative Politics in the Former USSR and Eastern Europe*, Westview Press, Boulder, CO.

Remington, Thomas F. (2000), 'The Evolution of the Executive-Legislative Relations in Russia since 1993', *Slavic Review*, vol. 59, no. 3.

Rybkin, Ivan (1997), *Rossiya Obretet Soglasie*, Znanie, Soglasie, Moscow.

Rybkin, Ivan (1998), *Rußland und die Welt Auf dem Weg zu Demokratie und Sicherheit*, Petro News Dr Harnish Verlag, Nürnberg.

Saikal, Amin and William Maley (eds) (1995), *Russia in Search of its Future*, Cambridge University Press, Cambridge.

Sakwa, Richard (1993), *Russian Politics and Society*, 2nd edition, Routledge, London.

Savchenko, Andrew (2000), *Rationality, Nationalism and Post-Communist Market Transformations: A Comparative Analysis of Belarus, Poland, and the Baltic States*, Ashgate, Aldershot.

Schleifman, Nurit (ed.) (1998), *Russia at a Crossroads History, Memory and Political Practice*, Frank Cass, London.

Schneider, Eberhard (1998), *Die örtliche Selbstverwaltung in der Russländlichen Föderation*, Berichte des BIOst, no. 15.

Shevtsova, Lilia (1999), *Yeltsin's Russia Myths and Reality*, Carnegie Endowment for International Peace, Washington, DC.

Smith, Steven S. and Thomas F. Remington (2001), *The Politics of Institutional Choice: The Formation of the Russian State Duma*, Princeton University Press, Princeton and Oxford.

Solnick, Steven L. (1996), 'The Political Economy of Russian Federalism A Framework for Analysis', *Problems of Post-Communism*, November/December.

Solnick, Steven L. (1998), 'Gubernatorial Elections in Russia, 1996–1997', *Post-Soviet Affairs*, no. 14, 1.

Soros, George (1998), *The Crisis of Global Capitalism*, Little, Brown, London.

Starovoitova, Galina (1997), *National Self-Determination: Approaches and Case Studies*, Brown University, Providence, RI.

Szajkowski, Bogdan (1994), *Political Parties of Eastern Europe, Russia and the Successor States*, Longman, Harlow.

Territorialnoe Upravlenie Presidenta Rossiiskoi Federatsii (1997), *Rossiiskie Regiony Posle Vyborov-96*, Izdatelstvo Yuridicheskaya Literatura, Moscow.

Tishkov, V. A. (1997), *Vynuzhdennye Migranty: Integratsiya i Vozvrashchenie*, Institut Etnologii i Antropologii Rossiiskoi Akademii Nauk, Moscow.

Treisman, Daniel (1998), 'Deciphering Russia's Federal Finance: Fiscal Appeasement in 1995 and 1996', *Europe-Asia Studies*, vol. 50, no. 5.

Treisman, Daniel (2000), 'Blaming Russia First', *Foreign Affairs*, November–December.

Urban, Michael (1997), *The Rebirth of Politics in Russia*, Cambridge University Press, Cambridge.

Valentei, Sergei (1997), 'Problemy otechestvennogo federalizma', *Federalizm*, no. 2.

Van Selm, Bert (1998), 'Economic Performance in Russia's Regions', *Europe-Asia Studies*, vol. 50, no. 4.

Vybory glav ispolnitelnoi vlasti subektov Rossiiskoi Federatsii 1995–1997 Elektornaya statistika (1997), Ves Mir Izdatelstvo, Moscow.

Waller, J. Michael (1994), *Secret Empire: The KGB in Russia Today*, Westview Press, Boulder, CO.

Wedel, Janine (1999), *Collision and Collusion: The Strange Case of Western Aid to Eastern Europe*, St Martin's Press, New York.

Wegren, Stephen K. (1998), *Agriculture and the State in Soviet and Post-Soviet Russia*, University of Pittsburg Press, Pittsburg, PA.

White, Stephen (2000), *Russia's New Politics: The Management of a Postcommunist Society*, Cambridge University Press, Cambridge.

White, Stephen, Graeme Gill and Darrell Slider (1993), *The Politics of Transition: Shaping a Post-Soviet Future*, Cambridge University Press, Cambridge.

Williams, Christopher and Thanasis D. Sfikas (eds) (1999), *Ethnicity and Nationalism in Russia, the CIS and the Baltic States*, Ashgate, Aldershot.

Yeltsin, Boris (1994), *Zapiski Prezidenta*, Ogenok, Moscow.

Yeltsin, Boris (1997), *The Struggle for Russia*, Time Books, New York.

Yeltsin, Boris (2000), *Midnight Diaries*, Weidenfeld & Nicolson, London.

Zergunin, Alexander (2000), 'Russia's Regions and Foreign Policy', *Transatlantic Internationale Politik*, no. 1.

INDEX